LINCOLN'S WAY

LINCOLN'S WAY

How Six Great Presidents Created American Power

RICHARD STRINER

ROWMAN & LITTLEFIELD PUBLISHERS, INC.
Lanham • Boulder • New York • Toronto • Plymouth, UK

Published by Rowman & Littlefield Publishers, Inc.
A wholly owned subsidary of The Rowman & Littlefield Publishing Group, Inc.
4501 Forbes Boulevard, Suite 200, Lanham, Maryland 20706
www.rowmanlittlefield.com

Estover Road, Plymouth PL6 7PY, United Kingdom

Distributed by National Book Network

British Library Cataloguing in Publication Information Available

Library of Congress Cataloging-in-Publication Data
Striner, Richard, 1950–
  Lincoln's way : how six great Presidents created American power / Richard
Striner.
    p. cm.
  Includes bibliographical references and index.
  ISBN 978-1-4422-0065-4 (cloth : alk. paper) — ISBN 978-1-4422-0066-1
(electronic)
  1. Presidents—United States—History. 2. Political leadership—United States—
History. 3. Federal government—United States—History. 4. Power (Social
sciences)—United States—History. 5. United States—Politics and government.
6. Lincoln, Abraham, 1809–1865—Influence. I. Title.
  JK511.S77 2010
  973.09'9—dc22   2010007265

∞™ The paper used in this publication meets the minimum requirements of
American National Standard for Information Sciences—Permanence of Paper for
Printed Library Materials, ANSI/NISO Z39.48-1992.

Printed in the United States of America

To my daughter's generation.

CONTENTS

Acknowledgments   ix

Introduction   1

1   Forgotten Paths in American Politics   5

2   From the Founders to Abraham Lincoln   23

3   From Lincoln to Theodore Roosevelt   47

4   The Legacy Crosses Party Lines: From Theodore to
    Franklin D. Roosevelt   81

5   The Legacy as Great Power Statecraft: From Truman
    to Nixon   129

6   The Legacy in Ruins: From Carter to George W. Bush   183

7   Horizons   233

Notes   249

Index   291

About the Author   301

ACKNOWLEDGMENTS

I wish to thank the following people for their contributions to the book. I am deeply grateful to James MacGregor Burns, James M. McPherson, Fred I. Greenstein, David A. Nichols, Richard Wayne Etulain, William D. Pederson, Joseph R. Fornieri, Adam Goodheart, Carl Reddel, Rocco C. Siciliano, Samuel C. O. Holt, Sara Gabbard, and my parents Herbert and Erma Striner for reading the manuscript in whole or in part. At Rowman & Littlefield, executive editor Niels Aaboe was a constant source of support and encouragement, and production editor Patricia Stevenson was extremely helpful. I wish to thank Wallace Dailey, curator of the Theodore Roosevelt collection at Harvard College Library, for his kind permission to use a splendid image from the collection. Special thanks to John W. Wright for his excellent suggestions. Any errors in the book are my own.

INTRODUCTION

Was Lincoln the greatest of our presidents? Many millions of Americans are fully convinced that he was, and for some excellent reasons. Lincoln was, after all, the Savior of the Union, the Great Emancipator, and a leader of remarkable character. But his greatness exceeded these achievements. For the case can be made that he took the young nation that the Founders created and positioned it for global power. He unleashed a potential in American life that would make the young republic a world colossus over time.

From the left and the right he borrowed wisdom. Then he used the vast power of our federal government in brilliant and extraordinary ways. In so doing, he created a tradition that would influence the twentieth century.

Historians, pundits, and political leaders have neglected this tradition, for its story has never been told. It is the story of an apostolic succession that moved from Lincoln to Theodore Roosevelt to Franklin Delano Roosevelt, who passed it on to Truman, Eisenhower, and Kennedy, all of whom learned from each other in sequence and developed ideas—superb ideas—that gave the world significant statecraft. Obama may add to this tradition.

This is a book about "men and ideas": *heroic* ideas and the people who put them to use. It's a book about leaders who believed in the American promise, but they also believed that only *powerful governance* could make that vision a reality. They fought tooth and nail against the people who believed that "the government that governs best, governs least."

They did not promote "government" mindlessly. They denounced the idea that more government is always the answer. But they believed that it was *sometimes* the answer when it came to the nation's necessities.

1

They knew the great dangers of chaos and they hoped to make Americans prepared for all kinds of surprises—and emergencies. They believed in the value of *coordinated* national life—in teamwork.

The presidents who followed in Lincoln's path blended *wisdom* and *power* from conservative and liberal thought, while discarding what was spoiled or dogmatic. Lincoln was in some respects *the first* of our presidents to synthesize the principles of left and right with a measure of success. Theodore Roosevelt was eager to revive this achievement. He declared at the end of his presidency that his work as a Republican leader had been "to take hold of the conservative party and turn it into what it had been under Lincoln, that is, a party of progressive conservatism, or conservative radicalism; for of course wise radicalism and wise conservatism go hand in hand."[1] Franklin D. Roosevelt made a similar statement in the course of a 1936 campaign speech: "'Reform if you would preserve.' I am that kind of conservative because I am that kind of liberal."[2]

Lincoln's way was adopted by the presidential Roosevelts and passed from the first to the second. "Lincoln is my hero," wrote Theodore Roosevelt to a friend in 1905.[3] In the very same year—1905—young Franklin Roosevelt exclaimed in a letter that "everyone is talking about Cousin Theodore saying that he is the most prominent figure of present day history."[4] From Lincoln to Theodore and Theodore to Franklin, the tradition continued to develop through World War II and beyond—from Truman all the way to Kennedy.

Then it vanished.

I believe that three particular themes in this legacy have served the United States well: (1) a convergence of the left and the right on certain fundamental issues that unite us; (2) an expansion of America's power to produce and consume, with an economic program to advance and accelerate the process; and (3) a conviction that the federal government can lead us in magnificent endeavors. Lincoln put all of these principles to use in his presidential years.

He used federal power in unprecedented ways—not only to preserve the American nation but also to reach down a hand to help liberate the downtrodden slaves. He supported the creation of the federal Freedmen's Bureau, a welfare agency that heralded the work of FDR. Even in the midst of total war—with its vast hardship—he supported the construction of expensive public works in the form of the transcontinental railroad. His financial method used a bold and largely successful mixture of taxes, deficit spending, and direct creation of money, the Civil War Greenbacks.

He unified the insights of left and right through the view of human nature he expressed in his fight to end slavery. He showed a grim and conservative recognition of the facts about *people at their worst*. The enslavement of others was for Lincoln a sign of monstrosity within the human spirit. Lincoln's open acknowledgment of human evil will stand for all time as a conservative reproach against utopian schemes and the naiveté that propels them. But throughout his career Lincoln's social ideals bespoke a true egalitarian optimism—the quintessence of the liberal outlook.

Was this double-sided attitude of Lincoln's inconsistent—or paradoxical? No. Lincoln simply believed in doing justice to the best and the worst of human nature. Consequently, it is vain to try to classify Lincoln as a clear-cut conservative or liberal. He was both.

So were the Roosevelts, and so was Harry Truman (who embraced what historian Arthur Schlesinger Jr. called the "vital center"), Dwight D. Eisenhower (who recommended a political creed that he called the "middle way"), and John F. Kennedy (who made Schlesinger a special presidential adviser to consolidate the "vital center").

For the record, I should state my political (or ideological) position openly and clearly: I believe rather firmly that America's status as a great global power is a blessing, to us and to the world. Notwithstanding some recent (and obvious) misadventures, our power has been useful to the world for the better part of a century. Does this need arguing? How else would the Axis have been stopped during World War II if the United States had been weak?

But I am not an uncritical enthusiast. America's strong global presence and the presence of a robust government in Washington can surely go astray, and we have all seen it happen many times. Government is not a panacea: like any other product or system, it is fraught with its own kind of dangers and we certainly know what they are.

Yet the seductive ideology of *minimal* government is wrong—completely inadmissible, in fact—for no great global power can sustain itself for long in the hope that things will simply "work out." And most Americans seem to understand this. What most of us acknowledge (when we know our own minds) is that well-founded governance is *necessary*. And when properly conducted, it can lead to inspirational results.

This book is intended for scholars and citizens of differing persuasions, conservatives and liberals who "live by ideas," as the poet Matthew Arnold expressed it. He explained this way of life as follows:

> When one side of a question has long had your earnest support, when all your feelings are engaged, when you hear all around you no language but one, when your party talks this language like a steam-engine and can

imagine no other,—still to be able to think, still to be irresistibly carried
. . . by the current of thought to the opposite side of the question.

My purpose here is clearly political. Some broad ruminations on a
national program are advanced at the end of this study. Only time will
determine if the legacy in question will empower our nation again. But
perhaps we will yet live to see it.

1

FORGOTTEN PATHS
IN AMERICAN POLITICS

One of the most consequential factors in election year 2008 was the sense that strong federal action—drastic action—was imperative. The economic emergency, the long-term national security and environmental challenges, the scandals in banking and finance prompted millions of American voters to demand governmental intervention.

The supporters of Barack Obama were responding to a very old mood—one that Theodore Roosevelt expressed back in 1910. After leaving the presidency, the Republican Roosevelt declared to a gathering of Civil War veterans in Kansas that Americans should "work in a spirit of broad and far-reaching nationalism when we work for what concerns our people as a whole. We are all Americans. Our common interests are as broad as this continent. I speak to you here in Kansas exactly as I would speak in New York or Georgia, for the most vital problems are those which affect us all alike." And in cases "where the whole American people are interested," he concluded, "the betterment which we seek must be accomplished, I believe, mainly through the National Government."[1]

From the 1970s onward, however, our leaders would declare the reverse: that "big government" ought to be rejected. Both Republican and Democratic presidents took this position. "Government cannot solve our problems," declared Jimmy Carter in his 1978 State of the Union address.[2] "Government is the problem," claimed Ronald Reagan in his first inaugural address.[3] "The era of big government is over," asserted Bill Clinton in 1996.[4]

By the close of the twentieth century, an anti-government mood took over our politics. Pundits and radio talk-show hosts heaped scorn upon the "nanny state," with its "tax-and-spend" behavior. Libertarian think tanks and laissez-faire economists encouraged the American people to regard the federal government as something of a weird and alien force. Elected leaders vied with one another in the politics of fiscal austerity.

But as events of the twenty-first century unfolded, the public moods began to change. Whatever one thought about the Bush administration's response to the attacks of 9/11, grave challenges would soon confront "the Feds"—and everybody knew it. Then four years later, in the aftermath of Hurricane Katrina, as Americans observed a great city, New Orleans, reduced temporarily to Third World conditions, the chorus of outrage arose all over the country: Where was Uncle Sam? Was America's status as a superpower starting to erode? Was America decadent? Can *any* great nation stay powerful—can any great nation stay *functional*—without a publicly grounded capacity to ward off danger to its citizens and cities?

The majority's answer was decisive in 2008—and so the outlook of Roosevelt returned.

This book will show that the governance philosophy of Roosevelt partook of a long and remarkable tradition. On the level of presidential politics, Lincoln was the first to "pull it off." This was obvious to Roosevelt, who grew up worshipping Lincoln. "Lincoln's way" became Roosevelt's ideal.

The tradition encompassed three elements: (1) a vigorous role for the federal government in building our prosperity and power; (2) an economic policy designed to increase the nation's wealth through the full employment of its citizens, along with an expansion of our money supply; and (3) a political and cultural synthesis to reconcile enough of the conservative and liberal traditions to soften the harshness of left-versus-right dialectics. This synthesis was strong, dynamic, and expansive. It should not be regarded as "moderate" any more than Lincoln—a leader of tremendous audacity—should be regarded as just a cautious "moderate."

Theodore Roosevelt was raised by his father in the Lincolnesque Republican tradition. According to historian John Milton Cooper Jr., the Republican Roosevelt aspired to be the "heir of Lincoln and Civil War Republicanism."[5] It was a source of immense satisfaction to Roosevelt in 1905 when John Hay—one of Lincoln's private secretaries during the Civil War—told him he was "one of the men who most thoroughly understand and appreciate Lincoln."[6]

By the same token, Franklin D. Roosevelt was deeply inspired by his older fifth-cousin Theodore. Much of the New Deal program—Social Security, for instance, which Theodore Roosevelt began to advocate forcefully in 1912—derived from what the elder presidential Roosevelt had called his "Square Deal." Several members of the FDR administration had been Theodore Roosevelt supporters in their younger years: Harold Ickes, for instance, and Henry Stimson, who was FDR's secretary of war during World War II (he was still a Republican).

The legacy developed both conservative and liberal principles. "'Reform if you would preserve,'" preached FDR (paraphrasing Thomas Babington Macaulay) in a 1936 campaign speech. "I am that kind of conservative because I am that kind of liberal."[7]

By the middle of the twentieth century, the legacy approached high tide. It made the United States of America the most powerful, the most promising, and the wealthiest nation in the world. And we could use that legacy today.

THE CONSERVATIVE AND LIBERAL PERSUASIONS

FDR's vision was defunct by the end of the twentieth century—and America was very much the worse for it. Consider what our rising generation took for granted in political life, at least before the transformational election of 2008: conservative and liberal warfare had been so intense that there was talk just a few years earlier (right after the election of 2004) about the "red state" and "blue state" Americans assailing one another for decades. It almost sounded like a kind of tribal war.

No doubt we can take a bit of comfort in the fact that this has happened before and to others. In Victorian England, for instance, Sir William S. Gilbert of Gilbert and Sullivan fame made sport with the notion that "nature always does contrive

> That every boy and every gal,
> That's born into the world alive,
> Is either a little Liberal,
> Or else a little Conservative!"[8]

Forgiving Sir William his imperfect rhyme, can we not for the most part agree that this phenomenon appears to be a governing force in modern life?

But the reality is far more complex. Conservative and liberal values have developed over centuries of continuity and change. And the histories of both of these traditions are fraught with some interesting surprises.

Though perennial themes of conservative and liberal thought have extended across the recent centuries, the *discontinuities* in both of these traditions have been stunning, if we pause to consider them. Two centuries ago, for example, the conservative and liberal preferences regarding the proper amount of governance were almost *the reverse* of what they are today: conservatives tended to be regulators—or even supporters of the "welfare state"—whereas liberals were free marketeers (they wanted maximum *liberty*).

That being the case, what definitive meaning can we give to "conservative" and "liberal"? What basis do we have for referring to conservative and liberal traditions? If conservative or liberal thought can reverse itself on something as basic as the proper role of government, what do the traditions consist of?

Conservative thought as it emerged in recent centuries embraced two determining attitudes: (1) a suspicious view of human nature at its worst, and (2) hierarchic proclivities. Liberal ideas were the reverse: they were hopeful in regard to the human condition and their mood was *anti-hierarchic*.

Consider some examples of the "classical conservative" outlook before the twentieth century. Historian Perry Miller once wrote that the Puritans of seventeenth-century New England "moved in groups and towns, settled in whole communities, and maintained firm government over all units. . . . Puritan opinion was at the opposite pole from Jefferson's feeling that the best government governs as little as possible. . . . They would have expected laissez-faire to result in a reign of rapine and horror."[9] Strong magistrates, according to the Puritans, were needed to control the wolfish tendencies of sinful humanity.

Conservatives defended hierarchic tradition with an emphasis on top-down governance at least through the middle of the nineteenth century. In the aftermath of the French Revolution, for instance, the acerbic British essayist Thomas Carlyle declared that "Obedience . . . is the primary duty of man." Consequently, he continued, "a government of the under classes by the upper on the principle of *Let-alone* is no longer possible in England. . . . The Working Classes cannot any longer go on without government; without being *actually* guided and governed; England cannot subsist in peace till . . . some guidance and government for them is found."[10]

But if counterrevoluntionary Toryism was patriarchal, it could also be benevolent for reasons that combined sincerity and cunning. The sincerity flowed from aristocratic values, especially the duties of noblesse oblige: the obligation of the Christian "lords temporal" to reach out with true Christian charity to commoners.

On the other hand, conservative benevolence could also be a ploy of self-interest: if the upper class wanted to prevent revolution, then why not eliminate the lower-class grievances that triggered unrest and revolution? Carlyle observed that it was "vain . . . to think that the misery of one class, of the great universal under class, can be isolated, and kept apart and peculiar, down in that class. By infallible contagion . . . the misery of the lowest spreads upwards and upwards till it reaches the very highest."[11] The logic for the "highest" was obvious: put an end to the misery below.

The result was a tradition of Tory reform; the British variation was described in some detail by the intellectual historian Roland Stromberg, citing the political opinions of Samuel Taylor Coleridge, who "believed in government regulation of manufacturers, government aid to education, the duty of the state to enhance the moral and intellectual capabilities of its citizens in all sorts of positive ways." The Coleridge agenda, in Stromberg's opinion,

> can be related to the rural squirearchy, was certainly not equalitarian or levelling . . . but was deeply humanistic and more likely than liberalism to support governmental welfare measures for the poor. The leading hero of factory reform and other humanitarian measures in early industrial England was the Tory, Lord Shaftesbury. The Coleridge tradition passed to . . . Benjamin Disraeli and his conception of a democratized Conservative Party leading the way to social reform on behalf of the workers.[12]

On the European continent, a similar impulse led Otto von Bismarck, the legendary "Iron Chancellor" of Germany—not a "liberal" by any definition—to institute social security. Years later, Kaiser Wilhelm II told Theodore Roosevelt that Germany's social reforms were overwhelmingly conservative in nature. Roosevelt recalled that when he spoke with the Kaiser in 1910 about "what Germany had done to protect its wageworkers in old age, and . . . when they are thrown out of employment," the Kaiser stated that he "thought it was the business of those who believe in monarchical government to draw the teeth of the Socialists by remedying all real abuses."[13]

Such was the nature of the "welfare state" as some conservatives began to develop it during the nineteenth and early twentieth centuries—a long-lost tradition indeed by the standards of twenty-first century conservative thought. It was surely this tradition that FDR was invoking when he said that he was "that kind" of conservative.

But what about the liberals—the classical liberals who preached laissez-faire or small government? The term "liberal"—aside from its early connotation of kindness or generosity—relates to the political cognates of "liberty."

The classical liberals embraced "laissez-faire," which was the creed of letting things alone. The slogan itself was derived from the writings of the eighteenth-century "Physiocrats": Enlightenment French reformers who preferred to "let nature take its course" in society.

Hence the liberal crusade to destroy regulation and replace it with across-the-board freedom: free speech and free press and free markets. Stromberg has said that while "there were several strains in early modern liberalism . . . they all tended to agree broadly on a negative conception of the state, on something approaching laissez-faire as an ideal."[14]

Furthermore, the liberal view of human nature rejected "original sin" and all the policies that flowed from such a doctrine. The liberal view was much sunnier and more optimistic. "Man, were he not corrupted by governments, is naturally the friend of man, and . . . human nature is not of itself vicious," wrote Thomas Paine in the 1790s: human nature is pure until society has somehow "corrupted" it.[15] So the liberal prescription was clear: improve the arrangements of society and peace would automatically prevail.

Small wonder that the liberals have flirted now and then with utopian schemes for reform. They have shown a perennial optimism in regard to the human condition and its prospects—perhaps we should call it a "progressive" state of mind—with an aversion to hierarchic values. It was surely *this side* of the liberal tradition (and not laissez-faire) that FDR was invoking when he called himself "that kind" of liberal in 1936.

The case can be made that the political philosophy of *both* of the Roosevelts derived from a very long tradition. And it began when our Founders reached an impasse.

HAMILTON AND JEFFERSON

Conservative and liberal views were important to America's first party system, which emerged in the 1790s: the system of the Federalist Party versus the Democratic Republicans. And of all the Founding Fathers, two particular leaders were exemplars of classical conservative and liberal thought: Alexander Hamilton and Thomas Jefferson.[16]

On the matter of governance, Jefferson embraced laissez-faire. "I own I am not a friend to a very energetic government," he had written to James

Madison in 1787. "[I]t is always oppressive."[17] Eleven years later, he advocated "a single amendment to our Constitution . . . taking from the federal government the power of borrowing."[18]

In 1800 he wrote that the "General Government" ought to be "reduced to foreign concerns only"; that is, the jurisdiction of the federal government ought to be nil in the domestic sphere. But even in foreign relations, he preferred to keep government's role to a minimum. "Let our affairs be disentangled from those of all other nations, except as to commerce which the merchants will manage the better, the more they are left free to manage for themselves," he continued, "and our general government may be reduced to a very simple organization & a very unexpensive one: a few plain duties to be performed by a few servants."[19]

Though Jefferson would never in his life speak the dictum that "the government that governs best, governs least"—that slogan would emerge years later at the height of Jacksonian politics—the views that he expressed in his pre-presidential years came extremely close to that maxim.

Hamilton's views were the reverse. In the *Federalist #70*, he wrote that "energy in the Executive is a leading character in the definition of a good government."[20] He had nothing but scorn for the creed of laissez-faire: the notion that "trade will regulate itself" was "one of those wild, speculative paradoxes, which have grown into credit among us, contrary to the uniform practice and sense of the most enlightened nations," he wrote.[21]

Trade could *never* just "regulate itself," said Hamilton. "If left entirely to itself," he warned, the activity of business might lead to "pernicious effects."[22] Historian Forrest McDonald has emphasized Hamilton's conviction that the "avarice of individuals" could push the flow of trade "into channels inimical to public interest." Hamilton also believed that without the leadership of government, "desirable enterprises might . . . not be undertaken for want of sufficient private capital, or when unexpected causes thwarted a prosperous flow of commerce," especially in times of economic depression.[23]

For all of these reasons, he espoused the creation of a wide-ranging public- and private-sector partnership, with a vigorous government to supervise. He convinced the first federal Congress to charter a powerful national bank—the first Bank of the United States—modeled closely on the Bank of England. He championed the creation of "internal improvements" such as roads and canals, observing that "inland Navigation" was "one of those improvements, which could be prosecuted with more efficacy by the whole, than by any part or parts of the Union." He asserted the "power of the national Government to lend its direct aid, on a comprehensive plan."[24]

He interpreted the Constitution so broadly as to claim that "whatever concerns the general Interests" was "within the sphere of the National Councils as far as regards the application of money."[25]

The Hamilton-Jefferson clash on governance related to their differing views of society. And their social views related to the left-versus-right dialectic that was starting to evolve.

In the 1790s, the triggering event in the political and cultural war between the left and the right was the raging revolution in France. "The French Revolution," wrote James Madison in 1799, "has produced such a ferment and agitation in the world, and has divided it . . . into such violent parties, that nothing depending on opinion, nor much even on facts, is received without a strong tincture from the channel through which it passes."[26]

The issues of the French Revolution reached America in 1793, when the French revolutionary republic—in the middle of its "Reign of Terror"—asked America to lend its assistance in the fight against counterrevolutionary Britain. Jefferson (who was serving at the time as George Washington's secretary of state) was sympathetic, whereas Hamilton (Washington's secretary of the treasury) was incensed. Under Hamilton's prompting, the administration patched things up with Great Britain and turned a deaf ear to the pleas of the French revolutionary leaders.

Jefferson resigned from the cabinet. Then he quietly lent his assistance to the founding of new "Democratic Societies" to stimulate friendship with revolutionary France.

In the very next year a domestic insurrection made the issues more urgent than ever. In 1794, a group of Pennsylvania farmers refused to pay an excise tax on whiskey that was one of the central features of Hamilton's revenue program. Hamilton warned that a "large and well organized republic can scarcely lose its liberty from any other cause than anarchy, to which a contempt of the laws is a high road."[27] Washington and Hamilton donned their old military garb and led troops to Pennsylvania to suppress the Whiskey Rebellion.

Washington himself viewed the rebels as part of a larger antigovernment insurgency. He wrote that "this insurrection is viewed with universal indignation and abhorrence; except by those who have never missed an opportunity by side blows, or otherwise, to aim their shafts at the General Government." He also wrote that "I consider this insurrection as the first *formidable* fruit of the Democratic Societies."[28]

Jefferson responded in kind; he wrote that the administration was controlled by crypto-monarchists—men who must be "perfectly dazzled

CREATING MONEY

If the method of Lincoln and Roosevelt employed "Hamiltonian means," then we should certainly examine those "means" from the standpoint of federal finance. Strong federal action is *costly*, and Hamilton was *eager* to emphasize the point. He was eager to place no constraints upon federal spending; in *The Federalist* #34 he declared that "there ought to be a CA-PACITY" in government "to provide for future contingencies as they may happen; and as these are illimitable in their nature, it is impossible safely to limit that capacity."[37]

The world of money and banking in Hamilton's time was quite different from its counterpart today. But there are reasons to probe into its nature. In the first place, money (as an economic thing-in-itself) is an evolving construction. Furthermore, the long and interesting history of money has everything to do with the gradual emergence of our nation into superpower status.

To understand the nature of American victory in World War II, for example, we must comprehend the methods of Hamilton. Indeed, the very basis for America's money supply in our own day and age (a topic so badly understood by the public and so badly explained by economists, generally speaking) has its roots in the era of Hamilton. In Hamilton's day, a new order of money was emerging; some have called it the "Financial Revolution."

For centuries, nations had produced official money in the form of gold and silver coins. This was "specie," as the bankers used to call it. It was "cold, hard cash": it was coin of the realm, and nothing less.

The possessors of silver and gold had the option of taking this treasure to the mint to have it melted and stamped into coin. This was how money (in its coin-based version) was launched into public circulation, as simple as that.

But it was not so simple from the standpoint of business, for the very thing that gave the coins their value—their precious metal content—made coinage by itself an inadequate basis for currency. Gold and silver were "treasure" because of their beauty and because of their *rarity*, which ironically meant that there would *never be enough* of these coins to facilitate exchanges in a growing economy. An extension of the money supply beyond coin was required by the marketplace.

There was also the matter of *convenience*. It was costly to the merchants who were forced to ship gold and silver abroad. Not so for the bankers: they would often melt coins into bars and then ship them abroad for re-coinage whenever they believed that the advantage of doing this—more "bang for the buck," so to speak, if you could coin your precious metal in a currency with far greater buying power, ounce for ounce—was worth the cost of oceanic shipping. Imbalances of trade could be another cause for shipping precious metal. But in most respects, it was a burden.[38]

One solution was the "bill of exchange," and it worked like this: merchant A in Boston owed money to merchant B in London. But merchant A had a debtor of his own in Great Britain, merchant C. So a bill of exchange was drawn up directing C to pay B the amount that was owed by A, thus streamlining everything.

Such bills became valuable in and of themselves: they were legal *directives to pay.* They would often change hands many times, for the sake of convenience, in the course of commercial transactions. Merchants quickly signed them over to others if the parties agreed to such a method of payment.

Hence the bills of exchange began to circulate as private "currency"— not official money, to be sure, and in no respect a form of legal tender. People didn't have to accept them. But for people who accepted them, they served as a surrogate for money, like the personal checks (directives to pay) that are still in use today for the payment of bills. In other words, the bills began to *function as money* and they catalyzed business transactions, like money.

Put another way, these pieces of paper were instruments of *purchasing power:* they conveyed a financial form of *energy.* They could call goods and services to life. No longer did the money supply consist of gold and silver alone.

These pieces of paper were in theory nothing more than mere *representations* of the gold and silver in banks. Yet they *added* to the circulating medium. They became a new addition to the business world's *power to pay*—a net *addition* to the world supply of money. By 1767, Sir James Steuart, a British economist, wrote that "MONEY" was essentially "any commodity . . . which acquires such an estimation . . . as to become the universal measure of what is called value."[39]

Behold exhibit A of the Financial Revolution of the seventeenth and eighteenth centuries: the extension of the money supply via paper bills of exchange. Now behold exhibit B: the paper banknote.

These notes were legal *promises to pay.* The banknote began as a *receipt* for a deposit in the bank, but it soon became something much greater—an instrument of lending—and it could work in two ways for a bank. When a bank *borrowed* money, it would issue a note that would become a contractual *bond*. It was a promise to *pay back the loan* by a stipulated date and at a stipulated rate of interest.

But then banks began to *lend out* money via promissory notes *that pledged to pay a certain sum "on demand."* These bank notes functioned as a surrogate for "money," like commercial bills of exchange: they were *promises to pay* that had *value* in commercial transactions. People readily accepted the notes of any bank that would pay off its notes "on demand."

Then a critical development occurred: *bankers issued more notes (via loans) than they could possibly redeem if all their notes were presented at the bank on the very same day.* That could happen sometimes, and when it did it was a "run on the bank," a disaster of the greatest proportions. The result was catastrophic for everyone concerned, except the people who got in the doors first.

But when bankers could pull the thing off—when they could manage to issue more notes via loans than they could back with their coin-based "reserves"—then the money supply of the world was expanded, and the power to call goods and services to life was enormously increased. In other words, *the banks were creating more money, and they did it through the practice of lending out notes beyond the limits of their specie deposits.*[40]

This sleight of hand, *which continues right now in an updated form that the economists and bankers call "fractional reserve banking,"* has been attacked by many as a fraud. It could certainly lead to horrific results in the event of mismanagement or crookedness: bankruptcy, lawsuits, and prison were the obvious risks. But if the banks were well-managed, the results could empower the economy. For as long as these notes were accepted as money, then they *constituted* money of a kind. They conveyed a real *power to purchase*. They created real services and goods that would otherwise never have existed. A ghostly power was at work around the world: a new *energy* was catalyzing wealth and creating new jobs through accounting tricks and pieces of paper. A blizzard of paper from the banks of the world was *expanding the money supply of the world* beyond the limits of its gold and silver coins.

But was it fraud? Only (under law) if the promise to pay should prove worthless when the notes were handed in at the bank. As long as these banks could make good upon their promise to pay, then the legal standard had been met under most nations' banking laws—and the money supply had been expanded.

Let us pause for a "reality check" and a crucial new piece of terminology. "Deficit spending" is the use of borrowed money—is it not? So . . . the people who spend what they borrow from a bank are in reality *deficit spenders*. Now the extension of money through the lending of banknotes facilitated this sort of spending. Consequently, through the methods we have just been describing, *the process of "deficit spending"*—in other words, *the use of borrowed money in the form of paper notes that were issued by banks—created more money*. It created more money since the issuance of notes far exceeded the world's supply of coin. Therefore under certain conditions, the process of deficit spending can create more money. Is this correct? Think it over, for the answer is important.

From this new financial world emerged the new Bank of England in 1694. Chartered in return for a loan to the Crown, it was an instrument for managing the "national debt" that the English were starting to incur. And this was Hamilton's model for the bank that was chartered by Congress in 1791, the first Bank of the United States.

The initial deposits for Hamilton's bank were brought in through the sale of bank stock. The federal government bought 20 percent of this stock. Then the bank made loans via banknotes, promises to pay. It made loans to the government by purchasing its bonds: its promises to pay. The bonds were backed up by the government's power to tax, and to borrow more money. A revolving debt had been created, on the model of the British experiment.

The system that we have been describing placed the primary stress upon *results*, both short term and long term. The real issue in incurring such "national debt" was the economic *use* to which the money would be put. If the borrowed money was invested in ways that created more wealth and *more money*—by catalyzing further rounds of loans that would be based upon the principle of fractional reserves—then the "national debt" could be the basis for a nation to attain great power and prosperity. It was "Hamilton's blessing," as the economic writer John Steele Gordon once called it.[41]

A blessing! That was how the British historian (and member of Parliament) Thomas Babington Macaulay viewed the national debt of Great Britain in the middle of the nineteenth century. His observations merit sharing at length:

> At every stage in the growth of that debt it has been seriously asserted by wise men that bankruptcy and ruin were at hand. Yet still the debt went on growing; and still bankruptcy and ruin were as remote as ever. When the great contest with Lewis [sic] the Fourteenth was finally terminated by the Peace of Utrecht, the nation owed about fifty millions; and that debt was considered, not merely by the rude multitude,

not merely by foxhunting squires and coffeehouse orators, but by acute and profound thinkers, as an incumbrance which would permanently cripple the body politic. Nevertheless trade flourished: wealth increased: the nation became richer and richer. . . . Soon war again broke forth: and, under the energetic and prodigal administration of the first William Pitt, the debt rapidly swelled to a hundred and forty millions. As soon as the first intoxication of victory was over, men of theory and men of business almost unanimously pronounced that the fatal day had now really arrived.

Macaulay's amusement could not be suppressed as he brought his long tale up to date:

The beggared, the bankrupt society not only proved able to meet all its obligations, but, while meeting those obligations, grew richer and richer so fast that the growth could almost be discerned by the eye. . . . While shallow politicians were repeating that the energies of the people were borne down by the weight of the public burdens, the first journey was performed by steam on a railway. Soon the island was intersected by railways. A sum exceeding the whole amount of the national debt at the end of the American war was, in a few years, voluntarily expended by this ruined people on viaducts, tunnels, embankments, bridges, stations, engines. . . . It can hardly be doubted that there must have been some great fallacy in the notions of those who uttered and of those who believed that long succession of confident predictions, so signally falsified by a long succession of indisputable facts. . . . *They saw that the debt grew; and they forgot that other things grew as well as the debt.* (My emphasis)[42]

This is heresy today by the lights of the economic *attitudes* that dominate our thinking. But it was nothing less than the way in which our "greatest generation" beat the Axis in the Second World War via massive deficit spending—and then emerged from that war to be the wealthiest people in the world. For our national debt after World War II was so huge due to wartime expenditures ($258.7 billion in 1945) that it was *actually greater than the gross national product* of the time ($213.4 billion).[43] And yet America went on to fund the Marshall Plan, the GI Bill, and the Interstate Highway System. (It bears noting that the interstate program was designed in part to foster full employment.)

The boom that quickly followed in the Eisenhower years was in many ways the best-grounded age of prosperity in all of our history, second to none. People spoke about our "affluent society."[44]

But no more. Americans have been justifiably frightened by the worst economic conditions since the 1930s. And our national debt is getting huge. There is no doubt at all that any national debt can be a drag if the money gets wasted. But if the money is invested in ways that increase our overall purchasing power, then "debt" can lead to superabundance that can spread right across the class lines. The issue in the age of Obama is whether continued deficit spending is the best (or the only) alternative to higher taxation.

CREATING LEGAL TENDER PAPER MONEY

But we are still not finished with money. Another new method of money creation emerged from the eighteenth century. Americans were truly "cash poor" in terms of gold and silver coins throughout much of the colonial period. Bills of exchange were not enough of a solution, so the colonists printed some money. Colonial governments printed the money, then they spent it (or lent it) into use.

Both in economic theory and in economic lore, "mere" printing press money created by government (paper money that is not backed in specie and is not created through the banks) has had a bad reputation. It has had the reputation for depreciating, quickly and disastrously. One thinks, for example, of the paper bills emitted by the Continental Congress in the course of the American Revolution ("not worth a Continental") or the "Confederate money" that the South tried to foist upon the world in the 1860s.

But at various points in American history, government money has succeeded. Pennsylvania in colonial times did an excellent job of *lending* printing press money into use. Secured by collateral, the bills that Pennsylvania lent into circulation were very well-grounded economically. And since the money was *lent*, it brought revenue back to the government (interest on the loans), which made taxation a great deal lighter. This system was supported energetically by Benjamin Franklin.[45]

Economist Richard A. Lester once lamented that "the standard works on American monetary and financial history" never mentioned the "satisfactory currency experiments" in colonies such as Pennsylvania: only obvious failures were of interest to the orthodox economists.[46] But Lester's own research suggested that "the price level during the fifty two years prior to the American Revolution and while Pennsylvania was on a paper standard was more stable than the American price level has been during any succeeding fifty-year period."[47] So much for the notion that inflation must result from any money-creation by government, instead of by banks. Economist John Kenneth Galbraith concurred. Pennsylvania and the other middle colonies, he wrote, "handled paper money with what must now be regarded as astonishing skill and prudence."[48]

Perhaps the greatest American experiment along these lines was America's creation of the famous Civil War Greenbacks. Though Confederate money was a failure, the governmental notes of the Union held their value as well as many banknotes.[49] The Greenbacks functioned as a major contribution to America's money supply—for decades thereafter.

We shall speak of these subjects again.

2

FROM THE FOUNDERS TO
ABRAHAM LINCOLN

The libertarian tradition in America—the impulse that leads to an aversion toward "government" as such—began in eighteenth-century
England and spread to the colonies. It emerged from a movement that was
fundamental in the politics that founded our nation: the politics of liberty.

In the 1600s English life was repeatedly convulsed by a long and bitter struggle for supremacy between the Crown (especially under the rule
of Kings Charles I and James II) and Parliament. In the so-called Glorious
Revolution of 1688, Parliament established its supremacy: England became
a constitutional monarchy, and so it remains. The victorious parliamentary
leaders of the time were called "Whigs," and their defeated royalist enemies
were the "Tories."

In the early 1700s, the Whigs ran the show in British politics—and on
the whole things settled down nicely. By the 1720s, a political consensus
was emerging, a consensus that the triumph of the Whigs had led Britain
to the best of all possible worlds, in political terms. British liberty was safe,
the British monarchy was tamed, and the supremacy of Parliament would
guarantee trustworthy governance.

But on the fringes of British political life a consequential minority dissented. A group that historians would later call the "Radical Whigs" was
convinced that the Whig revolution had been terminated much too soon.
The power of the Crown had been tamed, it was true, but the seductions
of power could corrupt the politicians in Parliament as surely as they turned
conceited kings into tyrants. According to the Radical Whig pamphleteers,
any gathering of power was a danger to precious English liberties. And so
they urged the British people to be watchful. They urged British subjects to
arise en masse whenever government curbed their prerogatives.

"They were the Cassandras of the age," in the opinion of Bernard Bailyn, the foremost American historian to study the movement.

> Few of them accepted the Glorious Revolution and the lax political pragmatism that had followed as the final solution to the political problems of the time. . . . They refused to believe that the transfer of sovereignty from the crown to Parliament provided a perfect guarantee that the individual would be protected from the power of the state. . . . They insisted, at a time when government was felt to be less oppressive than it had been for two hundred years, that it was necessarily—by its very nature—hostile to human liberty . . . and that it could be, and reasonably should be, dismissed—overthrown—if it attempted to exceed its proper jurisdiction.[1]

The most prominent Radical Whigs in the 1720s were John Trenchard and Thomas Gordon, whose pamphlet series *Cato's Letters* invoked the name of an ancient Roman senator, Marcus Porcius Cato the Younger, who committed suicide at Utica in 46 B.C. after Julius Caesar defeated Pompey the Great. Death, proclaimed Cato, was better by far than to live under Caesar's rule. The heroic image of Cato in eighteenth-century Britain (and America) was in part the result of an influential play, Joseph Addison's *Tragedy of Cato*, which was first performed in 1712.

According to Bailyn's research, these British pamphleteers made a huge impression in colonial America decades before the American Revolution put their theories into practice. "To say simply that this tradition of opposition thought was quickly transmitted to America and widely appreciated there is to understate the fact," according to Bailyn. In truth, the Radical Whig worldview was "devoured by the colonists. . . . From the earliest years of the century it nourished their political thought and sensibilities."[2]

This was the background to proto-revolutionary agitation in colonial America when "Sons of Liberty" denounced the new British imperial taxes as harbingers of a despotism that would steal away the liberties of Englishmen. This was the world in which Patrick Henry and Samuel Adams raised alarms and called for resistance. This was in many ways the ideological background to American nationhood—and so it stood to reason that American patriots would flinch from the prospect of granting much power to the government they made for themselves in the course of the American Revolution. On the contrary, the United States government established in our first constitution (the Articles of Confederation) was notoriously weak.

And so it failed. It failed so completely in the 1780s as to prompt such movers and shakers of the time as James Madison and Alexander Hamilton (joined in 1787 by George Washington, Benjamin Franklin, and many others) to agitate for stronger national governance. The upshot, of course, was the Constitutional Convention, which created a government with clearly articulated power to tax, to regulate interstate commerce, to establish a federal judiciary system, and more.

But the Constitution was fervently opposed by a wide range of "Anti-Federalists" (including such patriots as Patrick Henry and Samuel Adams) who continued to fear what a gathering of national power might eventually do to American liberties. It was largely to reduce the concerns of such people that James Madison agreed to the drafting of a Bill of Rights, which would be added to the federal Constitution in the form of the first ten amendments.

The Constitution triumphed, and the federal government was launched. But we have seen what happened in the next ten years: the feud among the Founders as leaders like Hamilton strove to move the nation toward great power status. In response, as we have seen, the dissenters like Jefferson warned against "consolidated" government. And before very long, James Madison began to change his mind—he rejected "consolidated" governance—and began his long alliance with Jefferson.

Though he never opposed the new federal Constitution, Jefferson was still in many ways an old-fashioned Radical Whig. But he was also affected by emergent liberal doctrines: free speech and free press and free markets. Maximum liberty was Jefferson's creed and so he fought tooth and nail against the dangers of the Hamiltonian program and thus became, over time, an iconic and legendary figure in America's long libertarian tradition.

But in his presidential years he quickly changed: he embraced the very measures he had warned against a few years before. He saw that liberty and power could be harmonized. And he liked the idea when he got a good taste of it . . . in office.

Though some disappointed followers of his—John Randolph of Roanoke, for instance—denounced him as a crass opportunist and a traitor to his very own principles, Jefferson chose to ignore them. The task of building an "empire of liberty" was far too enticing for Jefferson. So he continued to become more flexible. And he continued to attract more followers.

JEFFERSON'S CONVERSION AND ITS AFTERMATH

The first substantial use of Hamiltonian means for Jeffersonian ends would thus appear with the conversion of Jefferson. In his presidential years he began to be expansive and less doctrinaire about the proper scope of national governance. Indeed, well before Hamilton's death at the hands of Aaron Burr—who killed him in a duel that they fought at Weehawken, New Jersey, on July 11, 1804—the transformation of Jefferson was obvious.

It began in the previous year (1803) with the offer of Napoleon to sell the immense Louisiana Territory. In order to accept this offer, Jefferson—the advocate of minimal government—was obliged to make use of his government's power in unprecedented ways. For the Constitution said nothing with regard to the power to annex foreign lands. Consequently, Jefferson construed the Constitution broadly. Moreover, the purchase was financed through deficit spending or a clear variation thereof. Payment to Napoleon was made in U.S. bonds (promises to pay with interest). Napoleon cashed them in on the European bond market.[3]

This was merely the beginning of Jefferson's conversion to the use of Hamiltonian methods. In order to expedite the settlement of new western lands, he approved the use of federal funds to start a "National Road" that extended from Cumberland, Maryland, to Wheeling, Virginia—the first installment in the long and important history of federal support for transportation infrastructure. He authorized Albert Gallatin, his secretary of the treasury, to issue a report on roads and canals that would guide the nation's development.

The Gallatin Report that was delivered to Congress in April 1808, called for a great inland network of waterways and highways at the cost of $20,000,000. "The general utility of artificial roads and canals is at this time so universally admitted," Gallatin wrote, "as hardly to require any additional proofs." And since there were many circumstances that "naturally check the application of private capital and enterprise to improvements on a large scale," he continued, it was likely that the "General Government alone can remove these obstacles."[4] Hamilton had made the same point nearly ten years before.

By the end of his second presidential term, Thomas Jefferson was pushing even further. In his final message to Congress, he urged the legislative branch to consider the expenditure of federal funds for "the improvement of roads, canals, education, and other great foundations of prosperity and union under the powers which Congress may already possess or such amendment of the Constitution as may be approved by the states."[5] In the field of education, he endorsed an idea that George Washington suggested years earlier: the creation by Congress of a national university. James Madison agreed. He wrote that a "seminary of learning" should be "instituted by the National Legislature" since a "well-instructed people alone can be permanently a free people."[6]

Both Jefferson and Madison admitted the extent to which they used Hamiltonian devices. But Madison invoked the mitigation of changing circumstances, observing that "the Republican party has been reconciled to certain measures & arrangements which may be as proper now as they were premature and suspicious when urged by the champions of federalism."[7] Jefferson was more nonchalant: "I know . . . that laws and institutions must go hand in hand with the progress of the human mind," he acknowledged in 1816. "As that becomes more developed, more enlightened, as new discoveries are made, new truths disclosed, and manners and opinions change with the change of circumstances, institutions must advance also, and keep pace with the times."[8]

The War of 1812 interrupted any plans for civilian public works. Yet it added to the overall logic and momentum of proposals for national development. For the war was in many ways a narrow escape for America. American performance in the war was disappointing, and the reason was very clear to policymakers: the nation had never really mobilized itself for a major conflict.

After peace had been secured in the Treaty of Ghent (which was signed on Christmas Eve, 1814), a consensus developed for a national buildup to help the young republic defend itself in any future wars. A second Bank of the United States was chartered in 1816 (the charter of the first bank had long since expired in 1811). The call for a nationwide system of roads and canals became stronger. One of the most fervent advocates of such "internal improvement" was John C. Calhoun of South Carolina, who served in the Monroe administration as secretary of war from 1817 to 1825. The United States, he told Congress in 1817, was "rapidly, I was about to say fearfully, growing. This is our pride and danger—our weakness and our strength. . . . Let us, then, bind the Republic together with a perfect system of roads and canals. Let us conquer space."[9]

The times were auspicious for a national consensus, for the old party system was dissolving with remarkable speed. The Federalist Party fell apart in the aftermath of war, and all the major political figures who were rising in the Jefferson-Madison Republican Party were enthusiastic champions of public works. In addition to Calhoun, there was Henry Clay of Kentucky, who envisioned an "American System" in which a dynamic and activist government would harmonize the needs of all the regions. He echoed the plea of Calhoun for preparedness; Americans should "act, seriously, effectively act, on the principle that in peace we ought to prepare for war," Clay declared. He urged civilian public works as well; the nation, he said, should construct a "chain of turnpikes, roads and canals from Passamaquoddy to New Orleans," a network that would "intersect the mountains." The nation needed thoroughfares and roads that would "bind and connect us together."[10] As historian Robert V. Remini has said, Clay "offered a planned national economy responsive to the new industrial age."[11]

To facilitate the building of infrastructure, Clay advocated broad construction of the Constitution. "All the powers of this government," Clay stated in an 1824 speech, "should be interpreted in reference to its first, its best, its greatest object, the Union." And in that regard, he continued, "we believe that the government incontestibly possesses the constitutional power to execute such internal improvements as are called for by the good of the whole."[12]

Broad construction of the Constitution had Supreme Court approval. In the case of *McCulloch v. Maryland*, Chief Justice John Marshall (writing for a unanimous court) had handed down the following formula in 1819: "Let the end be legitimate, let it be within the scope of the constitution, and all means which are appropriate, which are plainly adapted to that end, which are not prohibited, but consist with the letter and spirit of the constitution, are constitutional."[13]

In 1824, a like-minded Congress passed a General Survey Act to update the Gallatin Report and smooth the way for public works funding. A related piece of legislation vested the U.S. Army Corps of Engineers with responsibility for improving the nation's river and harbor infrastructure.[14] 1824 was also an election year: James Monroe was about to retire from the presidency.

The next president, John Quincy Adams, recommended a massive public works program in his first message to Congress on November 25, 1825: a huge outlay for internal improvements, the founding of a national university and astronomical observatory, the creation of a new Department of the Interior, and more. He supported the "cultivation and encouragement of the mechanic and of the elegant arts, the advancement of literature, and the progress of the sciences," all under federal auspices.[15]

But it was not to be—not yet. For determined opposition killed the Adams proposals in Congress; indeed, the consensus for internal improvements fell apart by the 1830s. A major change in political culture was beginning, and another generation would have to elapse before the program that John Quincy Adams had proposed would be realized, if only in part, by Lincoln and the Civil War Republicans.

THE OPPOSITION TO PUBLIC WORKS AFTER 1824

The program of John Quincy Adams was defeated for two reasons: (1) the rise of a second party system, with one of the parties reviving all the principles of minimal government, and (2) a fear within the leadership circles of the South that a powerful government could fall into the hands of abolitionists.

The old Jefferson-Madison Republican Party was unable to contain the ambitions of rival politicians in election year 1824. Four candidates—John Quincy Adams, Henry Clay, Andrew Jackson, and William Crawford—campaigned for the presidency. Since none of them prevailed in the Electoral College, the election was thrown into the House of Representatives, where Adams and Clay made a deal: in return for his support, Adams pledged to appoint Clay secretary of state, which at that point was something of a springboard to the presidency. Adams himself had served as secretary of state under Monroe.

Andrew Jackson and his vocal supporters denounced this "corrupt bargain." They swore to drive the Adams administration out of office in the next election. Meanwhile, they thwarted the Adams program as much as they could. By 1828 they succeeded in toppling Adams: Jackson triumphed and the age of "Jacksonian Democracy" was launched.

A new party system was emerging: Adams and his followers had called themselves "National Republicans" in 1828, while the followers of Jackson revived the old Jefferson nomenclature and called themselves "Democratic Republicans." Before long, the followers of Jackson were known simply as "Democrats."

An integral part of Jacksonian political culture was revival of the old conservative-liberal enmity—so heavily based in the politics of economic class. Jackson and his followers persistently claimed that Adams was a haughty aristocrat, whereas Jackson ("Old Hickory") was a self-made man and the champion of common men everywhere. A Jefferson-Jackson affinity was touted by the Democrats in these years. They gradually revived the old Jeffersonian creed of laissez-faire (while dismissing or forgetting the conversion of Jefferson to public works measures later on).[16]

The Jacksonians claimed that strong government tends to protect the rich; consequently, the slogan of the party's *Democratic Review* was "That government governs best, which governs least," and the slogan of the *Washington Globe*, the journalistic house organ of Jacksonian Democracy, was "The world is too much governed."[17] Jackson vetoed internal improvements and destroyed the second Bank of the United States when its supporters tried to recharter it.

The leaders of the other party—the National Republicans—tried to do what they could to stem the currents of Jacksonian politics. They ran their best candidate, Henry Clay, in the election of 1832. But Jackson prevailed. His "common man" appeal was very hard for his opponents to beat, and so the National Republicans decided to turn the tables on Jackson if they could: they called him "King Andrew the First" and portrayed him as a presidential despot who vetoed the measures that the people, through their duly elected representatives in Congress, wished to enact.

This turn-the-tables logic led them to change their party's name by the middle of the 1830s to the "Whig" Party, thus invoking the English tradition of *limiting* the power of the monarch. What resulted was an interesting inversion of message: though the Whigs believed in *energetic* governance, their party's new name implied a program of *limited* governance. Because of these tactics ("if you can't beat 'em, join 'em") the principle of governmental stewardship was almost a truth that could not speak its name in the Jacksonian period.[18]

That changed to a certain extent when the Panic of 1837 caused the worst economic depression up to that time in American history. Old Hickory's destruction of America's central bank (the second Bank of the United States) had ruinous effects. For the central bank had performed a vital function in relation to the state-chartered banks of America.

According to economic historians Gary M. Walton and Hugh Rockoff, the private, state-chartered banks that were empowered "to issue their own paper money, redeemable in gold or silver," made extensive loans in the form of paper banknotes "that came to be accepted at widely varying rates." Since the banks were creating this money on the basis of fractional reserves, the notes' value depended on the size of the specie reserves (in gold or silver coin) that the bankers retained for the purpose of redeeming the notes when people turned them in for cash payment. Walton and Rockoff continue, "Notes of established, reputable, 'specie-paying' banks were taken at their face value—that is, at par—over wide areas. Bills of other banks were received at discounts ranging from 1 or 2 percent up to 50 percent or more."[19] Some of the so-called wildcat banks of the era kept little gold or silver in reserve. Such banks of course failed when a crisis occurred and their circulating notes became worthless.

The second Bank of the United States kept the system secure in three ways: (1) its notes were universally accepted; (2) it could function as a "lender of last resort" to state banks when they experienced problems; and (3) it made a practice of returning the notes of other banks, when it received them, for redemption at the banks that created them. This forced the state banks to keep large enough reserves to preserve their reputations and sustain their operations with sufficient cash "liquidity." As Walton and Rockoff have argued, "by the late 1820s, the paper money of the country was in a very satisfactory state."[20] But Andrew Jackson destroyed all this: with the central bank gone, people's confidence in bank money dropped. Consequently,

> more and more people returned paper for specie at their banks. When large numbers of noteholders attempted to do this, the banks were unable to make the exchanges, and banking panics occurred. (A strong second bank might have been able to nip these panics in the bud by acting as a lender of last resort.) The result was a sharp but temporary recession in 1837 and, finally, one of the worst depressions of the century from 1839 to 1843.[21]

Old Hickory's legacy was ruin for many farmers and merchants.

Jackson's Democratic successor, Martin Van Buren, was prevented by his party's ideology from sponsoring relief measures. But the Whigs proposed public works to improve the country's infrastructure and assist all the unemployed workers. Looking back, for instance, on the failure of his program during the 1820s, old John Quincy Adams lamented in 1837 that his policies "would have afforded high wages and constant employment to hundreds of thousands of laborers," and that "every dollar expended would have repaid itself fourfold."[22]

By the same logic, young Abraham Lincoln—a follower of Clay who was serving at the time as a Whig floor leader in the Illinois legislature—pushed canal- and railroad-building projects that would stimulate employment and turn the economy around.[23] It is striking to note the degree to which the Whig economic agenda for creating public works in the 1830s in many ways heralded the New Deal measures of FDR and the policies that John Maynard Keynes would recommend a century later. John Quincy Adams, Henry Clay, and Abraham Lincoln could all be called proto-Keynesians to some extent.

Despite some intermittent successes, the Whigs remained the opposition party for much of the antebellum period. The institutional growth of the federal government advanced with the creation of the Department of the Interior in 1849, and yet the public works agenda on the national level continued to languish. The Democrats—members of the anti-government party—continued to call the shots a great deal of the time.

Perhaps this is the place to observe that the Democrats *abandoned laissez-faire when it came to Indian removal*: they were quite prepared to use federal force on behalf of white settlers who coveted the Indians' land. The Indian Removal Act of 1830 codified a trend that had developed for years. It constitutes a race-based injustice of early America that cannot be excused or shrugged away. Granted, the culture clash between the very different ways of life—the "Indian" way and the "white" way—could be a problem at various times: some of the Native Americans were warlike. But others were peaceful and settled, and the peaceful Indians were treated quite shamefully by Jackson. The removal of the Cherokee Indians from Georgia in the 1830s was nothing less than a disgrace. Notwithstanding this particular recourse to federal force—military force—Jacksonians continued to oppose the principle of federally supported public works. And so the vision of John Quincy Adams and Henry Clay was unrealized.

The second major reason why the champions of internal improvements were defeated was the growing perception in the slave-holding South that a powerful government in Washington was something to be dreaded. After the Missouri Crisis that began in 1819, southern leaders were fearful that the ever-growing population of the free-state bloc would reduce the existing bloc of slave states to minority status in the Union. That being the case, pro-slavery leaders tried to thwart the creation of a robust government in Washington. They feared a government they couldn't control.

This is what propelled the spectacular 180° turn that changed John C. Calhoun from an ardent supporter of internal improvements to the militant states-rights theorist who wrote the "Exposition and Protest" against the federal tariff that was passed by Congress in 1828. But the tariff was largely symbolic—symbolic of the danger that a well-funded government could pose to the "southern way of life." Calhoun admitted that "I consider the Tariff, but as the occasion, rather than the real cause of the present unhappy state of things. . . . The truth can no longer be disguised, that the peculiar domestic institutions of the Southern States . . . [have] placed them in regard to taxation and appropriation in opposite relation to the majority of the Union."[24] As historian William W. Freehling has observed, pro-slavery militants feared that "the 'general welfare' clause would serve abolitionists as well as road builders."[25]

So the southerners began to be obstructionists. They sought to make certain that American life would be safely bogged down in the meandering ways of states' rights. John Quincy Adams observed that "when I came to the presidency the principle of internal improvement was swelling the tide of public prosperity, 'till the Sable Genius of the South saw the signs of his own inevitable downfall . . . and fell to cursing the tariff and internal improvement, and raised the standard of free trade, nullification, and state rights. I fell and with me fell, I fear never to rise again . . . the system of internal improvements by means of national energies."[26]

But a vestige of the Adams agenda—an institution to promote the diffusion of knowledge—came to pass in the antebellum years. It was created with help from abroad. In 1829, a wealthy British philanthropist died in Genoa. His last will and testament provided that if and when his nephew should die without heirs, his estate should be given "to the United States of America, to found at Washington . . . an establishment for the increase and diffusion of knowledge."

The nephew died in 1835—without heirs. Calhoun and his fellow southern militants opposed the idea of pursuing the British bequest: the idea was an affront to "states' rights." But John Quincy Adams led a tireless campaign to get the money, and he finally succeeded. The bequest was received at the U.S. Treasury in 1838.

Almost ten years later, in 1846, Congress passed legislation that created, under federal auspices, the institution envisioned by the wealthy British benefactor: James Smithson. The result was the Smithsonian Institution, which, through its popular museums on the National Mall, continues to exemplify (if only in part) the great vision that John Quincy Adams had expressed back in 1825.

LINCOLN AND THE "BLUEPRINT FOR MODERN AMERICA"

The young American republic—proclaiming to the world the self-evident truth that all men are created equal—was afflicted by a shameful contradiction that was very hard to confront: the presence of slavery. And the way in which Americans resolved the contradiction almost tore the United States apart.

American slavery of course would be destroyed at the *national* level—through *federal power*. And pro-slavery leaders had feared this development for years before it occurred. Their worst-case scenario was nothing less than this: an anti-slavery amendment to the Constitution.

With a free-state majority in place, southern leaders would be powerless to stop such a measure in Congress. And if the free-state majority eventually outnumbered the slave states in three-to-one terms, the amendment might be ratified.

To avert this development, defenders of slavery kept pushing the expansion of the South's "peculiar institution." Their goal was to increase the number of the slave states. Concurrently, opponents of slavery kept trying to *prevent* the expansion of the evil. They wanted *federal action* to stop it. So another "big government" issue appeared in American life: the issue of whether or not *the federal government possessed clear constitutional power* to stop the spread of slavery.

From the time of its founding in 1854, the Republican Party (which supplanted the older Whig Party) insisted that the federal government *did* possess such power. Republicans pointed out historical and legal precedents: the Northwest Ordinance of 1787, which prevented the extension of slavery into former colonial lands above the Ohio River, and the later Missouri Compromise, which drew a sharp dividing line across the Louisiana Purchase to separate the lands that were open to slavery from those that were not.

But John C. Calhoun began to work out a theory that would undercut such federal action. He began to argue that the *Fifth Amendment* to the Constitution made the federal government powerless to stop the spread of slavery.

The Fifth Amendment states, in part, that "No person shall be . . . deprived of life, liberty, or property, without due process of law." Slaves were a form of property. And if the owners of slaves were prevented by congressional action from bringing this property to federal lands (specifically, the lands within the western territories), they would thus be "deprived" of the property, according to Calhoun.

A rather far-fetched argument perhaps, but this was the doctrine that was solemnly affirmed by the United States Supreme Court in the infamous *Dred Scott* decision of 1857, which declared the Missouri Compromise unconstitutional and voided the power of Congress (or the territorial legislatures) to stop the expansion of slavery in federal lands.

Thus far we have seen how southern leaders were trying to *protect themselves from federal power.* It bears noting, however, that they also made attempts in the antebellum years to get *control* of federal power—and then *use it* to their own advantage. The most obvious example of this was the Fugitive Slave Law of 1850, which directed the federal government to interdict runaway slaves.[27] But a far more important example was a haunting "what-if" possibility—perceived by Lincoln and others—in the aftermath of *Dred Scott.*

On its surface, Calhoun's Fifth-Amendment doctrine (as employed by Taney and his Court) was a *hindrance* to federal power. But as Lincoln pointed out very clearly (most distinctly in his "house divided" speech), the *Dred Scott* decision had been grounded in the *Constitution*, the supreme law of the land. And if the Constitution, as construed by Taney, *protected the right to bring slaves into federal lands*, then perhaps southern advocates of slavery would start to declare that *the Constitution protected their right to bring their slaves into all of the states*—including the *free states*—and then keep them *there as long as they wished*. A pro-slavery twist to the Constitution could lead to pro-slavery actions by the federal government that would trump the power of the free states. Lincoln put it this way:

> "A house divided against itself cannot stand."
>
> I believe this government cannot endure, permanently half *slave* and half *free*.
>
> I do not expect the Union to be *dissolved*—I do not expect the house to *fall*—but I do expect it will cease to be divided. It will become *all* one thing, or *all* the other. Either the *opponents* of slavery, will arrest the further spread of it, and place it where the public mind shall rest in the belief that it is in course of ultimate extinction; or its *advocates* will push it forward, till it shall become alike lawful in *all* the States, *old* as well as *new*—North as well as *South*.[28]

The latter scenario could happen very easily, said Lincoln. "We shall *lie down* pleasantly dreaming that the people of *Mississippi* are on the verge of making their State *free*," he declared, but then "*awake to the reality*, instead, that the Supreme Court has made *Illinois a slave State*."[29]

There is reason to believe that Lincoln's fears were precisely on target. As political philosopher Harry V. Jaffa once wrote,

> there is no reason to suppose that, should slavery in the mines, foundries, factories, and fields of the free states have proved advantageous to powerful groups therein, new systems of discipline might not have been invented to make the exploitation of slave labor highly profitable. The totalitarian regimes of the twentieth century provide us with ample evidence of the variety of ways that this might have been done. . . . It is simply unhistorical to say that such a thing *couldn't* happen because it *didn't* happen. It didn't happen because Lincoln was resolved that it *shouldn't* happen. And nothing but his implacable will made it impossible.[30]

So the struggle over slavery devolved into a brawl over federal power. The American issue of slavery would turn upon the fortunes of the rival blocs of states—the free-state bloc and the slave-state bloc—that were locked in an all-out political struggle for control of the federal government.

The South was positioned to go either way: when the leaders of the South had federal power, the defenders of slavery invoked constitutional protections and hailed them as sovereign. But as soon as their spokesmen lost control or were ousted from their federal positions, southern leaders were prepared to renounce the Constitution and to champion the rights of the states.

When Lincoln prevailed in the election of 1860—and his party took control of Congress as well—southern leaders saw at once that they had lost any lingering control over federal power.[31] So they decided to break up the Union. And the result was the triumph of Lincoln and the Civil War Republicans, who stopped the secessionists, terminated slavery, and used the long-dormant power of the federal government.

The federal presence in the 1860s was colossal by antebellum standards. The Democrats of course were quite appalled. But the Republicans were eager to use the occasion to revive the great vision of internal improvements that John Quincy Adams and Henry Clay had espoused so many years before.

Historian James M. McPherson has observed the degree to which the new Republican Party "inherited from its Hamiltonian and Whig forebears a commitment to the use of government" for several purposes. Republicans supported the use of federal power "to foster economic development through tariffs to protect industry, a centralized and regulated banking system, investment subsidies and land grants to high-risk but socially beneficial transportation enterprises, and government support for education. By 1860 the Republican Party had also pledged itself to homestead legislation to provide farmers with an infusion of capital in the form of free land."[32] With Lincoln's support, the Republicans created what McPherson has called "an astonishing blitz of laws [which] did more to reshape the relation of the government to the economy than any comparable effort except perhaps the first hundred days of the New Deal."[33] Historian Leonard P. Curry has called it the "blueprint for modern America."[34]

Lincoln was a very keen supporter of internal improvements when he served in the Illinois legislature many years earlier. As a Whig floor leader, he was deeply involved in the creation and funding of canal and railroad projects in Illinois. And he also supported the creation of public works projects at the national level. He remained an ardent believer in Henry Clay's "American System."

When Lincoln was elected to Congress in the 1840s he touted such projects directly. On June 20, 1848, he made a speech on the floor of the House of Representatives rebutting Democratic objections to internal improvements and denouncing a public works veto by Democratic president James K. Polk. Lincoln was quick to dismiss Democratic allegations in regard to constitutional issues: "No one," said Lincoln, "who is satisfied with the expediency of making improvements, needs be much uneasy in his conscience about its constitutionality."[35]

Nor was Lincoln uneasy regarding his opponents' allegation that the taxes to support public works "would be *general*, while their benefits would [be] *local* and *partial*, involving an obnoxious inequality." Such petty objections were myopic, in Lincoln's estimation, and he offered a comparison to prove it:

> The Navy, as I understand it, was established, and is maintained at a great annual expense, partly to be ready for war when war shall come, but partly also, and perhaps chiefly, for the protection of our commerce on the high seas. This latter object is, for all I can see, in principle, the same as internal improvements. The driving [of] a pirate from the track of commerce on the broad ocean, and the removing of a snag from its more narrow path in the Mississippi River, can not, I think, be distinguished in principle.[36]

Lincoln admitted that Americans would always be inclined to disagree to some extent about *specific* internal improvements. And these arguments could lead to bitter quarrels. Lincoln gave some examples: "One man is offended because a road passes over his land, and another is offended because it does *not* pass over his. One is dissatisfied because the bridge, for which he is taxed, crosses the river on a different road from that which leads from his house to town; another can not bear that the county should be got in debt for these same roads and bridges; while not a few struggle hard to have roads located over their lands, and then stoutly refuse to let them be opened until they are first paid the damages."

But the way to overcome such "wrangling," said Lincoln, was to base all internal improvements on "*facts*" instead of "whim, caprice, or local interest." He exhorted the members of Congress to begin the work in earnest: "Determine that the thing can and shall be done," he suggested, "and then we shall find the way."[37]

Though Lincoln did not support deficit spending for improvements at the national level in the years before the Civil War—"I would not borrow money," he avowed in 1848—his support for active governance grew.[38] Lincoln said in the 1850s that "the legitimate object of government" was "to do for the people what needs to be done, but which they cannot, by individual effort, do at all, or do so well, for themselves."[39]

When the Civil War erupted, most congressional slave-state leaders resigned from the federal Congress: the oppositionists went down to Richmond. And since Republican majorities prevailed in both the Senate and the House after 1860, Republicans proceeded to enact (in updated form) the sort of program that John Quincy Adams and Henry Clay had espoused a generation earlier.

In 1862 they passed the Homestead Act and the Morrill Act creating the land-grant college system. They created the Department of Agriculture in preliminary form. They authorized land grants and loans to the newly chartered Union Pacific Railroad Company. And in 1863 they founded the National Academy of Sciences.

They expanded the money supply in 1862 through the Legal Tender Act—an emergency measure creating $150 million (expanded within six months to a total of $300 million) worth of paper "fiat" money, the United States notes that were known informally as "Greenbacks."

In 1863 they began to create a sophisticated system of national banks whose notes would total $300 million. In return for their charters, the banks were required to invest a percentage of their capital in federal bonds. Then the bonds would be placed on deposit in the Treasury. (The banknotes bore the statements "National Currency" and "Secured by United States Bonds deposited with the Treasurer of the United States.") The *New York Times* proclaimed that this new financial system was a "centralization of power, such as Hamilton might have eulogized as magnificent."[40]

The effects of the Republican program were momentous when compared to the paucity of federal action in previous decades. Historian Leonard P. Curry has said that "the measures dealing with the public lands and national support for public improvements were of far-reaching social and economic significance. The gigantic transportation works and the colleges and universities—good, bad, and indifferent—which were built in the years that followed, left nothing that they touched unchanged."[41] Senator John Sherman of Ohio reflected in 1863 that the new Republican laws "cover such vast sums, delegate and regulate such vast powers, and are so far-reaching in their effects, that generations will be affected well or ill by them."[42] He also proclaimed that "the policy of this country ought to be to make everything national as far as possible; to nationalize our country so that we shall love our country."[43]

The Union military effort in the Civil War—an immense undertaking for which Congress authorized $500 million in July 1861—was underwritten by deficit spending. Indeed, two-thirds of all the Union war revenues were raised in this manner.[44] Congress also passed the first progressive income tax in American history to finance the war. Meanwhile, Lincoln was a vigorous advocate of bond-financed efforts to rid the nation of slavery.

Well before he decided to issue the Emancipation Proclamation, he had tried to initiate a program to phase out the institution of slavery in border states loyal to the Union. From the very beginning, his financing depended on bonds. Late in 1861, he drafted legislation that he hoped would be enacted by Delaware, the smallest of the slave states. "Be it enacted by the State of Delaware," Lincoln's draft proclaimed, "that on condition the United States of America will, at the present session of Congress, engage by law to pay . . . in the six per cent bonds of the United States, the sum of seven hundred and nineteen thousand and two hundred dollars, in five equal instalments [sic], there shall be neither slavery nor involuntary servitude, at any time after the first day of January in the year of our Lord one thousand, eight hundred and sixty-seven, within the said State of Delaware."[45]

There is reason to believe that Lincoln's long-cherished vision of a slavery phase-out was based upon the method the British had used when they rid their empire of slavery. Parliament voted in 1833 to pay £20 million to all the slave owners in the British West Indies as they freed their human property.[46] In a private memorandum from 1858, Lincoln mused that "the abolition of the Slave-Trade by Great Brittain [sic] was agitated a hundred years before it was a final success. . . . School-boys know that Wilbe[r]force and Granville Sharpe, helped that cause forward; but who can now name a single man who labored to retard it?"[47]

In a feistier line, he consoled himself that the anti-slavery leaders in Britain had to face extraordinary obstacles; their program had

> its open fire-eating opponents; its stealthy "don't care" opponents; its dollar and cent opponents; its inferior race opponents; its religion and good order opponents. . . . All these opponents got offices, and their adversaries got none. [But] I have also remembered that though they blazed, like tallow-candles for a century, at last they flickered in the socket, died out, stank in the dark for a brief season, and were remembered no more, even by the smell.[48]

So he fortified himself to carry on: it was possible that "the higher object of this contest may not be completely attained within the term of my natural life," he wrote. But it would "come in due time."[49]

He seized the opportunity afforded by the war: the chance to start a great national phase-out of slavery, with compensation. When his Delaware ploy came to nothing, he convinced the Republican Congress to offer a buy-out plan to the slave states—even the rebel states—if they would phase out slavery. Republican Senator Charles Sumner rejoiced in the measure; "proceeding from the President," he wrote, "it must take its place among the great events of history."[50]

But not a single slave state, rebel or Unionist, adopted Lincoln's compensation plan. And so, in a steady but no doubt supremely angry frame of mind, he decided to free the Confederates' slaves by force. He pretended that emancipation was a measure to *save the Union only*. But this was surely a political deception: there were many other ways in which a president could have saved the Union, not least of all the Democrats' method of advocating peace talks to patch up the Union on distinctly pro-slavery terms. And the Democrats made this very clear.

Even after he had issued the Emancipation Proclamation on September 22, 1862—as a military measure, it was limited to slave states in active rebellion—Lincoln asked Congress to amend the Constitution for the purpose of creating a long-term voluntary phase-out program in the *non*-rebellious slave states. In his annual message to Congress of December 1, 1862, he encouraged a constitutional amendment providing that "Every state, wherein slavery now exists, which shall abolish the same therein, at any time, or times, before the year of our Lord one thousand and nine hundred, shall receive compensation from the United States."

Once again, Lincoln's method was deficit spending via bonds. He argued that prosperity resulting from our national growth would make the economic burden much lighter by 1900. By the turn of the twentieth century, he argued, "we shall probably have a hundred millions of people to share the burden, instead of thirty one millions, as now."[51] "Debt" was no impediment for Lincoln and price was no object when it came to his grandest objectives. At the end of the war, when Congress passed the Thirteenth Amendment—abolishing slavery everywhere—Lincoln flirted with the notion of *paying* all the slave states to ratify. The price tag: another $400 million.[52]

All of this was quite Hamiltonian. Historian Phillip Shaw Paludan has affirmed that the "more perfect Union" resulting from the work of the Civil War Republicans "was achieved chiefly through an extraordinary outreach of national authority."[53] But the outreach of national authority was often rather Jeffersonian in spirit: it sought to broaden the meaning of equality. "All honor to Jefferson," Lincoln had written in 1859, "the man who had the coolness, forecast, and capacity to introduce into a merely revolutionary document an abstract truth": all men are created equal.[54] In 1865, Republicans created a new social welfare agency: the Freedmen's Bureau, created with Lincoln's approval to extend humanitarian and legal assistance to the former slaves.

Surely Lincoln achieved a magnificent synthesis of Hamiltonian and Jeffersonian values. Indeed—as I have argued elsewhere at length—his audacity and brilliance as a magistrate remain unsurpassed in American history.[55] He was the greatest moral strategist our nation has produced, and he ended American slavery.

But there was more: in Lincoln-style governance, conservative and liberal attitudes regarding human nature were harmonized. One can certainly argue that Lincoln was *both* a conservative and liberal.[56]

The liberal side of Lincoln is easy enough to discern: in 1857 he said that when the Founders agreed to Jefferson's assertion that all men are created equal, "they meant to set up a standard maxim for free society which could be familiar to all, and revered by all, constantly looked to, constantly labored for, and even though never perfectly attained, constantly approximated, and thereby constantly spreading and deepening its influence, and augmenting the happiness and value of life to all people of all colors everywhere."[57] What statement more effectively distills the quintessential liberal spirit?

Lincoln's egalitarian side could be expressed with charisma. In 1858, when he tried to throw Stephen Douglas out of the Senate, Lincoln excoriated the man who had claimed that America's Declaration of Independence applied to whites only. No, said Lincoln, it applied to *all people everywhere*. (Note: Lincoln never referred to his opponent as *Senator* Douglas, but called him a "judge" for his earlier service on the Illinois Supreme Court. Lincoln sought in this manner to imply that the tenure of Douglas in the Senate would come to an end; his days in the Senate were numbered.) Here is Lincoln in action at a torchlight rally on the evening of July 10, 1858:

> Those arguments that are made, that the inferior race are to be treated with as much allowance as they are capable of enjoying; that as much is to be done for them as their condition will allow. What are these arguments? They are the arguments that kings have made for enslaving the people in all ages of the world. You will find that all the arguments in favor of king-craft were of this class; they always bestrode the necks of the people, not that they wanted to do it, but because the people were better off for being ridden. That is their argument,

and this argument of the Judge is the same old serpent that says you work and I eat, you toil and I will enjoy the fruit of it. Turn in whatever way you will—whether it come from the mouth of a King, an excuse for enslaving the people of his country, or from the mouth of men of one race as a reason for enslaving the men of another race, it is all the same old serpent, and I hold if that course of argumentation that is made for the purpose of convincing the public mind that we should not care about this, should be granted, it does not stop with the negro. I should like to know if taking this old Declaration of Independence, which declares that all men are equal upon principle and making exceptions to it where will it stop. If one man says it does not mean a negro, why not another say it does not mean some other man? If that declaration is not the truth, let us get the Statute book, in which we find it and tear it out! Who is so bold to do it! [Voices—"me" "no one," &c.] If it is not true let us tear it out![58]

In this sense, Lincoln's fundamental creed was surely liberal: antihierarchic. Yet this liberal quality in Lincoln was balanced by a grim and conservative instinct regarding the ugly side of human nature: the side of our nature that frustrates utopian visions. "Slavery," said Lincoln in 1854, "is grounded in the selfishness of man's nature, opposition to it in his love of justice. These principles are an eternal antagonism."[59]

Lincoln told the complacent in 1854 that "we cannot repeal human nature." We cannot repeal the side of human nature that revels in degrading and dominating others. We cannot repeal the side of human nature that proclaims, in the words of George Fitzhugh—an antebellum advocate of slavery—that "some were born with saddles on their backs, and others booted and spurred to ride them; and the riding does them good."[60] We cannot repeal the oppressive side of human nature, but we can *govern* it.

Here is the conservative Lincoln, who was able to look so unflinchingly at human evil and *call* it evil. In his first inaugural address he referred to "the better angels of our nature." But in his second inaugural address he invoked a more somber American tradition—a tradition handed down from the Puritans.

He spoke of the punishment inflicted on a wayward people for indulging the evil of slavery. A mighty and divine scourge of war, Lincoln said, had been sweeping the American land. And, "if God wills that it continue, until all the wealth piled by the bond-man's two hundred and fifty years of unrequited toil shall be sunk, and until every drop of blood drawn with the lash, shall be paid by another drawn with the sword, as was said three thousand years ago, so still it must be said 'the judgments of the Lord are true and righteous altogether.'"[61] As Harry V. Jaffa once observed, "a case against the people, as well as for them, was present in Lincoln's thought from beginning to end."[62]

In his second inaugural address this supreme proponent of democracy—"government of the people"—almost called in the manner of Carlyle for their moral *"obedience."* Jefferson said that his party had "cherished" the people while the other party feared and distrusted them. Lincoln "cherished" the people, but he clearly distrusted their tendency to do unto others what they wished to avoid having done to themselves.

He made an interesting speech about the politics of liberty in 1864. Freedom was a double-sided principle, the president explained. "The world has never had a good definition of the word liberty," Lincoln observed, "and the American people, just now, are much in want of one. . . . With some the word liberty may mean for each man to do as he pleases with himself and the product of his labor; while with others the same word may mean for some men to do as they please with other men, and the product of other men's labor. . . . The shepherd drives the wolf from the sheep's throat, for which the sheep thanks the shepherd as a *liberator*, while the wolf denounces him for the same act as a destroyer of liberty."[63]

It is therefore appropriate to say that Lincoln's governance philosophy was *balanced*, though still quite dynamic. Lincoln strove to do justice to the *best* and the *worst* of which our human nature is capable. Doing justice to the best of our nature, he believed that our government should help us—it should *underwrite* our human fulfillment. Doing justice to the worst of our nature, it must *regulate* tyrannical lusts. It must find effective ways to *restrain* them.

The triumph of American slavery was surely not averted by market forces, by the interplay of checks and balances, or even by moral protest. Protest of course was necessary, but only the decisive intervention of a genius using every Hamiltonian resource at his command could make America live up to its promises—the promises of Jefferson.

Through it all, a little child in Manhattan learned powerful lessons, as his civic-minded father expounded what Lincoln was achieving. Young Theodore Roosevelt revered Mr. Lincoln and his soldiers. Perhaps some notions in regard to his future were beginning to race through his mind already. He would champion the powerless, master all comers, and control human arrogance firmly. Perhaps a role more definite than this was beginning to work through his mind: presidential hero. He kept ponder-

Sweet victory: Abraham Lincoln as the end of the Civil War approaches. This picture was probably taken at the studio of Alexander Gardner in Washington, D.C., on February 5, 1865. Meserve # 100. Credit: Library of Congress.

ing the precedent that Lincoln had set—as he waited for his chance to measure up.

He would get his chance suddenly in 1901, with the murder of William McKinley. A Rooseveltian revival of Lincolnesque politics would launch the new twentieth century.

3

FROM LINCOLN
TO THEODORE ROOSEVELT

The historical bond between Lincoln and Theodore Roosevelt began very early when the future president's father—Theodore Roosevelt Sr.—left his home in upper-class Manhattan for a trip to the nation's capital in 1861. His purpose was to meet with the president.

Roosevelt and other philanthropic New Yorkers had developed a plan to create an allotment commission that would help the Union soldiers send a portion of their pay to their families. Roosevelt Sr. made overtures to John Hay—one of Lincoln's two executive secretaries. (Hay would later serve the nation as secretary of state under President Theodore Roosevelt.) "I explained my object in a few words," wrote the elder Roosevelt in a letter that he sent to his wife, "and was immediately shown into the next room where the President sat."

Lincoln approved of the allotment plan and so Roosevelt stayed in the nation's capital to lobby for its legislative enactment. He became close friends with John Hay. He also became a rather prominent member of the social circle that gathered around the First Lady, Mary Todd Lincoln.[1] James MacGregor Burns and Susan Dunn have written that the elder Roosevelt "enjoyed cordial relations with President and Mrs. Lincoln, joining them on carriage drives and sharing their pew in church."[2] Young Roosevelt heard all about it when his father came home, and there is reason to believe the boy witnessed the passing of Lincoln's funeral procession when it took its course through New York City on April 25, 1865.[3]

Burns and Dunn have observed that young Roosevelt grew up in a home "where the heritage of Lincoln was pervasive." So pervasive, indeed, was the heritage that all the great national figures who eventually emerged from the Roosevelt clan (Theodore, Franklin, Eleanor) were "inspired by Lincoln's example [to] define a new brand of pragmatic yet courageous political and moral leadership that would set a standard for American leaders—on the right and on the left."[4]

The influence of Lincoln on Theodore Roosevelt would last through the end of his life. And it was greater by far than the conventional reverence for Lincoln among the Republicans. Lincoln was Theodore Roosevelt's model of the ideal statesman. "As I suppose you know, Lincoln is my hero," wrote Theodore Roosevelt to George Otto Trevelyan in 1905.[5] He said the same thing to his own son four years later: "Lincoln is my great hero."[6] To another correspondent he wrote that "Lincoln has always meant more to me than any other of our public men, even Washington."[7]

His admiration for Lincoln went beyond appreciation of his personal qualities: his patience, brilliance, and courage. Theodore Roosevelt revered the work of Lincoln for ideological reasons. The demonstrable synthesis of left and right in Lincoln's statecraft became fundamental to the outlook of Theodore Roosevelt. In 1908—a year before the publication of Herbert Croly's landmark *Promise of American Life*—Roosevelt informed Sydney Brooks, a British-born journalist, that his "business" as a leader of Republicans had been "to take hold of the conservative party and turn it into what it had been under Lincoln, that is, a party of progressive conservatism, or conservative radicalism; for of course wise radicalism and wise conservatism go hand in hand."[8] In the very next year (apparently before he began to read Croly), Roosevelt praised the work of journalist William Allen White, who was working up a formulation of the Hamiltonian and Jeffersonian traditions that was similar to Croly's: "I think you have struck it exactly right as regards Jeffersonianism and Hamiltonianism. I have no use for the Hamiltonian who is aristocratic, or for the Jeffersonian who is a demagog [*sic*]. Let us trust the people as Jefferson did, but not flatter them; and let us try to have our administration as effective as Hamilton taught us to have it. Lincoln . . . struck the right average."[9]

It is interesting to note that these views—mature views expressed in his presidential years—were already taking shape in the mind of Theodore Roosevelt in early manhood. Looking back years later in his autobiography, he wrote of his political apprenticeship in the New York legislature, where he served in the early 1880s. He wrote about his friendship with Billy O'Neill, a state assemblyman from the Adirondacks, who shared his views on most issues. O'Neill had "thought much on political problems," and "we looked at all questions from substantially the same view-point," Roosevelt wrote. More specifically, "he admired Alexander Hamilton as much as I did, being a strong believer in a powerful national government; and we both of us differed from Alexander Hamilton in being stout adherents of Abraham Lincoln's views wherever the rights of the people were concerned."[10]

In some ways Roosevelt's character was quirky enough to prevent him from achieving the overall mastery that Lincoln displayed in his presidential years—he was far too impulsive at critical moments to achieve the self-control that made Lincoln such a consummate strategist. But he was staunchly determined to revive the prestige of the national government as Lincoln had used it before—to make "the State," as the poet Matthew Arnold expressed it, the instrument for summoning the nation's "right reason" or "collective best self."[11] No less than Lincoln, he would hold aloft American ideals—and enforce them.

RECONSTRUCTION AND THE GILDED AGE

Lincoln *enforced* our American ideals. He likened himself to a shepherd protecting the sheep from the liberty of wolves.

But in a free society the wolves have a say, and supporters of American slavery reviled Lincoln's so-called presidential tyranny throughout the Civil War. White supremacist "Copperhead" Democrats accused him in scathing terms of executive usurpation. They claimed he abused the Constitution he had taken an oath to defend.

Such charges have continued to resonate, left and right, to this day. A substantial cadre of Lincoln detractors—particularly strong in the southern states, but by no means restricted to the South—hold firm to this angry point of view.[12]

There are elements of truth in the notion that Lincoln had less regard—*slightly* less regard—for constitutionalism than his admirers might suppose. Lincoln obviously believed in the rule of *law*. And he knew that the law must be *construed*. He used all of his gifts as an attorney to defend his own emergency wartime measures—such as the suspensions of habeas corpus—with cogent constitutional logic. But holistic thinking made him view the Constitution as a means to a much higher end. It could never be an end in itself.

Lincoln's brand of constitutionalism went far beyond the penchant for "broad construction"—flexible interpretation—that he inherited from such distinguished forebears as Alexander Hamilton, John Marshall, and Henry Clay. The truth would appear to be this: Lincoln viewed the Constitution as possessing *less stature* than the Declaration of Independence—our nation's *freedom manifesto*. Lincoln made his veneration for our founding Declaration

very clear at many times in his life. In 1861, he declared at Independence
Hall that he had "never had a feeling politically that did not spring from
the sentiments embodied in the Declaration of Independence."[13] In feistier
language, he confessed that "all my political warfare has been in favor of
the teachings coming forth from that sacred hall. May my right hand forget
its cunning and my tongue cleave to the roof of my mouth, if ever I prove
false to those teachings."[14]

The Union itself was subservient in Lincoln's estimation to America's
purpose as the Declaration established it. In another speech that he made
in the early months of 1861, he told the Democratic mayor of New York
City that the Union was designed for a purpose beyond the mere existence
of the nation per se. He used a nautical metaphor to drive the point home
in his remarks:

> There is nothing that can ever bring me willingly to consent to the
> destruction of this Union . . . unless it were to be that thing for which
> the Union itself was made. I understand a ship to be made for the
> carrying and preservation of the cargo, and so long as the ship can be
> saved, with the cargo, it should never be abandoned. This Union itself
> should likewise never be abandoned unless it fails and the probability of
> its preservation shall cease to exist without throwing the passengers and
> the cargo overboard.[15]

At Independence Hall, Lincoln made the same point. The purpose of
the Declaration of Independence, he contended, "was not the mere matter
of the separation of the colonies from the mother land." It was "something
in that Declaration giving liberty, not alone to the people of this country,
but hope for the world for all future time." Then he startled his listeners as
follows: "If this country cannot be saved without giving up that principle,
I would rather be assassinated on the spot than to surrender it."[16]

Consider now a statement by Lincoln in response to a critic in 1864.
In the course of a letter that he wrote to this critic, Lincoln placed the continued existence of the nation (with its deep and intrinsic moral purpose)
far above the Constitution in value. He told his correspondent that emergency conditions made him act upon the theory "that measures, otherwise
unconstitutional, might become lawful, by becoming indispensable to the
preservation of the constitution, through the preservation of the nation."
He was saying, in effect, that American survival trumped the Constitution
in importance: if the nation (with its promise of freedom) went down to
defeat, then the Constitution went with it. For that reason, constitutional
haggling should yield to more significant statecraft.[17]

It is useful to articulate the hierarchy of values that Lincoln appeared to be invoking: it was the *Declaration of Independence*, with its "sacred" equality principle ("the standard maxim of free society," as Lincoln had called it in 1857), that Lincoln revered, whereas the Constitution—an *amendable* package of provisions—was essentially *derivative*. Here is the progression, in descending order of importance: the Declaration (setting forth the nation's moral purpose at the Founding), the Union (providing the framework of nationhood itself), the Constitution (a framework of legal mechanics, replacing an earlier framework, the Articles of Confederation).

It is useful as well to remember Lincoln's readiness to *change* the Constitution to adapt it to the nation's development. For this reason Lincoln fervently supported the Thirteenth Amendment, which abolished slavery forever and placed power to prohibit involuntary servitude in federal hands.

Thus began a constitutional revolution-through-amendment—a revolution in American jurisprudence that the Radical Republicans continued in the manner of Lincoln by forcing through the Fourteenth and Fifteenth Amendments to the Constitution during Reconstruction. Historian James M. McPherson has described the reversal of thrust that these amendments would give to constitutional law:

> Nearly all of the first ten amendments to the Constitution apply the phrase "shall not" to the federal government. . . . But beginning with the Thirteenth Amendment in 1865—the amendment that abolished slavery—six of the next seven amendments radically expanded the power of the federal government at the expense of the states. The very language of these amendments illustrates the point: instead of applying the phrase "shall not" to the national government, every one of them grants significant new powers to the government with the phrase that "Congress *shall* have the power to enforce this article." (italics added)[18]

Federal action to protect basic rights was an integral part of the Republicans' "blueprint for modern America." The Fourteenth Amendment, with its promise of "equal protection," would be vital to the various "equal rights" revolutions of the twentieth century. Hamiltonian means for Jeffersonian ends: in the long run, it took a substantial outreach of *national* power to protect the basic rights we take for granted. Take "freedom of speech": *it was only in 1925* that the Supreme Court applied the Bill of Rights *to the states* (in the case of *Gitlow v. New York*) by means of the Fourteenth Amendment's equal protection clause. Until 1925, any state could suppress a person's freedom of speech, as the slave states had done by suppressing abolitionist writings. The sweeping protections of the Constitution's First Amendment (as the language of the First Amendment makes clear) applied only to federal actions—and not to any actions by the states.

It was largely to protect the former slaves from *the states* that Republicans drafted the Fourteenth and Fifteenth Amendments to the Constitution in the 1860s. Slavery itself had been a legal institution that was sanctioned under *state law*. Supporters of slavery had used *state action* to suppress the abolitionists by making anti-slavery speech a *state crime*. It was through *state action* that the planter aristocracy attempted to resurrect slavery after Appomattox through the newly established "Black Codes." Under some of these codes, which of course were passed as *state laws*, former slaves who refused to work for white employers could be jailed as "vagrants." They would then have to work for any white man who paid their fine. Involuntary servitude was back—or so it seemed.[19]

But the Republican Congress refused to permit the stealthy resurrection of slavery. Consequently, as Republicans drafted their amendments, the *states* became the primary targets. Consider section 1 of the Fourteenth Amendment, passed by Congress in 1866 and ratified in 1868:

> All persons born or naturalized in the United States, and subject to the jurisdiction thereof, are citizens of the United States and of the State wherein they reside. No state shall make or enforce any law which shall abridge the privileges or immunities of citizens of the United States; nor shall any state deprive any person of life, liberty, or property without due process of law, nor deny to any person within its jurisdiction the equal protection of the laws.

The language of the Fifteenth Amendment, passed by Congress in 1869 and ratified in 1870, was roughly comparable:

1. The right of the citizens of the United States to vote shall not be denied or abridged by the United States or by any State on account of race, color, or previous condition of servitude.
2. Congress shall have the power to enforce the provisions of this article by appropriate legislation.

The intent of these amendments was clear. And yet their language was in many ways defective. A great tragedy of postwar Reconstruction was the faulty language—the faulty legislative draftsmanship—of the new constitutional amendments. For by treating the *states* as the primary culprits, the amendments opened up significant loopholes for white supremacist behavior that was *not* put forth through the overt actions of states.

This was why the civil rights law that Congress passed in 1875—a law prohibiting discrimination in public accommodations—was overturned in 1883 by the Supreme Court: per the Fourteenth Amendment, only *states* were prohibited from acts of invidious discrimination. If *citizens* wished to behave unkindly, the Supreme Court reasoned there was nothing that the federal government could do to prevent such action.[20]

The Fifteenth Amendment was rife with comparable weaknesses. When Congress sent military force to protect the voting rights of blacks from intimidation by night-riding terrorists—via the "Enforcement Acts" of 1870 and the Ku Klux Klan Act of 1871—the Supreme Court voided such action in the 1876 cases of *United States v. Cruikshank* and *United States v. Reese.* The Supreme Court ruled that the acts of mere hoodlums (*private citizens* rather than *states*) were a matter for state or local action, not federal action.

Even clear and explicit actions *by the states* to suppress black voting—through devices such as literacy tests and poll taxes—were upheld by the courts due to "strict construction" of the new constitutional amendments. The Fifteenth Amendment was explicit in declaring that the right to vote could not be denied by the states *on the basis of race, color, or previous condition of servitude,* which of course left the states quite free to suppress people's voting rights for *other* reasons, like illiteracy and poverty.

Historian Patricia Lucie has confirmed that the language of the Fifteenth Amendment resulted from intensive congressional maneuvering: "The Fifteenth Amendment, ratified in 1870, was the survivor of a whole gamut of proposals ranging from nationally guaranteed universal suffrage and the right to hold office all the way down to a version that would have permitted states to exclude citizens on grounds of previous slavery, though not on race alone."[21] The final language represented an unfortunate political compromise. It was the best that the Radicals could manage in 1869. The Fourteenth Amendment was likewise a compromise—and many of the Radicals disliked it.[22]

For a long time the Radical Republicans were viewed—both within the historical profession and by the public—as all-purpose villains: as the perpetrators of corrupt "misrule" in the defeated South. But in the past half-century the Radicals have won great praise from historians as torchbearers of civil rights: idealists who grappled head-on with the culture of nineteenth-century white supremacy. Most of them had participated in the anti-slavery movement. One of them, Thaddeus Stevens, wrote into his will a provision to inter him in an integrated cemetery so that even in death he could promote the cause of racial equality.[23]

Men such as these had a very brief "window of opportunity" after the Civil War to advance the cause of civil rights. With Lincoln gone, they had to further their cause with all deliberate speed before a white supremacist backlash occurred. They were truly in a race against time. As historian Kenneth M. Stampp has observed, even the Republican Congress "could support an experiment in social engineering for only a few short years, and it had to be justified on the grounds of an unprecedented emergency."[24]

The Radicals were plagued with bad luck: four years went to waste as they were forced to grapple with Andrew Johnson, who inherited the presidency from Lincoln. Johnson had been placed on the ticket with Lincoln in 1864 at a time when Republicans were worried about their electoral chances—so worried that they changed their party's name for the season to the National Union Party. They also dumped Vice President Hannibal Hamlin—a staunch anti-slavery Republican—and replaced him with a southern Democratic Unionist: Andrew Johnson of Tennessee. The Republicans were running scared.

Little did they know that after Sherman's capture of Atlanta, the Republicans would triumph in a landslide. Little did they know that a white supremacist assassin would kill the reelected president barely a month after his inauguration. Booth's murder of Lincoln put a white supremacist Democrat in power—a Democrat who still believed in the maxim that the government that governs best, governs least.

What followed was the all-out war between Johnson and the Radical Republicans. In response to the creation of the Black Codes, the Republicans extended the existence of the Freedmen's Bureau. Then they passed a strong civil rights law. Johnson vetoed both of these actions, condemning them as unconstitutional. The Radicals overturned the vetoes and drafted the Fourteenth Amendment to "settle the hash" about constitutionality.

In 1867, the Republicans put all but one of the former rebel states under temporary military rule for the purpose of enfranchising blacks. Johnson opposed this policy. The brawl between Johnson and the Radicals continued through 1868.

In the election of 1868, the Republicans won back the White House. But their candidate, Ulysses S. Grant, was almost beaten by an unrepentant Copperhead, Horatio Seymour of New York—a man who had opposed Lincoln's wartime policies—and the Democrats' rhetoric was drenched in white supremacist hatred. In the opinion of historian Eric Foner, "it is more than likely that Seymour carried a majority of the nation's white electorate."[25] And he did this in a race against Grant, the Union's foremost hero. The white supremacist backlash was under way, and the Radicals were running out of time.

In Grant's first term they created the Fifteenth Amendment and sent the United States Army in pursuit of the Ku Klux Klan. But support for Reconstruction kept dwindling. In 1872, Congress let the ex-Confederates vote again. Democratic gains in Congress—along with the major distraction of another economic depression—forced cutbacks in funding that crippled any further Reconstruction. By 1877 it was over. In truth, the duration of "Radical Reconstruction" had been brief.

What were the successes and the failures of Reconstruction? Former slaves were permitted to vote and hold office in the ex-Confederate states. But their freedom to vote was short-lived: it declined with the departure of the federal troops who protected their rights from coercion.

By the standards of American white supremacy, empowerment of blacks was, of course, regarded as a "failure"—an affront to white political rule—and this was one of the reasons why the so-called failure of Reconstruction gave a very bad name to "big government."

What else? Under Reconstruction the infrastructure of the ex-Confederate South was rebuilt and modernized. But this leads us to another of the stock attacks that were directed at Reconstruction: Reconstruction was supposedly "corrupt." Its public works were attacked as "boondoggles" that were building up a staggering "debt." This was the stereotype of Reconstruction—the Reconstruction of carpetbaggers and scalawags—that Americans remembered down the years.

There *was* some corruption during Reconstruction; Louisiana and South Carolina had the worst of it, according to the best and most reliable research. But in other parts of the ex-Confederate South, the result was different: Mississippi had the cleanest government in years under Governor Adelbert Ames, a so-called carpetbagger (Yankee), and Governor James Alcorn, a so-called scalawag (native-born Southerner).[26]

The issue of corruption leads straight to a much broader issue: for American life *in general* (not just in the occupied South) was overwhelmed by scandals in the postwar years—from the federal level to the local, in government and business alike. This was the dawn of the Gilded Age, a historical phenomenon that marred Reconstruction enormously.

In New York City, the Democratic machine (under boss William M. Tweed) stole so much money that the city faced bankruptcy. In the private sector, some members of the board of the Union Pacific Railroad perpetrated white-collar theft that engendered a political scandal. They set up a subsidiary company to do the actual construction of the railroad—they called it "Crédit Mobilier of America"—with themselves as interlocking directors (that is, they held seats on the boards of both companies). Then they caused the construction company to overcharge the parent company outrageously. The difference between what it cost to build the railroad and the charges that were foisted on the Union Pacific went straight into the pockets of the thieves via Crédit Mobilier stock.

How did this private-sector scandal intrude upon politics? Simple— Union Pacific was a federally chartered concern. The company profited immensely from low-interest federal sweetheart loans and from beneficent federal land grants. To forestall public scrutiny that might lead to over-sight hearings, the thieves began to share their loot with politicians—with members of Congress. The scandal broke in 1872, when Grant was up for reelection. Other scandals, like the New York City "Tweed Ring," were erupting at the very same time.

These scandals were appalling to upright people. Before very long a major "honesty in government" movement appeared in both parties. But the effects of the scandals were more far-reaching than that. Thought-ful Americans searched their souls in response to what appeared to be an episode of national declension. As early as 1871, the poet Walt Whit-man declared that "we had best look our times and lands searchingly in the face, like a physician diagnosing some deep disease. Never was there, perhaps, more hollowness of heart than at present, and here in the United States."[27]

What could account for the disgrace? Some reformers thought they had the answer: too much government. Big government increased the opportunities for theft, the reformers believed. After all, in the Civil War and Reconstruction, the United States government had grown to unprec-edented size. Never before had Americans experienced "so much govern-ment" for so long. It was, in the view of these reformers, "unnatural."

In the election of 1872, a faction of self-styled "Liberal Republicans" argued that public affairs should "return to normal" under strictly *liberal* precepts: the precepts of minimal government. The first step was end-ing Reconstruction. The Amnesty Act of 1872 was a direct result of this movement. And it led to a major new infusion of Democratic strength as ex-Confederates voted again and reclaimed their old seats in Congress. This hurt Reconstruction even more.

But there was something even larger (and sadder) than this in the mood swing of Gilded Age politics. Ages of heroic crusading eventually "run out of steam" and "burn out." A great many people get weary of the trumpets and the banners. The result can be a vigorous backlash.

Consider the case of Senator Roscoe Conkling from New York. A Republican who dallied for a time with the Radical Republicans, he had even played a role in the drafting of the Fourteenth Amendment. But he soon became the swaggering leader of the brash new "Stalwart" faction that emerged in the Republican Party. As more Republican scandals developed during Grant's second term, the tough Stalwarts were completely unfazed. In 1877, Conkling made a bold and provocative speech to the Republican convention in New York State. He made merciless fun of "good government" reformers, whom he viewed as mincing buffoons. He called them the "man-milliners, dilettanti and carpet knights of politics." He declared that "parties are not built up by deportment, or by ladies' magazines, or gush."[28] About a decade later, Senator John J. Ingalls of Kansas called the anti-graft reformers political eunuchs: they were "endowed with the contempt of men and the derision of women, and doomed to sterility, isolation, and extinction."[29]

"Good government" reformers won a round in 1883 with the creation of the U.S. Civil Service Commission. And yet political machines remained powerful. Accordingly, the reputation of government declined.

It was not *Reconstruction-based* "corruption" that had launched the postbellum Gilded Age: *it was the Gilded Age that killed Reconstruction.* And the values of the age found higher vindication in the ideological changes taking place within conservative thought.

THE CONFLICTED CONSERVATIVE MOOD AND ITS LIBERAL COUNTERPART

The welfare state as a conservative creation took shape in Great Britain and in Europe. And the concept of Tory reform was explicitly traditionalistic. The goal was to stop revolution—and to thwart the incipient "leveling" tendencies of international socialism. The antidote was social reform—from above. But along with self-interest and calculation, there was great moral fervor in this upper-class reform movement.

The factory acts of Great Britain began as early as 1802 when Parliament began to control the conditions in the textile mills that employed little children as workers. The famous factory acts of the 1840s brought protection to mine workers. Anthony Ashley Cooper, the seventh Earl of

Shaftesbury, was the great moving force behind these latter bills. In 1847 he persuaded Parliament to establish a ten-hour day in the factories.

This tradition continued with the leadership of Benjamin Disraeli, the famous first Earl of Beaconsfield, prime minister, and leader of the British Conservative Party in the middle of the nineteenth century. Disraeli led the fight to enfranchise two million men from the lower classes—he gave them the vote—and he championed in his second ministry (1874–1880) additional factory acts along with reforms in housing and public health.

As early as the 1860s, a program for a full-blown welfare state emerged from the pen of John Ruskin, the prominent social critic and aesthete, who called himself a "violent Tory of the old school" at certain times. He insisted that the upper classes of England should take responsibility for social welfare through the state.[30]

In 1860 he published a series of articles in *Cornhill Magazine* that would appear in book form two years later as *Unto This Last*. His proposals merit quoting at length in the form of the following excerpts:

(1) First,—that there should be training schools for youth established, at Government cost, and under Government discipline, over the whole country; that every child born in the country should, at the parent's wish, be permitted (and, in certain cases, be under penalty required) to pass through them [in order to be taught] the following three things: the laws of health . . . habits of gentleness and justice . . . and the calling by which he is to live.

(2) Secondly,—that, in connection with these training schools, there should be established, also entirely under Government regulation, manufactories and workshops for the production and sale of every necessary of life, and for the exercise of every useful art. And that, interfering in no whit with private enterprise, nor setting any restraints or tax on private trade, but leaving both to do their best, and beat the Government if they could,—there should, at these Government manufactories and shops, be authoritatively good and exemplary work done, and pure and true substance sold; so that a man could be sure, if he chose to pay the Government price, that he got for his money bread that was bread, ale that was ale, and work that was work.

(3) Thirdly,—that any man, or woman, or boy or girl, out of employment, should be at once received at the nearest Government

school, and set to such work as it appeared, on trial, they were fit for. . . .

(4) Lastly,—that for the old and destitute, comfort and home should be provided; which provision, when misfortune had been by the working of such a system sifted from guilt, would be honourable instead of disgraceful to the receiver.[31]

Such proposals emerged from the Tory milieu that encompassed the insistence of Thomas Carlyle that every man had the right to be given decent work and that government's duty was *governing*, wisely and decently: sustaining moral law and preserving social stability. These principles correlated well with the creation, some twenty years after Ruskin's manifesto, of the social security system in Germany by Otto von Bismarck. And they related to the element of Tory reform, with its genuine infusion of *noblesse oblige* that we will find in the American statecraft of well-to-do American reformers like the Roosevelts.

But in mid-nineteenth century Britain a countermovement was rising: a conservative movement to establish and defend a brutal hierarchy through dog-eat-dog competition and minimal government. This movement drew the laissez-faire principle across the political spectrum from the left to the right. It began the long tradition of conservative free marketeering that became to a large extent canonical—and remains so to this day—among American conservatives.

"Survival of the fittest" was the maxim, and it entered the realm of ideology well before the publication of Darwin's *Origin of Species* in 1859. The progenitor was Herbert Spencer, a British philosopher who coined the phrase in 1850. He was a champion of laissez-faire. He opposed all Tory reforms as interference with natural selection. State interference on behalf of the poor results in the triumph of the "unfit," according to Spencer. "The whole effort of nature is to get rid of such, to clear the world of them, and make room for better," he wrote. Under nature's laws, all are put on trial: "If they are sufficiently complete to live, they *do* live, and it is well that they should live. If they are not sufficiently complete to live, they die, and it is best they should die."[32]

We can see in these statements the ferocious state of mind that Charles Dickens had attacked with such passion in *A Christmas Carol*. For present purposes, though, it behooves us to witness in Spencer's writing the transformation of laissez-faire from a liberal doctrine to an outlook that would please some conservatives.

To a certain extent, laissez-faire had arisen in the left-of-center milieu, in the *equality* ideal. Early liberal politics espoused an equality of *liberty—maximum* liberty. Libertarian policies would elevate the downtrodden masses, the liberals believed. Libertarian politics would aid the self-empowerment of common men everywhere on earth. This was the belief of Jefferson—*before* his conversion to the positive uses of the state.

Now compare this vision to the use of laissez-faire by Spencer: in Spencerian doctrine, the noninterference of government *builds up* the powerful and *grinds down* the weak and "unfit." The goal is the *reverse* of equality. In Spencerian politics, the doctrine of minimal government erects a large hierarchic structure. Through Spencer, the doctrine of laissez-faire became hierarchic, and thus conservative. But it was totally at odds with the politics of Tory reform. As historian Richard Hofstadter noted more than half a century ago, the Spencerian doctrine was propagated internationally. Yet it caught on here in America more than in Britain, where Spencer introduced it.

It became an ideology that historians dubbed "Social Darwinism." Hofstadter called it "one of the leading strains in American conservative thought." But he also noted that "it lacked many of the signal characteristics of conservatism" in its old-fashioned form. Hofstadter continues: "A body of belief whose chief conclusion was that the positive functions of the state should be kept to the barest minimum, it was almost anarchical, and it was devoid of that center of reverence and authority which the state provides in many conservative systems."[33]

Spencer's ideas were adopted by American opinion-makers such as William Graham Sumner, a sociologist, and Edward Livingston Youmans, the founder of *Popular Science Monthly* in the 1870s. Spencer himself paid a visit to America in 1882. He was given a hero's welcome by the wealthy. Gilded Age leaders were especially smitten with his doctrines. Steel magnate Andrew Carnegie reminisced about the effect of reading Spencer: "Not only had I got rid of theology and the supernatural, but I had found the truth of evolution. 'All is well since all grows better,' became my motto, my true source of comfort."[34]

Other Americans saluted Herbert Spencer in a manner that was far more aggressive. William Graham Sumner declared that "'the strong' and 'the weak' are terms which admit of no definition unless they are made equivalent to the industrious and the idle. . . . If we do not like the survival of the fittest, we have only one possible alternative, and that is the survival of the unfittest. The former is the law of civilization; the latter is the law of anti-civilization."[35]

It should not be surprising that the doctrines of Spencer were embraced by American conservatives. Americans had little experience with governmental stewardship. John Quincy Adams had been dead for many years and the Civil War Republicans' experiment had run out of steam. The ferocity of Gilded Age values made it hard for Disraeli-style Tory reform to inspire transatlantic imitation.

But within the Republican Party, the principles of Hamilton— transmitted via Lincoln—made it possible for thoughtful young patricians like Theodore Roosevelt to learn from a tradition of conservative values that was different from the Gilded Age norms. And a growing religious movement—especially strong among wealthy Americans—challenged Spencer on behalf of Christian ethics.

Across the denominations in the 1880s spread a movement known as the "Social Gospel," and it preached the extension of Christian charity in updated forms. Ministers such as Washington Gladden among the Congregationalists and Walter Rauschenbusch among the Baptists were eager to challenge Social Darwinist maxims. From the Social Gospel emerged a new wave of altruistic activity. It was strong in those upper-class circles where philanthropy retained a place of honor. In 1889, Andrew Carnegie— who prided himself on his altruism as an employer—wrote an essay called "Wealth" (it was published in Britain as "The Gospel of Wealth"), in which he touted the virtues of philanthropy. His early idolization of Spencer had succumbed to some strong second thoughts.

Young Theodore Roosevelt had learned from his father that the upright and well-to-do man should make provision for the weak and infirm. Eleanor Roosevelt—the future president's niece—became active in the cause of "social justice." At Groton young Franklin Delano Roosevelt absorbed a Christian gentleman's version of the Social Gospel from the Rector Endicott Peabody.

The church-based critique of Social Darwinism—so obviously different from the Christian fundamentalists' war upon Darwinian *science*—had a strong academic correlation. Economist John R. Commons was the author of a book titled *Social Reform and the Church* that was published in 1894. The author of the book's introduction was another young economist, Richard T. Ely. In 1886 Ely had included in the draft of a prospectus for the new American Economic Association the following statement: "We regard the state as an educational and ethical agency whose positive aid is an indispensable condition of human progress. While we recognize the necessity of individual initiative in industrial life, we hold that the doctrine of laissez-faire is unsafe in politics and unsound in morals."[36]

Two years later, a best-selling novel—it sold millions of copies and advanced the Social Gospel agenda—gave Americans a vision of a future where greed, instability, and poverty had all been banished. *Looking Backward* by Edward Bellamy was published in 1888. It was set in the year 2000. A Gilded Age Bostonian named Julian West has a Rip Van Winkle experience: he awakens to a Boston that is nothing less than utopia, for there is no poverty at all. Everything is planned at the national level through cooperative and democratic methods. It was socialism with a very significant difference: everyone was *rich*. Indeed, the life of great wealth is shared *equally*. The wisdom of the left and the right had been brought into a stunning convergence: with everyone prospering, equality prevailed—*through wealth*.

After a modicum of service to the nation, each citizen receives the same annual stipend: an *enormous* annual stipend. The state can easily afford it. For the colossal productivity of twentieth-century America produces an extravagant extent of abundance. Nothing is wasted, and everybody's talent is fulfilled to its utmost extent. A system of government schools and workshops—Ruskin's proposal, but expanded like a vision out of science fiction—makes American life luxurious.

Toward the end of the story, Mr. West has a terrible dream: he is back in Gilded Age Boston. He cannot tell reality from fantasy: he imagines that *the glory he has seen in the future was the dream, and the Gilded Age is his reality*. The prospect of living in Gilded Age Boston is unbearable now: "The twentieth century had been a dream. I had but dreamed of . . . the glorious new Boston with its domes and pinnacles, its gardens and fountains, and its universal reign of comfort." He was back in the dreadful Gilded Age:

> The festering mass of human wretchedness about me offended not my senses merely but pierced my heart like a knife. . . . As I observed the wretched beings about me more closely, I perceived that they were all quite dead. Their bodies were so many living sepulchres. On each brutal brow was plainly written the *hic jacet* of a soul dead within. As I looked, horrorstruck, from one death's head to another, I was affected by a singular hallucination. Like a wavering translucent spirit face superimposed upon each of these brutish masks I saw the ideal, the possible face that would have been the actual if mind and soul had lived.

But he awakens: *his illusion of returning to Gilded Age Boston was the dream*, and he is saved—saved by the future.

Bellamy gave the great system he depicted in his novel a non-socialistic name: nationalism. The author himself was a descendent of clergymen on both sides of his family. When he was twenty-four years of age he wrote an essay called "The Religion of Solidarity." Fourteen years later he published *Looking Backward*. It swept the country, and it led to the formation of Bellamy clubs across America.

So far we have seen the deep chasm that developed in conservative thought in the second half of the nineteenth century: the gulf between the new Social Darwinist creed and the older tradition of Tory Reform, as revivified and given new force through the Social Gospel movement with its mandate of upper-class benevolence. We have seen how the spiritual force of such preaching could harmonize the left and the right, as in Bellamy's utopia, where wealth and equality are blended.

It is time to catch up with the transformation of the liberals. For the liberals experienced a conflict as deep and intense as the struggle among the conservatives. As conservatives began to make use of laissez-faire, the deep left-of-center impetus to strive toward equality began to make use of the state.

Winston Churchill observed that British liberals experienced a crisis of conscience—and ideology—toward the end of the nineteenth century:

> The great victories had been won. All sorts of lumbering tyrannies had been toppled over. Authority was everywhere broken. Slaves were free. Conscience was free. Trade was free. But hunger and squalor and cold were also free; and the people demanded something more than liberty. The old watchwords still rang true; but they were not enough. And how to fill the void was the riddle that split the Liberal Party.[37]

An early indication of change was the 1848 declaration of John Stuart Mill that "the admitted functions of government embrace a much wider field than can easily be included within the ring-fence of any restrictive definition."[38] Historian David Harris has sketched the continuation of the change, observing that "after Gladstone was gone, the British liberal party became converted to the doctrine of the state as an engine of social betterment."[39]

Something similar happened in America. But it took much longer than in Britain. It began as the values of Gilded Age America created a crisis that engendered great anger from the source of all liberal concern: the "common people." And "the people" were crying out for governance.

GRASSROOTS INSURGENCY

The activist governance philosophy that Lincoln had championed diminished in the 1870s. But it produced a few significant results as it faded through the decade.

The Justice Department was created in 1870. The first of our national parks—Yellowstone—was created by Congress in 1872. In the very next year the creation of a federal forestry commission foreshadowed the creation, in the 1880s, of the Forestry Division in the Agriculture Department, which in turn foreshadowed the creation of "forest reserves" by President Benjamin Harrison, pursuant to an 1891 law.

In 1879, the United States Geological Survey was founded, and the *ad hoc* Mississippi River Commission laid the groundwork for future governmental action in the field of flood control. The Army Signal Corps began to do meteorological work that would lead to the creation of the U.S. Weather Bureau in 1890.

Furthermore, the ideal of governmental stewardship survived (briefly) in American jurisprudence: the Supreme Court decision in *Munn v. Illinois* (1877) validated government regulation of commerce at the state level. Chief Justice Morrison R. Waite declared that when "one devotes his property to a use in which the public has an interest, he, in effect, grants to the public an interest in that use, and must submit to be controlled by the public for the common good."[40]

The *Munn* case arose in response to state laws that were known as the Granger laws. The Grange (its formal name was the National Grange of the Patrons of Husbandry) was a society organized by farmers in 1867 for mutual assistance. By the 1870s, Grangers had forced through a series of state-level laws to stop railroads from practicing "rate discrimination."

The American Gilded Age railroad industry was ruthless as often as not. In comparison to the best of the American railroad companies before the Civil War—which often met extremely high standards for probity (the Pennsylvania Railroad was the model)—Gilded Age railroads were rife with malfeasance and crookedness.

The Grangers' complaint was that the railroads were charging exorbitant rates in certain parts of the country where no competition existed. The Granger laws were designed to protect the American farmer from extortionate shipping rates. But the Supreme Court suddenly reversed its support for these laws a decade later: in the case of *Wabash v. Illinois* (1886), the Court decided that since most of the railroads in question were interstate lines, the state Granger laws usurped the right of Congress to regulate interstate commerce.

In direct response to this decision, the Interstate Commerce Commission (ICC) was created by Congress in 1887. The ICC was the first of the great modern regulatory commissions at the federal level. But the commission's authority was weak, at least in the beginning. Another response to complaints about monopoly arrived with the passage of the Sherman Anti-Trust Act of 1890. But its provisions were vague, and so the grievances of farmers intensified.

The railroads figured in a number of other upheavals in Gilded Age America. It was principally loans that were extended to some shaky and ill-managed railroads that triggered the financial Panic of 1873, which caused the worst economic depression up to that time in American history. Economic desperation led to hunger marches and a series of spectacularly violent railroad strikes in the summer of 1877.

The "Great Railroad Strike" of that year began in West Virginia, and it spread to other parts of the country. The violence and destruction were particularly bad in St. Louis and Chicago. Eighteen men and boys were killed in Chicago and millions of dollars worth of property got destroyed. According to many accounts, it was cuts in the wages of railroad workers that triggered the outbreak.

Workers in other American Gilded Age industries were desperate by the 1880s. The steel industry adopted the following standard schedule for unskilled workers: twelve hours a day, seven days a week. Urban poverty spread as unprecedented waves of impoverished immigrants flowed into the hastily built new tenement districts in America's larger cities. Many were trapped in the life of the "sweatshop." Others were tricked into company towns, where their debts to the "company store"—which overcharged them—were designed to exceed their salaries.

The company store had its counterpart in the "New South" on southern plantations where the sharecropping system had replaced the old chattel slavery system. Under the so-called crop-lien arrangement, sharecroppers (of both races) were promised a "share of the crop" in lieu of wages. In the meantime, however, they had to eat. So the planter (or a "furnishing merchant") would set up a store that would furnish them with all the necessities. Then, at the end of the growing season, their share of the crop would be assessed. The planter would compare the market value of their share to the value of the goods that had been furnished. Then, surprise! The value of their share was always *less* than the value of the furnished goods they had received. They had to stay—until they paid off their debts.

Farmers on the Great Plains discovered that their standard of living got worse every year as an epoch of falling commodity prices reduced their monthly cash flow. The more they produced, the lower the commodity prices. Historian Lawrence Goodwyn has summed it up: "As the hard times of the 1870s turned into the even harder times of the 1880s," it was clear to these farmers that their efforts "were not really going anywhere." Goodwyn continues, "Indeed, by 1888 it was evident that things were worse than they had been in 1878 or 1868. More and more people saw their farm mortgages foreclosed. As everyone in rural America knew, this statistic inexorably yielded another, more ominous one: the number of landless tenant farmers in America rose steadily year after year. . . . Hard work availed nothing."[41]

So again the farmers joined forces. Two farmers alliances—the National Farmers Alliance, which was strong in the Great Plains, and the so-called Southern Alliance (at first called the National Farmers Alliance and Industrial Union)—began to formulate plans for cooperative ventures by the end of the 1870s.

They planned to create huge buying and selling co-ops. Through the co-ops they hoped to get vastly better deals for the goods that they needed and the goods that they placed on the market. They would buy and sell in bulk—together. The idea had particular appeal in the South, but it made abundant sense to many farmers in the Plains states as well. The "Alliance-men" would pull their crops off the market and store them. This would force up the price of their goods, but it would also generate collateral—collateral to bring in the venture capital to launch the great co-op plan. This idea was largely the work of a self-taught economist, Charles Macune.

But the bankers demurred (in the South a great many of them were in cahoots with the local planters), so the angry Alliance leaders turned to the government instead. Goodwyn has called the resulting movement "the largest democratic mass movement in American history."[42]

The Alliance leaders got candidates for Congress to pledge their support for laws that would jump-start the co-ops with low interest federal loans. The loans would be provided to the farmers via federal Greenbacks—new money created by the government. In Goodwyn's opinion, "intellectually, the plan was profoundly innovative . . . far too much so for Gilded Age America."[43] Congress never took action on the plan.

So the two alliances merged and then they reached out to organized labor. Between 1890 and 1892, they founded their own political party—the Populist Party—to force the government action that they wanted. The Omaha Platform that Populists endorsed in the 1892 election demanded intervention by government to help the nation's workers and curb the kind of corporate power that was keeping "the little guy" down.

The Populists demanded that "the powers of government . . . should be expanded . . . as rapidly and as far as the good sense of an intelligent people and the teachings of experience shall justify."[44] They demanded support for the agricultural co-ops. They demanded much better regulation of the railroads. They even called for the outright nationalization of the railroads if regulation should fail. They called for an income tax that would hit the rich harder along with an expansion of the money supply to ease the growing burdens of debtors. And they demanded anti-trust action.

In 1893 yet another financial panic erupted, and it ushered in another economic depression—the worst one yet. The next year a maverick Ohio reformer named Jacob Coxey led an "army" of unemployed workers to Washington. The marchers were asking for jobs—government jobs— through public works, to be financed through Greenbacks. Instead, they got arrested—at the Capitol.[45]

In the same year a strike at the Pullman Palace Car Company—a strike in response to a series of devastating wage cuts without compensatory cuts in the rents that were charged in the company town—spread into a railroad strike across the country. The strike was led by the American Railway Union (ARU). President Grover Cleveland smashed this strike by sending in troops. He and his attorney-general, Richard Olney, invoked the Sherman Anti-Trust Act *against the unions*, deeming them "conspiracies in restraint of trade." As he languished in jail, the angry union president, Eugene Victor Debs, read pamphlets on European socialism. A few years later, he founded the American Socialist Party.

As these tensions of the 1890s increased, many well-to-do Americans prepared themselves for class war: a war of the "have-nots" against the "haves." They reminded one another that the French Revolution's Reign of Terror had occurred just a hundred years earlier. Perhaps the "tramps" and the "down-and-outs" would notice the fact and act accordingly. The times had become apocalyptic.

In the election of 1896, the Populist Party was eclipsed (and before very long driven out of existence) when the Democratic candidate stole the Populists' thunder. He was William Jennings Bryan, a congressman from Nebraska.

In his speech at the Democratic convention, Bryan worked up the crowd in a manner that would never be forgotten by the people who heard him that day: "We have petitioned and our petitions have been scorned; we have entreated and our entreaties have been disregarded; we have begged, and they have mocked when our calamity came. We beg no longer, we entreat no more, we petition no more. We defy them!"[46]

Though Bryan went down in defeat and the Populist Party declined, the agitation of the 1890s brought results. The apocalyptic mood of the decade made scores of Americans demand a new reconciliation of the classes.

Wise business leaders started telling one another that America's social conflicts were out of hand.

Industrialist Marcus Alonzo Hanna—who raised immense sums for the man who beat Bryan in the 1896 election, William McKinley—condemned the autocratic behavior of his fellow industrialist George Pullman by declaring in the middle of the Pullman strike that "a man who won't meet his men half-way is a God-damn fool."[47] Hanna went on to play a role in the founding of the National Civic Federation, a group of business and labor leaders organized in 1900 to mediate labor-management conflicts.[48]

Americans in many walks of life were concluding that a new coordination—a new efficiency based upon a higher understanding of Christian ethics—was urgently required. The American republic seemed poised at the edge of an abyss. Perhaps the downward slide was beginning, as Americans assailed one another like a gang of savages. A revival of the better American values was needed—a summoning back of the heroic. Americans were ready once again to demand a true civic mutuality—a beneficent order to defend against the dangers of chaos.

From the drive to promote the new Pledge of Allegiance to the new "City Beautiful" movement—a movement to restore the great principles of classical grandeur to urban design—American culture was pervaded by demands for a worthy and cohesive social order. Perhaps the first of the necessary steps should be reform in response to just grievances.

Slowly, and then with increasing momentum, the measures that the ill-fated Populists espoused were addressed through legislative action. In 1894 Congress enacted an income tax—a tax that the Supreme Court declared to be unconstitutional the very next year (*Pollock v. Farmers' Loan and Trust Co.*). But then a constitutional amendment providing for an income tax cleared Congress in 1909 and was ratified in 1913.

Stricter regulation of railroads arrived with the Elkins Act of 1903 and the Hepburn Act of 1905. And a series of federal loans to rural co-ops (1916, 1923, 1929, and 1933) paved the way for more sweeping agricultural reforms in the New Deal. The ravages and fears of the 1890s made the Gilded Age values untenable.

TR AND THE "PROGRESSIVE" RETURN OF BIG GOVERNMENT

To young Theodore Roosevelt, the Gilded Age was repulsive. But he was also responsive to its influence. He was torn between the new Social Darwinist creed and its antidote, the Christian Social Gospel. He saw value in both of these movements by applying the teachings of his father.

His father was a wealthy philanthropist, whom TR revered. He had taught his son early that the Christian obligation of the gentleman was service to the poor. In New York, the future president's father helped to found the Children's Aid Society, the State Charities Aid Association, and a special orthopedic hospital to help poor children.[49]

But he had also taught his son the transcendent importance of *fitness*. In his boyhood, the future president suffered from debilitating sorts of problems: asthma, poor eyesight, a puny physique. His father taught him to build himself into a colossus. "You must make your body," he taught him.[50]

Thus began the long career of Theodore Roosevelt, the "man's man": the outdoorsman, boxer, wrestler, cow-puncher, champion of "the strenuous life." But through it all he sought to be a hero of the weak and infirm. He sought to help them as his father once helped them.

For the rest of his life he would promulgate the gospel of strength. And he promoted this gospel as a patriotic imperative. He hoped to see America become a great global power with a two-ocean navy and a massive industrial base. *Power* was the key to our future, he believed, since the fate of mankind was to live within a process of struggle. So he preached the "survival of the fittest," up to a point.[51]

But the *use* of great power in the hands of the noble must be *service*— service to others. TR propounded a demanding and stern Social Gospel. He would enter public service in the armor of a knight: as a modern Christian soldier giving battle in the name of the Lord. He would, as he told himself at Harvard, be nothing less than a "brave Christian gentleman."[52]

It became the intellectual achievement of Roosevelt to counteract the Gilded Age vices by rescuing some elements of *Gilded Age wisdom*—the wisdom contained in its competing upper-class philosophies. He blended Social Darwinist and Social Gospel theory into unified policy.

After college he plunged into politics. He launched his career with a stint in the New York legislature, where he served for two years, from 1882 to 1884. One of the causes to which he devoted his idealism was honesty in government. As remedial action began at the federal level with Congress's creation in 1883 of the U.S. Civil Service Commission (which placed at least a modicum of federal jobs off-limits to grafters and spoilsmen), TR fought the grafters in Albany.

Another issue to which he turned his attention was the degradation of workers in New York City's sweatshops. He championed a bill introduced by a cigar-makers' union to prohibit the making of cigars in the tenement houses, where conditions were filthy, as TR discovered when he made an inspection on the Lower East Side. The law passed—only to be overturned by the courts.

His crusading continued. Appointed to the U.S. Civil Service Commission by President Benjamin Harrison, he launched vigorous investigations of fraud, chicanery, and incompetence. "I have made this Commission a living force," he exulted, "and in consequence the outcry among the spoilsmen has become furious."[53]

TR the holy terror in Washington returned to his hometown, New York City, in response to an offer in 1895 to serve as the president of the city's Board of Police Commissioners. The holy terror continued. At night he prowled the streets incognito to spy upon cops who were loafing. He recruited minorities—women and Jews—to serve the force in leadership positions. He founded a School for Pistol Practice (later the Police Academy). He prowled the tenement districts with reformers like Jacob Riis to refamiliarize himself with the terrible crisis of the slums.

It was a work of *noblesse oblige*, an aristocratic undertaking. In the social crisis of the 1890s, TR was openly contemptuous of radicals, Populists, labor leaders, or the sort of political "demagogues" (like Bryan) who threatened to stir up the masses and incite them to possible violence. It was only in his presidential years that he would seek to accommodate "conservative" and "radical" ideas at the highest level.

After McKinley's victory in the election of 1896, TR used his various Republican connections to get himself a high-level job: assistant secretary of the navy. In this position he could advocate naval expansion and modernization to make the navy more efficient. But in 1898, with the outbreak of war against Spain, he stepped down and formed the cavalry outfit that journalists quickly dubbed the "Rough Riders."

By the end of the summer, TR was a military hero. Hardly pausing for breath, he ran for office again—the governorship of New York. His presence on the campaign trail was heralded by uniformed Rough Riders blowing bugles. The effect was electrifying, and so was his performance as governor.

Back in Albany, the crusader was soon hard at work on behalf of good causes, old and new: clean government, taxes on private utilities, regulation of the miserable conditions in the sweatshops. The "Old Guard" Republicans hated it, and managed to kick the reformer upstairs in the election of 1900: they put him on the ticket with McKinley. But when McKinley was killed in 1901, TR got his chance to revive the great Lincoln tradition.

He soon found himself at the head of the "Progressive movement" that developed early in the century, a bipartisan reform crusade. As he finished what would have been McKinley's second term, he commenced a demonstration of power on behalf of reform.

He used the Sherman Anti-Trust Act in 1902 to smash a railroad monopoly, the Northern Securities Company, recently organized by financier and industrial consolidator J. Pierpont Morgan. Roosevelt defied the most powerful capitalist in America—and prevailed when the Supreme Court upheld the prosecution two years later. Over forty other anti-trust prosecutions followed, including a suit that eventually broke up John D. Rockefeller's Standard Oil Company.

He also took unprecedented action in 1902 to mediate a labor-management dispute, a strike by the anthracite coal miners of Pennsylvania. Roosevelt summoned both sides to the White House and asked them to state their positions. The union leader, John Mitchell, was receptive to the concept of binding arbitration, but the owners, led by George F. Baer, were contemptuous. They said that troops should be sent to break the strike.

TR was furious—with the owners. Years later he recalled that they were "insolent": they dared to speak in his presence using language that was both "insulting to the miners and offensive to me."[54] That was a mistake. TR wrote to Mark Hanna that "the attitude of the operators is one which accentuates the need of the government having some power of supervision and regulation."[55] TR planned to intervene. He would send in the troops, but to *seize the mines from their owners*. When the news of this plan reached J. P. Morgan, he pressured George Baer into yielding. Roosevelt won.

It was the very first time that a president had sided with labor in a strike. But a larger point had been made: Roosevelt had dramatized his growing belief that social justice required governmental supervision of business. In 1903, he got Congress to pass legislation creating a Department of Commerce and Labor along with a "Bureau of Corporations" to investigate problems. (The Commerce and Labor Departments were separated ten years later.)

His belief in the mission of the federal government went far beyond regulation. He wanted federal *action*—action in the areas where private enterprise could not deliver—action in the realm of public works. In 1902 he had sided with Nevada Democrat Francis Newlands and pushed through Congress the epochal Newlands Reclamation Act, which set aside money from land sales to fund irrigation projects in the West. This act became the basis for future projects like Hoover Dam. In 1903, he commenced his

Global vision: Theodore Roosevelt in the White House, 1903. Credit: Theodore Roosevelt Collection, Harvard College Library. Used with permission.

great signature project, the Panama Canal—a miracle of brilliant engineering that would prove itself vital to American victory in World War II.[56]

Roosevelt's support for what we now call "infrastructure"—his support for modern projects to tame an unruly environment—was dynamically balanced by his ardent support for conservation. In 1903, by presidential order, he established the first of the federal government's wildlife refuges on Pelican Island off the eastern coast of Florida.

Throughout his completion of McKinley's second term, he was constantly assessing his leadership relative to Lincoln. He cultivated John Hay, Lincoln's wartime secretary. Hay had been serving as McKinley's secretary of state, and Roosevelt kept him on. It was immensely significant to Roosevelt in 1905 when Hay told him he was "one of the men who most thoroughly understand and appreciate Lincoln." Hay presented Roosevelt with a ring containing strands of Lincoln's hair that had been shorn on the night of the assassination.[57] At the same time, planning for the Lincoln Memorial began as a federal commission (the McMillan Commission of 1901–1902) and revived the classical vision for Washington, extending it with new City Beautiful embellishments.

Historian John Milton Cooper Jr. has described TR as a "self-anointed heir of Lincoln and Civil War Republicanism" who meant to "exalt the power and prestige of the federal government."[58] As Hay and other Civil War Republicans congratulated Roosevelt, a new generation of "Progressive" Republicans responded to his vision of a re-empowered Uncle Sam. Henry Stimson, who would later serve both Herbert Hoover (as secretary of state) and Franklin Delano Roosevelt (as secretary of war), reminisced that the elder President Roosevelt was "the most commanding natural leader" he had ever known. Stimson told Yale alumni at a class reunion in 1908 that when he left private legal practice for public service under TR, his "first feeling was that I had gotten out of the dark places where I had been wandering all my life, and got out where I could see the stars and get my bearings once more."[59]

Immensely popular, Roosevelt won reelection in 1904, and then the power demonstration resumed. In 1905, through adroit maneuvering, he strengthened the Interstate Commerce Commission by securing congressional passage of the Hepburn Act. He created the United States Forest Service in the Agriculture Department, appointing his friend Gifford Pinchot as chief forester. He offered his services to mediate the Russo-Japanese War—and won the Nobel Peace Prize.

But then a furor developed that brought out a "radicalism" in Roosevelt, a radicalism coinciding with the old conservative instinct to regulate the ugly side of human nature. In 1906, Upton Sinclair's "muckraking" novel *The Jungle* made startling allegations in regard to the meatpacking plants in Chicago. Sinclair, a socialist, alleged that the meatpackers bulked out the sausages by grinding in dangerous sweepings from the factory floor,

including rat dung and poisoned rats. Roosevelt ordered an investigation by
Commissioner of Labor Charles P. Neill and attorney James B. Reynolds.
Their report was so shocking that Roosevelt insisted on action. He wrote
to the chairman of the House Agriculture Committee as follows:

> I have recently had an investigation made by Commissioner Neill of the
> Labor Bureau and Mr. J.B. Reynolds, of the situation in the Chicago
> packing houses. It is hideous, and it must be remedied at once. I was at
> first so indignant that I resolved to send in the full report to Congress.
> As far as the beef packers themselves are concerned I should do this now
> with a clear conscience, for the great damage that would befall them in
> consequence would be purely due to their own actions. But the dam-
> age would also come to all the stock growers of this country and the
> effect of such a report would undoubtedly be well-nigh ruinous to our
> export trade in meat. . . . I do not wish . . . to give publicity at this time
> to the report, with the certainty that widespread damage will be caused
> not merely to the wrongdoers but to the innocent. Nevertheless, it
> must be distinctly understood that I shall not hesitate to cause even this
> widespread damage if in no other way does it prove possible to secure
> a betterment in conditions that are literally intolerable. I do not believe
> that you will have any doubt on the matter. If you have, I earnestly hope
> you will see me at once.[60]

The result was the passage of the Pure Food and Drug Act and Meat Inspection Act, along with the creation of the Food and Drug Administration
(FDA).

Through it all Roosevelt asked himself what kind of businessmen—
what manner of miscreants who passed themselves off as sober citizens—
would permit such conditions to exist in the factories they owned. How
could wealthy men poison their neighbors and then sleep the undisturbed
sleep of the righteous? Roosevelt's rage at the meatpackers was the rage of
an old-fashioned Tory at the "malefactors" who were giving his class a bad
name. It was also the rage of a Tory who was not at all surprised about the
worst that human nature had to offer.

In 1907, TR gave a speech called "The Puritan Spirit and the Regulation of Corporations." He likened himself to a Puritan magistrate of old.
The Puritan, he said, was

> no laissez-faire theorist. When he saw conduct which was in violation
> of his rights—of the rights of man, the rights of God, as he understood
> them—he attempted to regulate such conduct with instant, unques-
> tioning promptness and efficiency. If there was no other way to secure

conformity with the rule of right, then he smote down the transgressor with the iron of his wrath. The spirit of the Puritan was a spirit which never shrank from regulation of conduct when such regulation was necessary for the public weal; and this is the spirit which we must show today whenever it is necessary.[61]

In his final message to Congress, Roosevelt observed that "the chief breakdown" in American society derived from "the new relations that arise from the mutualism, the interdependence of our time. Every new social relation begets a new type of wrongdoing—of sin, to use an old-fashioned term—and many years must always elapse before society is able to turn this sin into crime which can be effectively punished at law."[62]

This related to Lincoln's old mission: protecting the sheep from the liberty of wolves. Or, as TR put it himself, it was the duty of the magistrate to curb the "perfect freedom of the strong to wrong the weak."[63]

All of this was quite conservative—in a sense. TR had told the members of Philadelphia's Union League Club in 1905 that "the great development of industrialism means that there must be an increase in the supervision exercised by the Government. . . . Such men as the members of this club should lead in the effort to secure proper supervision."[64]

Such conservatism—the conservatism that was handed down from Carlyle, Ruskin, and Disraeli—was lost on the kind of Social Darwinists who thought that protection of *carte blanche* property rights should be the highest care of the statesman. Such latter-day conservatives—the Republican Party's Old Guard at the turn of the century—were spoiling for a fight against Roosevelt the "radical" or "wild man."

Moreover, Gilded Age values were alive and well in the American judiciary system at the time. *Lochner v. New York* made this clear in 1905. In this case the Supreme Court overturned a New York state law to limit working hours, thus continuing a trend that would last until FDR's great fight against the "nine old men" in black robes.

TR became a lame-duck president—and at the very height of his power. Right after the election of 1904, he made a foolish and impulsive promise: he promised he would never run again. By 1907, the Old Guard knew that his time was almost up, so they thwarted him at every turn. Moreover, a financial panic occurred in that year—a panic that was stopped by J. P. Morgan and friends, who persuaded TR to help them prop up the banks by depositing federal funds to the tune of $150 million. It worked. But the wealthy critics of Roosevelt of course blamed his "radicalism" for the crisis.

As conservatives in Congress began to defy him, TR returned their defiance. He sent his "Great White Fleet" of new battleships around the world as congressional enemies threatened to cut off the funding. He put millions of acres of public land into the national forest system—right on the eve of congressional action that would tie his hands in the matter. At the end of his presidency, 150 million acres had been sequestered in the national forests. A million and a half acres of water-power sites were set aside. Five more national parks had been created, as were eighteen national monuments pursuant to the National Monuments Act of 1906. As election year 1908 rolled around, TR convened major study commissions—commissions on conservation, inland waterways, country life—to guide the nation's future development.

And he fired back abuse at the men he regarded as the smug representatives of greed. They had called him a "radical." Well, the old Tory was *feeling* like a radical compared to these "conservative" warlocks. Years later—after a brief but extremely consequential defection from the Grand Old Party in 1912—he wrote that he had "endeavored to make the Republican Party the radical progressive party, as it had been in the days of Abraham Lincoln." He continued, "I feel no less that I was loyal to my principles when I opposed the Republican party because it had fallen into the hands of the Bourbons and corruptionists, who had made it stand, not for the principles for which Abraham Lincoln stood but for the latter-day application of the principles represented in Lincoln's time by Buchanan and Pierce and Fillmore. I am, as a matter of fact, in my ideas very radical indeed."[65]

TR's journey to "radicalism" was beginning in 1908. It was clear to his fellow "progressives" he had made a big mistake when he had promised not to run again. When he kept that promise in 1908, the mistake was foolishly compounded. He should have thought about Lincoln's observation in the very last speech of his life: "Bad promises are better broken than kept."[66] But Roosevelt kept the foolish promise. He passed the torch to a mild-mannered friend and associate: William Howard Taft. With TR's endorsement, Taft won the election of 1908 against the Democrats' William Jennings Bryan. Then TR took off to hunt big game on safari in Africa.

In the bush he began to read Croly's *Promise of American Life*. The theme of Hamilton-Jefferson reconciliation struck a very responsive chord in the mind of TR. Already he had written to a friend that "wise radicalism and wise conservatism go hand in hand," and he restated the theme in his final message to Congress. At this point in his life he felt a very strong conviction that the nation required *mediation*. As historian Richard Hofstadter once observed, TR knew "how to act as a balance wheel between what he considered to be the most irresponsible forces of left and right."[67] The most important thing in the mind of TR was to provide the American people with a "Square Deal," as he put it in 1904: a well-grounded plan for mutuality.

Such a vision was appropriate, in Roosevelt's view, to the urgent task of helping the United States *modernize*, to evolve in more *efficient* directions as it faced the great challenges of modern mass-based society. As he pondered the message of Croly, Great Britain was instituting social security in 1910. Young Winston Churchill (an erstwhile Tory) was working with the Liberal David Lloyd George on behalf of the reform.

When Roosevelt returned from his travels abroad—on the way back from Africa he met with the Kaiser to talk about Germany's system of old-age pensions and unemployment compensation—he gave a speech to some Civil War veterans in Osawatomie, Kansas. Known forever after as his "New Nationalism" speech (a phrase that he borrowed from Croly), it outlined a vision of industrial-age coordination. "I do not ask for overcentralization," TR said, "but I do ask that we work in a spirit of broad and far-reaching nationalism when we work for what concerns our people as a whole."

The old trust-buster said that he had changed his mind; he had come to the conclusion that breaking up monopolies was probably retrogressive. It would be better by far to *control* them. "Combinations in industry are the result of an imperative economic law which cannot be repealed by political legislation," he asserted. "The way out lies, not in attempting to prevent such combinations, but in completely controlling them in the interest of the public welfare."[68]

Three years later, in his *Autobiography*, he offered a sweeping diagnosis of the needs of mass society:

A simple and poor society can exist as a democracy on the basis of sheer individualism. But a rich and complex industrial society cannot so exist; for some individuals, and especially those artificial individuals called corporations, become so very big that the ordinary individual is utterly dwarfed beside them, and cannot deal with them on terms of equality. It therefore becomes necessary for these ordinary individuals to combine in their turn, first in order to act in their collective capacity through that biggest of all combinations called the government, and second, to act, also in their own self-defense, through private combinations, such as farmers' associations and trade-unions.[69]

Roosevelt the theorist was squarely in line with the latest Darwinistic teaching. For the newest Darwinian thinking had turned its back upon hyper-individualism. Instead, "progressive" Darwinians were eager to point out *cooperative* themes—teamwork—in the way that different species had flourished. In the human species, the arts of intervention—agriculture, medicine, planning—could be models for a much larger order. It was TR's hope to advance this mission, but he no longer had the power—the power of the presidency.

Perhaps the falling-out between Roosevelt and Taft was inevitable. Roosevelt was nursing sore envy of Taft—and regret over his own bad decision to relinquish presidential power. Though Taft was in many ways successful in fields such as anti-trust prosecution and conservation, in the eyes of TR he failed. He lacked gusto.

Against the advice of many friends, TR challenged his own successor: in 1912 he "threw his hat in the ring" for the Republican presidential nomination. Here was yet another grand mistake in strategy. If TR had managed to restrain himself for just four more years, he could have led the United States in World War I, instead of looking on with such bitterness as Woodrow Wilson, in TR's opinion, botched the job.

But he challenged Taft in 1912, and when he failed to dislodge the presidential incumbent, he bolted the Republican Party and formed a new "Progressive" Party. TR's followers in that year—among them young Harold Ickes, Alfred Landon, and Dean Acheson—were euphoric as Roosevelt combined some conservative and liberal principles in thundering terms:

> We are for human rights and we intend to work for them in efficient fashion. Where they can be best obtained through the application of the doctrine of States' rights, then we are for States' rights. Where, in order to obtain them, it is necessary to invoke the power of the nation, then we shall invoke to its uttermost limits that mighty power. We are for liberty. But we are for the liberty of the oppressed, and not for the liberty of the oppressor to oppress the weak and to bind burdens on the shoulders of the heavy-laden. It is idle to ask us not to exercise the power of government when only by the power of government can we curb the greed that sits in high places, when only by the exercise of government can we exalt the lowly and give heart to the humble and the downtrodden.[70]

One of the Progressive proposals that Roosevelt advanced in 1912 was social security. Another was the popular "recall" (by plebiscite) of bad judicial decisions. TR's message of "efficiency" was so compelling that a powerful industrialist, George W. Perkins (a former Morgan partner), became an ardent follower.[71]

But the race was hopeless. With Taft and Roosevelt dividing the Republicans, the presidency (along with the control of Congress) passed to Woodrow Wilson and the Democrats. TR would never hold office again. He died in his sleep on January 6, 1919, at the age of only sixty.

Journalist Mark Sullivan remembered him as follows:

> His every gesture counted, his every blow went to the mark, or started there, and if he had to retreat, he knew—to the surprised dismay of those who thought they had him beaten, the precise moment when he could turn. Roosevelt in battle—which was Roosevelt most of the time—was a huge personality endowed with energy almost abnormal, directed by an acute intelligence, lightened by a grinning humor, engaged in incessant action. The spectacle, occupying the biggest headlines in the daily newspapers, gave to the life of that day a zest and stimulus and gaiety such that average Americans who lived through the period carried it as a golden memory, and, in their elder years, recalled it as the ancient forty-niners remembered California, sighing "there'll never be another Roosevelt."[72]

But there *would* be another, of course—and his plans were already in the making.

4

THE LEGACY CROSSES PARTY LINES: FROM THEODORE TO FRANKLIN D. ROOSEVELT

Franklin Delano Roosevelt experienced a very sheltered life as a child. He had a sickly father, a kind but domineering mother, and luxurious surroundings—all too luxurious—at the splendid estate in Hyde Park that his parents called "Springwood." When he went off to prep school at Groton in his teens, he felt the painful limitations that resulted from the overprotective regime at his parents' estate.

So the rugged life of his older cousin Theodore, who hailed from the Oyster Bay side of the Roosevelt clan, was the kind of inspiration—the kind of antidote—that he needed.

When FDR was fifteen, his cousin Theodore visited Groton. He regaled the students with tales of his adventures fighting crime when he served as president of New York City's Board of Police Commissioners. "After supper tonight," wrote FDR to his parents, "Cousin Theodore gave us a splendid talk on his adventures when he was on the Police Board. He kept the whole room in an uproar for over an hour, by telling us killing stories about policemen and their doings in New York."[1] In the course of this visit Cousin Theodore invited young Franklin to visit him at Oyster Bay and stay over on the Fourth of July. Franklin accepted.

The hero worship—and the long-term influence—had begun. As James MacGregor Burns and Susan Dunn have written, "For Franklin, Oyster Bay was everything that Hyde Park was not."[2]

Then Theodore began his ascent: assistant secretary of the navy, volunteer colonel of the Rough Riders, governor of New York, vice president of the United States, and then, with the assassination of McKinley, the president.

The association of Franklin and Theodore Roosevelt became even closer. On New Year's Day in 1903, Franklin visited his cousin at the

White House: "Dinner at White House & have talk with the President," he wrote in his diary.[3] Soon afterward, Franklin became engaged to young Eleanor Roosevelt, Theodore's niece. So Cousin Theodore became "Uncle Ted." Then in 1904 Franklin cast his first vote in a presidential election—for Theodore Roosevelt. Though "my father and grandfather were Democrats and I was brought up as a Democrat," FDR stated years later, "I voted for the Republican candidate, Theodore Roosevelt, because I thought he was a better Democrat than the Democratic candidate."[4] But he was also, of course, Cousin Theodore.

A few months later, Franklin and Eleanor married—and it was Theodore who gave the bride away. "Well, Franklin," he quipped at the end of the ceremony, "there's nothing like keeping the name in the family!"[5] In the course of their honeymoon in Europe, Franklin wrote back to his mother, informing her that "everyone is talking about Cousin Theodore saying that he is the most prominent figure of present day history."[6]

After the honeymoon, Franklin got a job as a clerk in a New York law firm—and he was bored. In 1907, he revealed to his fellow clerks that he intended to be president. And he would do it by copying Theodore—to the letter. He would follow the very same pattern; he would occupy the very same positions that had served as such stepping stones for Ted. Years later, one of Franklin's fellow clerks, Grenville Clark, reminisced about it all:

> I remember him saying with engaging frankness that he wasn't going to practice the law forever, that he intended to run for office at the first opportunity, and that he wanted to be and thought he had a very real chance to be President. I remember that he described very accurately the steps which he thought could lead to this goal. They were: first, a seat in the State Assembly, then an appointment as Assistant Secretary of the Navy (an office held by Theodore Roosevelt early in his career), finally the governorship of New York.[7]

As Burns and Dunn have observed, "the stunning similarities between Theodore's and Franklin's careers were no coincidence. . . . Both attended Harvard, studied law and were bored by it, entered politics in their twenties, served in the New York legislature, won appointment as assistant secretary of the navy, married well, fathered six children . . . served as governor of New York, and ran for vice president of the United States. That the two patterns are identical is perhaps less extraordinary than one might think, for Franklin deeply admired TR and fervently wished to emulate him."[8] Or perhaps, as Frances Perkins (FDR's secretary of labor) speculated, Franklin had a secret and perhaps unconscious desire "to outshine Ted."[9]

In 1910 he was approached by the Democratic Party and decided to run for the New York legislature. Much has been made of his Democratic pedigree. But Burns and Dunn have convincingly argued that a flip of a coin could have changed things: "Both Sara [FDR's mother] and Eleanor had been raised as Republicans. . . . Young Franklin took after his father politically, but his Democratic loyalty was tenuous, having enthusiastically backed Cousin Theodore every time TR ran for office. . . . Franklin was so positioned in 1910 that he could be a candidate in either party."[10] But the Democrats got to him first.

Nonetheless, Uncle Ted was delighted with FDR's victory. "Just a line to say that we are all really proud of the way you have handled yourself," wrote Theodore in the aftermath of FDR's election to the legislature.[11] And one of the very first things that FDR did was to summon Gifford Pinchot, Theodore's friend and chief forester, to advise him on conservation matters. Conservation and the public construction of hydroelectric dams became FDR's major priorities during his years in Albany. Both of these priorities built upon the interests of Theodore and both of them foreshadowed crucial measures of the New Deal.

After the election of 1912, Franklin moved to the next political milestone. Still following the footsteps of Theodore, he got himself appointed assistant secretary of the navy in the Wilson administration. Theodore remained attentive: "It is interesting to see that you are in another place which I myself once held," he wrote to Franklin.[12] Josephus Daniels, Wilson's secretary of the navy, wrote the following notes in his diary: "His distinguished cousin TR went from the place to the Presidency. May history repeat itself."[13]

THE WILSON ERA

America's rise to superpower status had advanced under Theodore Roosevelt. At home, strong efforts were made to force a new cohesion of the left and right along with greater economic efficiency—through socioeconomic teamwork. In global terms, the nation's capabilities increased. The Panama Canal was completed in 1914—in the presidency of Woodrow Wilson. It was Wilson's fate to both advance and retard the global role of the nation, while advancing and retarding the role of its federal government.

The ambiguous results of the Wilson regime were in part symptomatic of the shifts within the liberal tradition, which America's Democratic Party exemplified. As in Britain, so in America: the old free-market "classical liberal" maxims started yielding to the ways of state regulation and even (to some extent) to the ways of the "welfare state." Wilson in his youth had been a Democrat reared in the Jefferson-Jackson tradition. Wilson as a nominal "progressive" became more flexible—or more conflicted.

In 1912 he called his program the "New Freedom." It was largely a restatement of American classical liberalism—free trade, states' rights—with a major new "progressive" departure: vigorous anti-trust enforcement. But the purpose of the anti-trust action was the restoration of free-market forces. When "monopoly" was crushed, private enterprise would solve the nation's problems.

Two years later the president began to change his mind. He supported the creation by Congress of the Federal Trade Commission (FTC). The FTC was designed to function as a supplement to anti-trust action. Wilson had proposed to make the old anti-trust prohibitions of the Sherman Act more specific. The result was the Clayton Anti-Trust Act of 1914. But if the Clayton Act proved ineffective, then the FTC would step into the breach with its cease-and-desist orders.

According to historian Arthur S. Link, the Clayton Act was ineffective indeed: its provisions were watered down by Congress. Wilson didn't do very much to resist this process. In Link's opinion, he was actually "uncertain as to the manner in which the broad objectives of his program should be accomplished."[14] When his adviser, the attorney and free-wheeling social reformer Louis D. Brandeis (whom Wilson later elevated to the Supreme Court), persuaded him to support the creation of the FTC, "Wilson seemed to lose all interest in the Clayton bill."[15]

But his support for the FTC was also lukewarm. He appointed ineffective commissioners, much to the disgust of Brandeis, who condemned the appointments in private later on as "stupid."[16] It was only over time that the agency fulfilled its potential.

Far more important than the FTC or the Clayton Act was the creation in the early Wilson years of a momentous apparatus for advancing American development: the Federal Reserve System, established through intensive give-and-take between the administration and congressional leaders in 1913. The operating methods of "the Fed" are sufficiently important to deserve an extended explication.

The banking community itself had demanded reform. After the Panic of 1907, bankers called for the creation of a central bank that could act as the "lender of last resort" as the second Bank of the United States had once done. The economic writer William F. Hixson has observed that "by 1914, banks held as reserves only about $10.50 for every $100 of deposits; and if only about a tenth of all depositors demanded cash, a bank would be forced into default."[17]

The increasingly perilous nature of fractional-reserve banking resulted from a change in the outward mechanics (and the secret metaphysics) of lending. As economic historians Walton and Rockoff explain, the old method of issuing banknotes was gradually replaced in the nineteenth century by "checkable deposits": the checking accounts and the "lines of credit" that we know and use today. Just as banks using fractional reserves had created new money—out of thin air—by lending banknotes beyond their deposits in coin, banks gradually began to "create new deposits" with the stroke of a pen and then issued the borrower a checkbook. As Walton and Rockoff have written, "when a bank made loans to its customers, it gave them the proceeds either in the form of its own notes, which then circulated as cash, or as a deposit credit against which they could draw checks."[18] By the 1870s, most commercial banks had "long since discarded the practice of issuing notes. . . . After the Civil War, bank deposits (checking) were far more important than notes in cities; by the mid-1870s, banks in all but the backwoods areas could extend loans simply by crediting the deposit account of the borrower."[19]

To be sure, these bankers were obliged to pay depositors, borrowers, and creditors cash (in the form of real coin) when either banknotes or checks were presented to them for redemption. But checks, as opposed to the circulating banknotes, were *brought to the banks for redemption as a matter of course*—they were never intended to circulate as hand-to-hand currency. So, demands upon the fractional reserves of the banks were accelerated, thus increasing the need for liquidity.

In 1907, the system began to explode, as panic drove the depositors to pull out their cash en masse. Hixson has observed that

> many of these banks, perhaps most of them, were solvent. Given time to collect repayment on their loans, they would have been able to pay cash to all depositors demanding it. But there is not time to collect repayment when a run on a bank occurs. . . . Their "fractional reserves," being only a small fraction of their deposits, were inadequate to meet the demands for cash from all depositors who mistakenly thought they had "money in the bank," and default ensued.[20]

The crisis caused bankers to demand a new national bank that could act as a lender of last resort. The short-term result was the creation of a National Monetary Commission headed by Senator Nelson W. Aldrich. Banker Paul M. Warburg called for a new central bank, to be named the "United Reserve Bank." Many bankers were hoping to create a new federal bank of this sort—a bank that would function like the Bank of England, the Banque de France, and the Reichsbank.

In 1912, the commission sent Congress a report with recommendations. It proposed the creation of a National Reserve Association with fifteen regional branches. Controlled by bankers, this "association" would hold as a part of its capital substantial deposits from the U.S. Treasury. The plan was opposed by sufficient Progressive Democrats (and the Democrats had won control of Congress) to force a compromise. The solution—worked out in consultations between key congressional sponsors (especially Senator Carter Glass of Virginia), President Wilson, members of the cabinet (especially William Gibbs McAdoo and William Jennings Bryan), and Wilson advisers (especially Louis Brandeis)—developed during 1913. The Federal Reserve System emerged as a partially decentralized institution with regional reserve banks, which would lend to the member banks. But it was also capped by a Federal Reserve Board appointed by the president. Later on, this board would get the power to set interest rates and reserve requirements directly. Finally, the banknotes issued by the system, which would operate through fractional reserves, would function as legal-tender *cash*, unlike any previous notes that had been issued by American banks.[21]

Our extraordinary monetary system thus emerged as a federal-and-private creation that is far more *integrated*—more synthesized in institutional terms—than the first or second Banks of the United States had been. Through the workings of the Federal Reserve System, it is no longer possible to speak about a "pure" free enterprise system. The truth: our money supply is created by the government and banks *together*. The liquid *capital* that fuels our particular version of *capitalism* is as much governmental as private-sector in its origin. It is a public-and-private economic creation: a hybrid.

And it enters circulation via fractional-reserve lending to this day. Walton and Rockoff have summarized: "Nowadays . . . banks no longer issue notes, and the paper money that passes from hand to hand is issued by the Federal Reserve; moreover, whenever a firm borrows money today it takes the proceeds as a credit to its account."[22] We all know the everyday mechanics: we take the plastic card that we receive from the bank to an ATM machine and get Federal Reserve notes, cash. Our "line of credit" constitutes the loan.

But do we understand the principle of "credit"? The term—a universal usage—is a hocus-pocus term from the occult. It is a *euphemism* for the hide-and-seek process of money creation by banks. On occasion, an economist has cut through the fog and let the public in on the secret; Irving Fisher, for example—one of America's foremost monetary theorists in the early twentieth century—explained "deposit creation" as follows: "When a bank grants me a $1,000 loan, and so adds $1,000 to my checking deposit, that $1,000 of 'money that I have in the bank' is new. It was freshly manufactured by the bank out of my loan and written by pen and ink on the stub of my check book and on the books of the bank. . . . Except for these pen and ink records, this 'money' has no real physical existence."[23]

To be sure, banking *starts* with an infusion of "capital." But then "extension of credit"—"deposit creation"—takes over through some fancy sleight-of-hand. All incoming cash—augmented by credit advanced by the Federal Reserve—can position a bank to create new money through a stroke of the pen (or a computer keystroke today). Economists William J. Baumol and Alan S. Blinder have spoken of the "modern alchemy of deposit creation" under Federal Reserve management—what critics of the system might regard as slick tricks of accounting—through a simple but pointed demonstration. A man deposits $100,000 in his checking account. Remember that: $100,000. So "the bank has now acquired $100,000 more in cash reserves, and $100,000 more in checking deposits." Note the entrance right here of *an accounting method that has multiplied the money by two*: $100,000 in "cash reserves" and $100,000 in "checking deposits." Take care: though the terms may appear to be synonymous—two equivalent terms—*that is not the case at all*, as we shall see.

The economists continue. They presume for a moment that the Federal Reserve's "reserve requirement" is 20 percent. That being the case, the bank's "*required* reserves are up by . . . $20,000, leaving $80,000 in *excess* reserves." So the bank lends the $80,000. Now watch what happens to our money supply: the depositor can write checks to the tune of $100,000. Remember that: he is free to spend his money when he wishes—every bit of it. Yet the *loan* has now entered circulation. *Another* $80,000 must be counted. The economists sum it up quickly: "There is now $100,000 in checking deposits and $80,000 of cash in circulation, making a total of $180,000. The money-creation process has begun."[24] And the $80,000 may result in yet *another* deposit in a bank (let us say that the *borrower* deposits his loan), which in turn provides the basis for *another* bank to make loans—creating *more* money. And it all takes place under federal auspices, thanks to the Federal Reserve.

In addition to this major contribution to the growth of American power—in this case financial power—Wilson and Congress expanded the role of the federal government in other ways as well. They created new agencies, like the National Park Service, established within the Interior Department in 1916. In the same year the Federal Farm Land Bank Act gave financial assistance to farmers. And in World War I, the vast array of new mobilization entities—the War Industries Board, the U.S. Fuel and Food Administrations, the War Labor Administration, and the Railroad Administration, which presided over a temporary nationalization of the industry—supplied a lesson in economic planning that many participants (not least of all Assistant Navy Secretary Franklin Roosevelt) remembered in the 1930s. There was also the matter of *deficit spending*: the national effort in World War I was so massively financed through the sale of bonds that our national debt soared twenty-fold—from $1 billion in 1915 to $20 billion by 1920.[25]

So much for the positive thrust, in institutional terms, of America's wartime experience under Wilson. But the experience was not completely happy. Wilson—and there is no way to put the matter kindly—was inept as a wartime leader, both in national and international terms. He was temperamentally averse to contingency planning, which meant that America was poorly prepared for the possibility of war before 1917. Though American troops (most of them newly inducted through the draft) reached France a few months after Congress's declaration of war, they did not reach the war's frontlines for a year because they needed such extensive training. Wilson had little sense of "lead time" in military matters.

On the home front, things were bad as well. Historian John Morton Blum put it gently when he wrote that Wilson "had to feel his way toward the creation of agencies sufficiently powerful" to manage the wartime mobilization; "the absence of forehandedness made the task enormous." Blum continues, "When the war came, the army lacked data even on the uniforms and shoes it would need; neither military nor civilians had an inventory of resources or a plan for priorities."[26]

The situation reached scandalous proportions in 1918. According to Blum, "several worried Democratic senators and most Republicans supported a bill to create a war cabinet of three distinguished citizens which was, in effect, to exercise the powers Congress had conferred upon the President. Had this measure passed, Wilson would have become a figurehead."[27]

Wilson counterattacked and got a different bill passed that empowered him to try again—through reorganization. By summer things began to straighten out and the mobilization hit its stride. But things could (and should) have been better from the start. Critics like Theodore Roosevelt continued to make this point in scathing terms.

The same aversion—is it time for us to call it incompetence?—to contingency planning in the years that *preceded* the mobilization led Wilson to ignore the task of planning for intelligent *de*mobililization. The result was a postwar unemployment crisis as millions of servicemen doffed their uniforms and found themselves without jobs. Inflation (due to shortages of goods) was a problem as well, and so the Federal Reserve banks hiked up their interest rates to counter it. This led to economic contraction. The crisis, which began in 1919 and was followed by a sharp recession in 1920 and 1921, led in part to the creation during World War II of the GI Bill as a way to forestall a new depression.

Wilson's ineptitude extended to moral leadership as well. Americans were deeply divided on the merits of entering the war. Wilson worsened the situation by supporting, as security measures, new laws that resulted in repression so severe as to prompt the creation of the American Civil Liberties Union in response.

According to historian John Milton Cooper Jr., "violations of civil liberties from 1917 through 1919 constituted a great failure for Wilson as a war leader, and they left the ugliest blot on his record as president."[28] Cooper cites, in particular, the 1918 Sedition Act, which "contained a sweeping ban on 'uttering, printing, writing, or publishing any disloyal, profane, scurrilous, or abusive language' against the government or the armed forces."[29]

The story gets worse. Mid-term congressional elections occurred in 1918. Wilson issued a statement asking voters to vote Democratic as a patriotic gesture. As Cooper has affirmed, "no other single action of Wilson's received such near-unanimous condemnation. . . . Republicans at once denounced the statement as a cheap partisan trick. . . . Wilson's staunchest defenders later deplored the appeal as a lapse of judgment and gesture of ingratitude toward Republicans who had supported his war policies."[30]

A lapse of judgment? Was it not just another demonstration of the president's aversion to contingency planning—his temperamental lack of foresight? When he made his appeal, the conclusion of the war was approaching; indeed, it was imminent. Surely Wilson should have sensed that if Republicans controlled the next Congress, he would need every bit of bipartisan support that he could get for any postwar treaty with ambitious long-term objectives. But apparently he never even thought about that. He never thought about the risk that he was taking when he made his foolish pitch to the voters. And it backfired. The Republicans took control of Congress.

Surely now he would realize his error and work with the Republicans? No, he declined to take a single Republican along with his delegation when he left for the Paris peace conference.

Wilson's failure went beyond the sad mistakes that are the typical results of mere stubbornness, myopia, and contempt for all the messy details. Wilson was impatient with the messy details because he viewed himself as God's agent: an agent of Providence. Far more than any other of the "Christian soldiers" who were active in Progressive-era politics—Theodore Roosevelt, for instance, whose followers sang "Onward, Christian Soldiers" at the 1912 Progressive convention—Wilson believed that his cause could not fail: God would see to that. So he never did worst-case contingency planning; he believed that such a thing was superfluous.

Listen to his words as he crusaded for the Versailles Treaty (while refusing to consider any talks with Republican leaders to ensure the treaty's passage in the Senate). On July 10, 1919, he told the Senate that his recent diplomacy was nothing less than God's will: "The stage is set, the destiny disclosed. It has come about by no plan of our conceiving, but by the hand of God who led us into this way. We cannot turn back. We can only go forward, with lifted eyes and freshened spirit, to follow the vision."[31]

Wilson's view of the world became utopian—millennial—by the summer and autumn of 1919. He had this to say about the League of Nations and its global promise in the very last speech that he made before he suffered his paralytic stroke: "Nothing less depends upon us, nothing less than the liberation and salvation of the world. . . . We have accepted that truth and . . . it is going to lead us, and through us the world, out into pastures of quietness and peace such as the world never dreamed of before."[32]

Compare this vision to the statement of Theodore Roosevelt in 1908 to the effect that "every new social relation begets a new type of wrongdoing—of sin." This realistic view of human nature (with its never-ending propensity for sinister behavior) precluded the ethereal notions that preoccupied Wilson toward the end. TR advanced a much *tougher* foreign policy, grounded in *realities of power*: power through national teamwork, power advanced through U.S. hegemony in Latin America (a heavy-handed legacy, of course), power extended through imperial possessions in the far-away Pacific, and the list could go on and on. TR's formula for global order was the old-fashioned balance of power—augmented by "sphere-of-interest" politics. It was a deeply conservative formula.

Wilson's vision, though he also engaged in hemispheric interventions for a while, was much simpler. It was the vision of grand global law to be enforced by the League of Nations. But this was not to be. The price to be paid for all the miscalculations of Wilson extended through the next twenty years. Another cultural backlash against the heroic was soon under way in America.

In the pivotal election of 1920, great numbers of Americans discovered that they wanted "not nostrums, but normalcy," as Warren Gamaliel Harding summed it up. The result was not only a reaction against more "progressivism" in domestic affairs but against international involvements. America's rise to superpower status was retarded for another generation, thanks to Woodrow Wilson's ineptitude—and his arrogance.

FROM WILSON TO HOOVER

The Gilded Age pattern was repeated in the 1920s: an age of crusading was followed by a postwar backlash. In the Gilded Age manner, it began with sleaze: scandals in Warren Harding's Washington served as a reiteration of the Grant era. The signature Gilded Age scandal had been Crédit Mobilier; the signature Harding scandal was Teapot Dome. Harding's interior secretary, Albert Fall, took bribes from some oil tycoons and then helped them to gain improper access to naval oil reserves.

As the Grant era crookedness yielded to an aftermath of minimal government, the Harding era yielded to drift. Calvin Coolidge, Harding's successor, believed that "rigid economy" in government served the people best, and the voters approved. Americans were sick of all the turmoil—so they "kept cool with Cal" in the election of 1924.

A great many voters were frightened by the prospect of "radical" changes for another reason: the Bolshevik triumph in the Russian Revolution had ushered in a brief "Red Scare." The scare abated, but the wariness lingered: the rise of the Soviet Union under Lenin and Stalin made a lot of Americans fearful of "statist" solutions.

Augmenting the new anti-government mood was resentment of Prohibition—a "progressive" reform that was instituted during World War I and then enforced, albeit sporadically, during the 1920s. Prohibition, though it shut down distilleries and breweries, was largely ineffective at interdicting "bootleggers," closing "speakeasies," or, it need hardly be added, engendering respect for the law—or government. The general response to Prohibition was derisive cynicism.

In the realm of international relations, the American mood was equally cynical: foreigners should solve their own problems. So too with the issue of preparedness: Americans were fed up with war, and professional soldiers took the cue, with a few exceptions. The watchword in military circles was political caution. When George S. Patton and Dwight D. Eisenhower called, as young officers, for bold new designs and new tactics for the use of tanks in combat, they were reprimanded.[33] The court-martial of General William ("Billy") Mitchell in 1925 became a warning to other smart reformers. Mitchell had commanded the American expeditionary air force in World War I. In the early 1920s he called for an independent air force and warned that America was falling behind in air power. He arranged the sinking of warships by dive-bombing planes as a warning against what we all know eventually happened at Pearl Harbor. His criticism of the top brass was too vocal—so he was punished.

Others made quiet preparations for the next great war, which they sensed was somehow "in the wind." Far away in the Panama Canal Zone, an erudite and visionary general named Fox Conner gave his bright young subordinate Dwight D. Eisenhower lessons in world history—as preparation.[34]

Others tried to do what they could to fill the vacuum of Coolidge-style politics. One of the rising political "whiz kids" of public service in the 1920s was Herbert Hoover, the secretary of commerce. Hoover was a wealthy mining engineer who had entered public service in the 1910s because of his reputation for efficiency. In 1914, he headed a "Committee for the Relief of Belgium," which distributed food and supplies to over five million people in the war-torn land. Hoover's success prompted Wilson to appoint him food commissioner in World War I; again, Hoover's work was superb. In 1919, as head of the American Relief Administration that sent food and supplies to the devastated regions of Europe, Hoover once again garnered international renown for feeding the hungry.

As secretary of commerce under Harding and Coolidge, Hoover was a moderate "progressive." He urged regulation of the nascent radio and aviation industries. Historian David Burner has observed that Hoover proposed the creation of a federal department of public works and a federal employment bureau. He "worked for the expansion of water-power facilities," urging action by the Reclamation Bureau in the Boulder Canyon of the Colorado River—a vision that led (later on) to the construction of the massive western dam that bears his name.[35] Burner has observed that "both as Commerce Secretary and President he put particular effort into getting a St. Lawrence Seaway."[36] He also played a role in the expansion of flood control efforts in the aftermath of the devastating Mississippi River flood of 1927.[37]

But there were limits to the work that even "whiz kids" like Hoover could do for a president like Coolidge. Coolidge had no real interest in a big and expensive construction project like Hoover Dam. And he turned a deaf ear to proposals by Republican senator George Norris for federal production of hydroelectric power on the Tennessee River.

There were other strong calls for new federal action in the 1920s. The auto manufacturers were interested in road development. Others shared this interest. A national "good roads" movement had developed from the 1913 proposal of businessman Carl Fisher (owner of the Indianapolis Motor Speedway) to construct a transcontinental highway.

Fisher's idea sparked the Lincoln Highway project. The president of Packard suggested that the highway should be named after Lincoln, and attempts were made to secure funding. But construction lagged. In 1916, the Federal Aid Road Act emerged from Congress, creating a new Bureau of Public Roads, but funding was meager.

Then in 1919, Secretary of War Newton Baker launched a transcontinental motor convoy of military vehicles to build up support for the highway project and to dramatize the bad condition of America's roads.[38] Those who made the harrowing journey never forgot it. One of them, Lieutenant Colonel Dwight D. Eisenhower, got his chance in the 1950s to provide what many people were calling for in the 1920s: transcontinental superhighways.[39]

But it didn't happen in the 1920s—at least not to the extent that the "good roads" advocates demanded. Congress passed a new Federal Highway Act in 1921, and yet it funded no federal construction. Instead, it fell back upon the method of granting assistance to states: grants to build roads that would not exceed 7 percent of all roads in a particular state.

Farmers began calling for remedial action as they had in the Gilded Age. Prices for crops started falling again, and a bad agricultural depression hit rural America. Assistance to farmers was increased to some extent by the Agricultural Credits Act of 1923 and even more through the Agricultural Marketing Act of 1929, which established a Federal Farm Board endowed with $500 million to lend to agricultural cooperatives. Herbert Hoover supported it.

But the big agricultural proposal that emerged in the 1920s was defeated. This was the McNary-Haugen Farm Relief Bill, which proposed to boost prices by creating a federally chartered corporation to buy the agricultural "surplus" and store it—or market it abroad. Farmers themselves would pay a tax to subsidize the process. Congress passed the measure in 1927, but Coolidge vetoed it.

Many have seen the agricultural depression of the 1920s as a harbinger of the Great Depression that began in 1929. For a while, the obvious "farm problem" stood out in sharp relief against the overall "Coolidge prosperity." But by mid-decade, a real estate slump had begun.[40] Some observers in the 1920s had reason to believe that the mainstream prosperity was hollow and that grave weaknesses lurked beneath the superficial glitter of the "Roaring Twenties" boom.

Such views were expressed in *Business Without a Buyer*, a book coauthored by William Trufant Foster (a former college president) and Waddill Catchings (an iron manufacturer) in 1927. Their warning: paychecks were not keeping pace with productivity. "We cannot sell the goods," they wrote, "because the people who would like to buy them do not have sufficient incomes."[41]

While some feared that "overproduction" would lead to a recession, Foster and Catchings insisted that the real issue was *purchasing power* and the problem of *underconsumption*. Smart businessmen attempted to control their costs, including labor costs, as standard method. But such micro-economic logic led to macro-economic dysfunction if America's workforce failed to reach its full potential for *buying*. Off-loading "excess" production through export sales (which Hoover, as commerce secretary, advocated) was not good enough: *our citizens had to come first*. Foster and Catchings's solution, as revealed in their 1928 sequel, *The Road to Plenty*, was public works spending by the government to stimulate purchasing power.

This was not a new idea: Foster and Catchings were working in the economic tradition of "contra-cyclical" theory, which had long since become international. In Victorian England, Walter Bagehot (the editor of the *Economist*) had argued that the Bank of England, through its monetary policies, should even out the business cycle and offset pernicious excesses: it should do this by tightening credit to avert "over-heated" expansion while serving as a "lender of last resort" to counteract recessions.[42]

The British economist John A. Hobson went further: he argued that the flip side of "overproduction" was a shortage of purchasing power: underconsumption. This, he contended, was the primary problem of depressions.[43] Government should solve the problem through increased spending: *fiscal* policy should supplement *monetary* policy to put the unemployed back to work.

The idea had American antecedents, as we know: the antebellum Whigs (Henry Clay, John Quincy Adams, and Abraham Lincoln) made proposals along these lines in the 1830s, and Jacob Coxey, the maverick reformer, campaigned for the principle in 1894 with his "army" of unemployed veterans. But no one had actually *tried* such a thing before at the federal level.

By the 1920s, the idea became of interest once again. As commerce secretary, Hoover had suggested more government construction to take up the slack in the postwar recession that occurred in the Harding years. At the national Governors' Conference in 1928, Governor Ralph Owen Brewster of Maine proposed establishing a federal-state-municipal public works "reserve" fund of $3 billion to serve as an economic "balance wheel."[44]

So the rudiments of "Keynesian" economic theory were in place before the Great Depression started. But such thinking was still in its infancy. In hindsight, America was stunningly ill-prepared for its greatest economic calamity. In the first place, America lacked a strong historical tradition in support of economic *planning*. Mere *financial* planning that was worthy of the name had been a slapdash affair at the federal level.

The Hamiltonian tradition was more or less disabled through the nineteenth century. And though disputes about economic issues were perennial and often explosive in American politics—Americans had disagreed sharply as to how (or whether) the imposition or reduction of tariffs, alterations in the coinage, or the issuance of legal-tender Greenbacks ought to be used by the government to help one group or another, or to help out the country as a whole—the closest that America had come to an ongoing economic policy had been the creation of the Federal Reserve as an instrument for quelling future bank panics and for issuing a more "elastic" currency. The only real interlude of government control and allocation of production was in World War I. By the 1920s, the Federal Reserve system was experimenting with hit-or-miss monetary policy. The Bureau of the Budget was created in 1921. But that was all the preparation that Americans had for the vast economic chain reaction that would lead, in a few short years, to economic collapse.

Though the earlier depressions in American history were brutal, the depression that began in Hoover's first presidential year was nothing less than horrific. The destruction was almost unbelievable. From 1929 to 1933, America's gross national product was cut by a third. Industrial production was *cut in half*. The output of durable goods fell from an index level of almost 100 in 1929 to 24.[45]

The level of unemployment rose from roughly 1.5 million to 13 million (a fourth to a third of the full-time workforce) and the crisis was worsening by 1933.[46] Millions of people lost their homes through bank foreclosures.

But foreclosures did not always save the banks: by 1933, one half of America's commercial banks had failed. America's money supply went with them: 40 percent of all "checkable deposits" in commercial banks (created via fractional reserve lending) simply vanished into thin air by 1933.[47] It was shockingly apparent that the Federal Reserve had not shored up the system, as its various creators had hoped.[48]

Economic historians Walton and Rockoff have observed that "in the four years between 1929 and 1933, the American economy simply disintegrated."[49] As it went, sudden poverty spread like a disease.

The reality suggested by the national figures was documented in detail. And the details were sickening. Thousands of middle-class Americans built shacks at their local city dump and then fought one another for the putrid remnants of food that the garbage trucks had left. Historian William E. Leuchtenburg relates that "in Chicago, a crowd of some fifty hungry men fought over a barrel of garbage set outside the back door of a restaurant; in Stockton, California, men scoured the city dump near the San Joaquin River to retrieve half-rotted vegetables."[50]

Thousands "rode the rails" as ragged hoboes. Men who for years had been "providers"—breadwinners—were thrown out of once-secure jobs. Then they and their families were thrown right out into the street. Big-city life was just as desolate as life in the countryside: according to Arthur Schlesinger Jr., "one out of every two workers was without a job" in Chicago by 1932. Around the country quiet tragedies unfolded, as Schlesinger relates:

> In the Pennsylvania coal fields, miners kept up a subdued battle against starvation, freezing in rickety one-room houses, subsisting on wild weed-roots and dandelions. . . . In Oakland, California, four-year-old Narcisson Sandoval, who had been living on refuse, died of starvation. . . . In Northampton, Massachusetts, Anthony Prasol, the father of eight children, killed himself because he had no hope of work.[51]

All of these events were taking place in the most advanced industrial nation that the modern world had ever seen. The situation was shocking to the point of being ludicrous. The *potential* for continued American productivity remained: that was perfectly obvious. No bombing or invasion had destroyed all the factories and farms of the United States. No plague had been killing off the workforce. No disaster had destroyed the raw materials. The ingredients for national abundance were all around—factories, farms, raw materials, people. Yet the *system itself* had broken down.

Leuchtenburg summarized the economic ironies—the bitter ironies—that were hammering away at the American mind in the last horrible months of Hoover's term: "While the jobless wore threadbare clothing, farmers could not market thirteen million bales of cotton in 1932. While children trudged to school in shoes soled with cardboard, shoe factories in Lynn and Brockton, Massachusetts, had to close down six months of the year. With ten billion dollars in bank vaults, hundreds of cities felt compelled to issue scrip because there was not enough currency in the town. . . . While people went without food, crops rotted in the fields."[52]

Before the Depression began, and for several years thereafter, efforts were made by the Federal Reserve to steer the nation's economy. Economists naturally differ as to whether the decisions of "the Fed" were misguided or not, and they also differ as to whether mere monetary policy could stop such a brutal chain reaction once it had begun.

By the time the Great Depression had arrived in full force, it was much too late to revive the economy through "easy money": through attractive interest rates. As economic historians Lester S. Levy and Roy J. Sampson have observed, "during most of the 1930s an easy money policy was pursued in the hope that recovery from the depression could be promoted." But although "large amounts of excess reserves were pumped into the banking system [the] reserves remained unused. So severe was the depression that sound business people were reluctant to borrow and banks were hesitant about lending to the daring entrepreneurs who solicited loans."[53] Why lend any money to reopen closed factories when market prospects were dismal?

Herbert Hoover tried to do what he could to promote reinvestment. But as the situation worsened, he became more isolated—more remote. And he seemed to be largely "in denial" in regard to the suffering. The man who fed the starving millions in Europe now opposed direct federal relief. He uttered bromides about "self-reliance." And he insisted on balancing the budget.

Late in the game, he supported the creation of a "pump-priming" agency, the Reconstruction Finance Corporation (RFC), to lend money to business and even to support public works. But it was barely a drop in the ocean. With such a massive wipe-out of purchasing power, the stimulus provided by the RFC could do little to revive the economy.

The nation's mood was turning ugly. Unemployed workers led a protest march upon the River Rouge plant of Henry Ford, which was closed for retooling; what they got was bullets and tear gas. Unemployed veterans of World War I marched to Washington demanding an early payment of a bonus. When Congress demurred—the bonus bill would unbalance the budget—angry members of the "Bonus Army" threw rocks at the cars of recalcitrant congressmen, and Hoover called out the army. Chief of Staff Douglas MacArthur chased the veterans away, using bayonets and tear gas to force the "mob" out of town. Then he torched the encampment of tents where they had been living.

Around the country unrest boiled over; Leuchtenburg recounts the stunning incidents of 1932: "At Storm Lake, Iowa, rope-swinging farmers came close to hanging a lawyer conducting a foreclosure; in the LeMars area, five hundred farmers marched on the courthouse steps and mauled the sheriff and the agent of a New York mortgage company. . . . In the Blue Ridge, miners smashed company store windows and storekeepers were given the choice of handing out food or having it seized." Some theorists wondered if "the long era of economic growth in the western world had come to an end."[54]

But a very different theorist was building up the doctrine of purchasing power on his way to international fame. The British economist John Maynard Keynes began preaching the doctrine of deficit-financed public works. If a wartime emergency could justify increasing the national debt—whatever it took to beat the Kaiser—why insist in the middle of a peacetime emergency on rigidly balancing the budget?

"There will be no . . . escape from prolonged and perhaps interminable depression," warned Keynes in 1932, "except by direct state intervention to promote and subsidize new investment" through deficit spending on a scale commensurate with war:

> Formerly there was no expenditure out of the proceeds of borrowing that it was thought proper for the State to incur except for war. In the past, therefore, we have not infrequently had to wait for a war to terminate a major depression. I hope that in the future we shall not adhere to this purist financial attitude, and that we shall be ready to spend on the enterprises of peace what the financial maxims of the past would only allow us to spend on the devastations of war. At any rate, I predict with an assured confidence that the only way out is for us to discover *some* object which is admitted even by the deadheads to be a legitimate excuse for largely increasing the expenditure of someone on something![55]

But Keynes's worst prediction came true: it took World War II to pull America out of the Depression.

THE DEMOCRATIC ROOSEVELT

In 1928, the same year in which Hoover won the presidency, FDR won the governorship of New York, thus continuing his emulation of Theodore. He succeeded Al Smith in the governorship—Al Smith, whom the Democrats had run against Hoover. Out of office, Smith dabbled for a while in real estate development (becoming a promoter of the Empire State Building project). He was bitter. But at least he didn't have to "face the music," like Hoover did: journalist Frederick Lewis Allen quipped that "Governor Smith must have felt like the man who just missed the train which went off the end of the open drawbridge."[56]

FDR tried to mitigate the Great Depression at the state level, and he soon became one of the nation's most dynamic governors. He created the first state relief agency to swing into action after 1929: the Temporary Emergency Relief Administration (TERA). He asked a social worker, Harry Hopkins, to run it. With another social worker, Frances Perkins, he developed state plans for unemployment compensation and old-age pensions. He also worked on conservation and hydroelectric power.

This was an appropriate beginning in FDR's preparation for the New Deal. But Roosevelt was uncertain regarding economics when he ran against Hoover in 1932: his campaign speeches were so contradictory that Walter Lippmann called FDR "a pleasant man who, without any important qualifications for the office, would very much like to be President."[57] He seemed to lack the intellectual force of his relative Theodore. "It is useless to blame this very unrooseveltian Roosevelt for having no ideas," wrote a Washington journalist; "he tries his best to have them."[58]

At the moment, though, it didn't matter: Roosevelt was charismatic. His magnificent voice—deep, well-projected, with a warm and honey-toned timbre—was inspiring, and so was his dynamic bearing. (He concealed his paralysis by means of hidden leg braces and other stratagems.) In any case, Hoover was doomed.

After the election, FDR assembled a "brain trust" composed of some Columbia professors, along with other advisers. As they deliberated, the air was full of expectation—and radical proposals.

In light of the massive contraction of the money supply that occurred when the deposit creation of the system reversed itself in catastrophic bank panics, some economists called the whole system into question and proposed a different kind of money, or a different kind of banking, or both. Henry C. Simons of the University of Chicago declared that

> we should characterize as insane a governmental policy of alternately expanding rapidly and contracting precipitously the quantity of paper money in circulation. . . . Yet that is essentially the kind of monetary policy which actually obtains, by virtue of the usurpation by private institutions (deposit banks) of the basic state function of providing the medium of circulation. . . . It is no exaggeration to say that the major proximate factor in the present crisis is commercial banking. . . . The state has forced the free-enterprise system, almost from the beginning, to live with a monetary system as bad as could well be devised.[59]

Precedent existed for direct governmental creation of money: the Civil War Greenbacks. Perhaps the time had arrived for Uncle Sam to take the monetary plunge and just print a batch of new money and spend it (or lend it) into circulation. In the early months of 1933, almost half the members of the House of Representatives had signed their names to a petition in support of Greenbacks.[60] The elderly economist John R. Commons endorsed the idea, declaring that "in order to create the *consumer demand*, on which business depends for sales, the government itself must create . . . new money and go completely over the head of the entire banking system by paying it out directly to the unemployed, either as relief or for construction of public works."[61]

Some insisted on a more comprehensive reform of the monetary system. Economist Irving Fisher of Yale—at the time a celebrity figure—joined Simons in condemning the fractional-reserve tradition. "The banker lends money of his own creation," wrote Fisher, and the concept was gross and unjust, as well as dangerous when bank panics spread. "Everyone except the banker who lends money lends pre-existing money, not money of his own creation. . . . The government should take away from banks all control over money creation."[62] Against complaints that his position was "radical," Fisher denied it. His view was "the opposite of radical," he wrote, for "what it asks . . . is a return from the present extraordinary and ruinous system of lending the same money 8 or 10 times over, to the conservative safety-deposit system."[63]

Fisher's system, which he touted as "the 100% reserve plan," would have set up a federal "currency commission" that would

> *turn into cash* enough of the assets of every commercial bank to increase the cash reserve of each bank up to 100% of its checking deposits. In

other words, let the Government buy (or lend money on) some of the bonds, notes, or other assets of the bank with money, especially issued through the Currency Commission. . . . This new money (Commission Currency, or United States notes), would . . . give an all-cash backing for the checking deposits. . . . So far as this change to the 100% system would deprive the bank of earning assets . . . the bank would be reimbursed by a service charge made to its depositors.[64]

Lending would continue via *savings* deposits in commercial banks—and via savings and loan institutions as well as investment trusts. But the creation and expansion of our nation's money supply would no longer occur via banks: "new loan funds would come out of savings but no longer out of thin air."[65]

Others had a simpler idea: a sweeping nationalization of the banks. It bears noting that the Bank of England was nationalized in 1946: the stockholders of the bank were paid off with government bonds.

In the so-called winter of despair (1932–1933), the nation seemed to confront the greatest threat to its institutions since the Civil War. Some heeded the Greenwich Village prophet Howard Scott, who was calling for scientific management of the economy; he called his program "technocracy." Some dreamed of going "back to the land" through cooperative farming or homesteads. Some were calling for an outright dictatorship.[66]

"Even the iron hand of a national dictator," said Republican Alfred M. Landon (who was destined a few years later to oppose FDR as the Republican presidential nominee in 1936), "is in preference to a paralytic stroke."[67] Leuchtenburg has said that "even businessmen favored granting Roosevelt dictatorial powers when he took office."[68]

Early in 1933, a new political film was released: *Gabriel over the White House*. Largely the work of William Randolph Hearst, the film was released by MGM. It depicted a president named Judson Hammond (played by Walter Huston), who persuaded Congress to suspend the Constitution and let him save the country single-handed. He put the unemployed veterans to work: he organized them as the "Army of Construction." And he balanced the budget.

This was partially the context of FDR's first inaugural address ("the only thing we have to fear is fear itself") when he declared that if all other measures should fail, he would ask the Congress for "broad Executive power to wage war against the emergency, as great as the power that would be given me if we were in fact invaded by a foreign foe."[69] The Republicans were right behind him: the arch-conservative Hamilton Fish told FDR that Congress should give him "any power that you may need."[70]

As the "first Hundred Days" of the New Deal commenced, legislation was *shouted* through Congress with Republicans in full support. One Republican congressman had this to say: "The majority leaders have brought us a bill on which I myself am unable to advise my colleagues, except to say that this is a case where judgment must be waived, where argument must be silenced, where we should take matters without criticism lest we may do harm by delay."[71]

He was talking about some emergency legislation to save the banks. And what was remarkable—in light of the fact that FDR could have had almost any legislation on banking that he wanted, even nationalization—is that he turned right away to a bevy of Hoover advisers and concocted a package that would prop up the status quo. He sent the legislation (the Emergency Banking Act of 1933) to Capitol Hill, and then, as Leuchtenburg describes the scene, "with a unanimous shout, the House passed the bill, sight unseen, after only thirty eight minutes of debate."[72] Republican Senator Bronson Cutting of New Mexico later remembered the events of that day "with a sick heart. For then . . . the nationalization of the banks by President Roosevelt could have been accomplished without a word of protest."[73]

Before very long, however, Congress passed some more banking legislation. And in the law that eventually emerged (the Glass-Steagall Act) was a powerful provision for insurance of bank deposits, a provision that FDR viewed with suspicion. The creation of the Federal Deposit Insurance Corporation (FDIC), as proposed by Senator Arthur Vandenberg of Michigan and Representative Henry Steagall of Alabama, was viewed by some as inadvisable. Over time, however, it became an essential provision for viable—indeed, for sane—commercial banking, and it constitutes a major part of the New Deal legacy.

The important point here is the conservative side of FDR—conservative, at least, in the old-fashioned sense of upholding traditional practices whenever possible. In the old-fashioned spirit, he positioned himself as a unifier—a patriot—in 1933. Americans saw him as a leader who was operating far above class, above party, and above the vested interests. And yet his policies in many ways *saved* the vested interests from truly radical changes.[74]

His advisers were a highly eclectic group, and they disagreed with one another constantly. Among them: Raymond Moley, a political economist; Rexford Guy Tugwell, an authority on agriculture and planning; Henry Wallace, a farm reformer whose father served as agriculture secretary under Harding; Adolf Berle Jr., an expert on corporate organization; Henry Morgenthau Jr., an economist and agriculture expert; Harold Ickes, a progressive Republican and conservationist who cheered for TR in 1912; Frances Perkins, the social worker who became the first female cabinet member (secretary of labor); and her fellow social worker Harry Hopkins.

FDR's *modus operandi* was to put these advisers into sharp *competition*—to "let the fur fly" for many months. He gave each and every one of his advisers a *measure* of what they recommended. There was method in the madness, to some extent: in his first inaugural address he had pledged himself to "bold, persistent experimentation." The result was a cacophony of wildly inconsistent policies.

Like Hoover, FDR was firmly committed to balancing the federal budget. Austerity edicts were handed down with regularity. On the other hand, he was also committed to *action* that would put the unemployed back to work. Among the big job-creation projects in 1933 was the Tennessee Valley Authority (TVA), a huge and majestic project giving life to the ten-year-old vision of Republican George Norris (who had called for a program of federal hydroelectric power-creation), while expanding that vision to encompass flood control. Another job-creation venture was the Public Works Administration (PWA), which channeled federal money into bricks-and-mortar projects of various types around the country. Of lesser scope was the Civilian Conservation Corps (CCC), a joint project of the War and Interior Departments putting unemployed men to work on reforestation and conservation projects under military discipline. For those left out, direct relief (welfare) was provided through FERA, the Federal Emergency Relief Administration, headed by Harry Hopkins.

But other high-visibility projects had little to do with public works. The NRA (National Recovery Administration) was a venture in national planning via labor-management price and wage codes established under government auspices. The program was voluntary. But for businesses willing to cooperate ("We Do Our Part" was the slogan), the benefits were great: the NRA suspended anti-trust prosecutions for price-fixing. The whole idea of the NRA was inflationary: both prices and wages would be propped up high, so that business and labor would benefit.

Here, without a doubt, was a dose of the old "New Nationalism" that Theodore Roosevelt espoused in 1912. It was the very same vision of national teamwork to build up American power through scientific efficiency. This was the sort of idea that attracted industrialist George W. Perkins to Theodore Roosevelt. Competition, said Perkins, had become "too destructive to be tolerated. Co-operation must be the order of the day."[75]

Perkins admired the German cartel system, and in 1912 he gave Theodore Roosevelt's campaign a gift of $250,000.

The New Deal's major agriculture project in 1933 was based upon similar premises. But its origins in the American reform tradition were different. The Agricultural Adjustment Administration (AAA) was set up to boost farm prices through collaborative planning between government and farmers. The idea was based upon the method of the Farmers' Alliance in the 1880s to push up farm prices by pulling crops off-market with governmental assistance. The McNary-Haugen plan of the 1920s was a kindred proposal.

Both of these agencies—NRA and AAA—enjoyed limited success on their own terms in 1933 and 1934. But both of them were highly regressive, in Keynesian terms. High prices (like high taxes) are generally bad for the suffering millions in a time of economic depression. And NRA—though it clearly boosted wages in American factories that *still remained open*—did nothing to *reopen* closed factories. The whole project was equivalent in some respects to a venture in "rearranging the deck chairs on the *Titanic*."

The effects of the AAA were worse: by paying farmers to cut back planting (they were paid from the proceeds of a tax), many tenant farmers and sharecroppers were thrown off the land because their services were no longer needed. This added to the unemployment problem. And since the AAA also paid many farmers to destroy existing crops or to kill some livestock in 1933, its critics complained that it resolved the contradiction of "starvation in the midst of plenty" by destroying the plenty. In response, some "surplus" commodities were shared with the poor through the newly created Surplus Relief Corporation (renamed the Surplus Commodities Corporation in 1935).[76] Still, the goal remained a cutback in "overproduction."

To be sure, the economic *stimulus* for recovery—the government action to restore the lost purchasing power of unemployed Americans—was supposed to be coming from the job-creation projects like the TVA and PWA. In the meantime, Hoover's old RFC was converted by Roosevelt, who appointed a maverick Texas banker named Jesse Jones to transform it into a major national lender: it bought bank stock and pumped more money, through loans, into many sorts of projects. It created a Commodity Credit Corporation to lend money to farmers. A few years later, it created the Federal National Mortgage Association—the famous Fannie Mae.

But the size of the unemployment problem was far too great for the scope of such programs to alleviate. The TVA was merely regional in its impact. As to the PWA, Leuchtenburg has written that "Secretary of the

Interior Harold Ickes, whom Roosevelt named to head the Public Works Administration, operated the agency with such extreme caution that it did next to nothing to stimulate the economy."[77] Recovery was stalling in the autumn of 1933—and the national mood began to darken.

With winter setting in, Harry Hopkins convinced his boss that strong emergency measures were required. The result was the Civil Works Administration (CWA), which created over four million temporary public works jobs, under Hopkins's direction. But FDR shut down the program as quickly as he could. According to Leuchtenburg, he was "alarmed about how much CWA was costing."[78] Four million men were out of jobs again, and the country slipped back into depression.

In many ways the problem was simple: the orthodox principle of balancing the budget was stunting the early New Deal. Orthodox thinking on the fiscal front made it difficult for FDR and his advisers to support a truly massive and sustained intervention. But with industrial production cut in half since the onset of the Depression, a tremendous effort was required.

Deficit spending made FDR very nervous. He didn't want it to become a "habit in this country," as he told his advisers.[79] Even the comparatively brief duration of the CWA entailed more deficit spending than FDR's budget director Lewis Douglas could bear. So he resigned, sending FDR the following communiqué: "I hope, and hope most fervently, that you will evidence a real determination to bring the budget into actual balance, for upon this, I think, hangs not only your place in history but conceivably the immediate fate of western civilization."[80]

Keynesian policies were still far away in the early months of 1934. Though Keynes had lamented that "the voices which . . . tell us that the path of escape is to be found in strict economy . . . are the voices of fools and madmen," his major work, *The General Theory of Employment, Interest, and Money*, had not yet been published when he wrote those vivid lines.[81] Keynes's *General Theory* would not hit the shelves until 1936. Marriner Eccles, a Utah banker whom FDR appointed as governor of the Federal Reserve Board in November 1934, was a Keynesian. But few other members of the FDR entourage could answer the description.

James MacGregor Burns has reflected that while Keynesian principles "might have provided a spectacular solution to Roosevelt's chief economic, political, and constitutional difficulties," FDR was "unable as a thinker to seize the opportunity that Keynesian economics gave him." Keynes himself had tried direct communication with FDR: "The Englishman had corresponded with the President, and he had talked with him in 1934. The two men liked each other, but the intellectual and the politician were cut from different cloth." More specifically, in Burns's opinion, "the idea of boosting spending and holding down taxes and of doing this year after year as a deliberate policy . . . seemed but another fanciful academic theory" to FDR at the time.[82]

So he supported other kinds of reform. In 1934, Congress passed the Securities and Exchange Act to regulate Wall Street. The new SEC would prevent misfeasance and conflict of interest among stockbrokers. Another act created the Federal Communications Commission (FCC) to regulate the radio industry.

Roosevelt also supported the insurance of home-loan mortgages through the newly created Federal Housing Administration (FHA). The FHA over time would, of course, transform the lending industry and bring home ownership within the reach of millions.[83] It bears noting that the National Housing Act of 1934, which created the FHA, was largely conceived by a committee of business leaders.[84] It also bears noting that the full effects of the program were still far away when FDR launched it.

In any case, it was the president's hope that the economy would slowly revive on its own. But the Depression continued, and the politics of unity collapsed. The patriotic aura that surrounded FDR had dissolved by 1934: he became "fair game" for his critics. Moreover, the left-versus-right dialectic reemerged, with the New Deal caught in the middle.

On the left, three emergent figures—Father Charles Coughlin, Dr. Francis Townsend, and Senator Huey P. Long of Louisiana—urged stronger, more "radical" measures. Coughlin pushed inflation through expanded silver coinage. Townsend pushed for old-age pensions that would boost the collective purchasing power of the elderly. Long pushed for "redistribution of the wealth": for confiscatory taxes that would cap the great fortunes and "share" the taxed wealth down below, eliminating poverty.

Long in particular was a significant menace to FDR. A brilliant demagogue, he led a political machine and controlled a great deal of his state by remote control from the Senate. His Louisiana enemies called him a "dictator." He developed an enormous following on radio (as did Father Coughlin) and encouraged the formation of "Share Our Wealth" societies across America.[85] He thundered in old-fashioned Populist style, condemning "Morgans and Mellons and Rockefellers" for their greed.

FDR too had established himself as a significant radio presence through his "fireside chats." Moreover, his charming manner in his frequent press conferences, which people could watch via newsreels at the cinema, gave an intimacy to his charisma. Both FDR and Long were star performers.

By 1934 a great feud between the two of them developed. Long, with his "countrified" humor, ridiculed FDR as a mama's boy, a pampered prince, and a dilettante whose convoluted policies had failed to "put the axe to the root": concentrated wealth.

Long was clearly positioning himself for a challenge to FDR in 1936. He would challenge him for the Democratic Party's nomination—or run as a third-party candidate. Some suspected that his plan was to ruin things for FDR, much as Theodore Roosevelt in 1912 had effectively ruined things for Taft. Long and FDR would split the reform vote. This would cripple the Democratic Party and throw FDR out of office. With FDR gone, a hapless Hoover-type Republican would dither for another four years. Meanwhile, Huey would be turning his state into a miniature utopia, with no more poverty or hunger. Then in 1940 he would offer his state as a model—for all America.[86]

Some believed him to be a wolf in sheep's clothing: a crypto-Fascist who would terminate American democracy. But Long called himself a man of the left. Other bona fide leftists—American Socialists and Communists—attacked FDR as a stooge of the bankers and tycoons.

On the right, more trouble was brewing. In 1934 a bipartisan conservative group emerged to challenge FDR; it attacked the New Deal as a bureaucratic nightmare. The American Liberty League was heavily funded by several wealthy families, notably the DuPonts. It issued pamphlets with titles like "Government by Busybodies." But this was just the beginning. After a while, a ferocious "hate Roosevelt" campaign was under way in certain upper-class circles.[87]

FDR, caught in the middle, swung back into action with a great new wave of legislation in 1935. Some have called it the "Second New Deal." The centerpiece was Social Security—the great conservative reform handed down from Bismarck, young Winston Churchill, and Theodore Roosevelt. Along with the old-age pensions came unemployment compensation and a measure of welfare.

A new banking act, drawn up by Marriner Eccles, gave the Federal Reserve Board more authority over the Federal Reserve banks—it gained complete authority to set the reserve rates. The act also gave the board effective control of the Open Market Committee (established in 1923 by the board to coordinate lending via purchases of bonds). Most important, the act made the FDIC permanent (Glass-Steagall set it up preliminarily) and hammered out the *quid pro quo* that was required in return for the benefits of the FDIC: to get deposit insurance, the member banks would have to submit to regulation and oversight. The FDIC board was empowered to examine each member bank's "financial history and condition," "the adequacy of its capital structure, its future earnings prospects, the general character of its management"—and so forth. Banks that were unsatisfactory would forfeit their privileges.[88]

Another act gave the Federal Power Commission (FPC) authority to regulate both interstate power transmissions and interstate utility transactions. The mission of the FPC was to ensure that electrical rates would be "reasonable, nondiscriminatory and just to the consumer."

A new agency, the Resettlement Administration, was created to build model suburbs that would demonstrate exemplary planning. The brainchild of Rexford Guy Tugwell, the agency planned to build an extensive network of "greenbelt towns" on the fringes of the nation's big cities. The flagship community of Greenbelt, Maryland, was built on the outskirts of Washington, D.C., in 1936 and 1937.

Another new agency, the Rural Electrification Administration (REA), lent federal funds to launch electrification co-ops in areas where private utilities refused to bring power (they deemed it unprofitable).

Other major items in the Second New Deal were more "leftist." For organized labor, the Wagner Act gave labor unions new federal support in their struggle to engage in collective bargaining—and to force recalcitrant owners to the bargaining table by going out on strike. A new entity, the National Labor Relations Board (NLRB), was created, with authority to supervise union elections and to take direct action against "unfair labor practices" by employers. Revealingly, FDR was a lukewarm supporter of the act until the very last minute.

Then there was the WPA (Works Progress Administration), another big job-creation effort that was headed by Harry Hopkins. FDR committed $5 billion to creating more jobs in 1935. The money was split between the PWA (which employed enough workers to complete particular projects) and the newer agency, which sought to *place a given number of unemployed men in new jobs*—almost any kind of jobs, just so long as the men were kept employed. Hence the Federal Writers' Project (set up within the WPA to hire unemployed authors), the Federal Theatre Project (set up to hire unemployed actors), and so forth.

It began to make a difference; the economy started to pick up. But there was also bad news for FDR: legal challenges regarding the constitutionality of his programs started reaching the Supreme Court. And the Court began terminating agencies, beginning with the NRA, which was toppled in 1935. The AAA was the next to go, in 1936. FDR was worried that the Wagner Act and Social Security Act would be next. But at least there was a major (if morbid) source of consolation for FDR in September 1935: Huey Long was shot dead.

Meanwhile, the critics on the right became more vocal—and more savage. In his study of the Liberty League, historian George Wolfskill paraphrased the nasty rhetoric that typified the new "hate Roosevelt" mania on the right. Roosevelt, to the patricians who loathed him, was

> a "cripple" [and] a "dupe." . . . From Newport to Miami, from Wall Street to Park Avenue, in country club locker rooms, in the cathedral-like hush of bank offices, in board rooms and carpeted law offices, the broad stories passed: Roosevelt was an inveterate liar, immoral (hadn't you heard of his affair with Frances Perkins?), a syphilitic, a tool of Negroes and Jews, a madman given to unbroken gales of immoderate laughter, an alcoholic, a megalomaniac dreaming his dreams of dictatorship.[89]

Some of the "Roosevelt stories" were obscene—so obscene that even members of the worldly Washington press corps were astonished.

In some ways the work of the Liberty League was a clear reiteration of the "Old Guard" conservative revolt against Theodore Roosevelt—the open breach that began in his lame-duck presidential years. There was a major difference, however. TR was a military hero, so the best that his enemies could do was to call him "the wild man." FDR was more vulnerable to a Social Darwinist assault: his detractors called him "weak." He was often insulted as "the cripple."

In a sense, the whole episode served as yet another Gilded Age replay: here again was conservatism in its Social Darwinist version ("survival of the fittest") at war with the tradition of Tory reform and the ethics of the Social Gospel, which FDR had imbibed in his youth from the Rector Endicott Peabody. Sociologist E. Digby Baltzell once perceived in the showdown of FDR and the Liberty League a confrontation of upper-class values: reformist aristocracy versus snarling, exclusionary "caste."[90]

FDR was both astonished and indignant at the right-wing vilification. In his own view, he had "saved the system of private profit and free enterprise after it had been dragged to the brink of ruin."[91] He told a Hearst reporter in 1935 that "I am fighting Communism, Huey Longism, Coughlinism, Townsendism. I want to save our system, the capitalist system."[92]

In truth, he had passed up a great many chances to alter "the American system" in ways that were radical. He could easily have nationalized the banks, but he decided to protect them. He often took the advice of "sound thinkers" in the business community. Historian Carl Degler once concluded that FDR was "a conservative at heart" in many respects.[93]

To be sure, FDR *as a Democrat* was responding to the liberal tradition. It was FDR's New Deal that would finally consummate the liberal embrace of the "welfare state" in America. The term "New Deal liberalism" is unavoidable, regardless of whether it is used as a term of honor, a term of abuse, or a term of description. The liberal lineage of New Deal culture was apparent in the paeans to Thomas Jefferson—not the Jefferson of minimal government, of course, but the Jefferson who championed the "common man"—that resounded in the culture of the 1930s. The Jefferson Memorial project approached its fruition at the very same time that James Stewart brought the character of "Jefferson Smith" to the screen in the Frank Capra film *Mr. Smith Goes to Washington*. Jeffersonian aesthetics were brought up to date through the common-man heroes depicted in the murals produced by the WPA, and in the lyrics of Woody Guthrie music. The list could go on. Surely themes such as these were a substantial part of the New Deal legacy—for liberals.

But there was clearly a conservative side to the New Deal: Burns has agreed with Degler that Tory reform was a significant presence in the leadership of FDR. Burns has remarked that while FDR's mind was "open to almost any idea" and "welcomed liberal and radical notions," he was "far closer to the conservative tradition than any other." He was in many respects "a conservative acting in the great British conservative tradition."[94]

He was a country squire who sought to practice noblesse oblige. He was a traditionalist who extended the legacy of classical architecture in the nation's capital. He conducted himself as a "Christian gentleman" who sought to uphold the community values of home and family. Burns has spoken of FDR's Burkean "belief in the unity of the past, the present, and the future," his "solicitous concern for the national heritage . . . that was passing through one generation of Americans after another."[95] For this reason, FDR was an enthusiastic supporter of the National Historic Sites Act of 1935.

He also supported law and order, encouraging J. Edgar Hoover to unleash the great force of the FBI (founded in 1908 as an investigative unit of the Justice Department and given its definitive name and acronym in 1935) against criminals like John Dillinger. The triumph of racket-busting "G-Men" was a theme of great consequence in the 1930s.

FDR was the sort of conservative who sought to create benign order—a conservative who believed that formations of order must protect us from chaos and savagery. He sought to *tame* the wild rivers that were flooding out the homes of poor families. He sought to *shelter* private property from surges of destruction in the great economic chain reactions. He sought to practice the Social Gospel. According to Burns, he got a pleasant and quiet sort of comfort from "hymns and Psalms, the order and routine of the church." This led him in turn to certain standards of deportment, of "gentlemanliness," that were quite traditionalistic.[96]

Leuchtenburg has written of the social ideals that FDR and his followers were seeking to instill in the American mind. They were the twin ideals of *safety* and *decency*—ideals that were shared in truly epic proportions through the vision of a landscape *tamed*. They were rendered picturesque (or even quaint) through the model communities the New Dealers built:

> The New Dealers . . . had their Heavenly City: the greenbelt town, clean, green, and white, with children playing in light, airy, spacious schools; the government project at Longview, Washington, with small houses, each of different design, colored roofs, and gardens of flowers and vegetables . . . most of all the Tennessee Valley, with its model town of Norris, the tall transmission towers, the white dams, the glistening wire strands. . . . Scandinavia was their model abroad, not only because it summoned up images of the countryside of Denmark, the beauties of Stockholm, not only for its experience with labor relations and social insurance and currency reform, but because it represented the "middle way" of happy accommodation of public and private institutions the New Deal sought to achieve.[97]

The middle way: surely Roosevelt was seeking to synthesize more than just the public and the private realms. He was seeking to harmonize conservative and liberal values, as the earlier practitioners of Hamilton-Jefferson reconciliation had done. The influence of TR was obvious here—and it made for bipartisan convergence. The dam-building programs of the 1930s were related to the path-breaking precedent set by the Newlands Act of 1902—authored by a *Democrat* and supported energetically by the Republican Roosevelt. The Civilian Conservation Corps was a latter-day salute to the tradition of the U.S. Forest Service that TR and Gifford Pinchot established, but it also related to the mission of the National Park Service, created under Woodrow Wilson. FDR was eager to practice bipartisan politics with Republicans like Ickes and Norris, and his bipartisan instincts continued to develop during World War II.

When FDR ran for reelection in 1936, he confronted a mild-mannered Republican opponent: Governor Alfred Landon of Kansas. FDR used the occasion to go after the Liberty League instead of Landon—the

Liberty League, whose venomous attacks became a major campaign liability
for the Republicans.

The Liberty League itself was bipartisan. Among its recruits was Al
Smith, the erstwhile progressive New York governor whom FDR had
nominated for the presidency in 1928 with the "happy warrior" speech.
Smith had steadily drifted to the right, and he gladly obliged the leaders of
the Liberty League by giving a speech that accused FDR of leading the nation down the path to Communism. On January 25, 1936, Smith told eager
listeners at a huge Liberty League banquet that "the young brain-trusters
caught the Socialists in swimming and they ran away with their clothes. . . .
There can be only one capital, Washington or Moscow. There can be only
the clear, pure, fresh air of free America, or the foul breath of Communist
Russia. There can be only one flag, the Stars and Stripes or the flag of the
godless Union of the Soviets."[98]

The right-wing accusation of "Communist sympathy" among the
New Dealers—the accusation that Whittaker Chambers and Joe McCarthy
would use to such spectacular effect after World War II—had emerged full-
blown in the middle of the New Deal itself.

On its face, the charge was nonsensical. But a genuine problem in the
1930s was confronting both the left and the right: the totalitarian regimes
at both ends of the political spectrum were exerting a strong and mag-
netic pull upon "true believers." On the right, in the 1930s, the regime of
Mussolini was regarded in utopian terms by Americans who longed for a
strongly hierarchic society. The poet Ezra Pound regarded Mussolini as a
latter-day Caesar Augustus, and a Fascist movement had been organized in
the United States by Lawrence Dennis. There were even Fascist paramili-
tary groups, like the "Silver Shirts" organized by William Dudley Pelley.
In Britain, the BUF (British Union of Fascists) had been led since 1932 by
a black-shirted aristocrat, Sir Oswald Mosley.

On the left, of course, it was the Soviet Union that served as the
utopian model. So in the very same manner that conservative sensibilities
(hierarchic) were seduced in the Fascist direction, the liberal sensibilities
(anti-hierarchic) were seduced now and then in the opposite direction in
the 1930s. Let a liberal speak for himself: the overwrought Lincoln Steffens, whose *Autobiography* (1931) urged liberals to regard the Soviet Union
as the vanguard of social justice through proletarian rule. In 1934 he told a
private correspondent that

> As a liberal bourgeois I have come to see not only that the Communist
> Party is the only organization in existence that really wants to deal with

our situation in *all* its phases, but I see also, as few liberals do, that the workers and peasants, the dispossessed . . . must lead, control, and carry through this program. . . . We liberals must not have power, not ever. . . . The liberals, all privileged persons, and all associates of the privileged, belong in the second line,—when their eyes are opened. . . . We, who have fitted successfully into the old culture, are to the very degree of our education and adjustment,—we are corrupted and unfit for,—the kingdom of heaven.[99]

The problem of a "Communist link" for the 1930s liberals (like the problem that the French Revolution once posed for the early liberals like Jefferson) was worsened by Joseph Stalin, who in 1934 launched the "Popular Front" as an international alliance of left-of-center movements against Fascism.

For these reasons, FDR took special steps to reject the support of any Communists in 1936. In one speech he declared that "I have not sought, I do not seek, and I repudiate the support of any advocate of Communism."[100] Harold Ickes wrote that "Fascism and Communism are equally abhorrent to us. Both are tyrannies."[101]

This was the occasion for FDR to tout his own "middle way": his pragmatism that could soften and meld the ideologies. I have cited the following statement already, but perhaps it should be cited once again, since the full historical context has now been developed: "Liberalism becomes the protection of the far-sighted conservative. 'Reform if you would preserve.' I am that kind of conservative because I am that kind of liberal."[102]

But in the midst of this rhetoric—and in many ways at odds with the feelings that prompted it—something very peculiar occurred in the outlook of FDR. He started talking like Huey Long. Perhaps the "Roosevelt stories" had been prompting him to hit back—hard—at the character assassins who had sullied his name with filthy lies. Perhaps he thought of what his tough cousin Theodore, defiant toward the "malefactors of wealth," might have done in the face of such abuse. But there was something more, something of *Huey*, in the language that FDR began hurling in the summer and autumn of 1936.

In June, before a crowd of many thousands, he lashed out at "economic royalists" as he accepted the Democrats' nomination for a second term. His enemies, he said, were nothing less than un-American in egomaniacal self-regard, in their autocratic lust for power: "It was natural and perhaps human that the privileged princes of these new economic dynasties, thirsting for power, reached out for control of the Government itself. They created a new despotism and wrapped it in the robes of legal sanction. In its service new mercenaries sought to regiment the people, their labor, and their property."[103] On Halloween, he chanted to a huge admiring throng that the "forces of organized money" were "unanimous in their *hate for me—and I welcome their hatred!*" The crowd roared. He continued, "I should like to have it said of my first Administration that in it the forces of selfishness and lust for power met their *match.*" More deafening cheers. He continued, "I should like to have it said of my second Administration that *in it these forces met their master.*"[104] The crowd almost went berserk.

FDR had never *sought* this kind of feud with the "royalists." He never *wished* to sound the themes of class war. But he probably believed that *they had started this war*—as an unprovoked act of aggression. Very well—FDR would *teach them.* He would show them how lucky they had been to have a leader like *himself* at the helm, instead of someone who was *truly* a radical, a leader with no inhibitions whatsoever—a leader like Long. The royalists were *ingrates*—and he would teach them the price of ingratitude. He would give them a good strong dose of what Huey Long might have given them.

One is tempted to engage in psychological speculation here. FDR had been a very "good boy" as a child, and his imposing mother Sara loomed as an enormous force in his life. He rebelled, if only for a while, through his emulation of Theodore. But then maternal domination resumed: Sara blighted his marriage with Eleanor, at least in its early and formative years.

FDR had abominated Huey while he lived: he was an uncouth scoundrel—a demagogue—to the Hudson Valley aristocrat. But perhaps there was some secret admiration? If so, there was nothing that could stop Franklin Roosevelt from walking around in Long's shoes, now that Huey was dead.

FDR was reelected in a landslide. And yet the populistic tone of his rhetoric had branded him, for better or worse. He found it difficult and awkward to pose as a "conservative" after this campaign. The *leftward* tilt of his war against the "royalists" confirmed, by the standards of the right, all the nasty things that the Liberty League had been alleging since 1934. A blow had been dealt against Tory reform in American conservative thought. FDR became a permanent fixture in conservative demonology. And the Toryism that he represented would yield more than ever to militant free marketeering in conservative culture.

Perhaps the struggle in American conservative culture had been lost already by the time of *Theodore* Roosevelt. Perhaps it was lost even earlier than that, in the Gilded Age, or in the days of John Quincy Adams. But the Hamilton-Jefferson reconciliation—the legacy of Lincoln and the Roosevelts—would endure in American life. It would flourish for another three decades in American history.

As he prepared himself for the next four years, Franklin Roosevelt decided the Supreme Court problem was his number-one priority. Why pass any new legislation when the court was predisposed to kill it? The result was the "court-packing" scheme that he proposed in the early months of 1937. He would push through Congress a bill to expand the court's size and thus humble—neutralize—the "nine old men" who had been striking down the New Deal programs.

There was nothing that was legally wrong with the bill: the Constitution says nothing whatsoever with regard to the Supreme Court's size. But 1937 was the Constitution's sesquicentennial. The court-packing scheme was a godsend to all the conservatives who claimed that FDR was a threat to American liberties. Here was proof: he was threatening our system of checks and balances, just like a dictator.

The proposal backfired: FDR's bill went down, and the humiliation of the court-packing episode harmed his second term enormously. Perhaps the baleful influence of Huey was partially to blame. Historian T. Harry Williams recounts a widely publicized answer that Huey once gave to a reporter who asked him, after the NRA had been toppled by the Court, to share some thoughts about what he might do "as President if the Supreme Court voided a Share Our Wealth law. 'Why,' he said, 'we'll just get a bill passed adding the whole membership of Congress to the Supreme Court and try the case again.'"[105]

Huey might have gotten away with it. But for FDR, ruthless action was largely out of character. Maybe that was the reason why he never developed an effective strategy for *winning* the court bill fight. He was only "going through the motions."

In any case, he paid a terrible price for the defeat. A new alliance of conservative Republicans and southern Democrats thwarted him, increasingly, in Congress. And his clumsy attempt to "purge" conservative Democrats in mid-term congressional elections backfired as well.

Still, FDR was successful in getting some important new legislation passed: the 1938 Fair Labor Standards Act, for instance, which established the basis for federal action to require a minimum wage. At the farm bloc's behest, a second Agricultural Adjustment Act reinstated production quotas. Federal loans were advanced to help the farmers pull some crops from the market. The "surplus" crops would be stored in the course of the boom years and then released in the bad years—thus creating an "ever-normal granary." The Bankhead-Jones Farm Tenancy Act of 1937 created a Farm Security Administration (FSA) to help tenant farmers purchase farms. In addition, the FSA created sanitary camps for migrant workers (a camp of this type was depicted in the 1940 film version of Steinbeck's *The Grapes of Wrath*).

The Housing Act of 1937 created a new U.S. Housing Authority to help fund public housing. Another new agency, the Civil Aeronautics Authority (a precursor to the FAA) was established to regulate aviation safety, which the Commerce Department had been regulating since the 1920s. Congress gave the new agency authority to regulate the fares that the airlines would charge and determine the routes that the airlines would travel.[106] So the second term of FDR achieved a few significant results.

There had even been a pithy sort of consolation in the side effects of the court-packing fight: FDR, though defeated, had prompted some significant soul-searching—perhaps mixed with a modicum of fear—among Supreme Court justices. One justice, Owen Roberts, began to switch sides: he voted to uphold the constitutionality of the Wagner Act. Another justice, Willis Van Devanter, retired.

The result was a turning point in constitutional law: the Supreme Court's hitherto reactionary jurisprudence started moving in a different direction. The Gilded Age norms of strict construction were increasingly abandoned. In a series of decisions with vast implications for the future—*NLRB v. Jones* (1937), which upheld the Wagner Act; *United States v. Darby* (1941), which upheld the Fair Labor Standards Act; and *Wickard v. Filburn* (1942), which upheld the second AAA—the Court construed the Constitution's interstate commerce clause in broad terms. In preceding decades, the Court had used a narrow definition of "interstate commerce." After 1937, however, the Court began ruling that many different acts of individuals or businesses could fall within the scope of the clause, provided that the similar actions of others, when taken collectively, "substantially affected" the flow of interstate commerce.[107]

But this shift in jurisprudence held little consolation for FDR and his supporters in his dreary second term. Almost everything, it seemed, was going wrong, not least of all the macro-economic trends. The Depression started worsening again.

In 1937, Roosevelt did the same thing—made the same mistake—that had stunted economic recovery back in 1934. Confident again that the nation's economy was strong enough to let the private sector take over, he slashed public works in early summer. Two months later, a massive recession began. People called it the "Roosevelt Recession."

Then he tried to change course: he requested congressional funding for "seven little TVAs," but Congress refused. Leuchtenburg observed that at this point FDR "seemed nonplused by what course to take. . . . The economy continued to plunge downhill, and he did not know how to stop it. . . . In early 1938, many Americans once more neared starvation."[108]

Defeatism set in. Even Harry Hopkins started musing that perhaps this depression would be permanent. In 1937, Hopkins wrote that it might be "reasonable to expect a possible minimum of 4,000,000 to 5,000,000 unemployed men even in future prosperity periods."[109] Leuchtenburg has written that "by 1939 many had come to conclude that Hopkins was right—that millions of jobless would never find jobs again, not even if 're-covery' was finally achieved."[110] Conservatives were able to claim that the New Deal had thwarted recovery—a charge that resounds to this day.[111]

Years later, Thurman Arnold looked back with chagrin at the missed opportunity of Roosevelt's second term. Arnold had learned the great Keynesian lesson when he shared this candid confession: "We did not learn the real nature of our economic difficulties until the tremendous spending of the Second World War pulled us out of our static economy and made us the richest nation the world had ever known."[112] Arnold made the observation in the 1950s.

THE "MIGHTY ENDEAVOR"

The world could go to hell—and stay there—as far as many Americans cared in the 1930s: isolationism was the order of the day, and demobilization was the policy in military matters. As the savage imperial dreams of the Nazis, Fascists, and Japanese militarists were acted out, the democracies of the world seemed eager to prove the point of Hitler, who jeered that democracy was weak—and decadent.

The United States, though mobilized (up to a point) to fight its economic depression, had rejected any mobilization to help keep peace or maintain global order. FDR hated this state of affairs, but there was nothing he could do to change the public mood, though he tried. And a series of neutrality laws—beginning with the Neutrality Act of 1935—tied his hands.

All through his second term he had to watch imperial Japan devour major sections of mainland China while committing gross atrocities. He had to watch Hitler's massive rearmament, his bloodless conquest of Austria and Czechoslovakia, his psychopathic treatment of the Jews.

In 1939, as the Second World War was erupting in Europe, FDR assured his fellow Americans that the United States could keep out. But in truth, he believed the reverse. So he decided to seek another term—an unprecedented third term—in the hope that he could build a political base from which to mobilize American force. It was probably at this point that FDR and other anti-Fascist Americans began to feel a strong connection with Lincoln—not "Lincoln the savior of the Union," but rather the Lincoln who had warned in his "house divided" speech about slavery invading the North.

Historian Merrill D. Peterson has shown how the legacy of Lincoln helped people like FDR to confront the Axis menace. According to Peterson, Robert E. Sherwood's 1938 play *Abe Lincoln in Illinois* was "a big hit . . . because it struck a political nerve." The play's theme was "more allusive to the imminent threat of totalitarianism than to the southern slavocracy. . . . Raymond Massey, for whom Sherwood had written [the role] . . . remarked in an interview, 'If you substitute the word dictatorship for the word slavery . . . it becomes electric for our time.'"[113]

In 1940, FDR campaigned against Republican Wendell Willkie—a moderate. In the early months of this election year, Hitler overran Denmark, Norway, Belgium, and Holland (where the Nazis firebombed Rotterdam). In June France surrendered to Hitler, who moved rapidly on to the air bombardment of Britain—a prelude to invasion.

A top-secret conversation began: FDR and Winston Churchill began to communicate. Topic number one was Britain's very survival in the face of Nazi invasion plans. On May 15, Churchill wrote to FDR, warning of "a Nazified Europe established with astonishing swiftness."[114] He broached the topic of American assistance in repelling the onslaught to come.

FDR took preliminary steps for a mobilization, but he had to move carefully at first. Isolationists, strong in both parties, were forming the "America First Committee." Their aim was to warn their fellow countrymen against a repetition of World War I, when Americans were "suckered" into fighting in a foreign war that was none of their business.

Americans were frightened by "the European war," and with reason. Even if America should manage to keep its distance and avoid getting "dragged" into the European conflict, the nation might find itself alone (more or less) in an Axis-dominated world. Isolationists said there was nothing to fear if that should happen: "Fortress America" could ward off any foreign threat.

But Fortress America would have to be *created*, so the basis for American rearmament and mobilization was established with some grudging isolationist assistance. FDR moved decisively in 1940 to begin the big "defense" preparation. And it was federal spending for *defense* before Pearl Harbor—in 1940 and 1941—that provided the massive economic stimulus that ended the Depression.

Both FDR and Churchill were haunted by a secret technological nightmare: Hitler with nuclear weapons. Churchill knew about nuclear physics; Albert Einstein had visited him at his country home in the 1930s. In 1939 Einstein had written a letter to FDR that warned about the danger of nuclear weapons in the wrong hands. So the National Defense Research Committee was established by FDR in the summer of 1940. Federal research on the subject of nuclear fission was the top priority. Simultaneously, FDR set up a Defense Advisory Commission to guide the mobilization.

The Battle of Britain began in the summer of 1940, with Luftwaffe bombings to soften up the British Isles. Churchill told his fellow countrymen on BBC that "Hitler knows that he will have to break us in this island or lose the war. If we can stand up to him, all Europe may be free." But if we fail, he continued, "then the whole world, including the United States, including all that we have known and cared for, will sink into the abyss of a new Dark Age, made more sinister, and perhaps more protracted, by the lights of perverted science."[115]

All through 1940 the president warned about the threat from Nazi Germany. On May 16, he told Congress that if Britain were conquered, the North Atlantic would soon be infested with Luftwaffe bases—and then "from the fjords of Greenland it is four hours by air to Newfoundland; five hours to Nova Scotia . . . and only six hours to New England. . . . If Bermuda fell into hostile hands it would be a matter of less than three hours for modern bombers to reach our shores."[116]

The political race between FDR and Willkie was hard fought. The Roosevelt-haters had a catchy three-syllable slogan: "No Third Term." Though Willkie was an internationalist, the great strength of the isolationist faction in his party made him talk more and more like *them*. This phenomenon increased in the latter months of the campaign, when the race became bitter.

FDR had extended his bipartisan methods: in a ploy that struck some as amusing, he tried to get both of the Republican candidates from the ticket of 1936—Alf Landon and Frank Knox—into his cabinet.[117] Landon demurred, but Knox accepted: he became the new secretary of the navy. Republican Henry Stimson agreed to be the new secretary of war. Both were old TR Republicans, and Knox had even been a Rough Rider back in 1898.

In the midst of all this, FDR took two extraordinary risks. First, he asked Congress to institute the first peacetime draft in American history. General George C. Marshall, the army chief of staff, provided invaluable support in his congressional testimony. Marshall was a master of logistics and he spoke authoritatively about the crucial realities of "lead time." He had served during World War I as an aide to General Pershing in France and he had witnessed the terrible price that was paid for America's lag in preparation. The peacetime draft cleared Congress—just barely.

It was needed, for America's peacetime army was small by the standards of the time: by May 1940 it was number nineteen among all the world's armies.[118] Equipment shortages abounded—and the equipment was often out of date. Moreover, the manpower pool was unimpressive due to the ravages of the Depression; according to historian Robert James Maddox, "illiteracy rates [among the men who were drafted] were high, and a shocking number of young men had poor eyesight uncorrected by glasses, bad teeth caused by a lack of dental care, or a variety of ailments due to inadequate diet."[119] General Marshall had his hands full.

The second great risk that was taken by FDR was a bold decision to "swap" fifty older American destroyers in return for some leases that would give the United States access to certain British bases. The ships, which FDR had declared to be "surplus," would assist against a Nazi invasion of the British Isles. Churchill requested the ships on a now-or-never basis. FDR went ahead—and bypassed Congress.

There was hell to pay: the *St. Louis Post-Dispatch* called the presidential order "an act of war" by "America's first dictator."[120] Willkie started dishing out the charge that FDR was a warmonger; on October 30 he warned that a third term for Roosevelt would mean certain war within the next six months. FDR replied with a tricky disclaimer: "I have said this before," he intoned, "but I shall say it again and again and again: Your boys are not going to be sent into a foreign war."[121] The operative term here was *foreign*: if *American* forces were attacked, he reasoned, then the war would no longer be "foreign."

FDR's victory was solid, and he got the third term that he wanted. So he plunged right ahead with his plans to help defeat the Axis. In the early months of 1941, he got Congress to approve a huge military assistance package for Britain: "Lend-Lease." The weapons would be *given* or "lent" to the British instead of being sold to them outright.

FDR's sales pitch was simple and nationalistic, at least on the surface: it was *handy* for the British to be fighting the Nazis, for this kept them far away from our shores. So Americans should *help* the fighting British keep the Nazis away. The isolationists were not fooled: Senator Burton K. Wheeler of Montana declared that "the lend-lease-give program is the New Deal's triple A foreign policy; it will plow under every fourth American boy." FDR retorted that this was "the rottenest thing that has been said in public life in my generation."[122]

FDR resumed his warnings of Nazi capabilities. In May, he told a radio audience that Hitler possessed the power to "occupy Spain and Portugal," and then to threaten "the island outposts of the New World—the Azores and Cape Verde Islands," which were "only seven hours' distance from Brazil by bomber or troop-carrying planes."[123] In October he announced that intelligence agents had acquired "a map of South America and a part of Central America as Hitler proposes to reorganize it. Today in this area there are fourteen separate countries. The geographical experts of Berlin . . . have divided South America into five vassal states, bringing the whole continent under their domination."[124]

In June, after Hitler invaded the Soviet Union, FDR sent Lend-Lease aid to Russia as well as to Britain. He ordered naval vessels to accompany the convoys to guard against Nazi submarines. He was *ready* for war—indeed, he *wanted* American force to be thrown into the balance. He was frightened.

His worst-case scenario was this: global Axis victory comprising (1) a huge Nazi-ruled empire including Russia, all or most of northern Africa, and some of South America with air bases in the north and south Atlantic; (2) Japanese conquest of all or most of China, India, Australia, New Zealand, and the central Pacific archipelagoes, providing the Axis with massive supplies of raw materials and possibly manpower; and (3) Nazi nuclear weapons and the military means to turn them loose upon American cities. There was no way that even "Fortress America" could last very long in such a world. Human nature at its worst would turn the planet into hell: Hitler prophesied a "thousand-year Reich."

As Lincoln had spoken of a "house divided," Franklin Roosevelt spoke of a *world* divided into force-realms of slavery and freedom. Merrill Peterson observes that as he rose to his challenge "in global terms," FDR "grew increasingly conscious of treading in Lincoln's footsteps."[125] "Today," declared Roosevelt in 1941, "the whole world is divided . . . between human slavery and human freedom—between the pagan brutality and the Christian ideal."[126]

So, for God, country, and Christendom, he sent the U.S. Navy to confront the Nazi savages at sea. He expected a battle that might justify a declaration of war. Instead, what he got was Pearl Harbor, half a world away.

After the declaration of war, the full power of America's economy was mobilized as never before. In his 1942 State of the Union Address, the president spelled out enormous production goals for the year: sixty thousand planes, twenty-five thousand tanks, and six million tons of merchant shipping. For 1943 the goal was increased by FDR to one hundred twenty-five thousand planes, seventy-five thousand tanks, and ten million tons of merchant shipping.[127] New classes of powerful warships were in production—the majestic *Iowa* class of battleships, the *Essex* class of fast carriers—and production quotas were increased. (The navy planned a *Montana* class of superbattleships, but opted instead to increase the production of aircraft carriers.) By the end of the war, the United States alone was producing more weapons and armaments than all the Axis powers combined.[128] Millions of men and women entered military service.

Another vast array of new temporary agencies coordinated economic life, as in World War I. Among the most important were the War Production Board (WPB), National War Labor Board (NWLB), War Manpower Commission (WMC), Office of War Mobilization (OWM), Office of Price Administration (OPA), and Office of Scientific Research and Development (OSRD).

Through alliances with universities and corporations, the OSRD created technological breakthroughs. Swift advances in radar technology were matched by a host of new weapons innovations such as napalm and the radio proximity fuse. Moreover, the nuclear race was on: in the hope of beating the Nazis, the Manhattan Project was advancing.

Federal spending rose to astronomical proportions by prewar standards: $13.3 billion in 1941, $34 billion in 1942, $79.4 billion in 1943, $95.1 billion in 1944, and $98.4 billion in 1945.[129] The financial pool that produced such expenditure was *flush* with *brand new money*. And it happened via fractional reserves.

As economist Seymour E. Harris summed it up, "from 1940 to 1945 . . . the government created large supplies of money to support the government bond-market"; indeed, "in World War II . . . the task of the Federal Reserve was to manufacture money."[130] The Treasury Department sponsored bond drives, eight of them in all. The purchases of bonds were supported via bank loans. Economic historian Allen H. Meltzer has observed that "to ensure that bond drives were successful, banks lent money to finance bond purchases at interest rates below the bonds' yield. Many banks agreed to buy the bonds from their customers after the drive. Since the buyers could profit by buying the bonds, they oversubscribed the new issue. This gave the appearance of public subscription but depended on bank financing."[131]

Whenever it was necessary, the Federal Reserve stepped in; Walton and Rockoff relate that "the Federal Reserve took the extraordinary step of 'pegging' the rate of interest on government securities. It accomplished this by pledging to buy government securities whenever their price fell below predetermined support levels. . . . By 1945, about $24.3 billion in bonds were owned by the Federal Reserve system and some $84.1 billion by commercial banks."[132]

Behind the financing was the hidden metaphysics of deposit creation—money creation—through the principle of fractional reserves. Meltzer has observed that America's "monetary base doubled in the four years ending fourth quarter 1945."[133] Walton and Rockoff concur: "The stock of money in 1939 was only slightly higher than that of 1929, but by 1944 it had more than doubled."[134] They furnish some comparative analysis: "During the Civil War, the system by which the government created money had been straightforward: it simply printed greenbacks and spent them. During World Wars I and II, the system was more complex, but the results were similar. Instead of printing paper money, the Federal Reserve enlarged the U.S. Treasury's deposit balances."[135]

"The Fed" bought the government's bonds. It paid for the bonds by "creating deposits," and we all know the process by now. Presto—a stroke of the pen, and the brand-new deposits were created. With "money in the bank," Uncle Sam could write thousands of checks.

Behind it all—behind the bank loans extended by commercial banks to the public and deposit creation by the Federal Reserve for the purpose of buying the war bonds—stood the power of the Federal Reserve to pump credit (money) through America's financial system. It pulled the credit out of thin air.

In 1939, the staff of the Federal Reserve system had been candid enough to describe the hidden process in an informational primer: "Bank credit plays a vitally important part in modern economic life. As a source of bank deposits transferable by check . . . it is always interchangeable with legal tender money, but for the most part it is not derived from legal tender money. . . . Federal Reserve Bank Credit . . . is itself a form of money authorized for special purposes. . . . [It] does not consist of funds that the Reserve authorities 'get' somewhere in order to lend, but constitutes funds that they are empowered to create."[136] Create it they did during World War II, and the money creation worked swiftly to underwrite the war.

Federal taxes covered much of the wartime spending—about a third to a half (depending on the method of calculation).[137] According to Meltzer, Treasury Secretary Henry Morgenthau "wanted to finance 50 percent of the war through direct taxation" and "came close" to achieving this objective.[138] The balance of the wartime revenue was chiefly raised through borrowing. In 1945, the accumulated national debt of the United States was so great ($258.7 billion) that it actually surpassed the gross national product ($213.4 billion).[139] Of course, the debt would have been far less if the government had printed up Greenbacks and spent them into use. As it was, however, our national debt was Hitler's doom.

It was also our economy's salvation: our gross national product *doubled* in the course of World War II. From $100.4 billion in 1940, our GNP surged to $213.4 billion in 1945.[140] Industrial and agricultural production skyrocketed. And the nation achieved full employment: everyone who wanted a job in the United States during World War II had a job. Inflation was addressed through price controls.

The civilian benefits from economic growth were deferred: wartime rationing resulted in civilian austerity. But the fact remained that Americans were earning record incomes. And since they couldn't spend the money right away, they *invested* it in government bonds: they lent it to the government. Or else they *saved* it, creating new deposits. The backlog of purchasing power that arose during World War II was stupendous.

All the while economist Alvin Hansen and others were spreading the Keynesian gospel in the economic profession. A mass conversion was beginning, for Americans could *see* with their very own eyes the transformation the war had created. From the rotten stagnation of the Great Depression to the superabundance of a mobilized America, the difference was spectacularly clear.

In any given year of the Great Depression, such abundance could have been produced. Full employment could have been accomplished—very easily—throughout the period. *All the suffering had been quite needless.* As Hansen observed later on, "the war put the American giant to work, and once fully employed, we found that we were able to raise our standard of living . . . beyond any level previously achieved at the very time we were fighting a total war. This no one would have believed until it actually happened."[141]

In the dawn of this realization, the president talked more and more of an "Economic Bill of Rights"—with the GI Bill as phase 1. Henceforth,

Country squire: FDR at the wheel of a 1936 Ford V-8 Phaeton. Credit: History Pictures.

ONE OF SOUTH DAKOTA'S "BLACK BLIZZARDS"
1934

Chaos: A horrific duststorm enveloping a South Dakota town in 1934. Credit: Franklin D. Roosevelt Presidential Library and Museum.

Rescue: Civilian Conservation Corps workers planting trees in Beltsville, Maryland. Credit: Franklin D. Roosevelt Presidential Library and Museum.

Power: B-29 bombers awaiting flight tests at the Boeing plant in Wichita. Credit: Franklin D. Roosevelt Presidential Library and Museum.

the right to be employed would be a part of "the American Way." FDR never lived to put the proposition to use in civilian economics. But the Employment Act of 1946 vested the federal government with permanent responsibility for guaranteeing high levels of employment. It also created the Council of Economic Advisers.

From 1942 onward, the war had sent Americans into harm's way: at Midway, Guadalcanal, and the Solomon Islands, where expansion of the Japanese empire was stopped and a "roll-back" of Japanese power had begun; in North Africa, where Americans attacked at the fringes of the Nazi empire; in Italy, where the fighting against the Nazis became more intense. Then in 1944, D-Day: the largest seaborne armada in recorded history—five thousand ships, four thousand landing craft, and six hundred warships. Via radio, FDR led the nation in prayer:

> Almighty God: our sons, pride of our Nation, this day have set upon a mighty endeavor, a struggle to preserve our Republic, our religion, and our civilization, and to set free a suffering humanity. Lead them straight and true; give strength to their arms, stoutness to their hearts, steadfastness in their faith . . . Success may not come with rushing speed, but we shall return again and again; and we know that by Thy grace, and by the righteousness of our cause, our sons will triumph.[142]

There were failures amid the successes, lamentable lapses amid the moral grandeur. Lincoln had predicted as much when he observed near the end of the Civil War that "in any future great national trial, compared with the men of this, we shall have as weak, and as strong; as silly and as wise; as bad and as good."[143] But though some would remember just the horror of the war there was a great moral clarity for others—and inspiration. Poet Robert Fitzgerald recalled reading Virgil far away in the Pacific:

> There we were on our island in our fresh khakis, laundered and pressed, the little bars gleaming on our collars and caps, saluting the old admiral with his snowy Roman head and the urbane operations officer who held in his crystal mind the location, course, destination, and speed of every least landing craft over thousands of miles. The scene could not have been more imperial or more civilized.[144]

But Fitzgerald believed that he was destined for the coming invasion of Japan: "The next landings would be on Honshu, and I would be there. More than literary interest, I think, kept me reading Virgil's descriptions of desperate battle, funeral pyres, failed hopes of truce or peace."[145] This reflected a mood of resignation. But it was also a sense of being called into destiny and duty. An entire generation of Americans were summoned—summoned into service.

So they followed where the Roosevelts, Stimsons, and Nimitzes directed them in many different parts of the globe—to Augustan peace or to a world of unimaginable danger—and they took whatever else came their way. Some dreamed of a Pax Americana. Others merely hoped the fighting would be over. But they could feel the awful summons of history—and so they followed.

5

THE LEGACY AS
GREAT POWER STATECRAFT:
FROM TRUMAN TO NIXON

It almost happened again in the aftermath of war: a bitter mood swing against the heroic. A wave of disillusionment—a sense of burnout or even betrayal—was rife in the age of Harry Truman. And though the president tried to resist the strong trend, it brought a neo-isolationist mood to American politics by 1952. America's ascent to global power was a close call.

For a while, the isolationists were plunged into deepest disgrace. In the aftermath of Pearl Harbor, they were vastly unpopular figures: they were widely viewed as false prophets who had sold the American people a "bill of goods." They were vendors of soothing syrup: they had minimized the threat from the Axis at the cost of American lives. Concurrently, a major revival of Wilson began—he was touted by many as a leader who was far "ahead of his time"—and Americans began to think globally.

But with the rehabilitation of Wilson came a dose of his millennial vision. The impulse to fight a great "war to end war"—to make the whole world "safe for democracy"—reappeared in the 1940s. In an article written from a military hospital, a soldier named Clarence Weinstock expressed it this way:

> Today we fight a great just war of liberation. We do not idealize conquest like the Nazi historians. . . . We do not cry "War is beautiful," like the Fascist poet, Marinetti. . . . No, we did not pant for war like our enemies; but now we thirst for victory. The destroyers must be destroyed. The killers of Guernica, Lidice, Nanking, Pearl Harbor . . . have to be erased from our human world. Our hate will only burn out when it has dealt with them all, the "Leaders," the "Dukes," the Gauleiters, and the Squadristi, the Iron Guards, and the Samurai.[1]

Less vehement—though still quite passionate—was the conviction that America's duty to its soldiers was to lead in the creation of a new world order that would "make the world right." In the 1943 film *So Proudly We Hail* a nurse mourns the loss of her son, who was just killed in combat. His father had been killed in the First World War, as she explains in the course of her soliloquy:

> I bore a son; he's dead. I bore a son, a healthy muscular child; he was a good son. It used to break my heart just to look at him, he was so beautiful. The handsomest son in the world. And now I have no heart to break. Like his father, he died for what he knew was right. He *was* right—my son and his father. And *this* time . . . if we don't *make* it right . . . my son and his father and all our dead will rise up and destroy us.[2]

Other Hollywood films expressed the same near-millennial resolve to try to "fix" what was wrong with the world—once and for all. In the 1943 musical *This Is the Army* (starring Ronald Reagan, George Murphy, and Kate Smith, among others) a production number at the grand finale featured soldiers in uniform who promised the American people that "this time" would be "the last time": in this war to end war they would finish the job, "so we won't have to do it again."[3]

Small wonder that with feelings like these, great numbers of Americans experienced a sense of enormous letdown (or worse) when the Cold War developed in the 1940s. And then Americans were right back in combat again, just five years later, in Korea. The painful truth was that Americans had no real experience yet of bearing great-power burdens indefinitely. On the contrary, the overwhelming feeling after V-J Day was to bring all the husbands and fathers back home, just as fast as possible—a feeling that was perfectly wholesome, of course, and yet tinged with all-or-nothing histrionics. An enduring American role in world affairs could by no means be taken for granted in the Truman years.

LEFT AND RIGHT IN THE EARLY COLD WAR

After World War II, the cutting-edge ideological issue was *Stalinism*, or—to use the term that could set people's teeth on edge at the time—the global issue of *Communism*. FDR had spoken of a "world divided" into realms of slavery and freedom. With the Axis gone, Stalin's Soviet Union stood alone for a while as the world's preeminent police state—the police state with which the people of the "Free World" would have to come to terms.

A significant number of Americans rejoiced when the Soviets had joined the Americans and British to form the "big three": the Allies who were fighting the Axis. Wartime fervor in America imbued many people with respect for what "the Russians" were doing. Wendell Willkie had written in his 1943 opus *One World* that "Russia is an effective society. It works. . . . The record of Soviet resistance to Hitler has been proof enough of this to most of us . . . [and] we must work with Russia after the war. . . . There can be no continued peace unless we learn to do so."[4]

FDR shared this optimism. So did Henry Wallace, who was placed on the national ticket with FDR in 1940 and who served as vice president for most of World War II. After he was dumped from the Democratic ticket in 1944—he was deemed "too liberal"—Wallace unfurled the banner of "Progressivism" with a 1948 third-party quest for the White House. He urged rapprochement with the Russians.

But other left-of-center figures had been coming to the opposite conclusion by the 1940s. Long before the Cold War's emergence—indeed, long before George Orwell commenced his distinctly left-of-center attack against the Stalinist system in *Animal Farm* and its follow-up, *1984*—an anti-Stalinist movement in the liberal ranks was apparent. The 1939 Nazi-Soviet pact, along with the ugly Stalinist purges of the 1930s, had been shocking to a great many people on the left, as had the Soviet invasion of Finland. Then after the war the new Soviet repression in Poland, Hungary, and Czechoslovakia solidified a liberal anti-Communist movement.

An early expression of the movement was the founding in 1947 of Americans for Democratic Action (ADA). Created by Eleanor Roosevelt, Hubert Humphrey, John Kenneth Galbraith, and others, ADA was an expression of emergent "Cold War liberalism." So was the publication two years later of *The Vital Center* by Arthur Schlesinger Jr. "Today, finally and tardily," Schlesinger wrote, "the skeptical insights are in process of restoration in the liberal mind."[5] He urged American liberals to swear off utopianism—to renounce the old millennial vision of a world redeemed through the gentle ways of peace or through the rescue of the downtrodden masses. Instead, he endorsed the "neo-orthodox" teachings of theologian Reinhold Niebuhr.

Niebuhr himself was a *friendly* critic of the liberals. In 1952 he observed that "the tendency of a liberal culture to regard the highest human possibilities as capable of simple historical attainment"—through a war to eliminate war, for example, or a struggle to uplift the downtrodden once and for all (the lure of Communism)—"can find no place in its scheme of things for heroic action or heroic patience." Heroism, active or patient, he defined as an ability "to make sacrifices and to sustain endeavors without complete certainty of success."[6] He offered Lincoln as a consummate example of heroic statesmanship.

By the time the Korean War had broken out, the themes of Cold War liberalism were well-established in the Democratic Party and beyond, in the intelligentsia. Many Cold War liberals expanded their attack upon Communism to encompass a war against the Marxist left as a whole. They accused American Marxists of complicity with Stalin.

But none of this mattered to the *right* in the postwar years. To conservative Americans, the Cold War challenge was a heaven-sent chance to revive and intensify attacks against the New Deal values. Conservative laissez-faire doctrine was given a new infusion of force in the Second World War. A pair of Austrian economists revived the attack on "big government" as they revivified laissez-faire theory.

In 1944, Friedrich von Hayek published *The Road to Serfdom*, which argued that free marketeering was the best antidote to the challenge of totalitarianism. The same message appeared in *Bureaucracy*, by Ludwig von Mises, which was also published in 1944. He wrote the following:

> The main issue in present-day struggles is whether society should be organized on the basis of private ownership of the means of production (capitalism, the market system) or on the basis of public control of the means of production (socialism, communism, planned economy). . . . There is no compromise possible between these two systems. Contrary to a popular fallacy there is no middle way, no third system possible as a pattern of permanent social order. The citizens must choose between capitalism and socialism, or, as many Americans say, between the American and the Russian way of life.[7]

This was what Al Smith had proclaimed to the Liberty League in 1936. And this is what many Republicans continued to proclaim in the 1940s.

The exemplar was Senator Robert A. Taft of Ohio. The son of former president William Howard Taft, he was far less amiable than his father had been at his best. A critic of the New Deal, he had risen in political stature to the point where admirers were calling him "Mr. Republican." But his rhetoric could be shrill. "If Mr. Roosevelt is not a communist today," he proclaimed in 1936, "he is bound to become one."[8] An isolationist, Taft once declared that, "war is worse even than a German victory."[9] He regarded the Soviet Union as a much greater threat than Nazi Germany: "The victory of communism in the world would be far more dangerous to the United States than the victory of fascism," he wrote.[10] After World War

II, with the Axis gone, he could turn his mind completely to continued chastisement of the left.

So the work of the Liberty League would be resumed—even as Harry S. Truman was attempting to extend the work of his predecessor through the postwar "Fair Deal." Right-wing critics kept hearkening back to the warnings of the Liberty League, but with the cutting edge of their rhetoric sharpened by concerns about national security. In 1948, Whittaker Chambers—a confessed ex-Communist who became a fervent anti-Communist—fingered Alger Hiss, a former State Department official, as a long-term Soviet agent. But there was more: Hiss was just a representative specimen of leftist treachery, according to Chambers. "All of the New Dealers I had known were Communists or near-Communists," he declared in 1952. "None of them took the New Deal seriously as an end in itself. They regarded it as an instrument for gaining their own revolutionary ends."[11]

It was against this background of broad-brush libel that Peter Viereck, a conservative writer, tried his best to resurrect the tradition of Tory reform in the postwar years. He pleaded with American conservatives to be high-minded and magnanimous—to uphold "the *conservation* not of economic greed and privilege but of the value-heritage for which America rightly entered World War II." He pleaded the cause of "the great conservative social reformers, from the 7th Earl of Shaftesbury through Disraeli, as well as the necessary New Deal reforms of our own great Squire of Hyde Park." But it was largely in vain: Viereck later concluded that a "smug reactionary misuse of conservatism" was the rule in the United States.[12]

TRUMAN

Before their untimely deaths, both FDR and Wendell Willkie had discussed a party realignment. Willkie was becoming a major Republican advocate of black civil rights during World War II. At the same time, enraged southern Democrats were giving the president hell about the opportunities for blacks that the war effort was creating. By the midsummer of 1944, the rival candidates of 1940 began reaching out to one another. Willkie, along with old Gifford Pinchot, sent a feeler to FDR. The president discussed the matter with adviser Samuel Rosenman. James MacGregor Burns tells the story; according to Rosenman, FDR proclaimed it was

> Willkie's idea. Willkie has just been beaten by the conservatives in his own party who lined up in back of Dewey. Now there is no doubt that

the reactionaries in our own party are out for my scalp, too—as you can see by what's going on in the South. Well, I think the time has come for the Democratic party to get rid of its reactionary elements in the South, and to attract to it the liberals in the Republican party. Willkie is the leader of those liberals. He talked to Pinchot about a coalition of the liberals in both parties, leaving the conservatives in each party to join together as they see fit. I agree with him one hundred per cent and the time to do it is now—right after the election.[13]

But both of these forceful leaders died before the partnership began—Willkie in October 1944 and then FDR in April 1945.

So America's political landscape continued to include both "conservative" and "liberal" Republicans, along with "conservative" and "liberal" Democrats. Yet the ideological *convergence* we have noted many times in the course of this history—the Hamilton-Jefferson reconciliation, as achieved by Lincoln and the Roosevelts—continued through the leadership of Truman, Eisenhower, and Kennedy. In the case of the Democrats, the left–right convergence had an obviously "liberal" tilt—as the middle-range leadership of Eisenhower tilted slightly in the other direction. But the *continuities* in statecraft were greater than the discontinuities or clashes. And the overall result was America's coming of age in global power.

Historian Alonzo Hamby has argued that the politics of Truman encompassed an "intuitive embrace of vital center liberalism. Just as he disdained the extremism of both the Left and the Right in American politics, he drew no moral distinctions between the totalitarianism of the Left and the Right in foreign affairs."[14]

Though Truman was forceful enough in intellectual terms, he portrayed himself as just an "ordinary, plain-spoken man." For this reason he expressed some rather colorful views about ideological excess. He once told Clark Clifford that FDR had been surrounded by a "lunatic fringe."[15] He fretted about "parlor pinks."[16] Conversely, his scorn for conservative Republican ideologues was scathing. "Mr. Taft has succeeded in making a real fool of himself as have several so-called leading Republicans," Truman once wrote to his mother and sister. "I am of the opinion that the country has had enough of their pinhead antics."[17]

Journalist Robert J. Donovan characterized Truman as a pragmatist: reforms that "his contemporaries called 'liberal' Truman preferred to call 'forward-looking.'" He "stood in the tradition of Wilson and Roosevelt, but not at the time on its left flank." Indeed, he knew "that most of the leading New Dealers had not been for him as Roosevelt's running mate in 1944."[18] But he began to win some of them over.

After Roosevelt's death, the new president inherited the tasks of defeating Japan, establishing a decent international order under United Nations auspices, and mastering the reconversion of America's war economy without undue dislocation. As to FDR's Economic Bill of Rights, it would be up to Truman to administer the GI Bill (passed in 1944) and then follow up with as many new measures in the field of economic security as postwar politics permitted.[19]

Japan was defeated much faster than a great many people had predicted: war planners were ready for a full-scale invasion of the Japanese home islands (Operation Olympic) that would last all the way through 1947 at the cost of millions of lives. We know how this was averted. Then defeated Japan was rebuilt and converted to a more democratic culture in the years that followed.

The American economy, flush with the purchasing power of the wartime mobilization, did not relapse into depression. Unemployment was averted by the GI Bill, which sent over two million veterans back to college and graduate school, producing hundreds of thousands of engineers, doctors, teachers, scientists, and businessmen while providing tremendous housing benefits that triggered a construction boom.[20]

To be sure, the reconversion had its economic rough spots. The retention of wartime controls on prices and wages through 1946 (a precautionary measure) triggered anger in a great many quarters. And there were serious shortages of goods, along with inflationary pressures, as the wartime industries retooled for civilian production. But what could—or should—have been done? Ten years later, economist Alvin Hansen looked back upon the situation as follows:

> Following the Second World War we had, as we all know, a considerable price rise. There are those who regard this as simply due to war and postwar mismanagement. I do not agree. Granted that the controls had to be removed and that taxes had to be cut—that, politically speaking, they could not be continued for a year or so longer—then I think it follows that some considerable price rise was inevitable. This is true because of the accumulated backlog of unfulfilled demand and of postwar shortages. Under these circumstances price stability could not have been achieved unless indeed we had been prepared to cut employment.[21]

But the Employment Act of 1946 called for *maximizing* employment.

In any case, higher prices and shortages contributed to discontent that the Republicans used to get control of both houses of Congress in the 1946 elections. One Republican congressman stoked the fires this way: "Got enough meat? Got enough houses? Got enough OPA [Office of Price Administration]? Got enough inflation? Got enough debt? Got enough strikes? Got enough Communism?"[22]

Inflation subsided, and the fears of depression proved groundless: indeed, America's economy began its ascent toward the boom of the 1950s and 1960s.

Truman's "Fair Deal" program extended the policies of FDR. The Social Security amendments of 1950 expanded the program's coverage. The Housing Act of 1949 provided federal funds for slum clearance. And the price supports in agriculture were continued through the Agricultural Acts of 1948 and 1949.

The price supports were created via the New Deal's Commodity Credit Corporation (CCC), which made loans to farmers. The farmers offered their "surplus" crops as the collateral. With the surplus removed from the market and stored, the price of food began to increase. Over time, however, this surplus found its way into federal storage; when farmers began to default on their loans, they had to give up their stored crop collateral. They were perfectly pleased to do so.

By the Truman years, the CCC was *buying* the surplus crops, which the government stored. The old vision of the Farmers Alliance in the 1880s, as amplified in the 1920s through McNary-Haugen, was brought to a grand, if partial, consummation in the years between the New Deal and the Fair Deal.

Truman also built upon Roosevelt's cautious support for civil rights. On June 25, 1941 (under pressure from civil rights leaders like A. Philip Randolph), Roosevelt had issued Executive Order 8802, forbidding racial discrimination in defense industries. The order established a Fair Employment Practices Committee (FEPC) within the Office of Production Management (OPM). Truman's action was more comprehensive: he was a champion of racial equality. He established a President's Committee on Civil Rights; he ordered desegregation in the military through Executive Order 9981, which he issued in 1948; and he proposed a strong civil rights bill to fight job discrimination—a civil rights bill that congressional opponents defeated in 1949.[23]

Another defeat for Truman was the massive opposition to his plan for universal health care. Federal involvement in the field of public health (beyond military medicine) extended from the creation of the Public Health Service in 1912 to the founding in 1930 of its successor agency, the National Institute of Health (NIH) and the creation in 1937 of the National Cancer Institute. FDR had considered adding medical insurance to Social

Rising to the occasion: President Harry S. Truman in the Oval Office. Credit: Library of Congress.

Security but demurred because he feared a storm against "socialized medicine." And that was the charge of the American Medical Association when Truman told Congress in November 1945 that every American should have the right to medical care. But at least Truman floated the concept. It went nowhere.

The Republican Congress was hostile to most of the Fair Deal measures of Truman. Conversely, the Republican Congress passed laws that the president detested, most famously the Taft-Hartley Act of 1947, which was passed over Truman's veto. The act circumscribed labor unions: indeed, it empowered the federal government to interfere in strikes (reviving the precedent set in the 1894 Pullman strike) when they threatened the national interest.

For a while, however, Truman forged a bipartisan consensus in the field of foreign policy. Republican Arthur Vandenberg of Michigan was one of the president's staunchest supporters in the Senate. Conservatives, however, were busily creating their influential myth about a liberal "sell-out" at Yalta.

The issue, of course, was the oppressive domination of Eastern Europe by the Soviets. Many people were appalled by this: as early as March 1946,

Winston Churchill delivered his "Iron Curtain" speech in Fulton, Missouri. As to *Yalta*, however, when the conference took place in the early weeks of 1945—FDR, Churchill, and Stalin held discussions at the Black Sea Russian resort—the Soviets *already* had substantial control of Eastern Europe, through the fortunes of war. Churchill himself had agreed to a Soviet sphere of influence in the Balkans as early as October 1944.[24] In the Yalta accord were unenforceable agreements that alluded to early "free elections." But the only way for FDR (or his successors) to loosen the Soviet grip would be to wage (or to threaten to wage) the kind of Russo-American war that no sane politician would have started in 1945.[25]

After all, FDR was convinced that Soviet help might be needed in the coming invasion of Japan. It bears noting that nuclear weapons had not yet been tested when the Yalta meeting took place. Besides, even *after* the Japanese surrender, the American people overwhelmingly wanted quick peace, not a new major war: Representative John Rankin of Mississippi told the House right after V-J Day that "if the Congress does not get busy and expedite the release of these men from the armed forces—men who are needed at home, who have jobs to go back to, who have wives and children to look after or who have crops to gather, or young men who should finish their education—you will soon be in the hottest war you have ever been in since you have been in Congress—and ought to be."[26]

At first Truman tried to get along with the Soviets, but he gradually began to change his mind. Soviet expansionism threatened Iran, Turkey, and Greece. Averell Harriman, who had served as America's wartime ambassador to Moscow, feared and loathed Joseph Stalin and regarded the Soviets' intentions with suspicion. His views were influential with Truman, and so were the views of Russian expert George F. Kennan, who regaled his colleagues in the State Department with a highly pessimistic assessment of Soviet intentions that he sent in a famous long telegram in February 1946. Kennan wrote that in Stalinist Communism the United States was dealing with a dangerously paranoid force; it was "a political force committed fanatically to the belief that with the US there can be no permanent modus vivendi, that it is desirable and necessary that the internal harmony of our society be disrupted, our traditional way of life be destroyed, the international authority of our state broken, if Soviet power is to be secure."[27] This telegram was highly influential; it inspired the doctrine of "containment."

Key State Department figures were convinced. General George C. Marshall, whom Truman had appointed as his secretary of state in early

1947, joined with Undersecretary of State Dean Acheson to formulate a comprehensive policy. In February 1947, officials of the State, War, and Navy Departments wrote a working paper for Truman. This document—from which the "Truman Doctrine" was derived—recommended that the president announce it would be henceforth "United States policy" to "support free peoples who are resisting attempted subjugation by armed minorities or by outside pressures."[28] On March 12, 1947, Truman used these very words in a speech to Congress requesting assistance for beleaguered Greece and Turkey. This action would be supplemented quickly by the Marshall Plan to help the European nations that remained in a state of devastation after World War II. At first George Marshall had proposed that the Soviets should share in this assistance. But the Soviets dismissed the idea as an imperialist trick.

In the opinion of historian John Lewis Gaddis, "American leaders did not want a Cold War, but they wanted insecurity even less." Truman and his team "had reluctantly concluded that recent actions of the Soviet Union endangered the security of the United States." Consequently, in Gaddis's view, the Truman Doctrine was "shock therapy: it was a last-ditch effort to prod Congress and the American people into accepting the responsibilities of . . . world leadership."[29] Leaders like Acheson, in Gaddis's opinion, were sincerely convinced that "the Soviet Union was trying to impose its ideology on as much of the world as possible."[30]

In his memoirs, Acheson recalled a crucial White House meeting with some powerful members of Congress. Many of the legislative leaders (of both parties) were skeptical regarding the administration's point of view. "In desperation," Acheson recalled, he requested permission to speak, and then Truman signaled his approval. Acheson told the congressional leaders that in the previous eighteen months:

> The Soviet pressure on the Straits, on Iran, and on northern Greece had brought the Balkans to the point where a highly possible Soviet breakthrough might open three continents to Soviet penetration. Like apples in a barrel infected by one rotten one, the corruption of Greece would infect Iran and all to the east. It would also carry infection to Africa through Asia Minor and Egypt, and to Europe through Italy and France, already threatened by the strongest domestic Communist parties in Western Europe. The Soviet Union was playing one of the greatest gambles in history at minimal cost. It did not need to win all the possibilities. Even one or two offered immense gains. We and we alone were in a position to break up the play.[31]

In 1948, such fears gained a new plausibility: the Soviet-assisted coup in Czechoslovakia together with the Soviet blockade of West Berlin seemed a grim confirmation of the very worst fears about Stalin's intentions. What followed, of course, on the American side, was the round-the-clock airlift to save West Berlin and the creation of NATO in 1949. Along the way came a lot more federal power in the realm of national security: the National Security Act of 1947 created the Central Intelligence Agency, the National Security Council, and the Defense Department, which unified the military services, including a newly independent Air Force. Truman also started an "internal security" program to interdict "security risks." This was well before the Alger Hiss case.

Truman's come-from-behind reelection victory in 1948 was in many ways the high point of what journalist Cabell Phillips called a "triumphant succession."[32] And the Democrats regained control of Congress. In the two years that followed, however, Truman found himself in dire straits again as he faced new international crises—and Americans reverted, by and large, to their sour mood of 1946.

Truman was a very gifted leader; he was smart, courageous, energetic, and he built the morale of his team to the point where associates like Acheson served him with a passionate devotion. He was intellectually curious. He sought the facts to the best of his ability. He was funny. He divided the Republicans in 1948 by calling the conservative Republican Congress into special session to enact the progressive platform of the party's own presidential ticket.

In other times, he might have left the White House in triumph. But the American mood was too volatile after the Second World War—the American people were still too conflicted in regard to the nation's new role in world affairs—to prevent the newest problems that beset Harry Truman from destroying the bipartisan support for his foreign policy. Besides, after 1948, the most vengeful Republicans were simply out for blood, as events would show.

In 1949, the Communists took over in China and the Soviets got nuclear weapons (through the work of Soviet spies). Then, in 1950, the North Korean Communists attacked South Korea and America (under the United Nations banner) was at war again, only five years after V-J Day.

With war came remobilization, along with new controls on wages and prices. But a longer-term pattern with vast implications was established simultaneously in 1950. A top-secret memorandum from the National Security Council (NSC 68) advised Truman on long-range planning and called for "a Rapid Build-up of Political, Economic, and Military Strength in the Free World."[33] NSC 68 was largely the work of Paul H. Nitze, who headed the State Department's Policy Planning Staff after Acheson succeeded George Marshall as secretary of state in 1949. As historian Ernest R. May has observed, the implications of NSC 68 were drastic: "From the end of World War II in 1945, relations between the West and the Soviet Union had become increasingly hostile. Until 1950, however, the contest remained primarily political and economic. NSC 68 argued that, if it continued so, the West would lose. To check or turn back the expansion of the Soviet Union and communism, the document said, the West needed large, ready military forces."[34]

Truman's basic acceptance of NSC 68 (along with the short-term cost of the war in Korea) led to skyrocketing defense costs: in immediate terms, according to May, "U.S. defense spending tripled [and] for the next four decades, it would remain two to three times higher than in any previous periods of peace."[35] Truman authorized development of thermonuclear weapons (the "hydrogen bomb") and launched a program of foreign assistance that extended the precedent set by the Marshall Plan (and Lend-Lease). Through the Mutual Security Act of 1951, Congress gave its permission for a "foreign aid" program that would keep the Third World from "going Communist." In the same year the National Science Foundation was created.

But at the very beginning of this mobilization, "McCarthyism" started. It built upon the work of the Liberty League, the shrill rhetoric of Taft-school Republicanism, the Yalta myth, the Hiss case, the "loss" of China, and the tactics of up-and-coming Communist-hunters in Congress like Richard M. Nixon. Senator Joseph McCarthy of Wisconsin had been swept into Congress in the Republican victory of 1946. Four years later he attained great power: the power to inspire great fear. On February 9, 1950, he asserted in a speech that he made in Wheeling, West Virginia, that the State Department was infested with Communists.

He went on to smear dozens of people, though he never proved a single charge. At the height of his influence—which was enormous—he had the power to wreck people's lives, and his senatorial immunity protected him from libel suits. He convinced great numbers of Americans that Communism had subverted the federal government at the very moment when the government was led by an increasingly anti-Communist administration.

To be sure, concerns about Soviet espionage were justified. As journalist Richard Rovere pointed out about a dozen years later, Soviet spies had been (and continued to be) "part of a world-wide infiltrating movement, and some of them managed to get into governments policed a great deal more carefully than ours—Nazi Germany's, for instance, and Imperial Japan's."[36]

Cogent thinking and responsible analysis, however, were anathema to McCarthy, one of the foulest demagogues in our history. In his partisan mode, he once sneered that "the Democratic label is now the property of men and women who have . . . bent to the whispered pleas from the lips of traitors . . . men and women who wear the political label stitched with the idiocy of a Truman, rotted by the deceit of an Acheson, corrupted by the red slime of a [Harry Dexter] White."[37]

It bears noting that the last of these figures—Mr. White—had served FDR as an assistant secretary of the treasury. In 1944, he had worked with John Maynard Keynes at the conference on international monetary stabilization that was held in Bretton Woods, New Hampshire. Then, shortly before his death—and this was the issue—he had testified with thinly veiled contempt before the House Un-American Activities Committee (HUAC). The new Red-hunting superpatriots remembered his irascible tone, even after his death. McCarthy's slur ("red slime") was posthumous payback.

Others joined in this primitive abuse. Here is what Republican senator William E. Jenner of Indiana had to say when Truman called George C. Marshall out of retirement (after his service as secretary of state) for additional service as secretary of defense: "General Marshall is not only willing, he is eager to play the role of a front man, for traitors. The truth is this is no new role for him, for Gen. George C. Marshall is a living lie." Jenner went on to call Marshall "an errand boy, a front man, a stooge, or a co-conspirator for this administration's crazy assortment of collectivist cut-throat crackpots and Communist fellow-traveling appeasers."[38]

This was typical of what was generally known as "McCarthyism" after 1950 (the term was supposedly coined by the newspaper cartoonist Herbert Block). Many far-right politicians (and not all of them Republicans by any means) participated. Even the respectable Robert A. Taft came close when he spoke about the "pro-Communist group in the State Department who surrendered to every demand of Russia at Yalta and Potsdam, and promoted at every opportunity the Communist cause in China."[39]

McCarthyism bred (or responded to) hysteria—and a few years after McCarthy's demise, Rovere could reflect upon the fascinating strangeness of it all. As Rovere recalled it, McCarthy even started to suggest, "that the struggle against world Communism was a *diversion* from the struggle against the domestic conspiracy [my emphasis]."[40] Rovere observed that this "sort of talk" came close to a neo-isolationist illusion: it prompted the notion that "Communism was a danger, not *to* the United States, but *in* the United States, when in truth it was just the other way about."[41]

It was "the other way about" because "the enemy within" was on the run: Truman and his people pursued the "security risks," while J. Edgar Hoover at the FBI—a right-wing hero—pursued them as well.

It didn't matter. McCarthy dominated the headlines in 1950 and the years thereafter, throwing Truman ever more on the defensive. To make matters worse, the Korean War was going badly. United Nations forces led by General Douglas MacArthur scored an early triumph by landing behind the enemy lines at Inchon. The North Koreans retreated and MacArthur chased them all the way to the Chinese border. But then the Chinese intervened.

A counterattack by the Chinese and North Koreans reversed the United Nations victory: the enemy troops reentered South Korea in 1951. MacArthur fought them back to the 38th parallel—the border of the two Koreas. He wanted to invade North Korea again and requested Truman's permission for the bombing of some Chinese bases. But Truman—fearing a massive and horrendous land war with China—demurred. And so the general criticized Truman in public, and Truman relieved him of command. McCarthy called for the president's impeachment; MacArthur, after all, was yet another hero of the right. A series of MacArthur-for-president booms had occurred in the 1940s.

MacArthur appeared to be ready for a full-scale war with China, a war that in all probability would escalate to nuclear dimensions if the infantry losses were grim. MacArthur wrote to Joseph W. Martin (House minority leader) in 1951 to the effect that "Asia is where the Communist conspirators have elected to make their play for global conquest. . . . If we lose this war to Communism in Asia the fall of Europe is inevitable. . . . There is no substitute for victory."[42] But the president settled for the qualified victory of pushing back the North Koreans to the 38th parallel. Many viewed this achievement as a stalemate—or a defeat.

In many ways Asia turned out to be the Truman administration's Achilles' heel. Hamby has criticized Truman's record in Asia, alleging that "the failure of Truman's Asian policy must be laid to the administration's inability to meet the admittedly more difficult problems of Asia with the same perception and foresight that marked its handling of Europe."[43] China was the key to it all.

Truman had sent George Marshall to China in 1946; the president was curious—one is tempted to say naively curious—to see whether hands-on diplomacy could prompt the Chinese Communists to work with Chiang

Kai-shek and his nationalist regime. Marshall concluded it was hopeless. In Hamby's account, the administration then "decided to cut its losses, yet it did not prepare the American people for the certain denouement."[44]

With all due respect, one is tempted to ask what form of "preparation" would have worked. After all, Chiang Kai-shek had powerful links with the Republican Party's Taft wing. Such Republicans dismissed the views of Chiang's detractors, such as General Joseph ("Vinegar Joe") Stilwell—who had reported to Marshall during World War II that the Chinese army under Chiang was "rotten with corruption."[45] The "China lobby" in Washington thought otherwise. In light of this political fact, how could Truman have attempted to tell the American people—without being vilified as a defeatist—that saving Chiang was beyond the power of America?

In any case, the "loss" of China, combined with the Korean stalemate, fed the long-cherished presidential aspirations of Senator Taft. In domestic politics, Taft had shown surprising moderation since 1948; he had voted for the Housing Act of 1949 and told his fellow Republicans they ought to support at least "a minimum standard floor under subsistence, education, medical care, and housing."[46] But in foreign affairs, he was peevish and quite contradictory.

He opposed U.S. membership in NATO. His old isolationist instincts remained highly active. Yet, as Hamby has observed, "he was powerfully attracted to intervention across the Pacific": during the Korean War, he "at one point or another supported crossing the 38th Parallel after Inchon, advocated withdrawal from the peninsula after the Communist Chinese intervened, endorsed MacArthur's call for an air war against the Chinese, and argued in favor of using Chiang's troops for an attack upon mainland China."[47]

In all, it was a highly uneven record, reflective of an ill-considered view of world affairs. In Hamby's estimation, Taft's "surface contradictions" all flowed from a "controlling contradiction." It was a contradiction with roots running deep into American conservative history:

> A dedicated enemy of Communism, Taft was also a partisan hater of an administration that had proclaimed a global anti-Communist commitment and a conservative repelled by the means that a total offensive against Communism would require—expensive foreign aid programs, heavy military spending, big government. He dealt with this predicament by engaging in an increasingly obsessive search for scapegoats among the Democrats.[48]

By 1952, it appeared that Taft's hour had arrived: he was the early front-runner for the Republican presidential nomination. But no one could predict what he would do—or undo—in the White House. Some called him a "New Isolationist." Internationally minded Republicans were scared; indeed, they were worried enough to recruit an old hero for the purpose of stopping Bob Taft.

EISENHOWER

Many observers have written of the "terrible temper," the rage against stupidity, that Dwight David Eisenhower managed to conceal beneath the sunny facade that Americans knew in the 1950s. A career soldier, he had definite ideas about national and international politics. He had nothing but scorn for political myopia—the cowardice that seeks to evade the hard challenges of history.

In 1939 he wrote a scathing entry in his diary regarding the appeasers who placated Hitler. "For a long time it has seemed ridiculous to refer to the world as civilized," he wrote. "It doesn't seem possible that people that proudly refer to themselves as intelligent could let the situation come about." He poured out his wrath against Hitler and the Nazis as follows: "Hundreds of millions will suffer privations and starvation, millions will be killed and wounded because one man so wills it. He is a power-drunk egocentric, but even so he would still not do this if he were sane. He is one of the criminally insane, but unfortunately he is the absolute ruler of 89,000,000 people. . . . Hitler's record with the Jews, his rape of Austria, of the Czechs, the Slovaks and now the Poles is as black as that of any barbarian of the Dark Ages."[49] Ike was also, of course, quite disgusted with Soviet tyranny.

Like many Republicans, he warned against "regimented statism"; he expressed a continuing concern down the years about the growing role of "centralized government." In 1948, for example, he warned in his inaugural address as the distinguished new president of Columbia University that "a paternalistic government can gradually destroy . . . the will of a people to maintain a high degree of individual responsibility."[50] But he was not a believer in laissez-faire: in the very same speech he warned that a society lacking in able governance was nothing better than a "temporary truce with chaos."

Early in his presidency, he told his brother Edgar that despite his opposition to "centralization," he believed that "the Federal government cannot avoid or escape responsibilities which the mass of our people firmly *believe* should be undertaken by it." He continued: "Should any political party attempt to abolish social security, unemployment insurance, and eliminate labor laws and farm programs, you would not hear of that party again in our political history. There is a tiny splinter group, of course, that believes you can do these things. Among them are H. L. Hunt . . . a few other Texas oil millionaires, and an occasional politician or business man from other areas. Their number is small and they are stupid."[51]

Ike's intention was to seek and maintain a sound centrist political balance. Against those who demanded "an all-powerful government" and those who tended to "deny the obligation of government to intervene on behalf of the people even when the complexities of modern life demand it," Eisenhower called upon America's leaders to "proceed along the middle way."[52] He used the term often.

Historian Steven Wagner has argued that Ike's "middle way" was the expression of "a carefully considered political philosophy similar to Theodore Roosevelt's cautious progressivism."[53] It was much more than that, as we know: it emerged from a tradition of American statecraft that reached across many generations. For Ike's generation, in particular, the "middle way" distilled the great lessons that Americans had learned in the 1930s and 1940s. Ike spoke for many millions of Depression survivors when he pledged to maintain the great programmatic "floor over the pit of personal disaster in our complex modern society."[54] And he spoke for millions in rejecting isolationist attitudes.

Eisenhower sought to provide the American people with guardianship: he would work to protect the new prosperity and strength that Americans had won for themselves. He would do it as a master of logistics, of organizational management, of systems analysis; the American commander at D-Day was long since a democratic leader who had mastered the sheer art of *process*.

And he would pull it off discreetly, as a matter of preference: political scientist Fred I. Greenstein has written of the "unobtrusive guidance" that Ike could finesse, of his penchant for "minimizing open debate," of his "hidden-hand presidency."[55] The man who had controlled such anger in himself would calm the passions of Cold War America.

After World War II, he settled in for a while in his role as university president. But then Truman called him back to military duty when he tapped him for NATO command. Indeed, Truman wanted Ike for the Democrats in 1952, and he privately offered his endorsement for a presidential bid. But Ike was a Republican—a moderate Republican—and the moderate-to-liberal wing of the party wanted *him* to supplant Robert Taft as the national leader of the GOP. In the Eisenhower working group were capable movers and shakers such as Thomas Dewey, Senator Henry Cabot Lodge, Winthrop Aldrich, John Hay Whitney, and Herbert Brownell, among others.

Truman thought about the perils of the coming election, and he sounded out Ike. According to historian Stephen Ambrose, "Truman was keeping his options open. In late December, the President sent Eisenhower a handwritten note, saying that while he would like to retire his immediate duty was to keep the isolationists out of the White House. He wanted to know Eisenhower's intentions." Ike sent a noncommittal reply.[56]

The pre-convention jousting with Taft and his supporters was sharp: after Ike took exception to MacArthur's position on Korea (in effect, Ike endorsed the key decisions of Truman), certain Taft supporters launched a smear campaign against Ike along the following lines: "REDS, NEW DEALERS USE IKE IN PLOT TO HOLD POWER"; "IKE CODDLED COMMUNISTS WHILE PRESIDENT OF COLUMBIA UNIVERSITY."[57] The nomination struggle was a brawl and the Republicans' unity weakened.

This was probably the reason why Eisenhower echoed some far-right conservative rhetoric during the general election campaign, a fact that Truman remembered with bitterness for many years afterward. Ike's running mate, Richard M. Nixon, added more inflammatory rhetoric.

But as soon as Ike was safely ensconced in the White House, middle-way politics proceeded. Convinced that the strategic importance of Korea was not worth the risk of a general war, he negotiated a ceasefire. In April 1953 he told the American Society of Newspaper Editors that his paramount duty was preventing a thermonuclear holocaust. His secondary duty was averting "a life of fear and tension; a burden of arms draining the wealth and the labor of all peoples."[58]

While John Foster Dulles, his tough-talking secretary of state, warned the Communists of "massive retaliation" and spoke of rolling back the power of the Soviets, Ike strove to contain the growing arms race. True, he extended the containment policy by working out new international treaties such as SEATO and CENTO. And he pledged to support the anti-Communist Chiang Kai-shek in Taiwan. But he was seeking a new flexibility; he wanted freedom to consider all options.

Soon after Stalin's death in March 1953, Ike organized an important secret planning session—the "Solarium exercise," as it was called—in which teams of war planners were instructed to develop different strategies for dealing with the Soviet Union over time. Robert R. Bowie, Ike's director of the State Department's Policy Planning Staff, has described the give-and-take of the Solarium session, along with its basic result: "High level teams were tasked with developing the best possible cases for alternative strategies, including an active policy of rollback. As [Ike] probably intended, the exercise exposed the futility and high risks of such a policy and thus put the idea to rest."[59]

The mobilization that began in the Truman years was scaled back during Ike's first term. Eisenhower's preference, soon codified in NSC 162/2, was to keep the American posture in the Cold War *sensible*, avoiding unnecessary clashes that could escalate to nuclear war. To avert thermonuclear conflagration, the doctrine of *deterrence* would be used with the Soviets, whom Ike regarded as rational, at least after Stalin. Bowie elaborates:

> Eisenhower was convinced that any major war between the United States and the Soviet Union would inevitably and rapidly escalate into a catastrophic nuclear war, however it began. The threat of prompt nuclear response would ensure that Soviet leaders recognized this reality. If they did, they would not be tempted to start any conflict in Europe, conventional or otherwise. And the capacity to retaliate despite a first-strike would be assured by continental defense and later by the submarine-based Polaris missiles and the triad—sea-based and land-based missiles complemented by manned bombers.[60]

In the parlance of the time, Ike's security posture was called the "New Look." It was not very popular among the anti-Communist "hawks"—or among the Joint Chiefs of Staff. But as historian Dennis E. Showalter has observed, "a steadily growing body of evidence [is] establishing just how dangerous the Eisenhower years and their aftermath to 1963 really were. At several points World War III could have happened and almost did. . . . [Eisenhower] had to deal with a society unprepared for the kinds of long-term confrontation inherent to a Cold War between superpowers. Public opinion stampeding in any direction might trigger global thermonuclear destruction. Eisenhower's calm public demeanor . . . played no small role in helping the United States, and the world, develop a sense of perspective."[61]

Crucial to the New Look was Eisenhower's wish to avoid *over*spending or *under*spending on national defense: what he hoped was to give the United States *exactly* what was needed, insofar as that was humanly possible. To do this, he wished to have exact and objective data on the Soviets' strategic capabilities. Early in his presidency, he created a program for top-secret airborne reconnaissance, with plans for space-based surveillance. Historian R. Cargill Hall of the National Reconnaissance Office relates that

[w]ithin ten to twelve months of taking office, President Eisenhower authorized and a few trusted advisors had established a clandestine project in compartmented channels. . . . It involved conducting *in peacetime* periodic, high-altitude photoreconnaissance overflights of potential foreign adversaries. The Sensitive Intelligence security control system established for these missions, or SENSINT as it came to be called, was far more than a "hidden hand"; SENSINT was entirely "off the political table." Because aerial overflights of "denied territory" in peacetime violated international conventions to which the United States was a contracting party, these efforts were so closely held that only a select few . . . even knew of their existence.[62]

The New Look called for restraint in conventional warfare: Ike showed such restraint when the French faced defeat in Indochina in 1954. Stephen Ambrose observed that "under no circumstances was Eisenhower going to send American troops back onto the Asian mainland less than a year after signing the armistice in Korea."[63] He sent advisers and supplies, for he did not want the Communists to win. But a large-scale commitment was out of the question; Ike reflected years later that "the jungles of Indochina . . . would have swallowed up division after division of United States troops, who, unaccustomed to this kind of warfare, would have sustained heavy casualties."[64]

It was *peace* that Ike wanted, in a context of Cold War *security*. To achieve this peace and security, he worked up a *modus operandi* that displayed a holistic grasp of the socioeconomic process.[65] As Showalter writes, "Eisenhower was a master at orchestrating national resources on behalf of the country's security interests, securing support from a broad spectrum of individuals and constituencies in science, industry, education, business, and public service."[66]

Part of this mastery derived from the legacy of planning through teamwork that flowed from the inception of TR's New Nationalism through World War II. Economist John Kenneth Galbraith has written that in policy circles much discussion was centered after World War II on the question of how "wartime employment, output and achievement could be made to last into the peace. The locus of much of this discussion was the National Planning Association, a loose convocation of economists, public officials, trade-union and farm-organization representatives, with a sprinkling of liberal businessmen who provided the financial support. Especially it was the gathering place of the Washington Keynesians," men such as Gerhard Colm, Alvin Hansen, Walter Salant, Robert Nathan, and others.[67]

The Employment Act of 1946 was the legislative basis for projecting a Keynesian program into Cold War American policy. As Hansen observed later on in the 1950s, no sooner had the Eisenhower administration taken office than "a recession began to threaten. The business world wanted assurance that the government would not let the economy down. The Administration gave them this assurance and in so doing leaned heavily upon the machinery set up under the Employment Act. . . . The main significance of the 1954 Economic Report [of the President] was the firm declaration . . . that the government would use its 'vast powers to help maintain employment and purchasing power.'"[68]

In October 1954, Ike declared that "so long as any citizen wants work and cannot find it, we have a pressing problem to solve. This administration is working vigorously to bring about a lasting solution."[69] The result was the Interstate Highway System, a long-term project to upgrade America's infrastructure and generate a great many jobs in the process. Robert J. Donovan recounted the instructions Ike gave to his cabinet in 1954, instructions that bespoke his commitment to industrial and economic policy:

> The President informed the Cabinet that he had asked [Arthur F.] Burns to co-ordinate reports from the various departments and agencies on their plans for public works projects. It would be essential, he said, to have planning advanced sufficiently to insure that men would be put to work quickly. Too often, he said, preliminary planning, testing, and surveys delay start on work. . . . Projects actually under way, he noted, gave the government flexibility in speeding them up or stretching them out, as conditions required.[70]

Late in 1955, according to Ambrose, Eisenhower said that, "he wanted [the Commerce Department] to plan to use the Interstate System for managing the economy."[71] The old vision of Foster and Catchings was now policy—for a while.

The Interstate Highway System would constitute the largest public works effort in American history. Eisenhower's support for the "good roads" movement had begun in his youth with his service in the cross-country motor convoy of 1919. Then, after World War II, he saw the autobahn system in Germany; it put America's highways to shame. Some efforts had been made in the preceding decades to modernize America's roads: freeways in and around Los Angeles, inter-city parkways (mostly in the East), and the Pennsylvania Turnpike, which opened in 1940. But the need for better highways was obvious.

Ike appointed a blue-ribbon task force chaired by Gen. Lucius D. Clay to consider different options for the project. Legislation based upon the Clay Commission's recommendations was sent to Congress in 1955, where debate continued for almost a year. Most disputed was the financing method, with the options of tolls versus bonds at the center of discussion.

What emerged in the Federal Aid Highway Act of 1956 was a compromise: funding for the system, based on gasoline taxes, would be channeled through a federal Highway Trust Fund, from which 90 percent of the funding for construction would flow. States would pay the remaining 10 percent of the construction costs, pick the routes for the highways, and then take care of the maintenance, with help from the trust fund. Strict standards would be set by the Bureau of Public Roads.[72]

In Eisenhower fashion, it was all done without great fanfare. Yet the Interstate Highway System revolutionized American life. It also delivered economic stimulation on a massive scale. Business activity, employment, and output were all affected: cars, motels, gasoline stations, resorts, restaurants, and the colossal construction activity itself resulted in huge private-sector wealth creation.

Ike also helped to create the St. Lawrence Seaway, a 2,350-mile shipping corridor to link the Great Lakes with Atlantic Ocean trade routes. Operated jointly by the United States and Canada, the system was opened in 1959, with Ike and Queen Elizabeth II in attendance at the opening ceremonies. Such brick-and-mortar extensions of the activist government tradition were accompanied by further institutional development: Ike created the Department of Health, Education, and Welfare (HEW) in 1953, and supported the creation of the Federal Aviation Administration (FAA) in 1958, and the National Aeronautics and Space Administration (NASA) in 1959. He also signed the 1955 Air Pollution Control Act, providing funds for new research in the field of pollution abatement.

In Eisenhower's view, the developmental goal of his method was to furnish the American people in a *sensibly* conservative manner with the basis for continued prosperity—and modernization. The free-enterprise system in partnership with wise and intelligent government would demonstrate the power of America's achievement to "the Communist bloc," to "the Third World," and to future generations. At the heart of it all was the economy.

The Eisenhower boom was in many ways derived from the mobilization of the Second World War: America's wartime expansion of productive capacity, money supply, and middle-class purchasing power had created an immense expansive potential that blossomed in the Eisenhower years. But Ike kept the process in motion, using federal stimuli to guarantee maximum employment. Moreover, he supported yet another extension of the Social Security system's coverage in 1954, observing that "government, through social security and by fostering applicable insurance plans, must help protect the individual against hardship and help free his mind from anxiety."[73]

One could call his economic principles Keynesian—but without fiscal recourse to deficits. To rein in national debt and to counteract inflation, Ike used some contra-cyclical devices to slow down the boom when the risks of "over-heating" were evident. Galbraith provides the rough figures: "a budget deficit of just under $6 billion in 1954 was turned into a surplus of about the same size in the two following years. In 1958, the deficit had grown again to $10.2 billion; this was brought down to $1.2 billion the following year and turned into a surplus of $3.5 billion in 1960."[74]

Inflation was the number-one concern: Hamby has written that for "Eisenhower and his aides, inflation was the worst danger; they fought it relentlessly with conservative fiscal and monetary policies" that resulted over time in an "economic slowdown."[75] The slowdown became a recession by 1958, and the Republicans paid a stiff price for reining in the boom: growing Democratic majorities in Congress were attributable, at least in part, to the economic setback.

But Eisenhower felt it was important, as he put it, "to stabilize the buying power of the dollar, else the value of the pension, the insurance policy, and the savings bond is eroded away."[76] There were also global concerns; the Bretton Woods pact of the 1940s represented an attempt to create an international economy in which different currencies were readily exchangeable—at steady rates.

Inflation itself has a great many possible causes, but the "wage-price" spiral was the cause that was usually invoked in the 1950s. Galbraith attributed the postwar inflation to the "market power" of the large corporations and labor unions of the time; in America's economy—after the Depression—optimistic calculation in the business community was such that "long before full employment was reached, corporations had the power to raise their prices, and it was greatly to their earnings advantage to do so." The rising cost of living prompted unions to demand higher wages, whereupon the new "wage increases would soon be stimulating and justifying yet further price increases."[77] Inflation in the Truman years had been a short-term affair, but inflation in the Eisenhower years was a portent of serious problems that would dog the American economy for decades.

So too the tenacity of left-versus-right dialectics: Ike's middle-way politics were staunchly opposed by disgruntled conservative Republicans. After the death of Robert Taft, the Republican right carried on, and began to regroup. Joe McCarthy's charge that the Truman team was infested with Communists was turned right away upon his own party's new administration. Ike's hidden-hand response was to isolate McCarthy, fighting back in a covert campaign. In the Army-McCarthy hearings of 1954, Ike encouraged the Department of the Army to attain the high political ground and then repel every sally of the demagogue.[78]

The Republican right was dismayed at the extent to which Ike was promoting "big government." A new 1950s generation of conservatives inveighed against the ever-looming "statist" menace. In *The Conservative Mind*, Russell Kirk condemned the "unitary state" and proclaimed that true progress can only result from "the snail-slow influence of historical example and just constitutions rather than from deliberate legislation."[79]

William F. Buckley Jr. was more militant, declaring that "the statist solution" to American problems was "inadmissible." "I will not cede more power to the state," he avowed. "I will not willingly cede more power to anyone, not to the state, not to General Motors, not to the CIO. I will hoard my power like a miser, resisting every effort to drain it from me. I will then use *my* power as *I* see fit."[80] Republican conservatives mobilized under Barry Goldwater's leadership in Ike's second term. On the far right, a new group—the John Birch Society—organized the faithful.

There were justified concerns about the power of "the state" in the Eisenhower years. Individual liberties indeed could be threatened by the Cold War security regime. One thinks, for example, of the open-air testing of nuclear weapons, with little or no calculation of the risks to public health; of the high-handed tactics that the CIA was permitted to employ in its covert operations under the quirky leadership of spymaster Allen Dulles (brother of John Foster Dulles); of the odious power-mongering that J. Edgar Hoover, the FBI's leader for life, was allowed to carry on.[81] Characteristically, however, the American right was indifferent to such developments (or else it was in full and vocal support of them): after all, if *pinkos* were really the targets, then the much-vaunted libertarian standards (or pretensions) of the right could be accordingly relaxed.

On the left, there was a different kind of libertarian militancy in the 1950s, at least within radical circles. Perhaps to some extent because the Cold War liberals were justified in saying that American Marxists had been "soft" toward the tyranny of Stalin, a self-proclaimed "New Left"—anti-Stalinist—began emerging in the 1950s. Its politics were neo-anarchistic. The writings of radicals such as Paul Goodman prefigured the rage on the left that would erupt against conservatives and liberals alike in the 1960s.

Liberal dissatisfaction with Eisenhower was expressed through complaints about his "do-nothing" ways. To some extent, Democratic liberals were fooled by the Eisenhower preference for work behind the scenes; in other respects, there were genuine differences of temperament and values at work. Stylistically, it was the eloquence of FDR—or the feistiness of Truman—that the liberals expected from the White House; they regarded Ike's attitudes as stodgy. In comparison to Truman's team at its best—the superb but modest George Marshall, the elegant Dean Acheson—liberals detested a number of the rough-edged characters who populated Ike's establishment: the maladroit John Foster Dulles, the uninspired George Humphrey (secretary of the treasury), the abrasive Lewis Strauss (chairman of the Atomic Energy Commission).

Programmatically, it was *dramatic* extensions of the federal presence that the liberals desired; they found Eisenhower's caution ill-grounded. Their dispute, for example, with Ike about federal aid to education—which Eisenhower clearly supported, albeit in a strictly limited way—reflected genuine philosophic differences. The National Defense Education Act of 1958 was therefore a compromise.[82]

Another bone of contention was the farm program; both Ike and his conservative agriculture secretary Ezra Taft Benson found the price-support program distasteful. They hated its cost and they hated the fact that the government was storing a "surplus." But they dutifully carried out the program as they struggled to reduce the big surplus and work out a better way of helping the farmers. The Agricultural Trade Development and Assistance Act of 1954 (PL 480) authorized the overseas sale of $700 million worth of surplus crops, with the outright donation of another $300 million worth of crops to relieve world hunger. An analogous provision of the 1954 Agricultural Act set aside $2.5 billion worth of agricultural surplus to help relieve hunger in America.[83]

Eisenhower's long-term strategy for price supports was to cut back production, in the manner of the old AAA. He called his proposal the "Soil Bank"; its purpose was to pay American farmers to remove from production an estimated fifty million acres of land. He even toyed with the idea of attempting to buy back some land that had been given away in the Civil War's Homestead Act.

Ike battled the Democratic Congress over farm policy; he vetoed an act that he considered too rigid and expensive in 1956. But then he signed a revised piece of legislation: he believed that the Agricultural Act of 1956 in its final form was more flexible; it also set the stage for his Soil Bank.[84]

In other words, Ike was *willing to compromise*: he proved it. He perfected a politics that unified Cold War American culture to a very high degree. He had an in-house intellectual to assist in this work: speechwriter Arthur Larsen, whose 1955 book *A Republican Looks at His Party* promoted a vision of an up-to-date "New Republicanism" that was grounded in Ike's middle way.[85] Republican politics aside, Ike's method included a steady bipartisanship: he worked easily with the Democratic majority leader in the Senate, Lyndon B. Johnson, and with Speaker of the House Sam Rayburn after the Democrats regained control of Congress in 1954. And it was Ike's quiet bargaining with Democrats like LBJ that helped advance the cause of civil rights for blacks.

The liberal Democrats (as opposed to the southern segregationist Democrats) wanted Ike to *crusade* for civil rights, as opposed to finessing the issue in his usual self-possessed manner. Many legends have arisen in regard to Ike's relationship with Chief Justice Earl Warren in the aftermath of the epochal *Brown v. Board of Education* decision in 1954. It was true that Ike worried in regard to the disruptive implications of the "all deliberate speed" directive that the Court handed down in a supplementary decision of 1955. It was also true that after ordering federal troops to Little Rock, Arkansas, in 1957 to support the *Brown* decision—a very strong action—Ike justified the move in the comparatively minimalistic language of upholding the law.

This caution and reserve was anathema to the emotional impetus that drove many grassroots organizers; a religious imperative of prophecy was vital to the ethos of civil rights uplift. That being the case, the idealists and activists were often disappointed by the quiet ways of Ike in the White House: they wanted stirring endorsements and oracular words instead of probity.

But historian David A. Nichols has argued that Eisenhower's record on civil rights was extraordinary, at least in the context of the times. In the aftermath of Truman's order to desegregate the military, for example, compliance had been minimal or nil. Ike changed all that:

> Eisenhower . . . encountered opposition similar to what Truman had experienced, but the former general had the prestige to command compliance from reluctant military subordinates. . . . Despite the military's legendary resistance to change, Eisenhower accomplished the racial transformation of the nation's combat forces with breathtaking speed, although facilities involving civilians, especially naval bases in the South,

took longer. This was done in the Eisenhower style, without press releases, focused on quiet negotiations with military leaders.[86]

As to desegregation of the public schools, Supreme Court action was already scheduled when Ike took the oath of office. During 1953, the Court invited Ike's attorney general, Herbert Brownell, to give a formal opinion on the issues. Brownell, a civil rights advocate, convinced Ike quickly that the "separate but equal" doctrine of *Plessy v. Ferguson* was bad constitutional law and should be overturned. Ike gave him permission to proceed. And so with Ike's full approval, his attorney general submitted a brief in opposition to segregated schools.

In the midst of all this, Chief Justice Fred Vinson passed away. In selecting Earl Warren as Vinson's replacement, Ike acted with his eyes wide open: Nichols has written that, "contrary to legend, Eisenhower and Brownell knew Warren's political views. Brownell had managed Dewey's 1948 campaign, and he and Warren were friends. . . . Eisenhower knew that Warren was in favor of civil rights and had publicly supported [the] fair employment practices commission (FEPC)" during World War II.[87]

The quiet ways of Ike: President Dwight D. Eisenhower with his special assistant E. Frederic Morrow, the first African American presidential staff member. Credit: Dwight D. Eisenhower Presidential Library and Museum.

After *Brown*, Ike nominated more Supreme Court justices, all of them civil rights supporters. Nichols has argued that Eisenhower "consciously made appointments that would entrench *Brown* in the judiciary," including the appointment of Justice John Marshall Harlan II, a name that was "striking in its symbolism": Harlan, after all, was named for his anti-segregationist grandfather, who cast the lone dissenting vote in the *Plessy* decision of 1896.[88] According to Nichols, Ike also proceeded to pack the southern circuits of the federal judiciary system with anti-segregationist judges.[89]

With congressional leaders like LBJ, Ike pushed through the first civil rights bill to clear the opposition in Congress since the days of Reconstruction. The Civil Rights Act of 1957, which created a Civil Rights Commission and a civil rights division in the Justice Department, was (and is) rather easy to deride when compared to the epochal civil rights laws of the 1960s. But at least it was a major step forward: Truman, after all, had failed completely in his quest for civil rights legislation in the 1940s.

In all, the Eisenhower record was appalling to conservative Republicans. In 1957, Barry Goldwater openly broke with his party's presidential leader, scolding Ike for his "tax and tax, spend and spend" behavior, which was quite in tune with the "siren song of socialism."[90] Eisenhower was furious. All through his presidency he made entries in his diary as follows: "I think that far from appeasing or reasoning with the dyed-in-the-wool reactionary fringe, we should completely ignore it and when necessary repudiate it. . . . They are the most ignorant people now living in the United States."[91]

Ike's press secretary, James Hagerty, recorded a statement Ike made to him in private well before the Goldwater breach: "If the right wing wants a fight, they're going to get it. If they want to leave the Republican Party and form a third party, that's their business, but before I end up, either this Republican Party will reflect progressivism or I won't be there with them anymore."[92] With his chief of staff Sherman Adams, he occasionally mused that he might have to leave the Republican Party and organize a third-party movement himself.[93]

But there were very few hints of this in public; Ike retained the mental habits of ice-cold analysis and self-control that poor Theodore Roosevelt had lacked back in 1912 when he bolted the party. Ike stayed with the party, while distressed about its dangerous future.

Greenstein provides us with an elegy for General Eisenhower. After all of the presidential misfits who have haunted the White House beginning in the middle of the 1960s, Eisenhower looks quite remarkable in hindsight: "Vietnam and Watergate brought Lyndon Johnson and Richard

Nixon to grief. . . . Gerald Ford, Jimmy Carter, and George Bush [Bush the elder, of course] were defeated by the voters. The presidency of Bill Clinton was bedeviled by Clinton's failure to endear himself with much of the public. Even the two-term presidency of Ronald Reagan experienced notable dips of support. [But] from January 1953 to January 1961 . . . the United States did have a uniquely popular president" whose "record in winning and holding public support" was based in his "ability to bridge contradictions."[94]

The middle way of Ike was a short-term success and a long-term achievement of the highest political magnitude: it took the legacy of Lincoln and the Roosevelts further than ever. Our American system had a master manager in charge when we urgently needed one.

KENNEDY

The legacy of Lincoln and the Roosevelts continued in the leadership of John F. Kennedy and broadened in his "New Frontier." The *programmatic* themes for American development were strong in the 1960s. In addition, however, there existed in the "Kennedy style" some distinctive dimensions of *personal* leadership that drew upon the legacies of Lincoln, TR, and FDR in a manner that deserves special comment.

Far more than with Truman or Ike, it was thrust upon Kennedy to deal with the unfinished business of Lincoln's America: the issue of black civil rights. The Civil War centennial began a few months after JFK's inauguration. And the powerful insurgency of civil rights leaders at the grassroots level made Americans confront the sort of issues that Lincoln would have faced if he had lived. Both Lincoln and JFK were denounced in their times by impatient or militant reformers (and by like-minded critics down the years) for being "moderate"—in the tepid sense of that term—or even weak on the issues of the day. But the case can be made that they worked in a kind of synergistic partnership with militants. Both of them extended their political base by degrees until their instincts told them that the timing was right for bold action.

The comparison with Theodore Roosevelt is also instructive: Kennedy's charisma was heavily based in the spirit of youthful adventure. TR and JFK had been war heroes; TR had his moment of destiny at San Juan Hill and JFK achieved renown as the hero of PT-109 in the South Pacific. TR led the "strenuous life," as an explorer—out West, on safari, up the Amazon. JFK sought to win the new "space race" by fast-tracking Project

Apollo. TR was a family man, and the nation was charmed by the antics of his captivating children. JFK's little children had a similar appeal.

As husbands, of course, they were very far apart, as we know: TR exemplified fidelity (after the death of his first wife, Alice, he had vowed for a time that he would never even *think* about another woman again), whereas the ribald sex life of Kennedy (unknown at the time beyond extremely narrow circles) came straight from the world of Hugh Hefner and Ian Fleming.

Among the "might-have-beens" concerning Kennedy is the possibility of scandal. Given his compulsive philandering (a matter of arrested development, perhaps, or more probably a morbid addiction with deep psychological roots that were inflamed by prescribed medications, including testosterone) and precarious health (largely kept from the public), it is possible to speculate that JFK by the 1970s might have served as an object of widespread derision, or pity, or both, if he escaped assassination. Perhaps Jackie would have finally divorced him.

It is equally possible to speculate that nothing of the kind would have happened. LBJ's "credibility gap" launched an age of self-righteous investigative journalism that Watergate brought to fruition. The mastery of JFK with the press might have held off scandal to the end. And his youthful appeal might have done a great deal to preempt the emergence of the counterculture, a transvaluation of values whose effects upon American history (both good and demonstrably bad) are truly incalculable.

The JFK who gave the Peace Corps to youthful idealists was holding off a strong countertendency of youthful alienation. This was part of a cyclical undertow, as noted before: the tendency of most heroic ages to succumb to a backlash.

The heroism of the World War II generation was already under challenge in the 1950s. By the early 1960s, books such as Paul Goodman's *Growing Up Absurd* (1960) and Joseph Heller's *Catch-22* (1961) were creating, with a multitude of similar books, the "generation gap" of the 1960s.[95] A crucial part of Kennedy's achievement was to make "the heroic," as such, quite *attractive* again to many consequential members of the cultural elite—whose views are often influential with the young. The heroism of the Peace Corps volunteers—and of the first astronauts—was related to the Kennedy magic. In addition, of course, there was a *visceral* appeal to the young in the charisma of JFK: he had the charm of a hipster, combined with the physical appeal of James Dean and the stars of rock 'n' roll. He never lived to encounter the Beatles or the new Ford Mustang—but both would have surely made him smile.

Notwithstanding, he remained a young man of the Depression and World War II: a man from the age of FDR. It was a very clever twist in his inaugural address when he said that the torch had been passed to a new generation of Americans, for he surely had a foot in both camps, "generationally" speaking. Not only were his policies derived from the domestic and global legacies of Franklin Roosevelt, but his personal demeanor was also shaped by the FDR persona. The "Kennedy wit"—so successfully displayed in the press conferences that millions of Americans savored on a regular basis *as television entertainment* by 1962—owed much to the seductive manner that FDR had displayed in his dealings with the press. JFK had come of age in the 1930s. It is more than likely that he picked up the FDR "body English" from the *March of Time* at the cinema. Videotapes make it easy enough to compare the droll tactics that were used by FDR and then adapted by JFK.

As for conservative-liberal convergence, the work of FDR and his successors was essential to the New Frontier. Both the "ADA liberalism" of Truman and the "middle way" of Eisenhower were extended by Kennedy, who made Arthur Schlesinger Jr.—Mr. "Vital Center" himself—a presidential adviser. The perennial issues of left and right were finessed in an even-handed manner in the Kennedy years. On the labor-management front, for example, the Kennedy team held business and labor accountable in equal degrees: corrupt union officials like Jimmy Hoffa and the price-gouging leaders of U.S. Steel were regarded alike as public enemies.

Bipartisan politics continued in a number of ways. An example was Kennedy's treasury secretary, C. Douglas Dillon, a lifelong Republican whose father had founded the Wall Street firm of Dillon, Read and Company. Dillon had served in the Eisenhower administration in several capacities. When he signed on as Kennedy's treasury secretary, he asked to bring in an economic adviser, and Kennedy agreed. Dillon's choice was a Keynesian: Seymour Harris.[96]

The broad continuities of Cold War policymaking were also retained. In military matters, the mobilization that began in the Truman years was resumed under JFK: the New Look of Ike was thrust aside. As early as March 1961, the defense budget was increased. The fleet of Polaris submarines would be gradually expanded from six to twenty-nine; the number of nuclear missiles that they carried would expand from 96 to 494. Land-based nuclear missiles were increased from three hundred to six hundred.[97]

Part of this development was Cold War psychology and part of it was simply smart politics. Even after Sputnik and the allegation of a (nonexistent) "missile gap" gave the Democrats something of an edge in the politics of "keeping up with the Russians," liberals were on the defensive. JFK had been a war hero, true, but there was all the difference in the world between the record of Kennedy in World War II and the stature of Ike, the commander at D-Day, who had the sheer *prestige* at the Pentagon to make the New Look possible.

With Kennedy, of course, it was different; it *had* to be different. And the Bay of Pigs fiasco (inherited, of course, from the planning of Eisenhower's CIA director, Allen Dulles) didn't help. So to ward off the possibility—nay, the certainty—of right-wing complaints about liberal weakness in the global war against Communism, JFK made certain that the military might of the United States would be second to none.

But despite the rhetorical clarion calls to ascend the battlements, JFK was as cautious as Ike when it came to most foreign interventions. The last thing he wanted or intended was to "pay any price" or to "bear any burden," as he claimed in his inaugural address. To the contrary, like Eisenhower, he feared thermonuclear war and he distrusted the gung-ho types in the Pentagon, the saber-rattlers like Air Force General Curtis LeMay who sought to carry on the MacArthur tradition to the point of risking nuclear war. JFK sought Eisenhower's advice on a number of occasions—and received it. He sought to tame the unruly brass with a good strong dose of corporate management, just like Ike had done. Eisenhower had recruited Charles ("Engine Charlie") Wilson of General Motors as his secretary of defense; JFK appointed Robert S. McNamara from Ford.

The Bay of Pigs crisis in April 1961 was a salutary lesson. Kennedy decided—against the counsel of advisers such as Arthur Schlesinger Jr. and Chester Bowles (as well as Dean Acheson, whom Kennedy had asked for an opinion)—to give Allen Dulles and his deputy Richard Bissell approval to proceed with their plan for a covert operation to topple Castro. But Kennedy insisted that American military forces should not engage the Communists directly.[98] Bowles predicted that, "if the operation appears to be a failure in its early stages, the pressure on us to scrap our self-imposed restrictions on direct American involvement will be difficult to resist."[99]

This was almost exactly what occurred: when the CIA operatives (Cuban exiles) were thwarted on the Cuban beaches, Dulles and Bissell, along with Chief of Naval Operations Admiral Arleigh Burke, urged Kennedy to use direct force. But Kennedy refused. He was worried that direct intervention in Cuba might prompt Nikita Khrushchev to retaliate in Berlin.

Kennedy later confided to an aide that the CIA and the Joint Chiefs of Staff had seemed "sure I'd give in to them. . . . They couldn't believe that a new President like me wouldn't panic and try to save his own face.

Well, they had me figured all wrong."[100] He told journalist Benjamin Bradlee later that the lesson should be passed along to others: "The first advice
I'm going to give my successor is to watch the generals and to avoid feeling
that just because they were military men their opinions on military matters
were worth a damn."[101] He said the same sort of thing about the CIA, and
Allen Dulles was forced to retire.

Superb military men such as George C. Marshall and Ike were hard
to find in the 1960s. The great exception, in Kennedy's view, was General
Maxwell Taylor, a hero of World War II who had retired in the 1950s
because of his disagreement with the Eisenhower New Look. Taylor (who
wrote a book on the subject in 1959, *The Uncertain Trumpet*) thought the
strategy of Ike was top-heavy with nuclear deterrence and light on conventional war-fighting capabilities. To Kennedy, the Taylor approach provided
flexible options that could help avert nuclear war. Whereas Ike had been
worried that conventional clashes would *lead* to a nuclear conflict, Kennedy
regarded conventional forces as a *buffer* that could *stave off* nuclear conflict.

So he brought Taylor back to active duty and assigned him to conduct
a postmortem on the Bay of Pigs. Just before the Cuban missile crisis, he
appointed Taylor to be chairman of the Joint Chiefs of Staff. Taylor became
a close associate, not only of the president himself but also of his brother,
Attorney General Robert F. Kennedy.

The Bay of Pigs failure emboldened the Soviets in 1961; when Kennedy met with Nikita Khrushchev that year in Vienna, he was shocked by
the latter's aggressiveness. Just like the brass at the Pentagon, it seemed, the
Soviet leader thought Kennedy was weak. And so Khrushchev tried to play
hardball in ways that he would never have attempted with Ike.

As Hamby has written, "during the first year of the Kennedy presidency, U.S.-Soviet relations remained at a low point. Berlin was on the
verge of armed combat. Until the fall of 1962, the Soviet Union engaged
in deliberately terroristic open-air testing of huge nuclear weapons. Nikita
Khrushchev himself seized every opportunity to behave in a boorish, aggressive fashion."[102]

Historian Robert Dallek has argued that "the Berlin crisis as it evolved
during the summer of 1961 was arguably the most dangerous moment for
a nuclear conflict since the onset of the Cold War."[103] The Soviets were
trying to eject American forces from West Berlin, but Kennedy resolved
to stand firm.

Stark fears of a nuclear war became pervasive in 1961. A new craze
for the construction of "fall-out shelters" swept the nation. Throughout
the early 1960s, apocalyptic fears found expression in novels like *Fail-Safe*

and movies like *Dr. Strangelove*. The latter's portrayal of a lunatic Air Force general (obviously patterned on Curtis LeMay) related to a different fantasy of Pentagon power run amok: the novel *Seven Days in May*, which envisioned an attempted coup d'état by a general who seemed to be patterned on Douglas MacArthur. The president portrayed in this novel was struggling to deal with the Soviets while opening the way to détente.

JFK was determined to rein in the military saber-rattlers while taking a very strong stand in the crisis of Berlin. He told the Joint Chiefs of Staff in writing that he viewed them as "more than military men and expected their help in fitting military requirements into the over-all context of any situation, recognizing that the most difficult problem in Government is to combine all assets into a unified, effective pattern."[104] As Dallek has observed, "he wanted no part of a Pentagon plan that saw a ground war with Soviet forces as hopeless and favored a quick resort to nuclear weapons."[105] He would not take a chance with Armageddon.

Kennedy called up reservists for duty in Germany and sent unmistakable signals to Khrushchev: America would not back down. But he also sent intelligent signals to show that he understood the need for some face-saving gestures to facilitate a Soviet compromise.

In a televised speech to the nation on July 25, JFK stated that the policy choice in Berlin was "not merely between resistance and retreat, between atomic holocaust and surrender. . . . We do not intend to abandon our duty to mankind to seek a peaceful solution." Though Americans "cannot and will not permit the Communists to drive us out of Berlin, either gradually or by force," he continued, the West deserved "a wider choice than humiliation or all-out nuclear action."[106] Khrushchev slowly backed down—and the face-saving gesture he selected to cover the retreat was the erection of the new Berlin Wall.

The next superpower confrontation and nuclear scare was the Cuban missile crisis of October 1962. Kennedy's critics have complained that JFK was reckless in the course of this crisis. But as Hamby has argued, he was careful: he asked advisers to present him with a wide range of options in a manner that compares with the "Solarium exercise" of Eisenhower—but in this case with imminent danger. Moreover, he selected the least provocative actions from those that were offered, as Hamby has observed:

> It seems especially odd that he [JFK] has been criticized for impulsiveness when he sought the advice of an "executive committee" composed of most of the major foreign policy authorities of the United States or that he has been accused of playing out irrational machismo impulses

when he accepted the most pacific alternatives seriously offered to him. Faced with an act of appalling recklessness, he responded with balance and flexibility. He rejected the advice not only of military leaders but of no less a Democratic eminence than Dean Acheson, and he chose to blockade Cuba rather than unleash bombers and an attack force.[107]

In the long deliberations that accompanied the crisis, the notions of some Pentagon chiefs drew the ire of Kennedy again. When the president asked the Joint Chiefs to consider what the Soviet response to an invasion of Cuba might be, LeMay categorically stated that the Soviets would not respond at all. When the brass had departed, the president turned to aide Kenneth O'Donnell and said, "Can you imagine LeMay saying a thing like that? These brass hats have one great advantage in their favor. If we listen to them, and do what they want us to do, none of us will be alive later to tell them that they were wrong."[108]

Again, the Soviets backed down. In the following year an opportunity arose for the negotiation of a pact that had been sought since the Eisenhower days: the Nuclear Test-Ban Treaty of 1963.

On the basis of Kennedy's performance with Khrushchev, it can truly be said that he continued Ike's program of peace and prosperity—but in conditions that were vastly more dangerous. The international basis for American power flowed directly from the national power base of economic might, as it had since the 1940s. And on the economic front, the conundrum of balancing growth with control of inflation was addressed through a forthright embrace of the Keynesian method, or the "New Economics," as its advocates had started to call it. (The term was introduced by economist Seymour Harris, who coined it as the title of a 1947 anthology.)[109]

Kennedy selected the Keynesian economist Paul Samuelson to chair an economic task force after the election of 1960. He named three Keynesian professors of economics to serve on the Council of Economic Advisers: Walter W. Heller, James Tobin, and Kermit Gordon. With Heller, who served as the chairman, the president developed a policy of "wage-and-price guideposts." These were guidelines that he and his cabinet could use for direct negotiations with the leaders of business and labor. While the guideposts were legally (and nominally) voluntary, it was clear that they betokened a "hands-on" economic policy: the goals of full employment and stability of prices were not to be left to the caprices of the market, or to chance. John Kenneth Galbraith—a supporter of the policy—saw its early results as quite impressive: "In the Kennedy and early Johnson years the total output of the economy expanded at a steady rate. The resulting employment increased more rapidly than the labor force; in consequence, unemployment went steadily down. And by modest direct effort prices were held stable. This was the New Economics."[110]

It was also the context for Kennedy's war with "Big Steel." Labor Secretary Arthur Goldberg had worked out deals with the steelworkers in accord with the wage-price guideposts. Early in the spring of 1962, however, U.S. Steel—the industry leader—led an industry revolt with a price hike. An angry Kennedy condemned this move as unwarranted and in defiance of the public interest. Anti-trust action was threatened. U.S. Steel backed down, and inflation was averted.

With inflation averted, the economic boom could proceed. To stimulate growth—another recession had started in 1960, and Kennedy had pledged to get the country "moving again"—the president proposed a large tax cut. To avert the loss of federal revenue, judicious deficit spending would be used. The New Economics (both in premises and in results) prevailed so successfully during these years that Edwin L. Dale Jr., an economic writer, could report by the middle of the 1960s that "the big majority of economists, and a growing number of businessmen, bankers, and labor leaders, believe that the recent deficits in the Federal Budget have been good, not bad, for America."[111]

Another source of economic stimulation was Project Apollo. Kennedy's pledge to put a man on the moon by the end of the decade was more than just a method for competing with the Soviets and capturing the imagination of the world. Though hardly a traditional public works program, it would serve as an economic *stimulator* in a way that was comparable to the Interstate Highway System. Kennedy and Lyndon Johnson—whom the president tapped to chair the new National Space Council—knew what they were doing, both politically and economically. As Dallek observes, "space spending would also provide jobs, and the political gains in the South and West, where NASA would primarily spend its funds, were not lost on savvy politicians like Kennedy and Johnson."[112] Johnson answered the administration's critics with a strong rhetorical question: "Would you rather have us be a second-rate nation or should we spend a little money?"[113] The projected cost of Project Apollo was somewhere in the neighborhood of $40 billion.

Kennedy and Congress invested directly in programs to upgrade the skills of Americans. Federal aid to education was expanded during 1963 through a series of laws (such as the Higher Education Facilities Act) that paved the way for the epochal legislation of 1965.

Kennedy also took the very first steps toward a "war on poverty." "Structural unemployment" was perceived to be the primary problem. As early as the 1950s, Senator Paul Douglas of Illinois had proposed legislation that would offer assistance to "depressed areas" like Appalachia, where unemployment exceeded the national average. Additional concerns about workers who were thrown out of jobs by "automation" prompted Congress to pass a rather limited measure in 1960 that Eisenhower vetoed.

But in the very same year the crucial West Virginia primary brought JFK into a state that was suffering from massive poverty. Kennedy observed such squalor there that he made up his mind to support "the Douglas bill" in some form. The Area Redevelopment Act (ARA) of 1961 provided funds (both grants and loans) to "depressed" communities to help them attract new industries and retrain displaced workers.[114]

Friendly critics, however, complained that the program was inefficiently structured. Keynesian economists pushed for much stronger measures. Led by Senator Joseph A. Clark Jr. of Pennsylvania, these advocates pushed through Congress the Accelerated Public Works Act of 1962, which delivered more funds for community-level public works through a streamlined approval procedure. In addition, the president introduced a measure that resulted in the Manpower Development and Training Act (MDTA) in 1962. The act authorized $700 million over four years for the purpose of retraining eight-hundred thousand workers. The program was run by the Department of Labor.

Congress extended the life of the program in 1963 at JFK's behest and added new and special features that would target black unemployment. In the same year Kennedy sponsored a White House conference that resulted in the creation of the President's Appalachian Regional Commission. So the "War on Poverty" was launched in the Kennedy years—not the Johnson years.

So was Medicare. JFK proposed the measure in 1962, thus reviving (if only in part) a reform from which FDR had backed away in the 1930s. Truman failed completely in his bid to get comprehensive health care insurance for Americans; Kennedy limited his measure to assistance for the elderly. Once again, however, allegations of "socialized medicine" proved too strong to overcome and the measure seemed hopelessly stalled in Congress.

One extremely important measure cleared Congress in 1963: the Clean Air Act, which provided more funding along with new authority to generate standards to measure emissions.

But the greatest domestic challenge for Kennedy, of course, was civil rights. At first, he continued the policy of Eisenhower: he sent federal marshals and troops though without the overwhelming force that Ike had used at Little Rock. But Kennedy faced a different problem from anything that Eisenhower faced. The Democratic Party was profoundly divided; its southern wing epitomized a white supremacy tradition that the party embraced—indeed, championed—from the days of Andrew Jackson through the days of Woodrow Wilson. That changed during FDR's time.

From the 1930s onward, the division in the party was extreme. The problem was becoming so bad by the 1940s that FDR—under fierce assault by southern racists—began toying with the notion of a postwar party realignment. It bears noting that the "Dixiecrat" revolt of Strom Thurmond launched a different trend of realignment in 1948: a white southern exodus from the party. This began to take hold on a long-term basis with the so-called southern strategy of Nixon at the end of the 1960s. By the Nixon era, the conservative culture of the South began to switch parties. But for JFK, southern Democrats were still a problem.

At first he tried to handle the belligerent racists in the way he handled Khrushchev: with minimal force. But after several years of confronting the crude defiance of governors like George Wallace of Alabama and Ross Barnet of Mississippi—after several years of beholding the repulsive violence unleashed against blacks by Klansmen and white supremacist police—it was clear to Kennedy that tough and uncompromising action would be needed to destroy the ways of Jim Crow.

The result was what historian Carl M. Brauer calls the "second Reconstruction." Brauer relates that the "Ole Miss" crisis set Kennedy "wondering about the validity of his totally negative view of Reconstruction. In the following months he read some of the works of C. Vann Woodward, a prominent southern historian who had much greater concern for the plight of blacks than the historians from whom Kennedy had drawn his first impressions of Reconstruction."[115]

After meeting the family of Medgar Evers just after his murder, JFK told Arthur Schlesinger Jr. that "I don't understand the South. I'm coming to believe that Thaddeus Stevens was right. I had always been taught to regard him as a man of vicious bias. But, when I see this sort of thing, I begin to wonder how else you can treat them."[116]

By 1963—the year of the epochal civil rights march on Washington—Kennedy made his irreversible decision: he proposed the strongest civil rights law in the nation's history. On June 11, he addressed the American people on television:

> The heart of the question is whether . . . we are going to treat our fellow Americans as we want to be treated. If an American, because his skin is dark, cannot eat lunch in a restaurant open to the public, if he cannot send his children to the best public school available, if he cannot vote for the public officials who represent him, if, in short, he cannot enjoy the full and free life which all of us want, then who among us would be content to have the color of his skin changed and stand in his place? Who among us would then be content with the counsels of patience and delay?[117]

He continued with even greater eloquence:

> We are confronted primarily with a moral issue. It is as old as the scriptures and is as clear as the American Constitution. . . . One hundred years of delay have passed since President Lincoln freed the slaves, yet their heirs, their grandsons, are not fully free. . . . Now the time has come for this Nation to fulfill its promise. . . . A great change is at hand and our task, our obligation, is to make that revolution, that change, peaceful and constructive. . . . Next week I shall ask the Congress of the United States to act, to make a commitment it has not fully made in this century to the proposition that race has no place in American life or law.[118]

Kennedy grounded the proposed civil rights legislation in the Fourteenth Amendment, the Fifteenth Amendment, and the interstate commerce clause.

The civil rights bill would face very tough sledding, but Kennedy believed that it would pass in due time—like Medicare. In the fall of 1963 he was enormously popular: he seemed to be a shoo-in for reelection. Perhaps his "coattails" would sweep into office a reformist Congress of the sort that had launched the New Deal. On November 14, 1963, he predicted that his program as a whole would be swept through Congress in eighteen months or less. The expectations were high when it was suddenly over, on November 22.

It takes no misty-eyed sentimentality or cult worship—no "Camelot" mythmaking—to grasp the feelings of the people like Isaiah Berlin, the philosopher and intellectual historian who wrote that with Kennedy's death "the suddenness and the sense of something of exceptional hope cut off in mid-air is, I think, unique in our lifetime—it is as if Roosevelt had been murdered in 1935."[119]

Doomed: The Kennedys arriving in Dallas on November 22, 1963. Credit: John F. Kennedy Presidential Library and Museum.

A second Kennedy term could indeed have been a triumphant one. Political scientist Irving Bernstein has argued that when JFK "predicted on November 14, 1963, that his entire program would be enacted within eighteen months, he was right; if anything, perhaps a bit on the conservative side. He was emerging as a President of great stature when, eight days later, a mindless assassin in Dallas cut his life short."[120] Robert Dallek largely concurs: "If Kennedy had been running against Goldwater in 1964, which is more than likely, he would also [like Lyndon Johnson] have won a big victory and carried large numbers of liberal Democrats into the House and Senate with him. He would then have enjoyed the same success as Johnson in passing the major bills that were on his administration's legislative agenda. . . . The most important of the Great Society measures deserve to be described as Kennedy-Johnson achievements."[121]

But what of Vietnam? Schlesinger claimed that right after the election the war would have dwindled: "Among the revelations of the Pentagon Papers was Kennedy's plan for the complete withdrawal of American advisers from Vietnam by 1965—a plan cancelled by Johnson a few months after Dallas. Kennedy confided to [Senator] Mike Mansfield that his goal was total withdrawal; 'but I can't do it until 1965—after I'm reelected.' Otherwise the Republicans might beat him in 1964 over the 'loss' of Indochina."[122] Dallek is largely in concurrence with this proposition:

> His fears of turning the war into a struggle on the scale of the Korean fighting and of getting trapped in a war that demanded ever more U.S. resources became reasons in 1963 for him to plan reductions of U.S. military personnel. . . . No one can prove, of course, what Kennedy would have done about Vietnam between 1964 and 1968. His actions and statements, however, are suggestive of a carefully managed stand-down. . . . By November 1963, Kennedy had established himself as a strong foreign policy leader. After facing down Khrushchev in the missile crisis . . . Kennedy had much greater credibility as a defender of the national security than Johnson had. It gave Kennedy more freedom to convince people at home and abroad that staying clear of large-scale military intervention in Vietnam was in the best interests of the United States.[123]

In short, he would have stood by the *Eisenhower* policy: averting massive war in Indochina.

One has to remember here the lesson of the Bay of Pigs—the lesson that JFK planned to pass along to his successor, the lesson that a chief executive should always "avoid feeling that just because [generals and admirals] were military men their opinions on military matters were worth a damn." It was a lesson that Lincoln had learned very early in the Civil War.

Schlesinger remembered his presidential hero as "a skeptic and an ironist; he had understood the complexity of things from birth. . . . JFK was urbane, imperturbable, always in control, invulnerable, it seemed, to everything, except the murderer's bullet."[124] Who can say how far he might have gone?

We can certainly say that our history would now be different—completely different—and perhaps vastly better, if he lived. And we should certainly grieve over that.

TRIUMPH AND CATASTROPHE

By 1964, the United States of America stood supreme—the mightiest nation in the world. Prosperous and strong, Americans employed a great nexus of government and business to broaden the basis of prosperity. Pragmatic, Americans embraced the ways of planning to address the nation's various ills. The inevitable (and in some respects productive) tensions of the left and the right had been channeled through a long-evolving synthesis. Some wished to discard the two traditions altogether in light of this achievement.

Republican Senator Jacob Javits deplored the "web of confusion which has entrapped many thoughtful Republicans and Democrats about the meaning of the words 'liberalism' and 'conservatism,'" adding that a "gain in the conduct of political debates" would occur "if we dealt, rather than by such designations, with concrete proposals," asking questions such as the following: "Will the specific terms of this concrete proposal enlarge the areas of freedom and opportunity for the individual while serving the common good? Given the aim of this concrete proposal is it beyond the reach of private resources, and, therefore, must it be made a governmental matter? If a governmental matter, is it beyond the reach of local and state resources, and must it, therefore, be entrusted to the central government?"[125]

Lincoln's way had triumphed, for a time: the foremost government-basher on the right, Barry Goldwater, lost on a spectacular scale in the election of 1964. The primary free marketeer in economic circles, Milton Friedman, was regarded by many as a crank in the early 1960s. Had he not, after all, talked of selling off the national parks, suggesting in 1962 that if "the public wants this kind of activity enough to pay for it," then "private enterprises will have every incentive to provide such parks"?[126]

By and large, Americans scoffed at such fanciful views. By an overwhelming majority they supported Lyndon Johnson's "Great Society," which put the conservative welfare state, now effectively in liberal hands after many years of transformation, at the summit of policymaking and politics.

And this was "as good as it got." Lyndon Johnson and Richard Nixon—back-to-back failures—unleashed a tremendous series of mistakes from which the legacy of Lincoln could not recover. By 1976, the American people were increasingly demoralized. Another age of government-bashing had begun. The economy was troubled. Conservative-liberal enmity was consuming American politics. All told, the American people were losing the statecraft they needed to maintain their nation's supremacy.

A brief triumph preceded the storm. JFK's civil rights bill became the great Civil Rights Act of 1964. Then LBJ and the 89th Congress did the rest: the Urban Mass Transportation Act of 1964, the Voting Rights Act of 1965, Medicare, the Housing and Urban Development Act of 1965, the Elementary and Secondary Education Act of 1965, the Higher Education Act of 1965, the National Historic Preservation Act of 1966, and the creation of the National Endowment for the Arts and the National Endowment for the Humanities. New cabinet-level departments were created as well: HUD (the Department of Housing and Urban Development) and DOT (the Department of Transportation). And of course, there was the War on Poverty, launched on a comprehensive basis in the Economic Opportunity Act of 1964.

The latter was quite controversial, and so it remains. To some extent, a fair assessment cannot be rendered: funding was quickly interrupted by the exigencies of Vietnam. A welter of initiatives coordinated by Sargent Shriver (a JFK holdover in the Johnson years), the poverty war was developed through divergent programs such as Head Start, the Job Corps ("top-down," as it were, in special training camps), the Community Action program ("bottom-up," through local initiatives), and new institutional entities like the Office of Economic Opportunity (OEO).

Much of it was quite experimental. Much of it was confused by the public with "welfare": the old New Deal arrangement through which, pursuant to the Social Security Act, the federal government, joined by the states, provided aid for "families with dependent children" (AFDC).

Some programs derived from the poverty war would prove valuable over the years, though in limited ways, due to limitations of funding. A 1980s study of the Job Corps, for instance, found the program succeeded so well in turning unemployed youth into taxpayers that the Corps returned roughly a dollar and a half for every federal dollar that it spent.[127]

Some conservative critics complained that the poverty war was a result of utopian premises. Political scientist Edward C. Banfield drew attention to folkways existing in a number of subcultures that result, at times, in perverse and self-defeating patterns that can stultify development: in other words, he identified the issue of the underclass and its "attitude."[128] He was heatedly denounced by liberals.

The case can be made that he had a fair point, though he overgeneralized his argument, badly at times. The theme has resounded down the years outside of the orthodox ideological channels: it was repeated years later, for example, by the activist and entertainer Bill Cosby in a manner that trig-gered a serious national discussion.

Regardless, it would still have been interesting to see what inroads might have been achieved within the culture of the so-called underclass by a massively funded Job Corps. But no, it was not to be: LBJ's Gulf of Tonkin ploy, which was followed by the major escalation of the Vietnam War, drew resources steadily away from the war on poverty.

Vietnam, of course, was a supreme disaster—a spectacular case of wishful thinking gone wrong. And the failure would plague our nation for the rest of the twentieth century. The military history will doubtless be re-vised and rewritten many times: there are people, for example, who argue that the war might still have been won if the United States had "stayed the course" after "mid-course corrections." Lewis Sorley has written that the early misjudgments of General William Westmoreland were being overcome by the 1970s; the new strategies of General Creighton Abrams spelled doom for the Communist enemy due to Abrams's better grasp of the challenge.[129]

The conventional view was solidified by 1968: the view of people like Senators J. William Fulbright, Wayne Morse, Eugene McCarthy, and Robert F. Kennedy, who called the war the "wrong war in the wrong place at the wrong time." It was a war, they believed, in which hit-and-run enemies could hold off conventional troops and Special Forces almost indefinitely. It was a war with no front, a quagmire—with little in the way of importance to justify a vast outpouring of American lives and treasure. Indeed, there were military men—Generals James S. Gavin and Matthew Ridgway—who argued for de-escalation. It should also be noted that for-mer president Eisenhower (though reluctant to embarrass his successors) took a very dim view of the military prospects in Indochina.

Maxwell Taylor, however, whom Johnson had tapped to be ambassa-dor to South Vietnam, took a harder, pro-escalation line. Defense Secretary Robert S. McNamara joined in the optimistic thinking and his later am-bivalence was muted. His associate Townsend Hoopes recalled the situation a few years later: "Accurately regarded by the press as the one moderate member of the inner circle, [McNamara] continued to give full public sup-port to the administration's policy, including specific endorsement of suc-cessive manpower infusions and progressively wider and heavier bombing efforts. Inside the Pentagon he seemed to discourage dissent among his staff by the simple tactic of being unreceptive to it."[130]

It seemed as if the shrewdest advisers whom JFK had brought aboard—the people whom David Halberstam would shortly call the "best and the brightest," in scorn—were losing their instinct for worst-case contingency analysis (when it came to the military *options*, at least) with LBJ in command.[131] The only worst-case scenarios they seemed to consider were (1) the loss of prestige that they feared if they were held to be guilty of "losing" Vietnam, and (2) the projection of a worst-case "domino" effect as a result of a Communist victory.

The Tet offensive was shocking in 1968: it was painfully obvious to LBJ that he was deeply "in over his head." With assistance from Clark Clifford, who replaced Robert McNamara, he backed away from escalation.[132] He announced that he was willing to negotiate. Then he abdicated: he declined to run for reelection.

The blame for the mess was hardly LBJ's alone; he was badly advised in the earliest stages of the war. But even in the face of bad advice—very bad advice—a shrewd leader like Kennedy or Ike would have probably stopped before the brink. They would have scrutinized a broad range of options. Not LBJ—as with Woodrow Wilson so many years before, there was no "Plan B" as he began.

He seemed to feel until the very last year (1968) that there was really no choice for him to make—the issues were clear, and there was no need to reexamine premises. As Hamby has observed,

> His relevant experience, like that of other men of his generation, came from Munich and from the failure of Western nerve in the 1930s. It resulted in the still widely held assumption that tolerance of any aggression anywhere represented a grave danger to all peoples everywhere. . . . Johnson remembered vividly the way in which the Truman administration had been crippled for its alleged softness on Communism, and especially for the loss of China. McCarthyism had been the ultimate weapon against Truman's Fair Deal. Any losses in the Cold War, any signs of softness might wound the Great Society.[133]

There was no declaration of war in this case: the optimists believed that the fighting would be over quickly. There was no imposition of wage-and-price controls as there had been during World War II and Korea. There was no cultivation of opinion, no attempt to build a consensus, or to sound out the range of opposition. As Dallek observes, Lyndon Johnson was largely in a state of denial as the war went badly: "Intent on proving his critics wrong, especially Robert Kennedy, whose emergence as a political opponent revolved around differences over Vietnam, Johnson refused to acknowledge that he had led the country into a stalemate, which would require large additional commitments to break."[134]

The cost of the miscalculations—the misjudgments—was vast. In the first place, the war on poverty diminished, and its critics have been pointing to its so-called failure ever since. Race relations worsened. After black civil rights had been secured, the momentum shifted to the economic front, where Johnson failed to deliver, and the fact was duly noted and protested. Pent-up rage spilled over into summertime riots in the black urban "ghettoes."

Something else was occurring, however—a cultural catharsis after years of frustration on the part of so many black Americans. Success with civil rights blew the lid off. Hamby suggests that the new black militancy was "more than a protest against such relatively tangible matters as poverty and discrimination. . . . It was also an expression of alienation," in a new generational form: youthful militants were eager to distance themselves from the world of their dignified parents—their "Uncle Tom" parents.[135] If Kennedy had lived, he would surely have confronted this development. His younger brother Robert had a flair for reaching out to troubled youth. In any case, Johnson was dumbfounded—completely unprepared—stunned.

As all of this was happening, the economic trends were going haywire too. Galbraith elaborates: "Beginning in 1966, there were large increases in spending for the Vietnam War. To the natural reluctance to increase taxes there was added the greater reluctance to increase them for an unpopular war. Not until 1968 was a surtax for war spending finally voted. . . . At the same time, the moral authority of the government, which had now to recruit support for a widely rejected war, had been sadly weakened. So, as the need for the [wage-price] guideposts increased, their effectiveness diminished. . . . Soon the restraints both on prices and wages were dead."[136] The problem would be passed along to Nixon, to Ford, and to Carter.

The country was becoming extraordinarily polarized. Opposition to the war took a number of forms, and it is vital to keep them distinct. Some disputed the wisdom of the war, in the manner of J. William Fulbright. Others called the war immoral. Pacifist opinion merged with broader cross-currents to initiate the counterculture of the 1960s. Before very long the world of hippies, communes, and psychedelia spread across the land. Strange Greenwich Village apparitions spread a "new age" spirituality.

Perhaps it had resulted from the long-building fears of Armageddon: rock singers warned that the "Masters of War" were in control of the world (Bob Dylan), that the "Eve of Destruction" was at hand (Barry McGuire), unless the "Age of Aquarius" (Fifth Dimension) dawned. There were long-ago precedents for this sort of thing in European history. Fourteenth-century doomsday cults like the Brethren of the Free Spirit reacted to the imminent "end of the world"—which seemed to be at hand with the arrival of the Black Death—through mystical forms of disorder. The pattern was repeated in the 1960s, to the consternation of millions of parents, whose teenage kids had "dropped out" to experience "acid."

Worse was on the way, much worse. The New Left, emergent in the 1950s, saw its chance to get even with the liberals. As the Cold War liberals had taunted the radical left—they said that the radicals were guilty of covering for Joseph Stalin and his crimes—radicals could now hit back by asserting that the Cold War liberals had blood on their hands in the 1960s, the blood of Vietnam. Leaders of the Marxist Students for a Democratic Society charged that the war was "imperialism," even "genocide." New Left historians emerged with like-minded allegations. Gabriel Kolko, for instance, wrote in 1969 that "a coercive elite, quite willing to undermine democracy at home as well as abroad, will rule the society, even in the name of 'liberalism.'"[137] It seemed to make sense to many students, at least after 1968: radicals claimed that the "establishment" had shown its true colors in Chicago with the violence unleashed against the peaceful protesters at the Democratic convention. Chicago police beat the protesters savagely and Hubert Humphrey, the liberal candidate, was viewed by many people as complicit or in some respect tainted. New Left Marxists kept repeating the charge: the liberals had blood on their hands.

The New Left leaders chanted "Power to the People" as police fired volleys of tear gas into college campuses. The Weathermen and the Yippies called law enforcement officers "the pigs."[138] Fathers who had fought against Hitler in the Second World War were informed by their sons that they were "pigs." It was against this background that Richard M. Nixon took the oath of office in 1969.

LBJ blew it, but Nixon was a national disaster; others had been thrown out of office in disgrace, but Richard Nixon was the first to leave the presidency through resignation. A bully, he thrived on the politics of anger. He wanted "payback" for many years of personal slights, both real and imagined. He turned the White House into a fortress within which he scrawled down his pitiful "enemies list" and recruited a shady cast of moonstruck characters to carry out "dirty tricks" assignments. At his bidding, Vice President Spiro Agnew directed his alliterative scorn against "nattering nabobs of negativism" and "effete, impudent snobs"—what he called the "radical liberals."

The attacks were a cover for a long, slow retreat in Vietnam: "Vietnamization." In all probability, JFK could have done it in a clever and nearly painless manner; Nixon made it agony, slow and protracted. To buy time for the phase-out, he escalated bombings and extended American raids into nearby Laos and Cambodia. The internal divisions of America were worse than at any other time in living memory.

The most outrageous thing of all was that Nixon was not unintelligent. He listened to the counsel of advisers such as Henry Kissinger, the master of global *Realpolitik*, as well as Daniel Patrick Moynihan, a "neo-con" who regaled him in private with the legacy of Tory reform in Great Britain. Moynihan and other neo-conservatives like Irving Kristol and Norman Podhoretz were mostly ex-liberals who still retained enough of the left-of-center perspective to offer yet another rendition of American centrist politics. Nixon listened: he was something of a Keynesian in economic matters, and his record in the field of environmental protection became profound.

He supported the establishment of EPA, the Environmental Protection Agency, in 1970, and tapped an ardent conservationist, Russell Train, to chair a Council on Environmental Quality. He told Congress his environmental program would be "the most comprehensive and costly program in this field in America's history."[139] He signed the Water Quality Improvement Act in 1970, along with new amendments to the Clean Air Act that gave EPA enforcement authority. He supported the creation of the Occupational Safety and Health Administration (OSHA). In 1971, he went along with the federalization (through creation of a quasi-public corporation, Amtrak) of intercity passenger railroad service when private sector companies abandoned it.

He proposed to wage a "war on cancer" to the tune of $100 million. He supported universal health care insurance for Americans, proposing "a program to insure that no American family will be prevented from obtaining basic medical care by inability to pay."[140] His solution to the poverty issue, though simplistic, was interesting indeed by the standards of conservative culture: his Family Assistance Plan, with its "guaranteed annual income," would have given cash stipends to the poor. It would have amounted to a massive extension of welfare if Congress had passed it.

If Nixon had simply been a better and wiser human being, he could have launched a great revival in American conservative culture: a revival of Tory reform. The Goldwater fringe in the Republican Party was not at all pleased by his work as a nominal conservative. His national security policies—ugly and harsh as they became—made him largely immune to the themes of libertarian thinking. A conservative in the old-fashioned sense—a sense that predated the shift to Social Darwinist laissez-faire—he epitomized counterrevolutionary governance. He was willing to mobilize the power of the state to protect the status quo from upheaval. He lionized J. Edgar Hoover right down to the old man's death.

In truth, he was highly ambivalent regarding the nature and purpose of conservative political culture as it stood in the 1960s. On the economic front, for example, he overruled advisers such as Paul McCracken who touted free-market values (Herbert Stein, who succeeded McCracken, was far more flexible and open-minded). Nixon boldly instituted wage and price controls during 1971 and then continued them in 1972. A nationalist, he destroyed the "Bretton Woods" system by refusing any further exportation of gold to cover balance of payments deficits. A fervent anti-Communist, he sought a calm and rational rapprochement with the successors of Nikita Khrushchev. He opened the door to Red China. Though clumsy at home, he was able, and at times almost gifted, as an international diplomat: a practitioner of great power politics. The Nixon era was a weird and conflicted interlude in many respects.

One very odd result of the Nixon-era polarization took place in the Jim Crow South. Though Nixon used a crass form of southern strategy to edge out the Democrats there—it began with some truly obnoxious nominations of ex-segregationist judges to the Supreme Court (the Haynsworth and Carswell nominations, both of which failed)—the "second Reconstruction" took hold in these years, and the Jim Crow South began to fade. There were several reasons, and they coalesced quickly by the 1970s.

In the first place, the Voting Rights Act proved effective, and blacks were empowered at the polls. In the second place, Nixon pushed school desegregation with financial incentives to the South (while opposing the ploy of "forced busing"). But there were other strange forces at work—cultural forces—in the southern shift away from Jim Crow.

Alabama's George Wallace made a bid for the White House in 1968 with a flimsy new political party (the American Party) that was hastily contrived. His running mate was Curtis LeMay. He barnstormed the North with complaints about the long-haired hippies who were ruining America. (Ironically, the long-haired look became a craze before long among the country singers in Nashville.) Of course, Wallace was a "hawk" on Vietnam. The South, with its age-old military lore, had for years been strongly interventionist. Southern interventionists, for instance, had helped FDR in the Lend-Lease days to overcome the Midwestern isolationists.

The point here was this: southern "good old boys" who had waved the Confederate flag in the Kennedy years were now waving the *Stars and Stripes* on behalf of the "establishment." They could occupy the patriotic high ground at last: they could vilify the war resisters, feeling good about themselves as they did so. In short, they were rebels no more.

Psychology offers up a powerful clue—or at least it presents us with a theory to account for the long-term success of the second Reconstruction. In the ten years that passed between 1965 and 1975, the white South enjoyed a "breathing spell" in which to get its racial politics reformed—*quietly* reformed. *Vietnam and the inner city riots were distracting the nation; attention moved away from the South.* So the South was allowed to save face. Southern whites were no longer being placed on the spot, where they had previously felt the need to dig in their heels and thus prove a point of regional honor. The angriest of them could now vent their wrath upon the hippies; the rest could relax. At the end of the process, a southern white man—Jimmy Carter—was the president to chase the post-Watergate goblins away, and even Wallace began to admit that the civil rights movement was a blessing both to whites and to blacks. A long historical curse had been lifted.

Conservative culture was clearly in flux, and some remarkable changes could have happened with a different kind of leader in the presidency. The culture of the liberals was also in flux—very much so.

The McGovern campaign against Nixon used a noninterventionist slogan in 1972: "Come Home, America." As rhetoric it clearly fell short of extreme isolationist rant, but it was still a very clear, even stark, repudiation of the Cold War ethos of Truman, Kennedy, and Johnson. A noninterventionist preference appeared to be the new proof of liberal credentials in America. It would haunt the Democratic Party and stultify its candidates for many years.

The McGovernites were anxious to repudiate the ham-fisted characters who made the last party convention such a horror. They sought to prove themselves "clean" of any lingering "complicity" with Cold War "elitist repression." The New Left was very much at work here. The moral compass of the liberal mind began to swing. Truman-era liberals were tough when it came to human nature: they were largely immune to the fraud of aggressors who claimed to represent the downtrodden. This was soon about to change in the 1970s.

Whereas Cold War liberals were anxious in the 1940s to dissociate themselves from any lingering sympathy with Communism, the antiwar liberals were anxious to discard any lingering associations with *anti-Communism*—in any and all of its forms. They began to take some cues from the radicals. They sought to prove that they were equally "sensitive"—equally "responsive" to the needs of the powerless—and not "complicit" with the culture of "repression" that caused Vietnam. To *re-deem* the great liberal tradition and prove that it was *innocent and clean*—not *elitist*—was the goal of the McGovern-era liberals. The culture of left-wing "political correctness" was not far away.[141]

The Marxist New Left had been a libertarian movement—anarchistic, in reaction to the Stalinist police state system. The Goldwater right (now increasingly championed by up-and-coming figures like Ronald Reagan) was a different kind of libertarian movement. Both the left and the right were thus poised on the eve of the Watergate crisis to exploit what they sensed to be the imminent fall of Dick Nixon—the "imperial president"—and to use the momentum for the purpose of smashing "bureaucracy."

The Watergate scandal was an odious affair that revealed Richard Nixon at his very worst—demented and out of control. It was nothing less than presidential crime, or presidential complicity with palpable crime: burglary, obstruction of justice, perjury, and abuse of power. Vietnam and Watergate were hammer blows that crippled American pride in the 1970s. More hammer blows were soon on the way.

Revulsion at Nixon's abuse of power made the liberal embrace of libertarian precepts the mode in the Democratic Party. The tendency was furthered by some new revelations, to the press and to Congress, of abuse and malfeasance by the likes of Allen Dulles and J. Edgar Hoover in earlier years: MK-ULTRA, COINTELPRO, and other furtive horrors from "the Feds." In the minds of many young Americans (and older Americans as well), authority figures were becoming almost delegitimized in the 1970s—stripped of any moral authority. Many Hollywood films in these years (like *The Godfather* and *Chinatown*) showed American officials who were sinister, corrupt, and incompetent. In a climate like this, it was every man for himself.

Neo-populism—not the Populism of the nineteenth century that called for an expansion of the federal government to give some relief to "the people," but rather an ersatz version of the populist mood that embraced a new decentralization ("Power to the People")—put an end to the Democratic epoch that began with FDR and Truman. Gone was the "Vital Center" liberalism of the ADA in the 1940s. At hand was the neo-Jeffersonian simplicity of Carter. Jimmy Carter was an early example of the throwback process that would lead to the "neo-liberal" revolution of the 1980s.

Two convergent trends of the era revealed both the new libertarian allure and its threat to the nation's public interest: the new extremism shown by the National Rifle Association (NRA) on the right and the American Civil Liberties Union (ACLU) on the left.

At first nothing more than an association of sportsmen, the NRA in the 1960s came under the leadership of militant gun libertarians who fought fiercely and adamantly against any and all forms of gun control, and their rhetoric was even more belligerent ("the best defense is a strong offense") in the aftermath of the assassinations of JFK, his brother Robert, and Martin Luther King. Concurrently, the ACLU came under the leadership of zealots who abetted the national movement in the 1960s to deinstitutionalize the mentally ill—to protect their "right" to live in squalor in the parks and on the streets of America.[142] A powerful trend was thus established through the work of these very different zealots: it is now very difficult (impossible, in fact) to keep armed and dangerous lunatics away from our loved ones. Here was an apt libertarian convergence of the left and the right to make our public places as chaotic and dangerous as possible.

The most fateful new surge of libertarian power took place on the right, among conservatives determined to wrest back control of their movement from the temporizers like Nixon. Under the leadership of editors like Jude Wanniski, the *Wall Street Journal* in the 1970s began a campaign to restore the economic life of America to 1920s conditions. Wealthy donors founded laissez-faire study institutes and think tanks, such as the Cato Institute in Washington, to tout free enterprise and ridicule government.[143] And the rise of Milton Friedman, a conservative libertarian economist (a student years earlier of Henry Simons, but a simple-minded acolyte at best), launched a counterrevolution in the world of economics that would topple the influence of Keynes.

As journalist William Greider has written, the rise of Friedman was a sign of the times—a symptom of ideological flux, of the sea change in cultural attitudes: "Milton Friedman might have remained obscure and lonely, an eccentric thinker living in the wrong age. Instead, he won the Nobel Prize for economics in 1976. He became, if not a celebrity, at least widely celebrated as a prophet."[144] He was one among a multitude of prophets in the election year 1976.

Let us pause for a moment to consider the zeitgeist of the 1970s: the American people had been living through a nightmare in the years after Kennedy's death. The assassinations, the shock of the inner city riots, the failed war in Asia with its shame to the national honor, the division among the generations, the disgrace of the Watergate scandal, the bewildering shifts in American culture, the grieving and the horror—all this wrought havoc with much of the electorate. But a new flock of libertarian healers offered an old elixir—maximum liberty—on the eve of the nation's bicentennial. The elixir was offered up and taken as the deeds of Patrick Henry were remembered. The spirit of 1776 would be summoned back to help heal America. As a notion, it sounded so appropriate. So . . . fitting in the aftermath of Nixon.

The prescription was offered up and taken. And the American people drank deep. They awakened soon enough to the disquieting age of Jimmy Carter and a new world of troubles. It was "downhill" from there—in the age of Ronald Reagan, Bill Clinton, and other false prophets. The legacy of Lincoln unraveled with terrible speed.

6

THE LEGACY IN RUINS: FROM CARTER TO GEORGE W. BUSH

"Things fall apart," wrote William Butler Yeats in the aftermath of World War I, and "the centre cannot hold."[1] Achievements disintegrate; history is strewn with examples of declension. So it came to pass—thirty years after World War II—that Lincoln's way could no longer be sustained.

There was plenty of blame to go around for this loss, but two presidents—Jimmy Carter and Ronald Reagan—should be singled out for special treatment. Different as they were in certain obvious ways, they had a great deal more in common than people might suppose.

CARTER

If Nixon was an ogre, Jimmy Carter would be lovable indeed. He worked hard to create this effect. His singsong voice, sweet smile, and almost deferential manner were perfect for developing the counter-Nixonian theme of civic humility. In his inaugural address he was self-effacing: "your strength can compensate for my weakness," he told the American people, "and your wisdom can help to minimize my mistakes."[2] How much more anti-Nixonian could anyone possibly be? Gerald Ford, the immediate successor to Nixon, was a very pleasant man, but Jimmy Carter was the man of the hour in the next presidential election. He radiated *goodness*.

He had Christian piety as well, and he made this clear: Nixon and his darkness had been routed by sweetness and light. In hindsight, the piety of Carter was relatively harmless compared to the aggressiveness of the evangelicals who bullied their opponents in the 1980s, 1990s, and afterward. But the sweetness and light of Jimmy Carter were not truly wholesome.

Theologians have argued that the very best *attempts* at humility can become rather ostentatious instead—one becomes rather *proud* of one's humility before very long—and the pretension of Carter was a study in manifest irony. Theologian Reinhold Niebuhr once reflected on the problem in general: "If virtue becomes vice through some hidden defect in the virtue . . . the situation is ironic."[3]

Such was the irony of Carter's attempt to achieve (and display) true "born-again" humility. It was *ostentatious*—obviously so to discerning eyes—and it lost its appeal very quickly; Carter seemed weak, indecisive, and befuddled in the bad years that followed.

But he knew what he wanted to do: to get Americans "home again," in the manner of the good George McGovern. He wanted his fellow Americans to walk more humbly, to treat the earth gently, to live in a spirit of harmony, to show goodwill, and to pull themselves back from all forms of overextension. This included government, of course—government in general. "Government cannot solve our problems," said Carter in 1978. "Government cannot . . . provide a bountiful economy, or reduce inflation or save our cities."[4] He added a bit of fine print: a *partnership* between Americans and government was good. In this manner his government-bashing had a "now you see it/now you don't" quality. But the *tone* of what he said was very clear, and it made a strong impact.

There was little more for Reagan to assert after generalizations such as these; from the assertion that "government cannot solve our problems" to Reagan's more simple-minded assertion—"government is the problem"—the government-bashing moved along. Carter rolled out the carpet in a great many ways for Reagan in the 1980s.

That was not his intention, of course; he was a man of the left, but in 1970s terms. His admirers loved it for a while: the spirit of Jefferson appeared to be back just in time to guide the bicentennial. Government was "bad," as Mr. Jefferson taught, but "the people" were always to be trusted.

Certain groups among "the people," however, were demanding much more of Uncle Sam: poor farmers were in desperate straits due to lower agricultural price supports in the 1970s. The politics of ersatz populism ran quickly afoul of real Populism—the genuine article, 1890s-style—and its legacy in New Deal programs. Angry farmers drove to Washington in tractors.

Carter's life as a peanut farmer seemed to give him little grasp of their plight. These people were fervent and aggrieved; they were family farmers, crowded out increasingly by "agribusiness" (large-scale corporate farming), which flourished with the system of price supports as the poor farmers struggled and scraped.

To be fair to Carter, his actions were sometimes at odds with his anti-government rhetoric. In 1978, he supported the extension of the CETA program—a Nixon-era creation that provided, through the Comprehensive Employment and Training Act of 1973, funds to be used by the states for the purpose of job-training and job-creation, especially in the arts. Historian William Leuchtenburg observed that "Carter adopted a number of programs that could trace their ancestry to the New Deal."[5]

True, but there was something in the nature of Carter's post-Watergate, neo-Jeffersonian mood that prompted him to challenge, reverse, and annihilate portions of the programmatic New Deal legacy. Leuchtenburg concluded that he undermined the legacy of FDR far more than he supported or extended it: "Throughout his administration Carter rejected the New Deal as a model, save in the most limited respects. In formulating a reindustrialization plan he turned down recommendations for a public corporation modeled on the RFC, and he was appalled by Senator Adlai Stevenson III's proposal for an oil and gas corporation fashioned after the TVA which would provide a yardstick to determine the fairness of prices charged by private industry."[6]

Carter acknowledged this candidly. In an interview with journalist David Brinkley, he recalled later on that "I went into office demanding deregulation of the private enterprise system, and balancing budgets and . . . cutting back on some of the excessive social programs. . . . This was the biggest political problem when I was in office."[7]

Looking back from the 1980s, Arthur Schlesinger Jr. recalled the work of Carter this way: "He derided the federal service [and] advocated deregulation. . . . From a longer perspective, the differences between Carter and Reagan will seem less consequential than the continuities."[8] In certain ways, both of them paved the way for Clinton.

Carter's work as an ersatz populist continued in 1978. In a stunning reversal of the New Deal tradition, he proposed to deregulate the airlines. And then he pushed the measure through Congress.

Federal support for—and regulation of—aviation began in the 1920s. Herbert Hoover, as commerce secretary, advocated federal action in the field, and in 1926 the Air Commerce Act gave the Commerce Department some authority. In the 1930s the department regulated aircraft safety and assumed responsibility for air traffic control. Then the New Deal began to fund airport construction: Uncle Sam covered 70 percent of this work across the country during FDR's New Deal.[9] After World War II, the work continued. The Federal Airport Act of 1946 called for long-term planning of airports. Later, in the middle of the Nixon era, the Airport and Airway Development Act established a trust fund for long-term construction and renovation of airports in 1970.

Regulation of airfares and routes began with FDR in the 1930s. The 1938 Civil Aeronautics Act gave the federal government the power to determine the fares that the airlines could charge and the routes that the carriers would serve. By 1940 this authority was wielded by the Civil Aeronautics Board (CAB), and the agency continued its work until the time that Jimmy Carter destroyed it.

Even after the creation of the FAA and the Department of Transportation, the CAB retained its powers and its mission. And then, at the bidding of Alfred Kahn, Carter's chairman of the CAB, it was over, with Carter's approval: the Airline Deregulation Act of 1978 gutted the agency, scattered its powers to the winds, and left the airlines free to set whatever fares they chose and fly whatever routes they believed were most "efficient"—for themselves.

Free marketeers were ecstatic. More important, millions enjoyed the cheaper fares that resulted from a price war that spread among the airlines. But then a heavy new price was exacted.[10] By the 1980s, Americans confronted "overbooking" and a drastic cutback of service. The loss of airline meals and nice amenities became the least of it—to maximize "efficiency," airlines developed a "hub-and-spoke" system of routes. What that meant rather often was that passengers would have to change planes instead of flying directly where they wanted to go, as they had done routinely in the past. This was surely less *efficient* from the standpoint of *passengers*—whose time would now be wasted in airport terminal layovers—but Uncle Sam could do nothing to correct it anymore, thanks to Alfred Kahn and Jimmy Carter.

The whole process was highly destructive. There were bankruptcies: long-familiar corporations such as TWA and Pan-Am began to disappear. As they went, they took experience with them. Employment security diminished with extensive layoffs—"downsizing," as they called it. Amid the upheaval, some companies sacrificed safety; the crash of Valujet Flight 592 killed over a hundred people in 1996. Explosive cargo had been placed in the hold. It appears that such details had gotten lost amid the never-ending worries of cash flow that haunted the managers.

A whole new world of economic insecurity resulted from deregulation, especially in the field of banking (another major blunder for which Jimmy Carter should bear the blame, along with Reagan, who was even more to blame) and electrical power (Bush the elder and Clinton let it happen, though the groundwork was laid under Carter).

In truth, economic insecurity increased across the board in the 1970s. "Stagflation," for instance, was a problem inherited from Nixon and Ford: a worst-of-both-worlds situation that government and business alike seemed powerless to cure.

Part of the problem was foreign competition: the Japanese and Germans (with American help) had rebuilt after World War II, and their up-to-date factories and newer techniques were more efficient in a great many cases than their older American counterparts. Foreign goods were frequently better and cheaper by the 1970s. America's balance of payments suffered. Manufacturing began to decline within the overall economic mix of the private sector.[11] American firms that could not bear the strain bit the dust, one after another: "rustbelt" factory closings were a new source of "structural unemployment" (in hard-hit regions), especially for workers who needed retraining. Downsizing worsened the problem all over the country.

Late in the 1970s, a number of economists called for a "national industrial policy." The goal was to reverse the manufacturing decline through workforce retraining, protective tariffs, and creation of new institutions such as national development banks that would subsidize critical industries. But this was not Carter's *modus operandi*.

The *inflation* side of stagflation was a complex affair, a source of endless theoretical quarrels among the economists. Arguably, the problem began with LBJ's abandonment of the wage-price guideposts developed by Kennedy. When he failed to institute wartime controls with the Vietnam escalation, the situation worsened. Nixon slapped on the wage-price controls, but then inflation surged when he removed them. A recession started as well. Both Nixon and Ford could explain this development by citing the production cutbacks—followed by outrageous oil price increases—that the OPEC nations imposed upon the West to strike back after Israel's defeat of the Egyptians and Syrians in the Yom Kippur War of 1973. The "oil shock" ramified across the American economy: recession and inflation occurred at the very same time. And people had to wait in line for gasoline.

Nixon responded in a number of ways: he appointed an "energy czar," William Simon, who launched a new Federal Energy Administration. Nixon also tried to launch a special "Project Independence" designed to achieve true "energy self-sufficiency" by 1980. He cited the Manhattan Project as his model.

But no Manhattan-style project was created on the necessary scale in the 1970s. Even Nixon at his best never sought to find an energy source that would replace the old fossil fuels. Not only would the oil industry have probably blocked such a move, but any *massive* response to the economic warfare of OPEC would have reeked of "big government." And by Carter's time, big government was out of the question.

To Carter's credit, he did support some spending to develop alternative power sources like solar and wind power (nuclear power lost most of its allure in the aftermath of the 1979 meltdown at Three Mile Island). Carter even supported the creation of a new cabinet-level Department of Energy in 1977. But none of these actions proved sufficient to stimulate a real scientific revolution. They were adjuncts to private-sector action. And this *had* to be the case at the time—did it not?—with a president who told the electorate that "government cannot solve our problems."

In any case, the "oil shock" was one among a number of causes that propelled the great 1970s inflation. Economists wrangled interminably about the nature of the other major causes. Some blamed higher overhead costs (including the costs of environmental and safety compliance with all the new federal regulations) that were passed along to consumers. Others blamed corporate profiteering. Inflation was arguably "pushed" by a wide range of economic factors beyond the price of oil: taxes, wages, stockholder greed, or the burden of increased corporate debt.

Galbraith continued to stress the sheer "market power" of the big corporations and unions: he argued that concentrated power such as theirs could result in higher prices in *any* situation short of full-fledged 1930s-style depression. A veteran of price control work during World War II, he had an obvious propensity to intervene in the market.

Milton Friedman, of course, was a free marketeer: he hated government action regardless of the socioeconomic conditions. But his laissez-faire principles were channeled more and more in a distinctive new direction that was known by the 1970s as "monetarism," the theory that inflation is exclusively (or chiefly) created by a rapid expansion of the money supply in relation to goods, and his prescription was therefore a simple one: stabilize money creation at a slow and steady rate, and the market would work to perfection.[12]

This particular theory was at odds with a different right-of-center initiative: the tax-cutting creed that its supporters called "supply-side economics" by the time of Carter. Journalist Jude Wanniski, journalist-economist Paul Craig Roberts, and economist Arthur Laffer were the major proponents of the method. In contrast to Friedman (with his preference for slow and steady growth), they pushed for a *massive expansion* of production and argued that reduction of taxes for the wealthy would unleash economic vitality: the wealthy would invest all the money that they saved in a manner that would benefit everyone.

Laffer also asserted that the method would pay for itself: tax cuts would lead to more revenue. Roberts, Wanniski, and their friends at the *Wall Street Journal* agreed. In *The Way the World Works*, an eye-catching manifesto published in 1978, Wanniski served up an economic model of the world in which the struggle of production (creation of supply) against the punitive effects of taxation was the central theme of economic history.[13]

Back to inflation. By the time of Jimmy Carter, an ominous factor was added to the mix of causation: inflation was becoming *self-sustaining*. It fed upon itself in the manner of a self-fulfilling prophecy. Journalist William Greider recalled the essential dynamics nearly ten years later:

> American consumers, having lived with constant inflation for more than a decade, had absorbed a new common wisdom, now shared by the rich and poor and middle class alike. Steadily rising prices were considered a permanent fixture of American life, a factor to be considered in every transaction. . . . By the late 1970s, most citizens had drawn their own practical lessons from experience. It not only made sense to buy now rather than later; it also made sense to borrow money in order to buy things now. Even with higher interest rates, a loan made today to purchase an automobile or a television set or a house would be paid back tomorrow in inflated dollars that were worth less. . . . If inflation persisted, as everyone assumed, debtors would be rewarded and savers would be penalized.[14]

Greider showed how the buy-now mood drove inflation to double-digit levels. He gave the example of a jewelry manufacturer who "kept raising the prices on his luxury jewelry to keep up with the rising costs of gold and diamonds as well as wages. Each time he raised prices, he worried that he would kill his sales. Each time, his sales increased."[15] People paid the higher prices to avoid paying *higher* prices, which were surely just over the horizon. Ironically, they acted in a manner that would *guarantee* ever-higher prices.

When inflation reached the double-digit levels, economists feared that America would soon face a hyperinflation of the sort that wrecked the economy of Germany back in the early 1920s. And then a second great "oil shock" induced by OPEC began in 1978 and continued into 1979.

Social Security was affected: benefits soared with inflation (Congress had provided for new cost-of-living indexes), while payroll contributions were stagnant. A short-term fix was achieved in 1977 through adjustments of tax rates and benefits. But the overall problem of inflation was perceived to be a comprehensive national crisis.

So at last Jimmy Carter did something dramatic: he held a kind of citizen summit, an expanded "town meeting." To Camp David he summoned a wide range of public officials, advisers, and citizens to brainstorm and share ideas. Then on July 15, 1979, he addressed the American people on television.

Some of his televised address belied his record as a government-basher; to reduce dependence on foreign oil, he proposed to use the power of his office and he called for new forms of federal action. He imposed some import quotas and he called for an "energy mobilization board" like the War Production Board of the Second World War.

And yet—true to form—he kept wallowing in anti-government rhetoric: he couldn't or wouldn't let it go. Here are some examples: "Looking for a way out of this crisis, our people have turned to the Federal government and found it isolated from the mainstream of our nation's life. . . . The gap between our citizens and our government has never been so wide. . . . What you see too often in Washington and elsewhere around the country is a system of government that seems incapable of action."

But *of course* it was incapable of action when its leader kept trashing its reputation. How can government effectively "act" when its leader destroys its morale and keeps distancing himself from its work?

The part of the speech that many people remembered the most—the part that caused many observers to deride it as Carter's "malaise speech"—was when he spoke about a national "crisis of confidence." He tried to be inspirational at times; "we simply must have faith in each other," he declared, "faith in our ability to govern ourselves, and faith in the future of this nation." But then once again, he took back what he said and told Americans something very different—he began to question their motives: "In a nation that was proud of hard work, strong families, close-knit communities, and our faith in God, too many of us now tend to worship self-indulgence and consumption. . . . We've learned that piling up material goods cannot fill the emptiness of lives which have no confidence or purpose."[16]

Here was a Sunday school lesson, but Americans were not in the mood. As a proverb, the message was trite, like advice from Polonius. Even worse, it appeared condescending. It sounded like the president was saying that the quest for the good things in life was but a symptom of emptiness within. He almost seemed to be telling the American people to admit that they *deserved* their economic problems (God's providence at work), and that reducing their car trips would toughen their moral fiber—make them better, like ascetic self-denial.

A few months later, Carter did something more consequential: he appointed as chairman of the Federal Reserve Board a banker, economist, and long-time public official, Paul Volcker.

Volcker solved the inflation crisis, and for that he is justly remembered. But he did it in draconian fashion. He went after the growth of the money supply: he contracted the "excess *reserves*." Instead of raising the discount rate (the basic interest rate), he got the Federal Reserve Board to hike the *reserve* ratios. This forced the banks to put more funds off-limits in *required* reserves. Then interest rates rose automatically. He prevailed with regard to his objective: "tight money" succeeded in "wringing" the pernicious inflation out of the economy. But the cost was a severe recession in 1980 that resumed in Ronald Reagan's term. Walton and Rockoff summarize the economic trade-off: "Inflation had fallen from 13.3 to 8.9 percent between 1980 and 1981 and rates were below 6.0 percent through the first half of 1982. Seizing the opportunity to eradicate inflation, Volcker tenaciously held to his policy. . . . He did so despite an increase in unemployment from 5.8 percent in 1979 to 9.5 percent in 1982 (the highest rate since the Great Depression)."[17]

Of course the New Deal safety net was there: unemployment compensation eased *some* of the suffering, but many people suffered nonetheless. Part of this devastation was not really Volcker's fault: unemployment compensation is adjusted by the states and lost income was not replaced in full.[18]

It does bear noting that the policy of Volcker was a serious blow against the efficacy and legislative stature of the Keynesian-spirited Employment Act of 1946. By Volcker's time, however, that law was already stripped of force. It was superseded by the 1978 Humphrey-Hawkins Act—its formal title was the Full Employment and Balanced Growth Act—which placed the goal of maximum employment on an equal footing with stable prices, increased production, balanced trade, and a balanced budget. There was no recognition in the act that such goals might be inconsistent, at least from time to time. Carter signed it.

Americans were probably sick of Jimmy Carter already, but then, just in time for the election, the Iranian hostage crisis, the sad (never angry) response by Carter, and the rescue attempt that bogged down in the middle of the desert made Carter a political dead man. He was blown away by Reagan in the manner of chaff before a powerful wind.

Just before he went, he committed one final blunder: he helped initiate the bank deregulation that Reagan continued and worsened.

Inflation was a real, if invisible, tax upon lenders in the 1970s; banks were getting paid back with very "cheap" dollars that contained less purchasing power than the dollars that were lent at the beginning. Long-term lenders, like savings and loans, felt the pressure most keenly of all. To help them, deregulators picked the worst possible method: they let the S&Ls make riskier investments.

The Depository Institutions Deregulation and Monetary Control Act of 1980, which Carter supported and signed, was wildly ambiguous: though it terminated interest rate ceilings (thus legalizing outrageous interest rates that would have once been considered usurious), it also gave the Federal Reserve new authority to set the reserve requirements for *all* depository institutions, including S&Ls and credit unions. In this manner, the act both tightened and reduced regulation at the very same time.

In any case, the *deregulation* provisions of the act set the stage for the Reagan-era law that made the S&L catastrophe possible: the 1982 Garn–St. Germain Depository Institutions Act. This law—one is tempted to call it almost criminally reckless in light of the S&L scandal—broke a bargain that was struck in the 1930s: deposit insurance in return for sound banking practices.

Neither Carter nor anyone else could foretell how steep—how very steep—would be the price of the bank deregulation. It would only take Reagan and his followers a few more years to make the blunder horrendous.

REAGAN

If Carter was a loser—by the end he was very nearly pitiful—Ronald Reagan would be confident indeed: he would epitomize easygoing strength. It was easy to create this effect. It came instinctively. He had the gift of gab and a rugged masculine appeal. He was a breath of fresh air after years of bitter disillusionment. His very bearing—self-satisfied, but all the while charming, friendly, debonair—was a tonic after Carter's self-destruction. Most Americans *wanted* to like him, and the circumstances of the 1980s helped this along.

Americans supported him regardless of his weakness: he averted his eyes from some realities that challenged his creed—his simple faith in self-help and the providence of God. A great deal of the time he didn't see what he didn't want to see—a dangerous habit in a leader—with the single and important exception of military power. To his credit, he emphasized national defense preparedness and made it an important priority. But even here, there was myopia. For what Reagan cared about was "hardware": weapon systems. What he neglected was the national/industrial *infrastructure* that had interested Ike in the 1950s.

This was no way to lead a great nation. But largely due to luck, Reagan prospered. Granted, Ronald Reagan was a forceful leader on the issues he cared about the most. Yet on many occasions he was saved (or helped) by the actions of others, by fortuitous quirks of historical timing he did little or nothing to create, and by the national mood.

There were one or two rough spots: the recession in the first two years of his term made his popularity dip, and the Iran-Contra scandal toward the end was an embarrassing affair. But all told, he was a very lucky man—*too* lucky.

Many others made it easy for Reagan. Volcker wiped out inflation, albeit at the cost of the severe recession that Reagan inherited. But then the recession ran its course, and inflation did not reappear; moreover, the OPEC cartel became weaker. The Democratic Party was in sad disarray (the left played into his hands in so many different ways in the 1980s). And perhaps most important of all, Mikhail Gorbachev rose up to power in the Kremlin and began the work of *perestroika*.

Democratic majorities in Congress helped Reagan as well, though in ways that were ironic: they made it hard for him to act out the right wing's fantasy of gutting the New Deal tradition. So he got to strike attitudes for free; there was no real price for him to pay. He never faced the kind of fury that he would have unleashed if he destroyed the New Deal safety net—at least the parts that the middle class wanted.

Hamby has argued that Reagan was surprisingly pragmatic; though his slogans might sound irresponsible at times, he would work with the people who opposed him. He used "the tactic of making necessary compromises while continuing to profess broader objectives as a long-term goal." Indeed, writes Hamby, since his gubernatorial days in California, "his rhetoric tended to be more ideological than his policies; in fact, at times they rather clearly contradicted each other. Neither then nor later would he let reality stand in the way of a good campaign speech; but by the same token, once he had the power to govern, he would not let the good speech stand in the way of practical necessity."[19]

"Once he had the power to govern"—here was the rub. For one has to remember the critical fact that he faced Democratic legislative majorities, both in his Sacramento days and then in Washington—at least in the House of Representatives. Who knows how far he might have gone if the Republicans had captured both houses of Congress in 1980?

We will never know. Perhaps Reagan would have brought in the wrecking crew and smashed the New Deal legacy. Perhaps not—in a diary entry from 1982, he wrote the following private reflection: "The press is dying to paint me as now trying to undo the New Deal. . . . I'm trying to undo the 'Great Society.' It was LBJ's war on poverty that led us to our present mess."[20]

In writing these words, Ronald Reagan was displaying a habit. Call it what you will, it was perverse: mental hide-and-seek, or selective amnesia, or a slippery grasp of the facts. The problem was this: he recalled what he *wished* to recall, and then conveniently forgot what didn't fit. In this case, he seemed to be forgetting something very easy to remember: he had vilified the New Deal a great many times since his mid-life conversion from an ardent New Dealer and admirer of FDR (for whom he voted four times) to a militant conservative follower of Barry Goldwater.

Reagan had this to say, for example, in 1976, about Goldwater and his legacy: "Goldwater tried to tell us some things that maybe eleven years ago we weren't ready to hear. We were still wrapped in the New Deal syndrome of believing that government could do all these things for us."[21] In the same year he told a journalist that "Fascism was really the basis for the New Deal."[22] Oddly, he continued to venerate FDR, while convincing himself that it was somehow Roosevelt's *advisers*, almost behind the president's back (never FDR himself), who created his policies.[23]

Here was Reagan at his worst and most dangerous: a man who subsisted in a world of foggy memories, slipshod analysis, contempt for historical accuracy, and a penchant for self-serving cant.[24] A more sinister man might have taken such propensities to truly Orwellian dimensions. But Reagan wasn't sinister so much as he was *boyish*—in the very *worst sense*.

He was just a big *boy* in a many ways. He could be a bit destructive at times, but he could also show a sweet-natured side. At his worst he could be painfully simplistic. His sweet-natured side was reflected very often in his diary. As he recovered, for example, from the bullet of John Hinckley Jr., he wrote the following reflections in the hospital: "I realized that I couldn't ask for God's help while at the same time I felt hatred for the mixed up young man who had shot me. Isn't that the meaning of the lost sheep? We are all God's children & therefore equally beloved by him. I began to pray for his soul and that he would find his way back to the fold."[25]

What greater attestation of a generous spirit could there be, in such a situation? Reagan *knew* that he was generous in spirit—he could *feel* it, and he thanked his Creator. His conscience was therefore very clear. So with a very clear conscience he could follow a callous ideology. He could live in a world of smug dogma without any consequences that affected him. It was an easy and self-indulgent world in which Reagan chose to live—and all the while maintaining a sense of overwhelming *decency*. He had an answer for everything, a quip to answer any accusation. He had little curiosity regarding the facts; he believed what he *wanted* to believe, so he could take a flimsy anecdote and blow it up larger than life. There were no moral doubts a great deal of the time: how *could* there be without curiosity? Carter turned self-doubt into a kind of sick joke; Reagan countered with the joke of false certitude. When taken to task, he could make a reply like the following: "Today, I'm accused by some of trying to destroy government's commitment to compassion and to the needy. Does this bother me? Yes. Like FDR, may I say I'm not trying to destroy what is best in our system of humane, free government—I'm doing everything I can to save it; to slow down the destructive rate of growth in taxes and spending; to prune non-essential programs so that enough resources will be left to meet the requirements of the truly needy."[26]

It sounded plausible: surely issues like taxation, allegations of waste and inefficiency, the efficacy of individual government initiatives—such as welfare, vis-à-vis the culture of the underclass—should be revaluated honestly and steadily. But Reagan wasn't being dispassionate or fair; he was a self-labeled leader of an anti-government movement, with an "axe to grind."

That being the case, why pretend? Why talk about employing the government's "resources" (even after the scrapping of "non-essential" programs) if his aim was to escape, and help Americans escape, from the "New Deal syndrome of believing that government could do all these things for us"? If "government is the problem," as Reagan asserted in his first inaugural address, why use it at all? Why talk about "pruning non-essential programs?" Leave everything—except police protection and national defense—to charity. This is probably what Reagan would have liked, at least in his fantasies. The minds of laissez-faire theorists from Spencer all the way to Friedman have worked in this way.

But perhaps, through it all, he was deeply uncertain, as Hamby has mused, "about how far to the right he wanted to go."[27] In any case, his conscience seemed clear, once again; his interesting diary (unless it was a huge snow job that was foisted upon posterity with utter sangfroid) makes this obvious.

It would have been interesting, at least in a morbid kind of way, to see him face the American people in the midst of economic depression—to see his glib self-assurance blown away in a true social crisis. It looked for a while (in 1982) as if something like that might happen. It appeared that an

economic crisis of major proportions would give Ronald Reagan his come-
uppance. But then Volcker eased up on the money supply (for a time), and
the economic boom took off.

So the nonchalance of Reagan could pass unchallenged, except by the
likes of poor Walter Mondale—whom the Democrats entrusted with the
hopeless task of beating Reagan in 1984. Reagan treated the election as a
joke (a *good-natured* joke).

In almost everything, it seemed, he got away scot-free: his illusions
never made him an object of ridicule, at least where it counted the most—
among the voters who supported him. His gaffes—his statements that
80 percent of pollution is caused by trees, for instance—never registered
among the true believers. Historian Michael Schaller relates an incident
from 1984, when the voters reelected Ronald Reagan in a landslide:

> In 1984 correspondent Leslie Stahl ran a feature on CBS news that
> contrasted Reagan's attendance at the Handicapped Olympics with the
> fact that he pushed Congress into cutting federal support for the handi-
> capped. A short time after the story aired, a White House staffer thanked
> Stahl for the "great piece," calling it a "five-minute commercial" for the
> president. Stahl objected, "Didn't you hear what I said?" Richard Dar-
> man replied, "Nobody heard what you said. They just saw the five min-
> utes of beautiful pictures of Ronald Reagan. . . . Haven't you people
> figured out yet that the picture always overrides what you say?"[28]

As journalist Haynes Johnson lamented in the 1990s, the price to be
paid for Reagan was almost incalculable; the 1980s were "an age of illusions when America lived on borrowed time and squandered opportunities
to put its house in order."[29] The failures and the scandals of the 1980s—the
S&L disaster, for example—would be dumped into the lap of his successor,
the elder George Bush.

Reagan's work as a conservative leader was significant in ideological
terms. He never felt the inner conflict that Hamby ascribed to Robert Taft
in the 1940s: the conflict between the desire for a global anti-Communist
crusade and disgust at the administrative ramifications—big government—
of American mobilization. For Reagan, there was no contradiction; a huge
military buildup combined with rhetorical government-bashing came naturally and easily to him. After all, he was fighting "the left" both at home and
abroad, using strategies fit for the occasion. But in overall terms, Reagan's
policies led to an asymmetrical legacy.

Earlier Republican policies were far more congruent: TR, for example,
wished to see a strong assertion of federal power at home and all over the

world. Calvin Coolidge was in favor of a *weak* Uncle Sam across the board. Reagan flexed the nation's muscles—extensions of federal power—on the global scene, while deriding the federal presence in domestic affairs. Voters who succumbed to the Reagan appeal thus imbibed a rather schizoid prescription for American resurgence: federal action outside of our borders but little in the way of civilian logistics at home—manpower, infrastructure, and so forth. Compare this to Eisenhower's vision in the 1950s: a vision of *coordinated* national power. Eisenhower knew too much to be a free marketeer. He had studied and taught before World War II at the Army Industrial College, whose mission was to train army leaders in the work of civilian-side mobilization and supply—the work of *preparedness.*

In the realm of public works, slow dry rot began to set in by the middle of the 1970s: Ike's highways needed repairs. Public-sector infrastructure was neglected as a rule by Carter and also by Reagan. In the early 1980s, a study undertaken for the Council of State Planning Agencies argued that "America's public facilities are wearing out faster than they are being replaced," and that "in hundreds of communities, deteriorated public facilities threaten the continuation of basic community services."[30] Reagan was indifferent—his ideology caused him to avert his eyes and ignore the bad situation—so the problem worsened. Looking back from the early 1990s, strategic and defense analyst Edward N. Luttwak claimed that in the previous ten years "the burdens placed on . . . infrastructures have increased much more than the amounts spent to improve them. As a result, from sewage systems to interstate highways, many U.S. infrastructures are now deficient in quality or quantity or both."[31]

It was *weapons* that Reagan wished to build. When Reagan came to Washington he listened to a host of Cold Warriors who warned that the Soviet Union in the Brezhnev era had begun to outclass the United States in weaponry. Paul Nitze, in particular—a key architect of NSC 68 under Truman—helped revive an early Cold War lobbying group, the Committee on the Present Danger (CPD). People such as these kept warning of a "window of vulnerability." Their claims were (and are) disputed in the national security field, but Reagan paid close attention. In truth he needed no persuasion from Nitze or any of the others; he instinctively agreed with what they said. Indeed, for years he had said the same thing, from the Goldwater days to the Nixon years, when he condemned the politics of Kissinger/Nixon détente and called for Cold War victory. And so he acted.

With his secretary of defense, Casper Weinberger, he pushed through enormous increases in defense spending: a 71 percent increase overall by the end of his presidency. Most of it went into weapons: more and bigger bombers, nuclear submarines, aircraft carriers, and missiles. Some of these weapons and armaments—Trident submarines, cruise missiles—were already in the "pipeline" during the 1970s. Others, like the B-2 stealth bomber, were new.

With the buildup, however, came Reagan's supply-side finance. Though he toyed in certain ways with Friedman's monetarism—he encouraged Paul Volcker to slow the growth of the money supply—Reagan also embraced the supply-side theories of Arthur Laffer, as promoted by the *Wall Street Journal*.[32] He brought Paul Craig Roberts of the *WSJ* right into the Treasury Department to work out the legislative details. The result was the 1981 Economic Recovery Tax Act (ERTA), also known as Kemp-Roth for its congressional sponsors, Jack Kemp and William Roth. Reagan had proposed an overall 30 percent cut in individual taxes and other taxes to be phased in over three years; what he got was slightly less, but not by much.

The tax relief would benefit the wealthy more than others, per the *Wall Street Journal*'s candid formula: marginal rates in the uppermost brackets fell from 70 percent to 50 percent. Later on, in the Tax Reform Act of 1986, the rates in the topmost brackets fell to 28 percent. It remained to be seen whether tax relief for the wealthy would lead to new bursts of job-creating production, as supply-siders said that it would, or instead to more purchases of trinkets and toys for the rich—yachts, Rolls Royces, and the like—or speculation of the sort that leads to no job creation at all.

The most famous result of Kemp-Roth was the creation of the largest peacetime federal deficits up to that time. Reagan's budget director, David Stockman, hoped that reductions in taxes would be coupled with—or would force—reductions in overall spending. This did not occur; not only was Congress unwilling to make the major cuts, but even Reagan held back from proposing big reductions in Social Security and Medicare. With the big new spending for defense, Stockman's in-house computer projections showed a pattern of ever-mounting deficits. But Reagan was content to let it happen, blaming Congress for its lack of "fiscal discipline."[33]

Stockman confessed, in some interviews with William Greider, that he knowingly produced optimistic projections for public consumption (he "changed the economic assumptions fed into the computer model") that were totally at odds with what he knew or suspected. He was full of private doubts; "I've never believed that just cutting taxes alone will cause output and employment to expand," he admitted. He believed that "supply side premises were based upon wishful thinking."[34]

Stockman had tried to cut Social Security benefits to early retirees by as much as a third. He warned of a continuing crisis of solvency with the Social Security system. But the move was unpopular in Congress and Reagan was leery of tampering with Social Security—at least directly. So he formed a commission chaired by Alan Greenspan to study new adjustments to the system. Another compromise package of benefit cuts and payroll tax increases was worked out in 1983.

Reagan pushed deregulation. He created a Task Force on Regulatory Relief, chaired by Vice President George H. W. Bush. He appointed administrators who treated their departments and agencies with contempt. As chairman of the Securities and Exchange Commission, Reagan appointed John Shad, who cut enforcement and reduced staff. As chairman of the Federal Communications Commission, Reagan chose Mark Fowler, who destroyed the requirement for public service programs and the long-standing "fairness doctrine" that required a grant of equal time for spokesmen on opposing sides of issues.

To the Interior Department Reagan sent James Watt, who had founded the Mountain States Legal Foundation, an anti-environmental group. To EPA he sent Anne Gorsuch Burford, who shared the views of Watt. A few years later she resigned amid scandal after one of her subordinates raided the toxic clean-up Superfund and diverted the money into politics.

On the left, these actions were abetted by the "neo-liberals," a group within the Democratic Party that continued the reversion of Carter to eighteenth- and nineteenth-century liberalism—liberalism Jefferson-style. The neo-liberals agreed with the Reaganites much of the time; Charles Peters, for example, in his 1982 "Neo-Liberal Manifesto," proclaimed that he and his fellow neo-liberals—people such as Gary Hart and Paul Tsongas— "no longer automatically favor . . . big government," since "our hero is the risk-taking entrepreneur."[35]

These people did a great deal of damage in the Reagan years. The most damaging action, however, was the Garn–St. Germain Act of 1982, which Reagan supported with enthusiasm—the next installment in the S&L saga.

The deregulation of the "thrifts" under Garn–St. Germain was not total: the legislation—named for Senator Jake Garn and Representative Fernand St. Germain, its sponsors in the Senate and the House—left some power in the hands of the Federal Home Loan Bank Board, established in the Hoover years. The board retained the power to shut down failing S&Ls,

whose depositors would be reimbursed to an extent by the Federal Savings and Loan Insurance Corporation (FSLIC), established in 1934.

But Garn–St. Germain let the S&Ls switch from mortgages to speculation, some of it in real estate and some of it wherever else an "angle" could be found. With the S&Ls free to make riskier loans, they attracted huge brokered deposits from investors who were after the higher interest rates that the S&Ls were allowed to pay after 1980. S&Ls were purchased by real estate hustlers pushing fancy schemes in collusion with their pals: long-shot development projects without any interest due for several years. The trashiest deals were fancy frauds: land-flip schemes, for example, where a vacant piece of land could be made to change hands all day and at an ever-higher price each time as the manipulators worked.

S&L hustlers and junk bond artists often worked together in the 1980s; Charles Keating, for example, bought the Lincoln Savings and Loan in California with help from the infamous Michael Milken of Drexel Burnham Lambert. After buying the S&L with Milken's assistance, Keating bought a huge portfolio of junk bonds that Milken unloaded. The junk bonds abetted corporate raids.

Junk bonds are high-risk and high-interest corporate securities. They were often employed as the basis for "leveraged buy-outs" in the 1980s: the proceeds of junk bond sales were employed by the raiders to acquire enough stock to take over once-respectable companies. The raiders often boasted that they brought a new "efficiency" to management. But their "efficiency" often consisted of cost-reduction methods that were sleazy if not reprehensible. At the very least, their new methods—service cutbacks, reductions in staff, and elimination of benefits—degraded both the workplace and marketplace. Workers who survived the waves of firings and layoffs ("downsizing") often found themselves chiseled out of medical insurance and pensions. To the extent that the Reagan boom "created more jobs," about half were only part-time jobs paying minimum wage.[36]

Why did the unions let it happen? Unions were weakened by a number of trends in the 1980s, especially outsourcing—the replacement of in-house staff by contractors, who were also in a perfect position to chisel their employees out of benefits.

By the end of the 1980s, the gigantic cost of paying off depositors of failed (or crooked) S&Ls had thrown FSLIC into bankruptcy. A terrible mess was left over after deregulation.[37] The financial disaster was made even worse by the fact that Uncle Sam's obligations were increased at the very same time that the S&Ls were given more leeway: S&L deposit insurance had been raised from $40,000 per account to $100,000. The eventual cost of the S&L bailout would be astronomical.

Then a stock market crash occurred in 1987. At the same time the junk bond market began to collapse; Drexel led the way with an insider trading scandal that began in 1986. Arbitrager Ivan Boesky got in trouble, as did Michael Milken, who was fired by the firm and went to jail. In 1990, Drexel Burnham Lambert declared bankruptcy.

The most obvious flaw in supply-side theory was the premise—so obviously glib and self-serving on its face—that the wealthy, on the whole, will choose to spend their resources on productive endeavors that will broaden American prosperity. The S&L scandal showed that many will invest in utter trash: parasitic and predatory ventures that will benefit no one but themselves while degrading the rest of us.

The "Reagan boom" of the 1980s was a very mixed affair. It was genuine, at least to the extent that expansion occurred: the tax cuts, deficits, and military spending served to stimulate the economy. The effect was in some respects Keynesian, a fact that most conservatives would never admit. Moreover, the military spending gave a welcome boost to manufacturing.

All the same, the balance-of-trade situation got worse and American autonomy suffered as waves of foreign investment put American firms into the hands of foreign owners. International credit played an ever-more necessary role in American investment; indeed, America—formerly the world's leading creditor nation—became the world's biggest debtor. And in overall terms, the manufacturing and farming sectors of the economy continued to decline.

Low inflation and a rapid expansion of the money supply went together: Friedman's theory was disproved in the 1980s. Walton and Rockoff have observed that by the middle of the 1980s the American economy "seemed able to absorb a considerable amount of new money without experiencing a return to high rates of inflation."[38]

But the economic benefits were shared unevenly at best: the rich did better. So much so, in fact, that Kevin Phillips, a conservative who worked for Richard Nixon years earlier (he had served as a senior Nixon strategist in 1968), turned populistic in the 1980s and condemned the results of Reaganomics. "Corporate chairmen and presidents as a class feasted in the 1980s," he complained, "but the number of mid-level management jobs lost during these years was estimated to be as high as 1.5 million."[39] Downsizing accelerated; General Motors, for instance, cut its workforce in half by the early 1990s.[40] The discrepancies were harsh, Phillips noted, as the wealth was redistributed upward: "The 1983–89 boom was far from uniform. . . . Corporate chief executives' compensation set new records as workers' real hourly wages declined. . . . While speculators and corporate raiders took home huge sums, the average American family wound up fearing for the safety of its bank accounts, insurance coverage, home values, and pension coverage."[41]

A study in the 1990s making use of Congressional Budget Office data contended that the top 1 percent of America's families increased their annual income (after taxes) during the 1980s by 122 percent.[42] But according to the 1991 *Green Book* published by the House Ways and Means Committee, the median net worth of all other American families, as measured in monthly household income, fell in the 1980s.[43]

With conservative pundits and commentators touting the achievements of the Reagan boom—"It's Morning in America"—and with corporate profits and the value of stocks given widespread credence as the foremost signs of prosperity, millions were inclined to blame themselves instead of Reagan for their shaky economic situation. After all, if the economy is booming, why should anyone not "get along"? Once Reagan was gone, however, his successor caught the brunt of economic disaffection, as worsened by another recession: the elder Bush, once again, was left holding the bag.

A long succession of scandals followed Ronald Reagan: his disparagement of public service (*nonmilitary* public service) bred a massive contagion of sleaze. A 1988 probe by the Justice Department led to convictions of over fifty Defense Department officials and contractors on charges of rigging bids. Several officials at the Department of Housing and Urban Development were convicted of fraud and embezzlement.[44] Reagan's attorney general, Edwin Meese, exerted pressure to procure a Defense Department contract for the Wedtech Corporation. He was later cited by the Justice Department for "conduct, which should not be tolerated of any government employee, especially not the attorney general."[45] Moreover, the Iran-Contra scandal led to eleven convictions of senior staff to the president.

Reagan is remembered by millions as the leader who "won the Cold War," and it is true that the pressure he exerted on the Soviet Union gave leverage to Gorbachev, who rose to power in 1985; the two of them began a synergistic partnership—Reagan even called his counterpart "Gorby." But Reagan's policies had *changed* by that time; his *initial* approach toward the Soviet Union caused results that frightened even him.

In the 1970s, Nixon and Carter had negotiated arms limitations agreements with the Soviets: Nixon's Anti-Ballistic Missile (ABM) treaty, which restricted the development of "anti-missile missiles," the Strategic Arms Limitation Agreement (SALT I)—both of which were signed in 1972—and Carter's subsequent SALT II treaty of 1979. Reagan criticized all of these treaties. On January 29, 1981, he proclaimed that "détente's been a one-way street that the Soviet Union has used to pursue its own aims. . . . The only morality they recognize is what will further their cause, meaning they reserve unto themselves the right to commit any crime."[46]

Taking this view, Ronald Reagan proposed to push back. He institutionalized hard-line "defense guidance" plans that were secret at the time: National Security Defense Directive 32 (NSDD-32), which proclaimed it U.S. policy to undermine Communist control of Eastern Europe and the Soviet Union itself, and NSDD-66, which committed the United States government to destabilize the Soviet economy.[47] What Reagan wanted was to start a new armaments race that would bankrupt the Soviet Union.[48]

In 1983 he delivered his "evil empire" speech and called for a Strategic Defense Initiative (SDI) that would give the United States the power to shoot down Soviet missiles from space ("Star Wars").[49] Unfazed by the fact that even a system with an accuracy rate of 99 percent would let dozens of Soviet nuclear weapons rain down upon American cities, Reagan touted the idea as a way to end the nuclear nightmare. He offered to share the research with the Soviets.

At times, he appeared to be afraid that he was going too far; on April 6, 1983, he recorded in his diary that "some of the N.S.C. staff are too hard line & don't think any approach should be made to the Soviets. I think I'm hard line & will never appease but I do want to try & let them see there is a better world if they'll show *by deed* that they want to get along with the free world."[50]

And then, something frightening occurred: in November 1983, a joint United States and NATO war simulation maneuver called "Able Archer 83" caused the Soviets to overreact on a scale that caused the worst fear of nuclear war since the Cuban missile crisis. Reagan's rhetoric was taken seriously—very seriously—in Yuri Andropov's Kremlin. As historian John Patrick Diggins relates, "the Soviet leaders were certain America was planning a preemptive strike." Oleg Gordievsky, KGB chief in London, recounted receiving orders to be on the alert for the "immediate threat of a nuclear attack on the Soviet Union. . . . The planned deployment of American missiles in Europe convinced the Soviets that an attack was imminent. . . . Moscow placed its interceptor aircraft on high alert as well as units of the Soviet army and the Warsaw Pact."[51]

When word of these reactions was conveyed to Reagan, he was shocked. As it happened, he had just watched a made-for-television movie depicting the aftermath of a nuclear attack upon America. It seemed that for the first time in thirty-odd years—since his mid-life political conversion—Ronald Reagan had begun to rethink his political behavior. It appears that he was genuinely scared, and for that we should be thankful. In his diary he wrote that "we have to do all we can . . . to see there is never a nuclear war."[52] On November 11, 1983, he proclaimed, "a nuclear war can never be won and must never be fought."[53] A few days later he penned the following reflection in his diary: "I feel the Soviets are so defense minded, so paranoid about being attacked that without being in any way soft on them we ought to tell them no one here has any intention of doing anything like that. What the h—ll have they got that anyone would want."[54]

On January 16, 1984, in a televised national address, he embraced the idea of "a constructive working relationship" with the Soviets and called for a "dialogue as serious and constructive as possible." He observed that "our two countries have never fought each other. There's no reason why we ever should."[55] He was ready at last for a leader like Mikhail Gorbachev. The world was ready, too.

This is not the time or place to consider the extent to which Gorbachev (who astonished the world at the 1986 Reykjavik summit by proposing to ban all nuclear weapons) should receive equal credit with Reagan for the great events that followed: the dismantling of Soviet repression and the peaceful termination of the long and grueling Cold War.[56] Reagan's admirers are certainly right when they emphasize the way in which his constant pressure on the Soviet Union was a factor in disabling Communism in Russia. His crusade was conducted at considerable risk—he played a dangerous game with the lives of millions, and he recognized the fact himself—but it succeeded, with Gorbachev's help.

Yet what Reagan's admirers refuse to confront is the fact that he employed the power of the *federal government*—the diplomatic, intelligence-gathering, and military *aspects* of government—in his fight against the Soviet empire. Both to Reagan and conservative pundits the Cold War victory was simple and beautifully dialectical: it was the victory of *freedom* over "statist" repression and tyranny.[57] But without the *power of Uncle Sam*, how likely would it be that mere businessmen—through the mere force of buying and selling—could have brought down the Soviet Union? Free enterprise alone is quite helpless in the face of totalitarian power. Only military might can make the difference.

What Reagan used to win the global struggle—federal power—he degraded at home, and with no sense of any inconsistency. To ensure that his program would be carried forward, he employed a time-honored technique: he packed the judiciary. And to succeed Paul Volcker at the Federal Reserve he chose a libertarian conservative, Alan Greenspan.

The lopsided legacy of Reagan has served the United States badly in a great many ways. Despite the obvious short-term benefits—an ill-grounded economic boom and a Cold War victory that left the former Soviet Union a political and economic shambles for almost a decade (no Marshall Plan under Reagan or Bush)—with China poised to cause the United States political and economic harm down the years as a nominal "trading partner" (the Cold War victory stopped at Beijing) and Iran greatly strengthened by Reagan's illicit arms sales (arms for hostages), there was very good reason for American conservatives to pause in their gloating and reflect.

But few of them did. It was "morning in America" for them, and they had no intention of allowing any critical analysis to slow down or spoil the big party. Yet the morning after was approaching.

DECADENCE

One conservative who paused to reflect was the columnist George F. Will. In 1983, he joined the consequential succession of latter-day commentators—Peter Viereck, Daniel Patrick Moynihan—who tried to resurrect Tory reform. In the *New Republic* he declared that "if conservatism is to engage itself with the way we live now, it must address government's graver purposes with an affirmative doctrine of the welfare state," and with "a wholesome ethic of common provision" to promote "social cohesion."[58] In the presidential term of the elder George Bush, Will continued this effort with a special emphasis on infrastructure. In 1990, he avowed that "transportation and other infrastructure issues should bring out a strong Hamiltonian streak in American conservatives, who too often talk the anachronistic language of Jeffersonian small-government sentimentality." He invoked the legacy of Lincoln: "a crimson thread of consistency connects Lincoln's passion for internal improvements with his later mission of binding the nation together as a land of opportunity."[59]

Comparably, toward the end of the 1980s there was movement on the left to repudiate neo-liberalism and revive the old New Deal version of "social cohesion." Oklahoma's senator David Boren introduced legislation to revive the WPA; he called his program the "Community Works Progress Administration."[60]

In 1990, Bush's secretary of transportation released a report on infrastructure needs titled *Moving America*. In the following year Congress passed the Intermodal Surface Transportation Efficiency Act (ISTEA), which authorized $151 billion for transportation improvements and maintenance over six years. This was not very much when compared to the backlog of maintenance needs. Wall Street financier Felix Rohatyn observed that Americans had "not invested adequately" in either the "public facilities to provide the infrastructure required by a modern industrial society" or the "human capital to provide all Americans with the education and training to fill the available jobs." He proclaimed that a "more active role for government" was "an absolute necessity" unless Americans wished to experience a long-term decline in their standard of living.[61]

ISTEA was at least a beginning: the elder George Bush tried to do what he could to make up for Reagan's inattention to civilian-side problems. The most urgent task, of course, was cleaning up the sordid S&L mess. In 1989 Bush unveiled his comprehensive bailout plan, which resulted in the passage of the Financial Institutions Reform Recovery and Enforcement Act (FIRREA). This abolished the Federal Home Loan Bank Board and FSLIC, created an Office of Thrift Supervision (OTS) to regulate S&Ls, switched S&L deposit insurance to FDIC, and set up a Resolution Trust Corporation (RTC) to finance the bailout at taxpayer expense. In 1990 the Comprehensive Thrift and Bank Fraud Prosecution and Taxpayer Recovery Act (Bank Fraud Act) enhanced the regulatory powers of the Federal Reserve, FDIC, and other bank supervisory agencies. Moreover, the 1990 Crime Control Act mandated a study of the S&L crisis by a National Commission on Financial Institution Reform, Recovery, and Enforcement.

All of this amounted to a partial reregulation of banking. At the same time, however, the deregulation movement was proceeding in the field of electrical power, where the next wave of corporate sleaze was starting to germinate.

Beginning in the late 1970s under Carter—when the old Federal Power Commission was reorganized as the Federal Energy Regulatory Commission (FERC)—presidents appointed deregulators to positions of FERC authority. These people, at the agency level, began deregulation in a manner that Congress had never approved. They gradually (largely through case-by-case decisions) abandoned the commission's New Deal charter (as specified in the 1935 Federal Power Act) to make certain that interstate electrical rates would be "reasonable, nondiscriminatory, and just to the consumer."

Under pressure from electric utility lobbyists, deregulation proceeded, both at the state and the federal levels. The parasites and predators were back: the basis for the Enron scandal was created in the 1980s and 1990s. Manipulation, rigged shortages, profiteering, and "hedge market" betting cost billions in excessive electrical rates while draining the industry of funds that should have been plowed right back into production through the modernization and expansion of the nation's power plants.

The pressure in the 1990s for more deregulation was strong—far too strong to be overcome by a public works ethic of the sort that was propounded on the right by people like Will and on the left by people like Boren. Instead, on both the left and the right, the spirit of decentralization, deregulation, and free marketeering grew apace.

On the right, a Bush administration theorist named James P. Pinkerton touted a New Paradigm to unify conservatives and liberals around the principle of "breaking down centralized structures."[62] On the left, theorists like David Osborne created the slogan of "Reinventing Government." This slogan was based upon the premise that "centralized systems are too slow, too cumbersome, and too rigid."[63]

With coauthor Ted Gaebler, Osborne asserted that, "unless there is an important reason to do otherwise, responsibility for addressing problems should lie with the lowest level of government possible."[64] Osborne became a major figure in the Progressive Policy Institute, a Democratic Party think tank founded in the 1980s by presidential aspirant Bill Clinton and a host of other kindred spirits.

As the left and the right shared ideas about promoting decentralization, the conservative-liberal war began to rage on all the other fronts. "Political correctness," left and right, became a rigid new extension of the old antagonistic values. Masters of trash-talk abuse—blatherskites such as Rush Limbaugh and Al Sharpton—brought political discourse to ever-lower levels of crudeness.

When the right was ascendant in the Reagan era, many "movement conservatives" dished out abuse in the manner of the demagogue Spiro Agnew. Cultural conservatives like Jeanne Kirkpatrick and William Bennett called liberals the people who would "blame America first." They condemned what they regarded as liberal "relativism" and called for a moral reawakening. But what was darkly funny at the time was the way in which so many right-wing evangelicals pushed statist forms of regulation (the banning of abortion, for instance) as the basis for moral resurgence while the right-wing free marketeers were hailing anything that turned a quick buck. Presumably, the free-market system on the laissez-faire standard places no restrictions on pornography (or on abortion, for that matter), narcotics, prostitution, or any other market-driven vice. No matter: in the cause of defeating "the left," strange bedfellows got together easily. Cultural conservatives and free marketeers disregarded one another's doctrines. They did it for the sake of tribal unity.

The left played into their hands. The New Left had done its work surpassingly well, and the syndrome of Vietnam guilt prompted many liberals to do some extraordinary things to prove their devotion to the needs of the downtrodden masses. In the middle of the hostage crisis in Iran, for example, Ramsey Clark—one of Robert Kennedy's successors as attorney general under LBJ—took a trip to Iran and proclaimed that Khomeini's revolution was a "miracle for the century." He offered himself as a substitute hostage if Iran would negotiate with Carter. When this offer of martyrdom elicited no response from the terrorists, Clark suggested the Iranians lead an investigation of American imperialism.[65] What better way to prove the accusations of the right about the "blame America first crowd"? But what the right wing—especially the evangelical right—could never comprehend was the degree to which "limousine liberalism" was as much *faith-directed* (notwithstanding any secular pretensions) as conservative faith-based crusading: the liberal imperative to honor and assist the world's "downtrodden" flowed from ancient biblical injunctions, however distorted by misapplied zeal. Conservatives were blinding themselves in the 1980s and 1990s to the presence on the left of theological imperatives as keen and energizing as their own.

"Political correctness," left and right, was religious war of a kind: it was a process of mutual demonization that Ike in the 1950s and JFK in the 1960s would have found appalling. There was little mediation at the center as the rival versions of Judeo-Christian self-righteousness played out. With the legacy of Lincoln and the Roosevelts gone, the unraveling of civic culture could not be restrained.

By the 1980s and 1990s, conservative and liberal theorists established certain sacrosanct formulae or policy prescriptions that would serve as standard litmus tests among the faithful. The anti-abortion crusade on the right and affirmative action on the left were stock items in the ongoing feud.

Divisive crusades such as these left enormous numbers of people in the middle feeling robbed of their political "voice"—and averse to participation in what seemed a war of absolutists. They felt whipsawed back and forth between the sorts of propositions that George Orwell once dismissed as the "smelly little orthodoxies, which are now contending for our souls."[66] As journalist E. J. Dionne Jr. lamented in 1991, "the false choices posed by liberalism and conservatism make it extremely difficult for the perfectly obvious preferences of the American people to express themselves in our politics."[67] The result was growing alienation.

Moral crusades are appropriate when issues are demonstrably clear, like slavery. There is no ambiguity at all as to whether a person can be owned under law by another human being, in the manner of livestock. There is no such clarity, however, with an issue like abortion, at least in the early stages of a pregnancy: however dreadful it seems to "kill an unborn baby," there is no unanimity possible as to the metaphysical question of whether a collection of embryonic cells can be held to constitute a "person," complete with what believers regard as an "immortal soul." It is all very well for both Catholics and Protestants to hold this as an article of *faith*. But this faith became *religious war* when the issue was proclaimed to be "legalized murder," a charge with which millions of ethical people could not agree.

Religious war: hence the practice of the "militants" who murdered physicians at abortion clinics.

Political correctness on the left was insistent without being murderous. Notwithstanding, it was deeply corrosive. There was no valid national consensus on the merits of "affirmative action" as a tactic for advancing civil rights. Some viewed it as reverse discrimination, while others insisted that its loss would be a fatal blow to "fairness." The issue was endlessly divisive as early as the 1970s. John F. Kennedy had hoped to avoid this problem as he worked up the Civil Rights Act. At a 1963 press conference, he observed that "we ought to make an effort to give a fair chance to everyone who is qualified—not through a quota, but just look over our employment rolls, look over our areas where we are hiring people and at least make sure we are giving everyone a fair chance, but not hard and fast quotas. We are too mixed, this society of ours, to begin to divide ourselves on the basis of race or color."[68]

But "identity politics" was more and more the rage by the 1990s. When taken to extremes, it was grotesque. Take the case of Ward Connerly, who chaired a California initiative to end racial preferences in 1996. "I'm a black man," he said, but he also declared he had "Indian in me, I have French, some Irish. The choice of what I am should be mine. Yet I've had reporters call me African American. What does that mean?" It meant that he was vilified by zealots from one end of California to the other. "He's married to a white woman," a state senator complained; "He wants to be white. . . . He has no ethnic pride."[69] Old ADA liberals like Arthur Schlesinger Jr. could only shake their heads and groan. Schlesinger called this sort of thing the "dis-uniting of America."

It was all very well for defenders of affirmative action to argue that Americans have emphasized ethnicity or race in many *positive* ways or that liberals were justified in taking special steps to reach out to American blacks in the 1960s. The point (by the 1990s, at least) was the *price* that was paid for prolonging and institutionalizing a politics that emphasizes race—that emphasizes physical structure more than personality and mind.

It is one thing to take special cognizance of race as a *secondary* aspect of identity—as an aspect of life that one can emphasize, ignore, or take in stride. It is altogether different when race becomes viewed as a primary aspect of one's identity. That changes us from people into objects, as Connerly complained. But the proponents of affirmative action just never seem to get this point.

The shrillness of the cultural wars bred a widespread mood of disaffection. Waves of derisiveness and alienation spread over American life. Commentators spoke about the "cynicism" of the age.[70] An opinion survey conducted in the 1990s by the *Washington Post*, Harvard University, and the Kaiser Family Foundation concluded that "America is becoming a nation of suspicious strangers, and this mistrust of each other is a major reason Americans have lost confidence in the federal government and virtually every other major national institution."[71]

As is often the case with the *fin-de-siecle* mentality, a spirit of decadence made the rounds. The avant-garde seemed to lust for grotesquerie, the airwaves were filled with reprehensible trash (Howard Stern), the cable channels were rife with extraordinarily degrading fare, and the left–right culture war continued. Libertarianism was descending to the lunacy of right-wing armed militias. Fragmentation was everywhere.

The social common denominator seemed to be vulgarity, aimless and mindless. Gone were the blazers, striped ties, and pleated skirts of the Reagan-era "preppies." At hand was the new age of "Goth," tattoos, pierced nostrils, and "distressed" jeans. *Washington Post* reporter Martha Sherrill caught the mood with the following reflection: "We're a little hungry for . . . violence and destruction, for devourings, for crudity and unsweet sex. For snot and vomit and blown-up bits of skull. We want our world un-socialized. We want our establishments eroding. We want our characters unmannered. . . . Good taste is dead, *and was probably never alive to begin with*."[72] This trend continued; *Fear Factor*, a show in which people won prizes by submitting themselves to disgusting situations, premiered in

2001. It almost seemed as if the counterculture had returned, but this time stripped of any New Age ideals.

Poor Bush the elder! What could he achieve in an age that was anti-heroic? What manner of consensus could be build with his nasal voice, his managerial demeanor, his effete oratorical style full of syntax problems and ill-conceived promises—"Read my lips!"—that would come back to haunt him? The culture of the 1950s let Ike get away with a stodgy presidential style. No such luck for Bush the elder, who had to follow Reagan. Bush's talk about a "kinder and gentler" conservatism had no effect at all. And even he had resorted to some trashy tactics in his race against Michael Dukakis. He cut a very poor figure in the White House, even when Saddam Hussein gave Americans a chance to "support the troops" in a war that was brief, clear-cut, and successful.

The Desert Storm interlude—though it created some newly minted heroes such as Colin Powell and "Stormin' Norman" Schwarzkopf—blew over, while a new economic recession just lingered, eroding the political base of the Republicans and spawning the revolt of independent Ross Perot.

Could a clarion call of some kind reawaken American ideals? Bill Clinton thought he had a plan. He had charisma, a recession to weaken the incumbent, and the gift of gab, like Reagan. Who could tell, as he ousted Bush the elder, that his new administration would run out of steam so quickly? He would self-destruct like Jimmy Carter.

CLINTON

Clinton thought he had a new "third way" that would unify conservatives and liberals. It was a centrist approach that might steal the Republicans' thunder and help out the Democrats. He would offer bold *action* on the economic front while talking tough to the left about "political correctness": he would take a hard line in regard to public safety, where Americans had doubts about liberal instincts.

The "third way" encompassed much more: it encompassed the extraordinary strategy of *using and abusing* "big government"—all at once. Clinton would use the federal government in *certain* respects while continuing the anti-government rhetoric of Carter and Reagan in the overall image he projected.

This was risky business and it backfired. The *theoretical* justification came from David Osborne, who wrote that government ought to be decentralized "unless there is an important reason to do otherwise." Clinton proposed to decentralize *except* in those cases where he felt that he ought to do "otherwise." The *political* justification for the strategy came from his belief that decentralization would preempt the Republicans and offer good "cover" for his new initiatives.

It didn't work. In the first place, it worsened the Republicans' belligerence by validating Reaganesque standards of governance. In the second place, it worsened the overall fragmentation of American life. Clinton never seemed to understand this. In a farcical manner he continued in Reagan's footsteps; as Reagan had assigned Bush the elder to chair a special task force on "regulatory relief," Clinton tasked Al Gore with responsibility for "reinventing government." Gore and his advisers pushed dispersal of federal efforts ("devolution") in the form of decentralization, privatization, and free-trade globalization. As all of this proceeded, the Republicans could play one-upmanship: they could tell the American people they were better at all of these tasks.

Clinton's weaknesses undercut his talents at the level of strategy and tactics as well. He lacked good judgment and he lacked self-control where it mattered. It wasn't just the womanizing, which would largely ruin his second term. He lacked self-control on the *tactical* level, and he lacked real toughness where it counted. His sense of timing was off—he would wait until the optimal moment for action had passed, and then he talked too much in his long-winded speeches and interviews. He was everywhere at once—telling jokes, sharing anecdotes, projecting empathy, "hangin' out." He was often all talk; in reacting to the gutter tactics that Republicans used to destroy his presidential program, he was shockingly weak.

He was a great survivor, a "come-back kid"—but who cared, after all was said and done? After "bouncing back" from disaster, he confronted yet another defeat, and another.

He *sounded* rather strong when he had challenged the incumbent in 1992. He compared his mood to the impatience of Lincoln with generals too weak to use the gathering of power that was placed at their disposal: "A president ought to be a powerful force for progress. But right now I know how President Lincoln felt when General McClellan wouldn't attack in the Civil War. He asked him, 'If you're not going to use your army, may I borrow it?' George Bush, if you won't use your power to help people, step aside, I will."[73]

But *how* did he propose to use the presidency? He proposed to bring power much *closer* to the people through *decentralization of focus*. At Washington's expense, the American localities would flourish—or so he claimed.

Clinton accused Bush of failing to "streamline the federal government, and change the way it works." Bush would not "cut 100,000 bureaucrats and put 100,000 more police on the streets."[74] Clinton avowed that "the old ways won't work. Trickle down economics have failed. And big bureaucracies, public and private, have failed."[75] Above all, he pledged to balance the budget.

With an energetic *demeanor* he was serving up a warmed-over version of the Carter program, with the major exceptions of the economic stimulus and national health care initiatives. He launched these in 1993 and they were both doomed to failure.

In the early months of Clinton's first term, Charles Bowsher, comptroller-general of the United States, told Congress that "maintaining, renewing, and enhancing the surface transportation infrastructure will require on the order of a half trillion dollars as we approach the new century. The Department of Transportation estimates that about $280 billion would be needed just to maintain the nation's roads and bridges at 1989 conditions."[76]

While maintaining his promise of a balanced budget, Clinton called for a $16.3 billion economic stimulus package containing almost $3 billion in highway spending, $736 million for improvements to mass transit systems, $250 million in airport grants, $188 million for Amtrak maintenance and modernization, $235 million for repairs to veterans' hospitals, and $94 million for flood control, hydroelectric power, waterway, harbor, and environmental projects.[77]

Republicans never let it happen. Conservative pundits tore Clinton's proposals to shreds, and their leader was George F. Will—he who had championed big infrastructure spending when *Republicans* controlled the White House. With a *Democrat* in power, Will turned on a dime; without a shred of consistency he hammered away at the "omnipresent, officious, intrusive, bullying and expensive government" that Clinton was foisting on America. He assailed the "banality" of Clinton's "pork-laden stimulus package" and its place in a supposedly leftist agenda of "metastasizing government." He decried the further "melding of America's public and private sectors, in the name of industrial policy." The pundit who had written a conservative "Defense of the Welfare State" knew nothing of Tory reform in 1993: "Conservatives are predisposed to protect the market's allocation of resources," he preached, while "liberals are predisposed to expand government's scope."[78] There was nary a word of explanation from Will for this polemical reversal.

Republican tactics in Congress were equally crude: a Senate filibuster led by Republican minority leader Bob Dole kept the Clinton stimulus package in legislative limbo. Invoking Senate Rule XXII, Republican senators prevented any vote on Clinton's proposals by the Democratic majority. They could talk the Clinton program to death unless a supermajority of senators shut off debate.

Clinton had been slapped in the face—the long-standing Washington tradition of a presidential "honeymoon" was gone. The situation was obvious: he was being tested by thugs, and all the "ring-wise" veterans of Washington power-plays anticipated his response.

Certain Democratic strategists began to issue calls for a hardball response—lest the credibility of Clinton be destroyed at the start of his term. Lloyd Cutler, for example, a Washington attorney who had served as a presidential adviser, urged Clinton to employ an audacious technique for breaking the filibuster: the Democrats would claim that the filibuster rule is unconstitutional. Cutler's formula was simple and clever; here is how he sketched it out:

> If the vice president, the majority leader, and at least 49 other Senate Democrats want to challenge the constitutionality of Rule XXII . . . there is a potential scenario for doing it. The Senate Rules Committee, controlled by Democrats, would approve an amendment of Rule XXII. . . . When the amendment comes before the Senate, the Democrats would need to muster only 51 favorable votes (or 50 plus the vice president's vote). A Democratic senator would raise a point of order that this number is sufficient either to pass the amendment or to cut off debate against it, because the super-majority requirements of Rule XXII are unconstitutional. The vice president would support this view, backed up by an opinion of the attorney general. Following Senate custom on constitutional points, the vice president would refer the question to a vote of the entire Senate, where the same 51 or more votes . . . would sustain it.[79]

What could the Republicans do? Take the issue to the Supreme Court. In the meantime, Dole and his friends would get a good strong taste of how Clinton and friends could hit back: "If the administration and the Senate Democrats prepare to play this constitutional card, their bargaining position in the upcoming negotiations on the size and shape of the economic stimulus package would be stronger."[80]

But it seemed that Bill Clinton, Al Gore, and the rest were too weak to even think about playing the card, and so the stimulus package was destroyed. Clinton had flunked his first test. He was felled by a knee to the groin; he was beaten in a legislative street fight.

What did he do to recoup? He bragged about reducing the deficit. Then he joined the Republican free marketeers in pushing NAFTA: the North American Free Trade Agreement.

NAFTA was the cutting edge of "globalization," a spin-off trend in the free-market binge that had been gathering force since the 1970s. The origins of NAFTA could be traced to the Reagan years: Bush the elder had conducted the first negotiations.

In good neo-liberal fashion, Clinton hailed the NAFTA treaty as a victory for "free trade." He called it an opportunity for Americans to "compete." Detractors called NAFTA a Trojan horse: a corporate ploy to practice outsourcing on the international scale. Economist Jeff Faux observed that "there will always be someone in the world willing to work for less," and Democratic labor unions agreed.[81]

Globalization as a fad had been based upon some primitive generalizations. As essayist John Ralston Saul has observed, it encompassed the half-baked notion "that the power of the nation-state was on its way out, to be replaced by that of global markets." It also encompassed the simplistic idea "that the growth of international trade . . . would unleash an economic social tide that would raise all ships."[82]

In fact, globalization helped a great many corporations, both American and foreign, shirk important public obligations. Businessmen found that they could shift some operations to parts of the world where they could get away with shabby behavior. With the nation-state degraded by the new transnational entities, the thought of one's old-fashioned patriotic duty—a conservative value—became an afterthought in many business circles by the 1990s.

Among Clinton's Democratic supporters, NAFTA seemed an unsavory extension of the Reagan years: it aggrandized the rich at the expense of the working class everywhere. As Saul observed, the proponents of globalization made people uncomfortably aware of all the class-based economic trends that were overtaking them. They reflected on the fact that "abruptly, a middle-class family required two incomes. . . . In a mere twenty five years CEO salaries in the United States had gone from 39 times the pay of an average worker to more than 1,000 times."[83]

The connection here to Reagan-era politics was real, and Clinton paid a heavy price. At the same time he worsened the scorn of the Republicans who viewed him as an ideological poacher.

Another big price was paid for NAFTA: by making it his number-one priority after his defeat on the stimulus plan, Clinton lost precious time and momentum on the health care initiative. To Hillary Clinton he entrusted the task of preparing a national health care plan that would achieve what FDR, Harry Truman, and Richard Nixon failed to achieve.

Gore's "National Performance Review" to cut governmental red tape was completed in September 1993. And so, using deficit reduction and "reinventing government" as gestures to prove his credentials as a foe of bureaucracy, Clinton made a big speech to Congress advocating sweeping health care reforms. There was just a little problem: his proposals were not yet ready for the mill when he made his big speech, and so the oratory was wasted.

It was a blunder of extraordinary magnitude, a blunder of timing. Clinton lost irreplaceable momentum as the months rolled by and his enemies sniped at the never-quite-completed plan. As journalist Sidney Blumenthal observed, the "congressional speech was made in a political vacuum, for [Clinton] lacked a strategy for following it up."[84]

Medical insurers—business leaders in a field that is notorious for profiteering—launched an opulent counteroffensive. It was a televised campaign of propaganda with thirty-second "sound bite" ads in which characters called Harry and Louise alleged that Clinton's plan "forces us to buy our insurance through these new mandatory government health alliances . . . run by tens of thousands of new bureaucrats."[85] The sabotage was effective, since Clinton was working on NAFTA at the time and his wife ran the health care study "in secret." As Blumenthal lamented later on, "the closed door meetings of the task force . . . made it a sitting target, and its foes were able to raise early suspicions by turning its secrecy into an issue."[86] The health care plan was defeated in Congress in 1994.

At the halfway point of his first presidential term, Clinton had some modest legislative accomplishments: the small AmeriCorps youth service program and the Brady gun-control law. But otherwise, his program had been botched. Journalist E. J. Dionne Jr. recalled that in 1992

> Clinton spoke incessantly about economic pressures on the "forgotten middle class" and government's need to respond to fears of middle class collapse. Clinton talked about programs to retrain the work force, to educate kids for a more competitive new environment, to ease the transition from old jobs to new jobs. Clinton still loves this rhetoric, and a variety of programs have been launched. But mostly they are not very big or very visible, having been ground into small pieces by budget pressures. . . . The central threads of his presidency have disappeared.[87]

Right-wing strategists could brag about the way they rolled Clinton. In October 1994 Ann Devroy of the *Washington Post* reported that "one

GOP strategist, unwilling to allow his name to be used, said: 'I tell you, I wake up every morning happy. . . . And every time I think we are going too far, I think, hell, no, hit 'em again.'"[88]

The next month Republicans took control of Congress with their primitive "Contract with America." As Newt Gingrich became the new speaker of the House, Dick Armey, a Republican sidekick, summed up twenty-odd years of ideology: "The market is rational and the government is dumb."[89]

The new Republican revolutionaries were proposing to do things that Reagan never tried. Outside of the military sphere, their program amounted to the systematic uninvention of America's status as a civilized power. The sorts of people whom Eisenhower once described as "the most ignorant people now living in the United States" were now calling the shots in Congress. Their vision of the country seemed clear: a nation of gated communities and widespread squalor that was guarded by high-tech weaponry.

Much of the Republican plan had been written at the Cato Institute by followers of Milton Friedman. For starters, Republicans proposed to sell off two hundred of the national parks and to privatize the management of national parks that remained.[90] They proposed to abolish the Council of Economic Advisers.[91] They proposed a balanced budget amendment to the Constitution. They proposed to slash or eliminate scores of public works programs. They proposed the evisceration of environmental laws by forcing the government to compensate businesses subjected to pollution controls—to pay polluters not to pollute. They proposed a drastic weakening of food and drug regulation. Proposals for privatizing Social Security began to be floated—the first serious call for such a thing since the days of Barry Goldwater.

The balanced budget amendment came close to passage: it failed in the Senate by a margin of just one vote. Journalist Paul Starr had warned that the amendment's provisions would "severely weaken government's capacity to achieve any purpose." A "minority in either house would be able to impede preparations for national defense as well as spending for the poor. . . . It would be all the harder to find money for purposes that conservatives prefer, whether 'Star Wars' defense systems, more prisons or intensified border patrols." Above all, the amendment could leave the United States helpless in the face of a recession: "If revenue fell along with economic activity and three-fifths of Congress could not agree to run a deficit, the Government would be forced to aggravate the downturn by cutting public expenditures as well—a recipe for turning recessions into depressions."[92]

Even FDIC deposit insurance would have been affected. Richard Kogen, a fellow at the Center for Budget and Policy Priorities, showed how bank deposits could be jeopardized:

> Doesn't the FDIC charge annual fees to banks, building up large balances, which would automatically be available in a banking crisis? Not after the amendment. It prohibits spending borrowed funds [and] incredibly, it also prohibits using accumulated savings; it requires that all federal spending in any fiscal year be covered by that year's revenues. This requirement is like telling a family to finance a new house or a child's college tuition out of that year's wages, no matter how much money the family has in the bank.[93]

Clinton rolled with the punches: he suggested that Americans "read the fine print" in their contract. While opposing the Neanderthal amendment, he worked with the Republicans to hammer out a seven-year balanced budget plan.

A free-floating coalition of critics started taking on features of the Contract with America. Food safety experts cautioned that the contract legislation would halt the improvement of federal inspections of bacteria-contaminated meats that caused approximately four thousand deaths and five million illnesses every year.[94] Officials at the federal Centers for Disease Control warned that cutbacks would hamper the search for new antibiotics to fight mutant bacteria. "We're setting ourselves up for a major catastrophe," declared the Centers' Ruth Berkelman: "I'm talking about going in for a routine operation and dying from an infection."[95] Businesspeople like Alfred Zeien, the CEO of Gillette, complained that "devolution" of product labeling requirements and employment regulations to the states could cause chaos for companies doing business on the national scale.[96]

As early as March, polls showed that a growing number of Americans feared that the Republicans were going too far. And then came the Oklahoma bombing: it was suddenly clear that all the demonization of government had incited some demented killers.

A slow backlash against the Republican contract developed through 1995. Conservationists were up in arms about the plan to sell the national parks. Even gun owners helped in some improbable ways; hunters reacted to a bill to take 270 million acres of land from the federal Bureau of Land Management and turn it over to the states by launching a radio campaign to "keep public lands in public hands," and they prevailed.

Clinton instructed his cabinet members to target unpopular provisions of the contract for special attacks. But he could not let go of the anti-government rhetoric. Journalists Paul Taylor and Thomas B. Edsall reported that "no matter what their stripe, all Democrats are having trouble articulating a coherent message about the role of government—not only because of their internal fissures, but because many say they have no idea where the head of their ticket will finally come down on the issue."[97]

The "reinventing government" contingent was in no mood to back down; Clinton's secretary of housing and urban development, Henry Cisneros, and his National Park Service director, Roger Kennedy, sent Clinton a policy essay in 1995 urging him to "decentralize with a vengeance."[98]

Morale in the executive branch was approaching rock bottom. Public service seemed to be despised. Robert C. Gallo of the National Cancer Institute announced his intention to leave government with the observation that "government scientists used to be the golden boys, but those days are over. Government is the bad guy today."[99] Ronald C. Moe of the Congressional Research Service wrote that "the executive branch is today . . . an institution that has been poorly led and managed by Presidents for three decades and that presently functions under great stress."[100] Excellent people left government for good as Clinton downsized agencies—or outsourced work to make up the difference (no pensions or medical insurance would have to be paid to mere contractors)—in fulfillment of his balanced budget pledge.

In his 1996 State of the Union address, Clinton solemnly proclaimed, "the era of big government is over." Then he added a wishy-washy caveat: "But we cannot go back to the time when our citizens were left to fend for themselves."[101]

All through the 1996 campaign, Clinton stayed "on theme" with this ambivalent message as he sought a second term. He told reporters in a late summer interview that while he had "never been an advocate of a weak federal government," he had definitely advocated "a smaller one, where people got more for less. . . . That's why, even though I never expected it to have any traction, I guess, politically—and I don't think it has—this reinventing government effort has been very important to me."[102]

His Republican opponent, Bob Dole, dished out clichés. He explained that the "basic difference" between himself and Clinton was that "I trust the people. The President trusts the government." Dole repeated on the stump that Clinton "talks like a Republican, but he's a liberal"—a liberal nurturing "a million little schemes to spend your money and rob the future of all the young people." He proposed an across-the-board tax cut, so that the "government has to pinch pennies."[103]

The results of the 1996 election maintained the uneasy status quo. Clinton remained in the White House, but the Republicans retained control of Congress. Yet Republicans began a slow retreat from their extremist contract. "Government is the enemy until you need a friend," proclaimed Republican William Cohen as he prepared to retire from the Senate. "Is the public ready to say: 'Let the private sector handle everything'? Clearly not."[104]

Some carefully targeted Clinton initiatives expanded governmental regulation in crowd-pleasing ways. Federal meat inspection standards were tightened for the first time since Theodore Roosevelt's day. Clinton set up a national database to track convicted child molesters. Congress passed legislation to tighten drinking water standards; the bipartisan Kennedy-Kassebaum bill made health care insurance more portable, and it also limited the power of insurers to deny coverage to people with preexisting conditions.[105] On the devolution front, however, Congress and Clinton found common if controversial ground in welfare reform (the Personal Responsibility and Work Opportunity Reconciliation Act of 1996) and the phase-out of agricultural price supports (the 1996 Federal Agriculture Improvement and Reform Act).

More devolution talk was in the air: free marketeers began to target Social Security. Another advisory commission was examining the long-term solvency issues of the system, and talk of a "crisis" spread. So the privatizers started to lobby. Economist Henry Aaron complained that "brokerage houses and mutual funds, lusting after lucrative customers, are pouring millions into a campaign to convince Congress and the president to privatize Social Security."[106]

Historian Edward D. Berkowitz put the issues in long-term perspective. He admitted there were actuarial concerns. But he also pointed out that some modest adjustments could alter the long-term picture:

> It helps to remember that about 142 million persons will make contributions to the program in 1996 totaling about $380 billion. That means that even small changes made today will have large consequences. . . . If we begin to make small adjustments now, we will produce large consequences 25 years from now, much like a plane that adjusts its course by one degree as it begins a long journey. . . . In the case of Social Security, a tax rise of 2.2 percent of covered payroll . . . if undertaken right now, would solve the entire long-range problem.[107]

The advisory panel was divided, but the specter of privatization was averted in 1997. Social Security survived—to be attacked later on by Bush the younger.

Clinton's second term was largely wasted on the ramifications of the Monica Lewinsky scandal, the Kenneth Starr prosecution/persecution, and the tawdry drama of impeachment without conviction. All the while, Clinton's vision of the future—such as it was—was increasingly irrelevant. His talk of a "bridge to the twenty-first century" was boring and banal.

More exciting ideas began to come from thinkers on the right. Perhaps the failure of the Gingrich program had been liberating Tory sensibilities.[108] In 1997 Clinton proposed authorizing $175 billion over the following six years for infrastructure. This was little more than the feeble ISTEA authorization of 1991. But a Republican congressman, Bud Shuster, forged a bipartisan consensus to exceed this level. Shuster faced off against "balanced budget hawks," who kept calling him the "prince of pork."[109] But he prevailed.

On another front, Newt Gingrich called for the rebirth of America's space program. The ever-mercurial George F. Will applauded. In a column datelined "Hoover Dam," Will mused that "many people will be surprised, and certain kinds of conservatives scandalized, by the speaker's belief that government is competent for, and has a duty to attempt, the peacetime mobilization of people for projects explicitly designed to elicit nobility through collective action. . . . But he has much American history on his side."[110] Then Will rediscovered his earlier support for infrastructure, noting that "Eisenhower's championing of more than 40,000 miles of new highways reflected thinking with a long, strong Republican pedigree."[111]

In 1997, William Kristol and David Brooks wrote a column in the *Wall Street Journal* calling for a "National Greatness Conservatism" that "does not despise government."[112] They lectured Republicans, reminding them that Theodore Roosevelt's statecraft possessed a strongly conservative component. Brooks argued, "democracy has a tendency to slide into nihilistic mediocrity if its citizens are not inspired by some larger national goal." And since "the best conservative thought knows that without a sense of national community, we balkanize," civilized Tories should be striving for a politics of "effort, cultivation, and mastery," knowing that "ultimately the American purpose can find its voice only in Washington."[113]

Meanwhile, the Clinton era lurched to its conclusion. Some people loved Clinton for the enemies he made, and certain commentators struggled to extol his achievements. Sidney Blumenthal claimed that "Clinton's policies helped the nation to achieve the greatest prosperity in its history, the greatest reduction in poverty and increase in family income and wages since Johnson's Great Society." He drew attention to the legacy of Clinton's balanced budgets, hailing "the greatest budget surplus ever, earmarked for paying off the national debt and guaranteeing Social Security and Medicare."[114]

But the economic boom that would crest at the end of the 1990s was as transient as Reagan's boom. It was driven by stock speculation and the Internet explosion. When the dot-com boom became the dot-com bust, the euphoria subsided.[115] As for unemployment, the most widely touted figures excluded the people who had reached such a point of despair that they had *given up* looking for jobs: the "discouraged workers." But there were lots of them, subsisting in a makeshift world of dysfunction.[116]

As for the earning power of middle-class wages, many thousands of Americans continued to complain that it took two incomes to approximate—let alone equal—the standard of living that their families enjoyed with a single income in the 1950s and 1960s.[117] That being the case, a grinding rat race overtook middle-class life in many parts of the United States. Journalist Robert Kuttner observed that "an employee fearful of his job security and working several jobs has less time or inclination to volunteer for the Little League." There was "barely enough time to juggle work and family" in Bill Clinton's America.[118]

And then, in an eerie reprise of Jimmy Carter's mistakes, Clinton signed some legislation that would lead directly to the economic meltdown under Bush the younger—as Carter inadvertently paved the way for the S&L scandal of the 1980s. In 1999, Clinton signed legislation to repeal the Glass-Steagall Act of 1933, which (among its other provisions) separated commercial and investment banking. This legislation—introduced by Senator Phil Gramm—put commercial banks at risk by entangling their lending with Wall Street speculation.

Even worse, in 2000, Clinton signed the Commodity Futures Modernization Act, which exempted a type of "credit derivative" called a "credit default swap" (financial terms whose baleful significance was clear by 2009) from regulation.[119] Clinton's treasury secretary, Robert Rubin, and his deputy, Lawrence Summers, both supported this move.

At his worst, Bill Clinton was a terrible mess—he became his own worst enemy. He had a quick mind, but he accepted the trendy clichés without much in the way of analysis. His endless gyrations were ridiculous: the late-night comics had a field day. And the American people lost another opportunity to "get their house back in order." American life was still ragged, divisive, and harsh at the end of Clinton's term.

But it remained to be seen whether competent leadership waited in the twenty-first century.

GEORGE W. BUSH

In his campaign speeches in the summer and fall of 2000, George W. Bush had pledged to be "humble" and to keep the United States "humble." Who could tell that this conventional piety—conventional at least by the standards of the new religiosity—was a psychological giveaway?

There were similar giveaways in Bush's demeanor in the autumn debates with the Democratic candidate, Al Gore. Bush smirked—there was no mistaking the expression—and came off as a cracker-barrel know-it-all. (Gore came off as a different kind of know-it-all—the walking encyclopedia.) It was a dreary campaign, but Gore won—in the popular vote.

Then the quirky anachronism lurking in our system—the Electoral College—kicked in, and Bush, with some flagrant help from his brother, the governor of Florida, prevailed in that state amid charges of irregularities at the polls. The Bushes were upheld when the Supreme Court stopped the Florida recount.

And so it was that the humble George Bush gave America the first demonstration of his will to win at any cost. He and his vice president, Dick Cheney—assisted by their strategist Karl Rove—displayed a ruthlessness that would last almost down to the end. Who could tell that the ruthlessness would go along with monumental incompetence?

But perhaps it was not so very strange: incompetence and arrogance are often related, for the arrogant tend to make mistakes that more sensible people avoid. This was the administration that was fated to lead the United States when war came directly to our shores on September 11, 2001.

The horror of that day—the helpless people on the hijacked planes, the exploding towers, the mass murder, the heroism of the New York firefighters and police officers, the self-sacrifice of the ordinary/extraordinary people who gave their lives to bring down one of the airliners destined for Washington—was the sort of thing that can never be forgotten by those who experienced it; it was one of those events like Pearl Harbor that become historically iconic. But the *contrast* between Pearl Harbor and 9/11 was instructive.

At Pearl Harbor the Japanese attacked a *military base* that was thousands of miles from the continental United States. America's response was a declaration of war and the greatest mobilization of resources and people in the nation's history. On 9/11, terrorists launched a direct assault upon civilians in the nation's largest city, with another attack upon the nation's capital (the strike at the Pentagon appeared to be a last-minute switch from a plan to obliterate the Capitol or the White House).

What was the response of George Bush? It was certainly less than Rooseveltian: there was no declaration of war and no national mobilization. Bush vowed to bring the terrorists to "justice," and he told the American people to go about their business as professionals handled the matter.

A conservative commentator, Charles Krauthammer, spelled out the comparison in darkly humorous terms: "This is not crime. This is war. . . . Secretary of State Colin Powell's first reaction to the day of infamy was to pledge to 'bring those responsible to justice.' This is exactly wrong. Franklin Roosevelt did not respond to Pearl Harbor by pledging to bring the commander of Japanese naval aviation to justice. He pledged to bring Japan to its knees."[120] Robert Kagan, an associate at the Carnegie Endowment for International Peace, was equally vehement: "Please let us make no mistake this time. We are at war now. . . . The only question is whether we will now take this war seriously, as seriously as any war we have ever fought, whether we will conduct it with the intensity and perseverance it requires. . . . We should now immediately begin building up our conventional military forces."[121]

Senator Charles Schumer of New York argued that "September 11 awakened us to the reality that technology has enabled a small group of diabolical people living halfway around the globe to make large parts of our society vulnerable to attack." A whole new strategic architecture for national security would have to be developed. Consequently, he argued, "for the foreseeable future, the federal government will have to grow."[122] Robin Toner opined in the *New York Times* that in the aftermath of 9/11 "nobody wants to get government off their backs."[123]

Little by little George Bush and his people got the point; Bush proclaimed a "war on terror." But there was never a mobilization. And there was never a significant expansion of our troop strength, except for the call-up of national guardsmen.

Bush failed to send enough troops to Afghanistan to capture (or kill) the terrorist leaders. His defense secretary, Donald Rumsfeld, was hoping to win "on the cheap," using Afghan warlords to supplement U.S. Special Forces. This coalition of convenience succeeded in toppling the Taliban regime, but Sheik Omar, the Taliban leader, and Osama bin Laden, the Al Qaeda mastermind, slipped away. The response to 9/11 had been botched.

A Rooseveltian response—a true national mobilization, complete with an expanded citizen army (those who lost family and friends at the World Trade Center could have led the great recruitment drive)—might have swept away much of the nihilism that corroded American culture in the

1990s. Americans were ready once again for dedication to the common good: they were ready for hard work, sacrifice, and unity. Bush blew it.

His response to 9/11 revealed all the ideological divisions in modern conservatism: its libertarian and authoritarian trends were deeply at odds.[124] Bush's penchant for free marketeering made him weirdly reluctant to federalize airport security, even after the attack proved that private contractors could not be trusted with the job. It took pressure from Congress by Senator Joseph Lieberman (Gore's running mate), among others, to convince George Bush that a cabinet-level Department of Homeland Security was a good idea. Once Bush got going, however, his USA Patriot Act became distressing to civil libertarians. Here was the authoritarian side of conservatism. "Big government," at least in this sense, was back with a vengeance.

Bush supported a number of "big government" initiatives with no connection to the issues of national security. One of them was the No Child Left Behind Act. This program forced the states to accept new standards for educational attainment, standards to be set by the Department of Education (which had been separated from the old HEW in 1980). Critics complained that the act forced a lockstep approach to curriculum and teaching in the public schools. This was the sort of thing that Eisenhower had hoped to avoid when he supported federal aid to education in 1958. In 2003, Bush signed into law a massive Medicare prescription drug plan. Major flaws in the program, however, left a great many elderly Americans worse off than before.[125]

In other respects, Bush sought to weaken the government as much as possible at the behest of corporate interests and the rich. Former solicitor of the House of Representatives Charles Tiefer charged that Bush "entered office eager to accomplish a larger-than-suspected far-right agenda, delivering much more for his conservative bases than their limited political strength would seemingly sustain."[126]

He revived supply-side economics. He pushed through one of the largest tax cuts in our history in 2001, and, as usual, the rich got richer. But the economy was faltering. Deindustrialization continued, and so did the worst effects of globalization.[127] The dot-com bust caused computer companies to downsize drastically in 2002; computer jobs were shifted to India. The economic contraction in Bush's first term caused many states to cut funding for schools, libraries, and parks.

In response, Bush pushed through another big tax cut in 2003. Once again, the rich got special breaks. Bush repeated the contention of Arthur Laffer that the tax cuts would pay for themselves, a contention that was proven spectacularly wrong in the years that followed.[128] Critics like Paul

Krugman began to wonder whether Bush was actually trying to create a fiscal crisis:

> It's no secret that right-wing ideologues want to abolish programs that Americans take for granted. But not long ago, to suggest that the Bush administration's policies might actually be driven by those ideologues—that the administration was deliberately setting the country up for a fiscal crisis in which popular social programs could be sharply cut—was to be accused of spouting conspiracy theories. Yet by pushing through another huge tax cut in the face of record deficits, the administration clearly demonstrates either that it is completely feckless, or that it actually wants a fiscal crisis (or both). . . . We can be sure that the right will do whatever it takes to preserve the Bush tax cuts—right now the administration is even skimping on homeland security to save a few dollars here and there.[129]

Bush "skimped on homeland security" even as his "war on terror" unfolded. Question: Has any other president pushed for *reductions* in taxes in the midst of what he calls a major war? Did Wilson or FDR seek *reductions* in taxes to help them win the world wars? Did Lincoln seek reductions in taxes to defeat the Confederates?

In this and other measures, Bush revived the world of Reagan. Deregulation continued. Bush appointed Gale Norton, a foe of the environmental movement, to be secretary of the interior. He refused to support the Kyoto Protocol of 1997, aimed at reducing "greenhouse" gases that could cause global warming.

A California energy crisis (linked to the incipient Enron scandal) unfolded in 2001. Industry critics asserted that profiteers caused artificial shortages in order to boost prices.[130] A professional utility consultant hoped for swift justice. Gregory Palast rejoiced that the primary culprits, Southern California Edison (SCE) and Pacific Gas and Electric (PG&E), were facing bankruptcy: "I can't think of anything that would more joyously combine historical justice and good public policy. Why justice? Because SCE and PG&E executives, eager to reap the profits of deregulation, were in the forefront of the army of industry lobbyists fighting to establish the system that got California into this mess. And why good public policy? Because letting the utilities go bankrupt could be the first step toward returning California to the system of government price regulation that has given America some of the cheapest and most reliable electricity in the world."[131]

As the Enron scandal erupted in 2001, the public heard not only that the soon-to-be bankrupt energy company was rife with accounting fraud but also that Enron traders had prompted utilities to cause rolling blackouts by shutting down plants for *unnecessary maintenance*.[132] Another electrical crisis occurred in 2003: a brief blackout of the northeastern United States. The apparent problem this time was *inadequate* maintenance of the interstate power grid.

In 2003, Bush fomented war in Iraq with the false allegation that Saddam Hussein harbored "weapons of mass destruction." He invoked the "war on terror" to justify toppling a regime that had nothing to do with Al Qaeda. The invasion, however, made Iraq a sudden haven for all sorts of terrorists, including Al Qaeda.

The decision-making was disgraceful. The CIA was bullied into churning out rigged intelligence analyses. Secretary of State Colin Powell was duped into making baseless charges that ruined his career. Another career would be ruined, but not soon enough: the career of Donald Rumsfeld, perhaps the worst individual to serve as America's secretary of defense since creation of the department in 1947.

Rumsfeld convinced George Bush that the war in Iraq could be easily won, and so troops were sent into peril in insufficient numbers. It was Vietnam again: these men had learned nothing in forty years. There appears to have been no planning for a long occupation or counterinsurgency warfare. There was no plan B—no worst-case planning at all. The political price to be paid for this failure would be clear at the midpoint of Bush's second term: mass discontent with Bush's handling of Iraq gave the Democrats control of Congress in 2006.

But even in 2004, when Bush faced the voters again, his ineptitude as commander-in-chief was an issue. His opponent, John Kerry, a Vietnam combat veteran, made certain it would be an issue. Bush's response was bluster. Journalist Bob Woodward summarized the tactics, looking back a few years later: "All the perpetually upbeat talk and optimism—from 'Mission Accomplished,' through 'stay the course' . . . the barbs that anyone who questioned his strategy in Iraq did not support the troops and instead wanted America to 'cut and run' or 'surrender to the terrorists'—it was the same play, over and over."[133]

But there was another play: Bush surrogates who called themselves the Swift Boat Veterans for Truth complained that Kerry's decorations as a Vietnam hero had been undeserved, that his heroism (in contrast to Bush's skimpy service in the Air National Guard) had been a lie.

Kerry made a mistake in 2004, the same mistake that Bill Clinton had made back in 1993: he took a hit below the belt without retaliating through some street-fighting tactics of his own. He was far too much of a gentleman. One wonders what would have occurred if he had sued the Swift Boat people for libel, right in the midst of the campaign—sued them for millions of dollars for character assassination. Would Bush have been inclined to depict him as a "flip-flop" candidate after that? We will never know.

To help ensure victory, Bush and his adviser Karl Rove used every angle to exacerbate the culture war, to depict all liberals as enemies of home and of family, to mobilize the Christian right. The result was the infamous electoral division of the "red states" versus the "blue states."

Bush prevailed—he divided America as Nixon used to do, and, like Nixon, he continued his debilitating struggle on behalf of an unpopular war. Blumenthal observed that "campaigning in 2004 on the trauma of September 11, he won by the smallest margin of any incumbent president in American history. . . . In the chasm between his meagre win and his grandiose ambition, Bush might have decided to form a government containing some moderate Republican and Democratic cabinet members, claiming the gravity of the foreign crisis demanded national unity. But the thought apparently never occurred to him."[134]

Then Hurricane Katrina hit New Orleans in 2005. To all the world, America looked like a banana republic as the city was reduced to conditions of a Third World country while officials in Washington dithered. Secretary of Homeland Security Michael Chertoff blamed the U.S. Constitution by invoking the duty of governors and other state officials to take the lead in such matters.

In the aftermath of Katrina, Colin Powell's former chief of staff, retired colonel Lawrence Wilkerson, charged in a speech to the New America Foundation that in the case of a nuclear attack (especially one that was launched by terrorists) or a catastrophic epidemic (especially a bioterrorism attack), "the ineptitude of this government [would] take you back to the Declaration of Independence."[135]

It was downhill for Bush after that: his attempt to semi-privatize Social Security collapsed and Republicans lost their congressional majority midway through his second term.[136]

More disturbing revelations emerged. An investigation by journalist William Finnegan suggested that America's abandonment of port and terminal operations to foreign owners could leave our port cities open to nuclear attack if terrorists should put a nuclear device aboard a rogue freighter.[137] Dangerous imported goods from China left millions of Americans wondering why the leaders of the nation chose to shortchange federal inspections.

In 2008 there was a scandal at FAA. Southwest Airlines neglected to check its aircraft for fuselage cracks. When some FAA inspectors tried to remedy the situation, their superiors slapped them down. The inspectors went public; they complained that the agency "had gone from aggressively regulating airlines to treating them like customers."[138]

All the while, the preconditions for the great economic calamity of 2008 had shaped up. Sleazy mortgage brokers seeking quick commissions sold adjustable rate mortgages (ARMs) to low-income borrowers who would probably default when their rates began to climb. Then the mortgages were packaged into larger bundles ("collateralized debt obligations," or CDOs) that were sold to big investment houses. These investment "vehicles" were so complex that it was hard to understand what they contained. But a number of people saw the danger. A member of the Federal Reserve Board, Edward Gramlich, urged Alan Greenspan, the chairman, to force some restraint. Under the 1968 Truth in Lending Act, the board possessed some power to do this. But Greenspan, a glib libertarian appointed by Reagan and reappointed by Clinton, refused.[139]

Before the "sub-prime crisis" struck the housing industry—before the real estate foreclosures swept the nation—preconditions for the "credit derivatives" catastrophe were also shaping up. Rich speculators bet that the collateralized debt obligations would fail. And so they bought what amounted to insurance policies: "credit default swaps," a type of "credit derivative" that pays off when certain assets fail. The swap/derivatives were hawked by large financial companies like AIG. The idea was to milk the disaster for the greatest possible payoff. As the brokers pushed loans that would fail, these hustlers began to exploit them. They did it with their eyes wide open to enrich speculators. Indeed, the hustlers at AIG sold *multiple* credit default swaps on the same "assets." This would lead the financial firm (which would naturally have to pay out) to the brink of bankruptcy in 2009. Of course, the hustlers left before it happened. And responsible financiers predicted as much; Warren Buffett called credit derivatives "financial weapons of mass destruction."[140]

At first, however, these trends had little effect upon believers in laissez-faire. They continued to diminish the effectiveness of public institutions. Privatization and outsourcing grew under Bush, and so a strange new anomaly arose: as governmental efforts increased in some sectors, the presence of the federal *workforce* continued to shrink.

New York Times journalists Scott Shane and Ron Nixon reported in 2007 that, "without a public debate or formal policy decision, contractors have been a virtual fourth branch of government. On the rise for decades, spending on federal contracts has soared during the Bush administration [fueled] by a philosophy that encourages outsourcing almost everything government does."[141]

At its worst, this tendency was dangerous: it put us at risk. How can we hold our officials accountable when services are rendered by businesses that might cut corners? This, we should remember, was the reason why airport security was federalized after 9/11. And yet the Bush administration began to subcontract some functions of border protection—a vital component of our national security program—to Halliburton, Dick Cheney's old corporate home.

The civil servants accountable to *us*—or to Congress—were being phased out in favor of businesses. While certain sectors of the government grew—the size of the Justice Department's workforce increased about 25 percent since 1990, for example, and the growth in our "homeland security" workforce was obvious—others declined: the Defense Department workforce shrank by 35 percent since 1990. The Department of Health and Human Services cut its workforce in half. The NASA workforce dropped by 23.2 percent.[142] Many agencies, in order to cope with falling budgets, created "foundations" to help them raise funds. Uncle Sam became a beggar.

Our government had to pinch pennies—the dream of Bob Dole came true—and so our national readiness, our strength as a great global power, was weakened. Even obvious investments, like highway maintenance, were still under threat and under challenge.

When the latest bipartisan federal commission on infrastructure spending delivered its report, Mary Peters, Bush's secretary of transportation, dissented. Journalist Fred Hiatt wrote that her position, "cast backward . . . would suggest that President Dwight D. Eisenhower never should have built the interstate highway system; it should have been left to private companies to build roads wherever tolling could generate a profit."[143]

Such were the comparisons that often sprang to mind as a national memorial to Dwight D. Eisenhower moved through the planning stages. Eisenhower looked better and better over time, especially compared to the incompetence of Bush the younger.[144] Ike was a master of logistics as a military man; his invasion armada was the largest and best equipped force of its kind in history. He never sent troops into combat in insufficient numbers. As a president he faced a new security threat—nuclear war—and he created sane structures of defense that served America well for many years. Through a partnership of government and business he helped to bring unprecedented prosperity. And this continued in the work of his successor, John F. Kennedy.

Those were the days when America "led the free world," when American life was the standard by which many billions of people judged success. A half-century later, we were sunk in disarray: our industries were going or in dreadful decline, our economy was riddled with booby traps, and our culture made it hard for us to talk about the many things we had in common.

Public service was disintegrating rapidly; government was melting into nebulous deals with mere contractors, some honest and some reprehensible. Gone were the days when a man like Henry Stimson could recall that when he entered public service he had stepped into a world of bracing clarity, a realm where he could look up high and see the stars.

No more. Public service had become a realm of mush, obscurity, mendacity, and disillusionment. Honest civil servants saw their budgets cut back and their responsibilities trimmed as political hatchetmen (or -women) took over at the tops of their agencies. With government run like a down-sized business, the service cutbacks were inevitable. This was decadence.

Presidential incompetence had helped it along, and so did folly, malice, and greed. The grandeur of America's ascendancy was rotted away from within. Foreign enemies could not have done better in a war of subversion. But we were doing all this to ourselves. At least after Hurricane Katrina—notwithstanding the war between the "red state" and "blue state" mentalities—there was a widespread sense of America's decline.

The latest presidential incompetent, Bush, remained a tinhorn almost to the end. But as the sub-prime crisis and the credit derivative scandal caused a Wall Street panic that ramified all around the world—as investment firms tottered, and the chain reaction grew—the worst economic contraction since the 1930s spread over the country. The new chairman of the Federal Reserve, economist Ben Bernanke, together with Henry Paulson, Bush's treasury secretary, worked for months to stop the hemorrhage. They finally persuaded George Bush—he who had tried to semi-privatize Social Security—to propose the greatest economic intervention in the free-market system by government since the New Deal: the $700 billion bailout package that Congress passed in the midst of a presidential election.

The legacy of Carter and Reagan was toppling. Washington wags of the sort who had praised Alan Greenspan—Reagan's Federal Reserve chairman—as "the maestro" during the 1990s now dismissed the aging libertarian as "Mr. Laissez-Faire."[145] Greenspan confessed to an irate congressional committee that he "made a mistake" when he ignored the sub-prime "bubble." He said he was "shocked" by the Wall Street meltdown.[146] A professor of political economy observed that America's Reagan-era "model" was gone: "Under the mantra of less government . . . the financial sector [did] tremendous harm to the rest of society."[147]

The 2008 presidential candidates, John McCain and Barack Obama, played catch-up, struggling to invent new positions—new formulae—to placate the voters. But one thing seemed clear at the time: as Bush's treasury secretary put it, "raw capitalism is dead."[148]

7

HORIZONS

"America was still resilient, still responsive to a cure."

Thomas Wolfe, *You Can't Go Home Again*

In 2008, after forty years of decline, a political breakthrough occurred. Commentator Joan Didion rejoiced that "for the first time in the memory of most of us a major political party [has nominated] a demonstrably superior candidate."[1] Barack Obama was positioned to revive our American tradition of intelligent centrist governance. A black man who emphasizes unifying themes (and a leader who de-emphasizes race whenever possible), he was well-positioned to eradicate some of our divisions.

Writer George Packer observed that while Obama's creed emphasizes "activist government," the nominally "liberal" Obama shows a very strong "attachment to the institutions that hold up American society, a desire to make them function better rather than remake them altogether," which is "a pretty good description of what used to pass for conservatism."[2]

If Obama succeeds—if he serves two terms and delivers prosperity and national security—Lincoln's way could stand redeemed in our time. If he fails, the sources of America's national and global greatness will continue to erode.

He began well enough in some respects: a $3.6 trillion budget for national necessities. He pledged to deliver economic recovery, to prop up the failing auto industry, to invest on a massive basis in new "green technologies," to reopen the issue of health care reform. He attempted bipartisan consensus-building, though Republicans generally spurned him. And he made intelligent plans to phase out of Iraq while shifting troops to more important theaters of action such as Afghanistan.

233

But he also made questionable moves—from the start. To be chief of the recovery effort, he tapped Lawrence Summers, an economist complicit in the deregulation that caused the economic disaster. Summers (like Robert Rubin, his political mentor) supported the deregulation of "credit derivatives" in 2000. Timothy Geithner, Obama's pick as treasury secretary, triggered resentment for the way he administered TARP—the Troubled Asset Relief Program that was thrown together in the closing months of Bush's term. Obama had pledged to restructure the financial sector, using all the abundant leverage provided by the federally orchestrated taxpayer bailout to curb the excesses of Wall Street—the excesses of the speculators who dragged down the world's economy by gambling on trash. But Geithner's moves in this direction seemed minimal. Economist Paul Krugman complained that on Geithner's watch the pay for investment bankers in the stricken banks was returning to pre-crisis levels. And this was obscene: "Given all the taxpayer money on the line, financial firms should be acting like public utilities, not returning to the practices and paychecks of 2007."[3]

The recovery was painfully slow. Notwithstanding the enormous $787 billion stimulus package (which was added to the previous $700 billion financial bailout package), unemployment remained unacceptably high in 2009. By summer, people spoke of a "jobless recovery."[4] What was wrong? The weakened state of manufacturing was partially to blame, but Obama's judiciousness—an admirable trait in other circumstances—was also a factor. Many complained that the recovery money was spent too slowly. The Democrats were unduly worried by Republican charges of a "boondoggle." Vice President Biden held regular meetings with the cabinet to vet all the spending proposals. This was a throwback to Harold Ickes and the excessive caution he displayed when he ran PWA. What was arguably needed in 2009 was a *crash* effort like the mobilization of 1940 and 1941—the huge emergency effort that supplanted the New Deal's temporizing and *yanked* the country out of its doldrums. Obama's incrementalism precluded the sort of tactics that could have led to a full and rapid mobilization. In the summer of 2009, writer Kevin Baker took a worst-case view, opining that Obama was moving "prudently, carefully, and reasonably toward disaster."[5] The recovery continued, though with too much suffering by far.

Obama was trying out an interesting mixture of Eisenhower's easygoing style—to calm down the national mood after years of polarization—and Kennedyesque inspiration. A defining moment came when the debate about health care erupted into right-wing catcalls—blatant attempts to cause hysteria with charges that Obama would institute "death panels."

Here were the very same "big lie" tactics—guttersnipe tactics—that were used against Bill Clinton.

Obama just bided his time and then counterpunched in a powerful speech to Congress—a speech that was punctuated by Republican boo-ing and a gross interruption ("you lie!") by a South Carolina Republican. Obama followed up with cross-country appearances to recover his earlier support base and generate cover for the Democrats in 2010.[6] But libertarian "tea parties" were appearing all over America: demonstrations to oppose big government with ancient American rhetoric. By the end of 2009, both houses of Congress passed a health care bill that was acceptable to Obama. But just a few weeks afterward, the Democrats were crippled in the Senate (before the health care bills could be reconciled) when a special election to fill the seat made vacant by the death of Edward M. Kennedy went to the Republicans.

This meant that the Democrats had lost their ability to block filibus-ters. And everyone, including Obama, blamed the loss on severe economic discontent.

Obama's first year was not a triumph. It was clear that recovery—not health care—should have been (and should have *remained*) the number-one priority. It was clear that the recovery stimulus was too incremental: it should have been heavily frontloaded with projects (one thinks inevitably of the WPA) that would eradicate unemployment fast. Obama had the wrong economic adviser: instead of Lawrence Summers he could very well have tapped a more forceful and cogent Keynesian—like Paul Krugman. But he didn't. After losing the ability to overpower filibusters, Democrats developed a jobs bill that won some Republican support. And Obama chose to handle the health care issue by advising House Democrats to settle for something like the Senate-passed legislation. He prevailed—but the public reaction to this hard-won achievement may be subject to change.

A number of state attorneys-general launched challenges in court on the basis of the bill's constitutionality. And the "tea party" people were livid all over the country.

Constitutional challenges to controversial legislation are to be ex-pected. But the hatred expressed by a number of the tea party sponsors was a very different matter. What the tea party-goers failed to understand was that their free-floating phobias regarding big government could shake the foundations of America's great power status. By invoking the rhetoric of Samuel Adams in an era when Americans are groping to recover self-mastery, they challenge the legacy of Founders such as George Washington, who, by the 1780s, saw plainly that libertarian fanaticism could lead the

United States to chaos. Hence the scrapping of the Articles of Confederation, which left the United States helpless in the face of foreign enemies and grave domestic woes. Only in a mad hatter's tea party would Americans eulogize the weakness of an infant nation without the power to provide for the common defense, insure domestic tranquility, and promote the general welfare. If the tea party-goers could be teleported back to the 1780s, they would probably oppose the ratification of our Constitution.

Will Obama have the spirit to hurl such challenges right in the party-goers' faces?

He is judicious, self-controlled, and patient. He has some qualities that make for a triumphant presidency—but perhaps not in times like these. What we may need now is what Theodore Roosevelt possessed long ago: swashbuckling audacity, the vision to commence mighty works (like the Panama Canal) that kindle patriotic fervor, empower the nation, and convey the thrill of pioneering.

Only time will determine if the smart young man whom the voters have placed at the helm will fulfill his early promise. The stakes are excruciatingly high.

INSPIRATIONAL HORIZONS

Classicist Donald Kagan once observed that "only in ancient Athens and the United States has democracy lasted for as much as two hundred years. Monarchy and different forms of despotism, on the other hand, have gone on for millenia. . . . Optimists may believe that democracy is the inevitable and final form of human society, but the historical record shows that up to now it has been the rare exception."[7]

Kagan argued that three conditions were necessary for democracy to flourish: "the first is to have a good set of institutions, the second is to have a body of citizens who possess a good understanding of the principles of democracy [and] the third is to have a high quality of leadership."[8] Kagan offered Pericles of Athens as the highest exemplar, musing that "few eras in human history can compare with the greatness achieved by Athens under the leadership of Pericles."[9]

The center of Periclean leadership was public works—specifically, the building program that created the Parthenon and nearby monuments. According to Kagan, "this project was at the center of Pericles' policies. . . . Nothing in his magnificent career matched its importance to him."[10]

Pericles of Athens conceived the great Acropolis building program as the crowning glory of his age. He envisaged the architectural program in the second half of the fifth century B.C. It was designed to achieve two effects. The first of these was socioeconomic: the campaign was intended to create what might be called a proto-Keynesian expansion of wealth that would build the prosperity of Athens in a manner that would benefit all social classes. According to Plutarch, Pericles "boldly laid before the people proposals for immense public works and plans for buildings, which would involve many different arts and industries . . . his object being that those who stayed at home, no less than those serving in the fleet or in the army . . . should be enabled to enjoy a share of the national wealth." Consequently, as the project advanced, "the city's prosperity was extended far and wide and shared among every age and condition in Athens."[11]

The second purpose was political. Kagan has argued that the buildings, especially the Parthenon, were conceived to make "the greatness of Athens tangible and visible to all." Athenians were "caught up in the magnificence of the structures they were building," and "understood that the buildings would be a memorial to their democracy."[12]

Periclean methods—always at war in our culture with the force of libertarian extremism—have played a significant role in our history. The case can be made that our six greatest presidents were essentially Periclean leaders. The greatest of our public works projects have made America's greatness "tangible and visible to all." Indeed, the monumental buildings of our nation's capital express the idea for all time.

The iconography of ancient Greece and Rome has been a theme-giver in the architecture and planning of America's capital city from the earliest days of the L'Enfant plan to the revival and expansion of the plan in the days of Theodore Roosevelt. In 1901 and 1902, the congressionally chartered McMillan Commission laid out the great building program that would gradually encompass the construction of the Lincoln Memorial, the Federal Triangle project (including the National Archives building), the Supreme Court building, the National Gallery of Art, and the Jefferson Memorial. The last of these buildings were completed under the watchful supervision of an upper-class patron of classicism, FDR.[13]

The "picture postcard" city comprising the "federal enclave" of Washington retains its power to inspire. Tourists who have come from the farthest corners of America throng the Mall and their reactions can often approximate the wonder displayed by James Stewart in the 1939 film *Mr. Smith Goes to Washington*—a film that was released at a time when the

Lincoln Memorial was less than twenty years old and the Jefferson Memorial was still under construction.

The symbolic purpose of the national memorials was (and is) obvious, but even workday buildings in Washington constructed in accordance with the principles of McMillan-style classicism—the federal office buildings that were built before World War II—have a grandeur that even some hard-bitten residents of Washington can feel now and then.

So does the original planning of the city, with its avenues and vistas, especially the vista created by the Mall, sweeping westward as it does to the Lincoln Memorial and onward for those who may be gazing from the high ground of Capitol Hill, across the Potomac to the dark ridge that forms the horizon. Beyond that ridge is the westward expanse of the republic. Any meditative mind in the spell of such a gaze will reflect upon America's vastness.

In FDR's time our elected leaders were obliged to think in such terms. From the New Deal agencies a visionary spirit spread out to other parts of America, even in the brick-and-mortar projects that today we call "infrastructure," projects constructed in accordance with the functional principles of modernism, as opposed to formal classical design. No matter. Classical or modern, the structures were meant to inspire the American people. In the powerhouse of the TVA's Fontana Dam (the highest dam east of the Rocky Mountains), visitors passed along a row of gleaming dynamos and read, at the top of a sky-lit wall, the following words: "Built for the People of the United States of America."[14]

Though Depression-era buildings were constructed in the midst of a crisis, they conveyed an unmistakable expectation of soul-satisfying progress—progress achieved through pioneering. The murals produced by the artists employed by the WPA often juxtaposed themes of old-fashioned pioneering (covered-wagon days) with the themes of industrial technology.

In a 1939 guidebook to Washington, the journalist and artist Edwin Rosskam exuded the spirit of the times: "From Washington this unprecedented drive spreads out. The Capital is the nerve center of a nation determined to work its way and construct its way out of chaos." There was so much to do: "America needs re-housing—we are building new houses. America needs better highways—we are constructing them. America needs power dams—we make them. America must control its floods and its erosion—we are working to stop both. America needs employment—we are straining to provide it."[15]

On the outskirts of Washington a new model suburb arose. It was Greenbelt, Maryland, constructed on a crescent-shaped ridge by the federal government. The Resettlement Administration built it with FDR's approval (he visited the town) as a cooperative community in which some Americans could get a new start.

In 1937 the town's first newspaper published an address that was written by a resident. Titled "We Pioneers," it expressed the old theme of a city on a hill:

> Let us keep ourselves, our community, our city government, our ideals, as clean as our new, windswept roofs. Let us conduct ourselves and the management of our Greenbelt in such a way as to deserve the pride with which all America will be looking on. We who have been endowed with the greatest living heritage on earth by our ancestors still have that hardiness and determination underneath. Greenbelt will be a success, with the cooperation of her citizens and with the help of God.[16]

This spirit could inspire us again. Obama has tried to revive it—on Inauguration Day, and on innumerable occasions ever since. And if fate will not allow him to revive it, someone else will have a chance later on because our challenges are overwhelming.

If the science of global warming is correct (or anywhere close to correct), the American people will in all probability embark upon the greatest public works program in our history in two or three decades. If the worst-case scenarios are true, then our great coastal cities (and thousands of shoreline communities) will have to be protected by a massive and extensive system of sea walls, if our technology is up to the task. Flood control systems will have to be designed by the best engineers in this nation. What the Dutch did centuries ago will have to be approximated soon all over the world, upon the shorelines of all major continents.

Even right-of-center leaders will acknowledge this fact if the science is confirmed by experience. The sheer destruction of *property* alone will force conservatives to start to think heroically.

A Manhattan-style project to replace fossil fuels may commence before many more years. Forget the obstructionist power of the oil industry: the power of the *real estate and banking industries* will manifest itself if the sea levels start to rise. Perhaps research will not lead to any single solution any more than the fight to conquer cancer has produced a unified solution. But a great multiplicity of efforts and discoveries is not beyond our power to imagine.

But there is one thing more that either we or our children must begin to imagine in a decade or two: a strategy to pay for all this. The sheer money supply must be expanded again, as it was during World War II. But the expansion of the money supply must not lead us into hyperinflation. Can this be done?

REVISITING MONEY CREATION

There are three basic methods for financing federal action: the appropriation of revenue raised by taxes, the use of additional revenue raised through borrowing (deficit spending), and direct creation of money. Only the first two methods were employed in the twentieth century, with minor exceptions.

After the creation of the income tax through amendment of the Constitution, high taxes prevailed at least in wartime, until the policies of Bush the younger destroyed that particular tradition. Deficit spending is an intermittent if controversial tradition, employed by the left and the right for very different reasons, and with very different effects. Balancing the budget is a national tradition in *rhetorical* terms (and also in conceptual terms among economists and others who are unconvinced by Keynes), but only a select group of twentieth-century presidents—Coolidge, Hoover, Eisenhower, and Clinton, most prominently—have embraced the balanced budget as a fundamental verity of statecraft. Others tried adhering to the principle (FDR) or giving it lip service (Reagan), while piling up significant deficits. At least one of our presidents (Kennedy) regarded the balancing of budgets as simplistic.[17]

Economists differ in regard to the merits of deficit spending when conducted at the federal level. Some, like Charles L. Schultze, have argued that deficit spending and interest on the national debt take dollars out of private investment that would otherwise stimulate economic growth. Others, like Robert Solow and James Tobin, argue that deficit spending is justified so long as the money is invested in projects that generate prosperity. Still others, like Robert Eisner, have argued that national debt should grow steadily as a stimulant of GNP.[18]

Eisner, the former president of the American Economic Association, reasoned in the 1990s that, "as we grow richer, we can indeed afford more of everything. And we can grow much richer still. More and more businessmen and economists are recognizing that our potential for growth is significantly greater . . . if we do not have government policies—budgetary or monetary—to hold down that growth. Rather than insisting willy-nilly on budget balancing, we should invest more."[19] In 1992 a group of dozens of economists, including some winners of the Nobel Prize, recommended deficit spending to invest in infrastructure maintenance and workforce retraining. They argued that the use of borrowed money on projects that build the economy is different from the kind of misdirected borrowing that drains an economy. It all depends upon how the borrowed money is used—what it creates.[20]

In a separate but related study, economist David Alan Aschauer demonstrated that for every public dollar spent on infrastructure investment, an additional fifty cents worth of private sector investment will typically result.[21]

"Deficit spending" will always have an odious sound to Americans, regardless of how many mortgages or car loans they use in their quest for the good things of life. They seldom reflect that our system of capitalism is grounded in the practice by dint of the fact that the banking profession is expressly set up to facilitate the lending of money at interest and the business community will always require new infusions of capital.

In the case of our *national* debt, what matters the most is the *relationship* of such debt to our prosperity, which *may or may not* be advanced by deficit spending, depending on the economic conditions that happen to prevail.

It is endlessly instructive to remember that in World War II our accumulated national debt became greater than our GNP. And yet America emerged as the richest nation in the world. As Walton and Rockoff reflected some years ago, "by 1945 [national debt] had reached $258.7 billion, 121 percent of the gross national product. This fact is often cited as evidence that an economy can survive a huge debt, suggesting that . . . fears about the evil consequences of our current debt may be exaggerated."[22]

Under Reagan and also under Bush the younger, our deficits increased while our economic base was allowed to decline. But a public works campaign in the future—the building of the great coastal sea walls—might justify enormous increases in debt if the result serves to stimulate American manufacturing and get the American workforce fully employed. And these latter two goals are important in and of themselves. As industrialist Lee Iacocca reflected more than twenty years ago, "without a strong industrial base, we can kiss our national security goodbye."[23] So much for the Keynesian prescription.

But there remains a long-neglected idea—a heretical idea—for financing the public sector: direct creation and expenditure of money, the much-maligned system of "printing press money" (Greenbacks) that won endorsement from distinguished economists like Irving Fisher, Henry Simons, John R. Commons, Lauchlin Currie, Richard Lester, and others, many years ago. Few think about the heresy today—economist John H. Hotson and maverick businessman William F. Hixson are among the recent exceptions. Americans in general know nothing at all about the heresy.

The principle is simple: if banks create money through fractional reserves, and if expansion of the money supply via banks can occur without hyperinflation, then why not empower the federal government to use its own prerogative and generate money directly? As Hixson put it in the 1990s, "it *never* makes sense for the government to permit banks to create money and then borrow it from them at interest, since the government can create money just as cheaply and efficiently for itself and then have the use of it without a debt to repay and without any burden of interest."[24]

Orthodox economists reject this idea for several reasons. First, they argue that "printing press money" has a built-in inflationary risk. They cite the continental notes that financed the American Revolution, the dreadful farce of Confederate money, and the inflation that accompanied the Union's Civil War Greenbacks. Second, they argue that Greenbacks preclude the sort of monetary policy that government conducts through the Federal Reserve: bank-created money can be tightened or expanded through the operating policies of "the Fed," which are quite sophisticated. Third, they argue that a system of Greenback currency would rob the economy of credit that is needed for economic expansion.

Each of these objections can be answered, though the answers will depend upon the nature of the "printing press" proposal that is actually being advanced. Some Greenback proposals have encompassed the *replacement* of fractional-reserve lending (its total abolition). Others have merely recommended a *supplementation* of bank-created money by additional infusions of government-created money. Some Greenback proposals would have taken away the power of commercial banks to create new money; Irving Fisher's 100 percent reserve plan was an example. Others stopped short of such action.

Inflation is a problem that multiple causes can produce. It is perfectly true that "tight money" can eradicate inflation—Volcker's method in the 1980s was a good demonstration of this—and the Federal Reserve is very well-positioned to tighten up the money supply when the national interest requires it. The same is true of all central banks. High taxes may achieve the same effect, though the problem of pushing through a tax increase in the United States can be daunting.

Still, it bears noting that some very large increases in our money supply via *bank-created money* have occurred without significant inflation; such was the case in the 1980s under Reagan after Volcker had tamed the infla-

tionary pressures of the 1970s. It is also useful to compare the rate of Civil
War inflation in the Union, when Greenbacks were used, to the rate of
inflation in World War I, when Greenbacks were not in use at all. Historian James M. McPherson has observed that the inflation rate was roughly
the same: "For the [Civil War] as a whole the Union experienced inflation
of only 80 percent (contrasted with 9,000 percent for the Confederacy),
which compares favorably to the 84 percent of World War I." McPherson
attributed the Union's success in containing inflation to the strength of its
economy as well as the "enactment of a comprehensive tax law on July 1,
1862, which soaked up much of the inflationary pressure produced by the
greenbacks."[25]

It also bears noting that Fisher's proposal to abolish bank-created
money made provision for inflation control. Fisher's system, in fact, possesses such value as an exercise in "thinking outside the box" that he deserves to be quoted at length.

Fisher proposed in the 1930s to replace the Federal Reserve Board
with a U.S. Currency Commission that would bring the reserves of all
commercial banks to 100 percent by purchasing their assets with newly created U.S. notes. The Currency Commission would buy up the loans of the
banks, thus replacing the money that the banks had created (through loans
of various kinds) with new money created by government.

Fisher also made provision for continued deficit spending with a special provision for canceling the interest on the debt through some tricky
accounting. He gave this policy a self-perpetuating twist that would effec-
tuate monetary policy through open-market operations—the buying and
selling of bonds. (When a central bank buys bonds, it injects funds into the
economy by paying for the bonds. When a central bank sells bonds, it pulls
money out of the economy.)

Fisher proposed to let the federal government continue to raise new
revenue by selling its bonds. But then the Currency Commission could
buy up the bonds *with new money created for the purpose.* Once the Currency Commission had the bonds, it would *forego the interest,* making deficit
spending *interest-free.* It would also use the bonds for the purposes of monetary policy. Let Fisher speak for himself:

> In the process of putting 100% cash behind bank deposits, the Currency
> Commission could and should . . . concentrate on buying Govern-
> ment bonds [from the loan portfolios of banks]. . . . By owning (in the
> person of its Currency Commission) its own bonds, the Government
> would thus reduce its debt. . . . Even if all outstanding obligations of

the United States were to find their way into the hands of the Currency Commission, the simplest procedure would be for the Currency Commission to hold these intact until maturity. Maintaining the physical existence of the bonds during their "life" would supply the Currency Commission with easily saleable securities for use in case of threatened inflation. Meanwhile, the Currency Commission would, like every other bondholder, receive from the United States Treasury the interest on the bonds, which interest would then be turned back into the United States Treasury. Or rather, the two opposite payments would be book-keeping offsets against each other.[26]

Fisher proposed to establish a permanent capacity for monetary policy this way:

> The bonds, or other obligations, could be floated under the usual procedure of the Treasury and find their way later into the hands of the Currency Commission under the usual procedure of the Commission. The Treasury would then receive the purchase price from the public in pre-existing money, but the Currency Commission would issue *new* money for its purchase of the bonds from the public.[27]

Fisher boldly defended this extension of the government's sovereignty:

> If, in spite of depressions, banks now prosper by creating money (such as Federal Reserve notes and checking deposits) and investing it in bonds, promissory notes, etc., the same privilege in the hands of the Currency Commission should prosper the Government still more.[28]

Fisher won the endorsement of a number of bankers in the 1930s. The economist Lauchlin Currie even tried to insert this proposed system into the Banking Act of 1935. But it will probably never come to pass. The abolition of fractional reserve lending might cripple our economy if funds to be lent from mere *savings* should prove insufficient for economic health. All Fisher had to say about the volume of loans that could emerge from savings was that loans will generate additional loans, just as money will facilitate a multitude of purchases in any given business day. That is very small comfort in the face of recessionary pressures.

Still, the contemplation of Fisher's proposal is an interesting exercise: it limbers up the mind. It frees us to contemplate other proposals, more modest proposals, for creation of government money. Several proposals along these lines were advanced in the 1930s. Most were rejected, but one of them was partially adopted.

John R. Commons proposed to print Greenbacks and pay them directly to the unemployed, for relief and also as salaries in public works projects.[29] (In the depression of the 1890s Jacob Coxey had proposed the same thing.[30]) Congress provided for a limited issue of Greenbacks in the Agricultural Adjustment Act of 1933; an amendment to the act proposed by Senator Elmer Thomas of Oklahoma gave the president discretionary authority to issue Greenbacks.[31]

FDR rejected this option, though he did make use of some alternative authority conferred by the act: authority to issue new Silver Certificates in payment for silver (the government would purchase the metal from silver mines and pay with the Silver Certificates). This off-budget "federal spending" increased the U.S. money supply, but in a curiously indirect manner compared to the direct issuance of Greenbacks. The issuance of Silver Certificates flowed from the largely atavistic notion that creation of money must depend upon a precious metal backing. That theory is defunct nowadays.

So much for the historical precedents, in theory and practice, for direct creation by the federal government of "fiat money" or "printing press money" or "United States Notes" or "Greenbacks." This has been the path not taken: the Keynesian method has prevailed from the 1930s to the present. Hixson has ascribed this development to sheer political (and psychological) expediency:

> Keynes was properly distressed by the outrageously high levels of unemployment of the era and by hunger in the midst of plenty. He wanted to do something to relieve the distress and do it as quickly as possible. But he was a pragmatist. He was a believer in the adage that "politics is the art of the possible." My guess is that he believed he could get more people back to work and back to a full stomach, and do it faster, if he proposed government spending financed by loans than if he proposed government spending financed by government money creation. That is to say, he believed "borrow and borrow" would arouse less intense opposition (by bankers in particular) than "create and create." . . . Given the prevailing prejudices . . . he may very well have been right.[32]

But is it out of the question to entertain some *limited* use of such measures sometime in the future? Would it not be an interesting exercise to ask ourselves whether federal action to avert a catastrophe could be undertaken without more taxes and without piling up more debt?

Why couldn't some Greenback spending—or, to be up-to-date, a new system of direct electronic purchase credits, convertible to cash through the methods of the Federal Reserve—*overlap with commercial banking*? The Civil War method of Lincoln used the monetary triad of taxes, fractional reserve measures (war bonds sold to the newly created National Banks), and the experimental Greenbacks. Why couldn't we do this again?

Many proposals for direct creation of government money in the 1930s were based upon the all-or-nothing choice between bank-created money and money created by the government. But why suppose such an all-or-nothing choice? Why not have the best of both worlds?

We could pump the new government money *right into the banks*, so the government money and the bank-created money overlap to form a monetary pool. If the Federal Reserve can pump credit through the banks to facilitate private investments, then Congress could do the same thing—for public investments. As the Civil War Greenbacks were frequently deposited in banks, new government money could be sent electronically to *vendor and employee accounts in commercial banks*, thus building up their excess reserves.[33]

Would this create some inflationary pressures? Probably. But then something like Paul Volcker's method—the hiking up of reserve requirements, per authority granted to the Federal Reserve Board in the Banking Act of 1935 and expanded to include all "depository institutions" in 1980—could be put into place as a counterforce.

Here is how the system might work. Intensive consultations taking place between the Council of Economic Advisers, the administration, Congress, and the Federal Reserve would determine whether issuance of government money might be undertaken without excessive risk of inflation. Congress would then make provision for a limited expenditure: it would *make* the new money directly. It would spend it right into the appropriations for specific agencies.

These agencies (or the Treasury acting on their behalf) would send direct electronic deposits to the bank accounts of vendors (or staff) who are carrying out the will of Congress. Then—if inflationary pressures should actually emerge—the Federal Reserve could increase its reserve requirements. The requirements would rise in direct proportion to the increase in excess reserves. As deposits increased, the banks would put more money off-limits. The result could be a near-perfect offset. So we could pay for some necessities without raising taxes or debt.

Look at it this way. The Federal Reserve can pull money out of nothing and direct it right into the banks. The American people through Congress should have the same power. Congress should be able to create new money, which executive federal agencies—via payroll and via procurement—could channel right into commercial bank accounts.

Remember: the brand new money would be *spent into the banks*, where it would *overlap* with bank-created money. Once there, it would naturally be subject to the monetary tools that are used by the Federal Reserve to control inflation. This amounts to the system that we have in place now, except that *Congress*—in addition to "the Fed"—would have the power to create new money and spend it into banks.

This system would require a departure from the habits of "the Fed," which has managed through the years to gain a measure of institutional autonomy that is rare among the world's central banks. But consider: during World War II, under Marriner Eccles, the Fed was quite willing to coordinate its policies with Congress and the Treasury.[34] The same thing occurred in 2008 when Messrs. Paulson and Bernanke joined forces. In any event, once the government money has been placed in the banks, it will *automatically* change the calculations of "the Fed."

The shift to such a system could be done very slowly and experimentally—in fact, prudence would *dictate* a slow and incremental basis for a monetary change of such importance. The point is that a change such as this is conceivable. Any legal objections could be quelled through constitutional amendment.

Or is a system such as this inconceivable? Is our existing financial apparatus to remain *completely unaltered* for the rest of the twenty-first century? The twenty-second? The twenty-third?

THE PERILOUS HORIZON

In the twenty-first century our children may not be spared the worst. We owe it to them to prepare for—to take arms against—evils we can stop. We have seen too much to be seduced any longer by illusions from the past thirty years. We can offer the world the fine *guardianship* we were pleased to deliver long ago.

We are still a young republic in a great many ways, so it will come: a challenge to *command* us. New leaders will learn the old lessons for themselves and then apply them with visionary fervor. Strange times can bring the advent of genius. Even now, it may be, the bright prodigies are waiting to be born.

NOTES

INTRODUCTION

1. Theodore Roosevelt to Sydney Brooks, November 20, 1908, in *The Letters of Theodore Roosevelt*, Elting E. Morrison, ed. (Cambridge, Mass.: Harvard University Press, 1951), VI, 1369.

2. Franklin D. Roosevelt, address in Syracuse, New York, September 29, 1936, in *The Public Papers and Addresses of Franklin D. Roosevelt*, Samuel I. Rosenman, ed. (New York: Random House, 1938), V, 389–90.

3. Theodore Roosevelt to George Otto Trevelyan, March 9, 1905, in *The Letters of Theodore Roosevelt*, IV, 1132.

4. Franklin Delano Roosevelt to Sara Roosevelt, September 7, 1905, in *The Roosevelt Letters: Being the Personal Correspondence of Franklin Delano Roosevelt*, Elliott Roosevelt, ed. (London: George G. Harrap & Co., Ltd., 1950), II, 82.

CHAPTER 1: FORGOTTEN PATHS IN AMERICAN POLITICS

1. Theodore Roosevelt, "The New Nationalism," address in Osawatomie, Kansas, August 31, 1910, in *The Works of Theodore Roosevelt* (New York: Charles Scribner's Sons, 1925), XIX, 26–27.

2. Jimmy Carter, State of the Union Address, January 19, 1978, in *Public Papers of the Presidents of the United States: Jimmy Carter, 1978* (Washington, D.C.: U.S. Government Printing Office, 1978), I, 91.

3. Ronald Reagan, inaugural address, January 20, 1981, in *Public Papers of the Presidents of the United States: Ronald Reagan, 1981* (Washington, D.C.: U.S. Government Printing Office, 1982), 1.

4. Bill Clinton, State of the Union Address, January 23, 1996, *Washington Post* (January 24, 1996), A13.

5. John Milton Cooper Jr., *Pivotal Decades: The United States, 1900–1920* (New York: W. W. Norton, 1990), 36.

6. See *The Letters of Theodore Roosevelt*, Elting E. Morison, ed. (Cambridge, Mass.: Harvard University Press, 1952), IV, 1131, n1.

7. Franklin D. Roosevelt, Address in Syracuse, New York, September 29, 1936, in *The Public Papers and Addresses of Franklin D. Roosevelt*, Samuel I. Rosenman, ed. (New York: Random House, 1938), V, 389–90.

8. Sir William S. Gilbert (with Sir Arthur Sullivan), "Iolanthe" (1882).

9. Perry Miller, "Puritan State and Puritan Society," in *Errand Into the Wilderness* (Cambridge, Mass.: Harvard University Press, 1956), 143. The link between state regulation and a harsh view of human nature is quite venerable. Citing the opinion of a number of Church Fathers to the effect that "political authority was a consequence of man's corrupted nature, a punishment and at the same time a remedy for his sins," historian John B. Morrall has argued that this view was influential throughout the Middle Ages. See John B. Morrall, *Political Thought in Medieval Times* (Toronto: University of Toronto Press, 1980; originally published 1958), 19. Probably the most influential distillation of this general view was Thomas Hobbes's classic *Leviathan* (1651).

10. Thomas Carlyle, "Chartism" (1839), in Alan Shelston, ed., *Thomas Carlyle: Selected Writings* (London: Penguin Books, 1971), 218, 187.

11. Carlyle, "Chartism," 199.

12. Roland Stromberg, *European Intellectual History since 1789* (Englewood Cliffs, N.J.: Prenctice-Hall, 1975), 54. In addition to its sources in nineteenth-century reform conservatism, the idea of the "welfare state" derived from various left-of-center doctrines, especially those of pre-Marxian socialists.

13. Theodore Roosevelt to George Otto Trevelyan, October 1, 1911, in *Cowboys and Kings: Three Great Letters by Theodore Roosevelt*, Elting E. Morison, ed. (Cambridge, Mass.: Harvard University Press, 1954; repr. New York: Kraus Reprint Co., 1969), 93–94.

14. Stromberg, *European Intellectual History*, 69. For a long time commentators have linked the emergence of liberalism and the philosophy of John Locke. Louis Hartz, for example, in his influential book *The Liberal Tradition in America*, declared that "a liberal society" necessarily "begins with Locke" (Louis Hartz, *The Liberal Tradition in America* [New York: Harcourt, Brace & World, 1955], v, 5–6, passim). The contention that "Lockean liberalism" was the fountainhead of liberal culture has continued, along with the tendency of some academic writers to extend the argument of Hartz to the effect that liberalism has enjoyed a political hegemony in the United States. While Locke's importance to the liberal tradition is beyond dispute, his influence can be (and has been) overmagnified. Further, the contention that "Lockean liberalism" has dominated American political culture to the point of overpowering significant conservative traditions is not convincing.

15. Thomas Paine, "The Rights of Man" (1791), in *The Complete Writings of Thomas Paine*, Philip S. Foner, ed. (New York: Citadel Press, 1945), I, 397.

16. For the past several decades historians have engaged in heated debate regarding American "political culture" in the age of the Founding Fathers. Following Bernard Bailyn, some have emphasized the influence of English Radical Whiggism on the Revolutionary generation. See Bernard Bailyn, *The Ideological Origins of the American Revolution* (Cambridge, Mass.: Harvard University Press, 1967). Others have joined in a dispute between scholars who emphasize "classical republicanism" (a political outlook idealizing certain aspects of classical antiquity and touting a program of civic virtue) and those who argue that classical liberalism, with its emphasis on individual rights and opportunities, was the fundamental force in American politics. For key works exemplifying these schools of

thought, see J. G. A. Pocock, *The Machiavellian Moment: Florentine Political Thought and the Atlantic Republican Tradition* (Princeton, N.J.: Princeton University Press, 1976) and Joyce Appleby, *Liberalism and Republicanism in the Historical Imagination* (Cambridge, Mass.: Harvard University Press, 1992). In "The 'Great National Discussion': The Discourse of Politics in 1787," *William & Mary Quarterly*, third series, 45 (1988), 3–32, Isaac Kramnick presented a pluralistic view of American political culture at the time of the Constitutional Convention, arguing that none of the "discernible idioms of politics" identified by scholars in recent years really "dominated the field." Historian Forrest McDonald has said, with regard to the Framers of the Constitution, that "it is meaningless to say that the Framers intended this or that the Framers intended that: their positions were diverse and, in many particulars, incompatible. . . . Some of their differences were subject to compromise; others were not" (Forrest McDonald, *Novus Ordo Seclorum: The Intellectual Origins of the Constitution* [Lawrence: University Press of Kansas, 1985], 224). The best overall treatment of intellectual history relating to the politics of the Founding generation is Gordon S. Wood, *The Creation of the American Republic, 1776–1787* (Chapel Hill: University of North Carolina Press, 1969).

17. Thomas Jefferson to James Madison, December 20, 1787, in *The Papers of Thomas Jefferson*, Julian P. Boyd, ed. (Princeton, N.J.: Princeton University Press, 1955), XII, 442.

18. Thomas Jefferson to John Taylor, November 26, 1798, in *The Papers of Thomas Jefferson*, XXX, 589.

19. Thomas Jefferson to Gideon Granger, August 13, 1800, in *The Papers of Thomas Jefferson*, XXXII, 96.

20. Alexander Hamilton, *The Federalist* #70, March 18, 1788, in *The Federalist* (New York: Modern Library/Random House, 1937), 454.

21. Alexander Hamilton, *The Continentalist* #5, April 18, 1782, in *The Papers of Alexander Hamilton*, Harold C. Syrett, ed. (New York: Columbia University Press, 1962), III, 76.

22. Alexander Hamilton, *Report on Manufactures*, December 5, 1791, in *The Papers of Alexander Hamilton*, X, 296.

23. Forrest McDonald, *Alexander Hamilton: A Biography* (New York and London: W. W. Norton, 1979, 1982), 55.

24. Hamilton, *Report on Manufactures*, X, 310.

25. Hamilton, *Report on Manufactures*, X 303.

26. James Madison, "Political Reflections," February 23, 1799, in *Papers of James Madison*, Robert A. Rutland, ed. (Charlottesville: University Press of Virginia, 1977), XVII, 237.

27. Alexander Hamilton, *Tully* #3, August 28, 1794, in *The Papers of Alexander Hamilton*, XVII, 159. "Tully" was an English nickname for the ancient Roman statesman Marcus Tullius Cicero. Hamilton was posing as a latter-day Cicero, saving his republic from a modern Catiline conspiracy.

28. George Washington to Henry Lee, August 26, 1794, in *The Writings of George Washington*, John C. Fitzpatrick, ed. (Washington, D.C.: Government Printing Office, 1939), XXXIII, 475.

29. Thomas Jefferson to James Madison, December 28, 1794, in *The Papers of Thomas Jefferson*, XXVIII, 228–29.

30. Max Farrand, ed., *The Records of the Federal Convention of 1787* (New Haven and London: Yale University Press, 1911, 1937), I, 289, 288.

31. Thomas Jefferson to Elbridge Gerry, January 26, 1799, in *The Papers of Thomas Jefferson*, XXX, 646.

32. Thomas Jefferson to William Johnson, June 12, 1823, in *The Writings of Thomas Jefferson*, Paul Leicester Ford, ed. (New York: G. P. Putnam's Sons, 1892–1899), XV, 442.

33. Herbert Croly, *The Promise of American Life* (New York: Macmillan, 1909), 28–29. On the influence of Croly, see Edward A. Stettner, *Shaping Modern Liberalism: Herbert Croly and Progressive Thought* (Lawrence: University Press of Kansas, 1993); David W. Levy, *Herbert Croly of the New Republic: The Life and Thought of an American Progressive* (Princeton, N.J.: Princeton University Press, 1985); and Eric F. Goldman, *Rendezvous with Destiny: A History of American Reform* (New York: Alfred A. Knopf, 1952), chapter 9.

34. Croly, *The Promise of American Life*, 28–29.

35. Croly, *The Promise of American Life*, 168–69, 170.

36. Theodore Roosevelt, *An Autobiography*, in *The Works of Theodore Roosevelt*, XXII, 481.

37. Alexander Hamilton, *The Federalist* #34, January 4, 1788, in *The Federalist*, 205.

38. For a discussion of early modern coinage and bullion, see Roy Harrod, *Money* (London: Macmillan/St. Martin's Press, 1969), chapter 1.

39. James Steuart, *An Inquiry into the Principles of Political Oeconomy* (1767), cited in McDonald, *Novus Ordo Seclorum: The Intellectual Origins of the Constitution*, 120–21.

40. For accounts of money creation through "fractional reserve banking," see John Kenneth Galbraith, *Money: Whence It Came, Where It Went* (Boston: Houghton Mifflin, 1975), 18–21, 45, passim; and William J. Baumol and Alan S. Blinder, *Economics: Principles and Policy* (Fort Worth, Tex.: Dryden Press/Harcourt Brace & Company, 1979; sixth ed., 1994), 727–34. Galbraith summarized the matter in a pointedly simplified way: "The process by which banks create money is so simple that the mind is repelled. . . . [A] stroke of the pen would give a borrower from the bank, as distinct from the original depositor, a loan from the original and idle deposit. . . . The original deposit still stood to the credit of the original depositor. But there was now also a new deposit from the proceeds of the loan" (Galbraith, *Money*, 18–21). For a radical critique of money creation through banks as opposed to the issuance of pure legal tender paper "fiat money" (such as the Civil War Greenbacks) by government, see William F. Hixson, *Triumph of the Bankers: Money and Banking in the Eighteenth and Nineteenth Centuries* (Westport, Conn.: Praeger, 1993). As to fractional reserve banking, Hixson offers the following counterintuitive formulation:

> In its initial stages, the introduction of fractional reserve banking permitted the total money supply (specie plus banknotes) to increase very much faster than the specie supply. . . . It seems poorly understood that the essential function of banks is not to receive and disburse parts of a money supply that remains at a constant size but to preside over the expansion of the money supply. . . . In modern times, virtually all deposits consist of money originally created somewhere in the banking system in the process of making loans on the basis of fractional reserves. In an important sense, it is loans that give rise to deposits, not deposits that give rise to loans as most people seem to believe. (Hixson, *Triumph of the Bankers*, 63–64)

41. John Steele Gordon, *Hamilton's Blessing: The Extraordinary Life and Times of Our National Debt* (New York: Penguin Books, 1998).

42. Thomas Babington Macaulay, *The History of England (1849–1861)* (London and New York: Penguin Books, 1968, 1986), 494–97.

43. *Historical Statistics of the United States, Colonial Times to 1957*, Bureau of the Census, U.S. Department of Commerce (Washington, D.C.: U.S Government Printing Office, 1961), 711.

44. The phrase is John Kenneth Galbraith's.

45. See Benjamin Franklin, *A Modest Enquiry into the Nature and Necessity of a Paper Currency* (1729), and Walter Isaacson, *Benjamin Franklin: An American Life* (New York: Simon & Schuster, 2003), 63–64.

46. Richard A. Lester, *Monetary Experiments* (Princeton, N.J.: Princeton University Press, 1939), 141.

47. Richard A. Lester, "Currency Issues to Overcome Depressions in Pennsylvania, 1723 and 1729," *Journal of Political Economy*, vol. 46 (June 1938), 324–75.

48. Galbraith, *Money: Whence It Came, Where It Went*, 53, 114–15.

49. See James M. McPherson, *Battle Cry of Freedom: The Civil War Era* (New York: Oxford University Press, 1988), 445–47; Hixson, *Triumph of the Bankers*, 141; and Paul Studenski and Herman E. Krooss, *Financial History of the United States* (New York: McGraw-Hill, 1952), 147.

CHAPTER 2: FROM THE FOUNDERS
TO ABRAHAM LINCOLN

1. Bernard Bailyn, *The Ideological Origins of the American Revolution* (Cambridge, Mass.: Belknap Press of Harvard University Press, 1967), 46–47.

2. Bailyn, *The Ideological Origins of the American Revolution*, 43.

3. See Marshall Smelser, *The Democratic Republic, 1801–1815* (New York: Harper & Row, 1968), Harper Torchbooks edition, 95–96.

4. Albert Gallatin, *Report on Roads and Canals*, April 6, 1808, in *Selected Writings of Albert Gallatin*, E. James Ferguson, ed. (Indianapolis: Bobbs-Merrill Company, 1967), 229, 230, 232. For a comprehensive account of public works in the United States through the mid-twentieth century, see Ellis L. Armstrong, Michael C. Robinson, and Suellen M. Hoy, eds., *History of Public Works in the United States, 1776–1976* (Chicago: American Public Works Association, 1976).

5. Thomas Jefferson, eighth annual message to Congress, November 8, 1808, in *The Writings of Thomas Jefferson*, Paul Leicester Ford, ed. (New York: G. P. Putnam's Sons, 1892–1899), III, 484–45. It should be noted, however, that while Jefferson became reconciled to appropriations for public works before the end of his presidency, his reductions in federal spending did substantial damage to America's infant navy, damage that became increasingly apparent in the years leading up to the War of 1812.

6. James Madison, second annual message to Congress, December 5, 1810, in *The Writings of James Madison*, Gaillard Hunt, ed. (New York: G. P. Putnam's Sons, 1908), VIII, 127.

7. James Madison to William Eustis, May 22, 1823, in *The Writings of James Madison*, IX, 135–36.

8. Thomas Jefferson to Samuel Kercheval, July 12, 1816, in *The Writings of Thomas Jefferson*, XV, 41.

9. John C. Calhoun, quoted in William W. Freehling, *Prelude to Civil War: The Nullification Controversy in South Carolina, 1816–1836* (New York: Harper & Row, 1966; Harper Torchbook edition, 1968), 94.

10. Henry Clay, *Annals of Congress*, 14th Congress, 1st Session, 789–92, quoted in Robert V. Remini, *Henry Clay: Statesman for the Union* (New York: W. W. Norton, 1991), 137.

11. Remini, *Henry Clay: Statesman for the Union*, 228.

12. Henry Clay, speech on internal improvements, January 14, 1824, in *The Papers of Henry Clay*, James F. Hopkins, ed. (Lexington: University Press of Kentucky, 1963), III, 587, 591. See also Remini, *Henry Clay: Statesman for the Union*, 158–60, 225–28, 286–88; and Maurice G. Baxter, *Henry Clay and the American System* (Lexington: University Press of Kentucky, 1995).

13. *McCulloch v. Maryland* (1819), cited in Alfred H. Kelly, Winfred A. Harbison, and Herman Belz, *The American Constitution: Its Origins and Development* (New York: W. W. Norton, 1983), 191.

14. See Forest G. Hill, *Roads, Rails, and Waterways: The Army Engineers and Early Transportation* (Norman: University of Oklahoma Press, 1957).

15. John Quincy Adams, first annual message to Congress, November 25, 1825, in *The State of the Union Messages of the Presidents, 1790–1966*, Fred L. Israel, ed. (New York: Chelsea House/Robert Hector, Publishers, 1966), I, 248.

16. It must nonetheless be admitted that Jefferson relapsed into his old anti-government views in the years leading up to his death in 1826. For an interesting analysis of this development, see Joseph J. Ellis, *American Sphinx: The Character of Thomas Jefferson* (New York: Alfred A. Knopf, 1997), 270–73.

17. Arthur Schlesinger Jr., *The Age of Jackson* (Boston: Little, Brown, 1945), 511.

18. For a good account of the Whig Party and its politics, see Lawrence Frederick Kohl, *The Politics of Individualism: Parties and the American Character in the Jacksonian Era* (New York: Oxford University Press, 1989), especially 113.

19. Gary M. Walton and Hugh Rockoff, *History of the American Economy* (Stamford, Conn.: South-Western/Thomson Learning, 2002), 250–51.

20. Walton and Rockoff, *History of the American Economy*, 255.

21. Walton and Rockoff, *History of the American Economy*, 260.

22. John Quincy Adams to Charles Upham, February 2, 1837, quoted in Henry Adams, *The Degradation of the Democratic Dogma* (New York: Macmillan, 1919), 25.

23. See Abraham Lincoln, "Remarks in Illinois Legislature, Concerning Resolutions Asking Information on Railroad and Fund Commissioners," December 8, 1838, *Collected Works of Abraham Lincoln*, Roy Basler, ed. (New Brunswick: Rutgers University Press, 1953), I, 122–23. See also Stephen B. Oates, *With Malice toward None: The Life of Abraham Lincoln* (New York: Harper & Row, 1977), 36–37, and especially 54. For an unsympathetic treatment of Lincoln's support for public works in Illinois, see Paul Simon, *Lincoln's Preparation for Greatness: The Illinois Legislative Years* (Norman: University of Oklahoma Press, 1965), especially 50–53. Illinois's public works initiatives from 1837 through the early 1840s apparently suffered from poor planning and poor management. Moreover, due to the economic contraction that followed the Panic of 1837, the pressure on state governments to cancel their internal improvements programs and default on their loans became keen. Lincoln resisted these pressures. But in the absence of a comprehensive federal program for the purpose of stimulating economic growth to counteract the depression, the debts of the states became a hindrance rather than an asset in many instances.

24. John C. Calhoun to Virgil Maxcy, September 11, 1830, Galloway-Maxcy-Markoe Papers, cited in Freehling, *Prelude to Civil War*, 257.

25. Freehling, *Prelude to Civil War*, 127.

26. John Quincy Adams to Charles Upham, February 2, 1837, quoted in Adams, *The Degradation of the Democratic Dogma*, 25.

27. This law replaced an earlier fugitive slave law enacted in 1793.

28. Abraham Lincoln, "'A House Divided,' Speech at Springfield, Illinois," June 16, 1858, in *Collected Works of Abraham Lincoln*, II, 461.

29. Lincoln, "'A House Divided,'" 467.

30. Harry V. Jaffa, *Crisis of the House Divided: An Interpretation of the Lincoln-Douglas Debates* (Chicago: University of Chicago Press, 1959), 395.

31. The last southern attempt to use federal power to protect the slavery system was the demand of pro-slavery militants in 1859 and 1860 for the enactment of a territorial slave code by Congress.

32. James M. McPherson, *Abraham Lincoln and the Second American Revolution* (New York: Oxford University Press, 1991), 39–40.

33. McPherson, *Abraham Lincoln and the Second American Revolution*.

34. Leonard P. Curry, *Blueprint for Modern America: Non-Military Legislation of the First Civil War Congress* (Nashville: Vanderbilt University Press, 1968). Curry's estimation of the strengths and the weaknesses of Civil War Republican initiatives is generally shrewd. See also the analysis of Heather Cox Richardson in *The Greatest Nation of the Earth: Republican Economic Policies During the Civil War* (Cambridge, Mass.: Harvard University Press, 1997) and Richard Franklin Bensel, *Yankee Leviathan: The Origins of Central State Authority in America, 1859–1877* (Cambridge: Cambridge University Press, 1991).

35. Abraham Lincoln, "Speech in United States House of Representatives on Internal Improvements," June 20, 1848, in *Collected Works of Abraham Lincoln*, I, 488.

36. Lincoln, "Speech in United States House of Representatives on Internal Improvements," 483.

37. Lincoln, "Speech in United States House of Representatives on Internal Improvements," 488–89.

38. Lincoln, "Speech in United States House of Representatives on Internal Improvements."

39. Abraham Lincoln, fragment on government, in *Collected Works of Abraham Lincoln*, II, 221.

40. *New York Times*, March 9, 1863, 8. The use of federal bonds to secure the National Bank Notes led to some long-term ramifications regarding the national debt. As economic historian Thurman Van Metre observed in the 1920s, "the bonds which secured the bank-notes outstanding at the close of the nineteenth century nearly all were issued to reach maturity before 1909, and if the Government redeemed them as they fell due it meant that the bank-note currency must be retired. In order to prevent this from happening, Congress enacted a measure on March 14, 1900, providing that the bonds maturing in 1904, 1907 and 1908 should be refunded into thirty year bonds. . . . This act reversed the policy which the Government had always followed, of paying its interest-bearing debt as soon as possible" (Thurman W. Van Metre, *Economic History of the United States* [New York: Henry Holt, 1921], 581).

41. Curry, *Blueprint for Modern America*, 9.

42. John Sherman to William Tecumseh Sherman, March 20, 1863, in *The Sherman Letters: Correspondence between General and Senator Sherman from 1837 to 1891*, Rachel Sherman Thorndike, ed. (New York: Charles Scribner's Sons, 1894), 194.

43. John Sherman, quoted in Bray Hammond, *Sovereignty and an Empty Purse: Banks and Politics in the Civil War* (Princeton, N.J.: Princeton University Press, 1970), 326–27.

44. See James M. McPherson, *Battle Cry of Freedom: The Civil War Era* (New York: Oxford University Press, 1988), 443.

45. Abraham Lincoln, "Drafts of a Bill for Compensated Emancipation in Delaware," circa November 26, 1861, in *Collected Works of Abraham Lincoln*, V, 29–30.

46. R. K. Webb, *Modern England: From the Eighteenth Century to the Present* (New York: Dodd, Mead & Company, 1968), 219.

47. Abraham Lincoln, "Fragment on the Struggle against Slavery," circa July 1858, in *Collected Works of Abraham Lincoln*, II, 482.

48. Lincoln, "Fragment on the Struggle against Slavery."

49. Lincoln, "Fragment on the Struggle against Slavery."

50. Charles Sumner, "'Stand by the Administration', Letter to _____, June 5, 1862," in *The Works of Charles Sumner* (Boston: Lee and Shepard, 1870–1873), VII, 116–18.

51. Abraham Lincoln, "Annual Message to Congress," December 1, 1862, in *Collected Works of Abraham Lincoln*, V, 530, 532.

52. Abraham Lincoln, "To the Senate and House of Representatives," February 5, 1865, in *Collected Works of Abraham Lincoln*, VIII, 260.

53. Phillip Shaw Paludan, *The Presidency of Abraham Lincoln* (Lawrence: University Press of Kansas, 1994), 316.

54. Abraham Lincoln to Henry Pierce and others, April 6, 1859, in *Collected Works of Abraham Lincoln*, III, 375–76.

55. Richard Striner, *Father Abraham: Lincoln's Relentless Struggle to End Slavery* (New York: Oxford University Press, 2006).

56. For the liberal side of Lincoln's legacy, see James G. Randall, *Lincoln the Liberal Statesman* (New York: Dodd, Mead & Company, 1947). For conservative aspects of Lincoln's statecraft, see Norman A. Graebner, "Abraham Lincoln, Conservative Statesman," in *The Enduring Lincoln: Lincoln Sesquicentennial Lectures at the University of Illinois*, Norman A. Graebner, ed. (Urbana: University of Illinois Press, 1959). J. David Greenstone has argued, in *The Lincoln Persuasion: Remaking American Liberalism* (Princeton, N.J.: Princeton University Press, 1993), that Lincoln's thought was grounded in liberalism. But Greenstone also acknowledged that Lincoln's "unionism and his Whiggish politics had a deeply conservative side" as well (26, 276–85).

57. Abraham Lincoln, "Speech at Springfield, Illinois," June 26, 1857, in *Collected Works of Abraham Lincoln*, II, 406. Lincoln's understanding of Jefferson's intention was accurate. Compare Lincoln's words with the following statement by Jefferson in 1790: "The ground of liberty is to be gained by inches. . . . We must be contented to secure what we can get from time to time, and eternally press forward for what is yet to get." Thomas Jefferson to the Reverend Charles Clay, January 27, 1790, in *The Papers of Thomas Jefferson*, Julian P. Boyd et al., eds. (Princeton, N.J.: Princeton University Press, 1961), XVI, 129.

58. Abraham Lincoln, "Speech at Chicago," July 10, 1858, in *Collected Works of Abraham Lincoln*, II, 500–1.

59. Abraham Lincoln, "Speech at Peoria, Illinois," October 16, 1854, in *Collected Works of Abraham Lincoln*, II, 271.

60. George Fitzhugh, *Sociology for the South—Or, the Failure of Free Society* (Richmond: A. Morris, Publisher, 1854), Burt Franklin Research and Source Book Series, #102, 179.

61. Abraham Lincoln, second inaugural address, March 4, 1865, in *Collected Works of Abraham Lincoln*, VIII, 333.

62. Jaffa, *Crisis of the House Divided*, 190.

63. Abraham Lincoln, "Address at the Sanitary Fair, Baltimore, Maryland," April 18, 1864, in *Collected Works of Abraham Lincoln*, VII, 301–2.

CHAPTER 3: FROM LINCOLN
TO THEODORE ROOSEVELT

1. See David McCullough, *Mornings on Horseback* (New York: Simon & Schuster, 1981), 58–63.

2. James MacGregor Burns and Susan Dunn, *The Three Roosevelts: Patrician Leaders Who Transformed America* (New York: Atlantic Monthly Press, 2001), 1.

3. Edmund Morris, *The Rise of Theodore Roosevelt* (New York: Ballantine Books, 1979), 41; McCullough, *Mornings on Horseback*, 64.

4. Burns and Dunn, *Three Roosevelts*, 2–3.

5. Theodore Roosevelt to George Otto Trevelyan, March 9, 1905, in *The Letters of Theodore Roosevelt*, Elting E. Morison, ed. (Cambridge, Mass.: Harvard University Press, 1951), IV, 1132.

6. Theodore Roosevelt to Theodore Roosevelt Jr., February 6, 1909, in *The Letters of Theodore Roosevelt*, VI, 1506.

7. Theodore Roosevelt to Lyman Abbott, July 3, 1905, in *The Letters of Theodore Roosevelt*, IV, 1259.

8. Theodore Roosevelt to Sydney Brooks, November 20, 1908, in *The Letters of Theodore Roosevelt*, VI, 1369.

9. Theodore Roosevelt to William Allen White, February 19, 1909, in *The Letters of Theodore Roosevelt*, VI, 1527. See William Allen White, *The Old Order Changeth* (New York: Macmillan, 1910).

10. Theodore Roosevelt, *An Autobiography*, in *The Works of Theodore Roosevelt* (New York: Charles Scribner's Sons, 1925), XXII, 79.

11. Matthew Arnold, "Culture and Anarchy," in *Selected Poetry and Prose of Matthew Arnold*, Frederick L. Mulhauser, ed. (New York: Holt, Rinehart & Winston, 1953; sixth ed., 1962), 239.

12. See, for instance, Willmoore Kendall, "Source of American Caesarism," *National Review* (November 7, 1959), 461–62; Thomas DiLorenzo, *The Real Lincoln: A New Look at Abraham Lincoln, His Agenda, and an Unnecessary War* (New York: Crown Publishing Group, 2002); and Thomas DiLorenzo, *Lincoln Unmasked: What You're Not Supposed to Know about Dishonest Abe* (New York: Crown Forum, 2006).

13. Abraham Lincoln, "Speech in Independence Hall, Philadelphia, Pennsylvania," February 22, 1861, in *Collected Works of Abraham Lincoln*, Roy Basler, ed. (New Brunswick: Rutgers University Press, 1953), IV, 240.

14. Abraham Lincoln, "Reply to Mayor Alexander Henry at Philadelphia, Pennsylvania," February 21, 1861, in *Collected Works of Abraham Lincoln*, IV, 239.

15. Abraham Lincoln, "Reply to Mayor Fernando Wood, at New York City," February 20, 1861, in *Collected Works of Abraham Lincoln*, IV, 233.

16. Abraham Lincoln, "Speech in Independence Hall, February 22, 1861," in *Collected Works of Abraham Lincoln*, IV, 240.

17. Abraham Lincoln to Albert G. Hodges, April 4, 1864, in *Collected Works of Abraham Lincoln*, VII, 281–82.

18. James M. McPherson, *Abraham Lincoln and the Second American Revolution* (New York: Oxford University Press, 1991), 62–63.

19. See Eric Foner, *A Short History of Reconstruction, 1863–1877* (New York: Harper & Row, 1990), 93–94; Kenneth M. Stampp, *The Era of Reconstruction, 1865–1877* (New York: Vintage Books, 1965), 79–80.

20. It bears noting, however, that a broader interpretation of the Fourteenth Amendment was possible. As Patricia Lucie has observed, the Fourteenth Amendment could be read more expansively to justify laws that "reached not only the palpable actions of states to deprive citizens of their rights but also state wrongs of omission or inaction." In fact, as she notes, though "Justice Joseph P. Bradley's opinion for the Supreme Court in the *Civil Rights Cases* [1883] came to be read as raising high the barriers of federalism to allow federal correction only of wrongs in the laws and actions of states . . . even Justice Bradley had a broader theory that allowed for federal correction of private acts both where the state's inaction had left citizens' rights vulnerable to private deprivation and where legislation was based on the Thirteenth Amendment, which was free from any state action limit. It was left to twentieth-century judges to push these doors open, however." See Patricia Lucie, "The Civil War Constitutional Amendments," in *Legacy of Disunion: The Enduring Significance of the American Civil War*, Susan-Mary Grant and Peter J. Parish, eds. (Baton Rouge: Louisiana State University Press, 2003), 180, 183.

21. Lucie, "The Civil War Constitutional Amendments," 180.

22. See Stampp, *The Era of Reconstruction*, 141–42.

23. See Stampp, *The Era of Reconstruction*, 104; and Foner, *A Short History of Reconstruction, 1863–1877*, 147. For the rehabilitation of the Radical Republicans in historical literature, see Stampp, *The Era of Reconstruction*, and Hans L. Trefousse, *The Radical Republicans: Lincoln's Vanguard for Racial Justice* (New York: Alfred A. Knopf, 1969). The best overall treatment of Reconstruction is Eric Foner's *Reconstruction: America's Unfinished Revolution, 1863–1877* (New York: Harper & Row, 1988). See also Michael W. Fitzgerald, *Splendid Failure: Postwar Reconstruction in the American South* (Chicago: Ivan R. Dee, 2007).

24. Stampp, *The Era of Reconstruction*, 135.

25. Foner, *A Short History of Reconstruction*, 146.

26. For a good comparative analysis, see Stampp, *The Era of Reconstruction*, 174–84.

27. Walt Whitman, "Democratic Vistas" (1871), in *Walt Whitman, Prose Works 1892*, Floyd Stovall, ed. (New York: New York University Press, 1964), II, 369.

28. Roscoe Conkling, address at Rochester, New York, September 26, 1877, quoted in Matthew Josephson, *The Politicos, 1865–1896* (New York: Harcourt, Brace & Co., 1938), 246, 728, n32; and in Alfred R. Conkling, *The Life and Letters of Roscoe Conkling, Orator, Statesman, Advocate* (New York: Charles L. Webster, 1889), 540, 541.

29. John J. Ingalls, *Congressional Record* (March 26, 1886), 2786.

30. John Ruskin, "Fors Clavigera, Letter Ten: The Baron's Gate," September 7, 1871, in John Ruskin, *Unto This Last and Other Writings*, Clive Wilmer, ed. (London: Penguin Classics, 1985), 1997 edition, 306–7.

31. Ruskin, *Unto This Last*, 163–64.

32. Herbert Spencer, *Social Statics* (1850) (New York: D. Appleton & Co., 1864), 414–15.

33. Richard Hofstadter, *Social Darwinism in American Thought* (Philadelphia: University of Pennsylvania Press, 1944; Beacon edition, 1955), 7.

34. Andrew Carnegie, *Autobiography* (Boston: Houghton Mifflin, 1920), 339.

35. William Graham Sumner, *Essays of William Graham Sumner*, A. G. Keller and M. R. Davie, eds. (New Haven, Conn.: Yale University Press, 1940), II, 56.

36. Richard T. Ely, *Ground Under Our Feet: An Autobiography* (New York: Macmillan, 1938), 136.

37. Winston Leonard Spencer Churchill, *Lord Randolph Churchill* (New York: Macmillan, 1906), I, 269

38. John Stuart Mill, *Principles of Political Economy* (1848) (London: Longmans, Green, and Co., 1909), V, 800.

39. David Harris, "European Liberalism in the Nineteenth Century," *American Historical Review*, vol. LX, no. 3 (April 1955), 515–56.

40. See Alfred H. Kelly, Winfred A. Harbison, and Herman Belz, *The American Constitution: Its Origins and Development* (New York: W. W. Norton, 1983), 400–404.

41. Lawrence Goodwyn, *The Populist Moment: A Short History of the Agrarian Revolt in America* (New York: Oxford University Press, 1978), viii.

42. Goodwyn, *The Populist Moment*, vii.

43. Goodwyn, *The Populist Moment*, 92.

44. Omaha Platform of the People's Party, July 1892, in John D. Hicks, *The Populist Revolt: A History of the Farmers' Alliance and the People's Party* (Minneapolis: University of Minnesota Press, 1931), appendix F, 441. See also Charles Postel, *The Populist Vision* (New York: Oxford University Press, 2007).

45. See Franklin Folsom, *Impatient Armies of the Poor: The Story of Collective Action of the Unemployed, 1808–1942* (Niwot: University Press of Colorado, 1991), 180–86.

46. William Jennings Bryan, "The Cross of Gold Speech," in *William Jennings Bryan: Selections*, Ray Ginger, ed. (Indianapolis: Bobbs-Merrill, 1967), 41.

47. See Thomas Beer, *Hanna* (New York: Alfred A. Knopf, 1929), 132–33.

48. See Herbert Croly, *Marcus Alonzo Hanna: His Life and Work* (New York: Macmillan, 1912), 388–400, 444. Eric F. Goldman perceived in Hanna and successors such as George W. Perkins—a Morgan partner and director of International Harvester and U.S. Steel—contributors to the legacy of American liberalism. See Eric F. Goldman, *Rendezvous with Destiny: A History of Modern American Reform* (New York: Alfred A. Knopf, 1952; Vintage edition, 1997), 160–61. From a New Left perspective, James Weinstein maintained that "the growing maturity and sophistication" of men such as Perkins bespoke an enlightened conservatism: Perkins and his peers had "come to understand, as Theodore Roosevelt often told them, that social reform was truly conservative." See James Weinstein, "Big Business and the Origins of Workmen's Compensation," *Labor History*, vol. VIII (Spring 1967), 156–74. For a further study of the contributions of reform-to-conserve business leaders in the origins of the American welfare state, see Edward D. Berkowitz and Kim McQuaid, *Creating the Welfare State: The Political Economy of 20th-Century Reform* (Lawrence: University Press of Kansas, 1988).

49. See H. W. Brands, *T.R.: The Last Romantic* (New York: Basic Books, 1997), 13.

50. Brands, *T.R.*, 26.

51. See David H. Burton, "Theodore Roosevelt's Social Darwinism and Views on Imperialism," *Journal of the History of Ideas*, vol. 26, no. 1 (January–March 1965), 103–18.

52. Theodore Roosevelt, private diaries, September 1, 1878, quoted in Carleton Putnam, *Theodore Roosevelt: The Formative Years, 1858–1886* (New York: Charles Scribner's Sons, 1958), 150.

53. Theodore Roosevelt to Henry Cabot Lodge, June 29, 1889, in *The Letters of Theodore Roosevelt*, I, 167.

54. Theodore Roosevelt, *An Autobiography*, in *The Works of Theodore Roosevelt*, XXII, 532.

55. Theodore Roosevelt to Marcus Alonzo Hanna, October 3, 1902, in *The Letters of Theodore Roosevelt*, III, 337.

56. For an account of the Panama Canal project, see David McCullough, *Path between the Seas: The Creation of the Panama Canal, 1870–1914* (New York: Simon & Schuster, 1977).

57. See *The Letters of Theodore Roosevelt*, IV, 1131, n1.

58. John Milton Cooper Jr., *Pivotal Decades: The United States, 1900–1920* (New York: W. W. Norton, 1990), 36.

59. Henry L. Stimson and McGeorge Bundy, *On Active Service in Peace and War* (New York: Harper, 1948), 4, 17.

60. Theodore Roosevelt to James Wolcott Wadsworth, May 26, 1906, in *The Letters of Theodore Roosevelt*, V, 282–83.

61. Theodore Roosevelt, "The Puritan Spirit and the Regulation of Corporations," address in Provincetown, Massachusetts, August 20, 1907, in *The Works of Theodore Roosevelt*, XVIII, 94.

62. Theodore Roosevelt, eighth annual message to Congress, December 8, 1908, in *The Works of Theodore Roosevelt*, XVII, 604.

63. Theodore Roosevelt, *An Autobiography*, in *The Works of Theodore Roosevelt*, XXII, 481.

64. Theodore Roosevelt, address at the Union League Club, Philadelphia, January 30, 1905, in *Presidential Addresses and State Papers by Theodore Roosevelt* (New York: Review of Reviews Company, 1910), III, 217–24. The conservative elements in Roosevelt's statecraft have elicited both criticism and praise from American historians. Writing from a left-of-center perspective, Richard Hofstadter devoted a chapter to TR in his iconoclastic study *The American Political Tradition* (1948). In labeling Roosevelt "The Conservative as Progressive," Hofstadter tried to expose what he believed to be the shallowness of Roosevelt's "progressivism." John Morton Blum, writing in 1954, countered that Roosevelt's conservative qualities were far more admirable than liberal critics believed: "An institutionalist, a gradualist, a moralist, from the position he attained he ruled strongly and quite well. Learning the while, he developed large plans for the uses of power. These had one common, revealing objective: stability" (Blum, *The Republican Roosevelt* [Cambridge, Mass.: Harvard University Press, 1954; Atheneum edition, 1962], 6). By the 1960s, such reasoning brought Hofstadter around; in his preface to the 1967 edition of *The American Political Tradition*, Hofstadter acknowledged that if he were to rewrite the volume he would treat TR very differently: "In writing of Theodore Roosevelt, I was, I think, unduly taken with my 'discovery' of the element of sham in his progressivism. . . . Instead of viewing T.R. as a bogus progressive, suppose one were to begin with the assumption that he was indeed distinctly a conservative at heart, but a most flexible and adroit conservative?" (Richard Hofstadter, *The American Political Tradition and the Men Who Made It* [New York: Alfred A. Knopf, 1948; Vintage edition, 1974], xxx–xxxi).

65. Theodore Roosevelt to Raymond Robins, August 12, 1914, in *The Letters of Theodore Roosevelt*, VII, 797.

66. Abraham Lincoln, "Last Public Address," April 11, 1865, in *Collected Works of Abraham Lincoln*, VIII, 399–405.

67. Richard Hofstadter, *The Age of Reform: From Bryan to F.D.R.* (New York: Random House/Vintage, 1955), 252.

68. Theodore Roosevelt, "The New Nationalism," address in Osawatomie, Kansas, August 31, 1910, in *The Works of Theodore Roosevelt*, XIX, 18, 26–27.

69. Theodore Roosevelt, *An Autobiography*, in *The Works of Theodore Roosevelt*, XXII, 539.

70. Theodore Roosevelt, "The Purpose of the Progressive Party," address in New York City, October 30, 1912, in *The Works of Theodore Roosevelt*, XIX, 459.

71. The element of regulation in Progressive Era reform has been the subject of critiques from both the left and the right; critics have denounced Progressive "supervision" of America's new industrial order as both "liberal" and "conservative" in its character, depending on their own ideological orientation. From a New Left perspective, Gabriel Kolko argued that "the period . . . labeled the 'progressive' era by virtually all historians was really an era of conservatism" because "national political leaders during the period 1900–1916 . . . in virtually every case . . . chose those solutions to problems advocated by the representatives of concerned business and financial interests." Consequently, it was "business control over politics" rather than "political regulation of the economy" that typified the "triumph of conservatism" by businessmen seeking stability and predictability through the subterfuge of regulatory reform. See Gabriel Kolko, *The Triumph of Conservatism: A Reinterpretation of American History, 1900–1916* (London: Collier-Macmillan Limited, 1963), 2–3. Though at first inclined to view Progressive reform in similar terms, James Weinstein later argued that it was elitist liberals—rather than conservatives—who used Progressive reforms to stabilize the capitalist system: "Corporate liberalism . . . appealed to leaders of different social groupings and classes by granting them status and influence . . . on the condition only that they defend the framework of the existing social order." See James Weinstein, *The Corporate Ideal in the Liberal State, 1900–1918* (Boston: Beacon Press, 1968), xiv. Not surprisingly, conservative (especially libertarian conservative) scholarship is also inclined to attack Progressive regulation as the work of liberalism—or socialism—but to argue that regulation undermined the strength of private enterprise instead of supporting it. See Robert Higgs, *Crisis and Leviathan: Critical Episodes in the Growth of American Government* (New York: Oxford University Press, 1987), 116, although Higgs acknowledges that regulatory ideas were widespread at the turn of the century. For recent accounts of the Progressive Era, see Michael McGerr, *A Fierce Discontent: The Rise and Fall of the Progressive Movement in America, 1870–1920* (New York: Oxford University Press, 2003), and Maureen A. Flanagan, *America Reformed: Progressives and Progressivisms, 1890s–1920s* (New York: Oxford University Press, 2007).

72. Mark Sullivan, *Our Times: The United States, 1900–1925* (New York: Charles Scribner's Sons, 1930), III, 71.

CHAPTER 4: THE LEGACY CROSSES PARTY LINES: FROM THEODORE TO FRANKLIN D. ROOSEVELT

1. Franklin Delano Roosevelt to James and Sara Roosevelt, June 4, 1897, in *The Roosevelt Letters: Being the Personal Correspondence of Franklin Delano Roosevelt*, Elliott Roosevelt, ed. (London: George G. Harrap & Co., Ltd., 1950), I, 108.

2. James MacGregor Burns and Susan Dunn, *The Three Roosevelts: Patrician Leaders Who Transformed America* (New York: Atlantic Monthly Press, 2001), 56.

3. FDR diary, January 1, 1903, cited in Frank Freidel, *Franklin D. Roosevelt: The Apprenticeship* (Boston: Little, Brown, 1952), 85.

4. Franklin D. Roosevelt, "Address at the Jackson Day Dinner," January 8, 1938, in *The Public Papers and Addresses of Franklin D. Roosevelt*, Samuel L. Rosenman, ed. (New York: Macmillan, 1941), VII, 38.

5. Theodore Roosevelt, quoted in Nathan Miller, *Theodore Roosevelt: A Life* (New York: William Morrow & Co., 1992), 410. See also Mildred Adams, "When T. R. Gave His Niece in Marriage," *New York Times Magazine* (March 17, 1935).

6. Franklin Delano Roosevelt to Sara Roosevelt, September 7, 1905, in *The Roosevelt Letters*, II, 82.

7. Grenville Clark, in *Harvard Alumni Bulletin*, April 28, 1945, 47: 452, cited in Freidel, *Franklin D. Roosevelt: The Apprenticeship*, 86.

8. Burns and Dunn, *The Three Roosevelts*, 80.

9. Frances Perkins, quoted in Geoffrey C. Ward, *A First-Class Temperament: The Emergence of Franklin Roosevelt* (New York: Harper & Row, 1989), 499.

10. Burns and Dunn, *The Three Roosevelts*, 115.

11. Theodore Roosevelt to Franklin D. Roosevelt, January 29, 1911, Roosevelt Papers, cited in Arthur Schlesinger Jr., *The Age of Roosevelt: The Crisis of the Old Order, 1919–1933* (Boston: Houghton Mifflin, 1957), 334.

12. Theodore Roosevelt to Franklin D. Roosevelt, March 18, 1913, Roosevelt Papers, cited in Schlesinger, *The Crisis of the Old Order*, 344.

13. Josephus Daniels, quoted in Schlesinger, *The Crisis of the Old Order*, 344.

14. Arthur S. Link, *Woodrow Wilson and the Progressive Era* (New York: Harper & Row, 1954), Harper Torchbook edition, 70.

15. Link, *Woodrow Wilson and the Progressive Era*, 72.

16. Link, *Woodrow Wilson and the Progressive Era*, 74.

17. William F. Hixson, *Triumph of the Bankers: Money and Banking in the Eighteenth and Nineteenth Centuries* (Westport, Conn.: Praeger, 1993), 178.

18. Gary M. Walton and Hugh Rockoff, *History of the American Economy* (Stamford, Conn.: South-Western/Thomson Learning, 2002), 250.

19. Walton and Rockoff, *History of the American Economy*, 411.

20. Hixson, *Triumph of the Bankers*, 178.

21. Other crucial details of the original system have been summarized by Walton and Rockoff:

> Each Federal Reserve Bank was to be run by a board of nine directors. Three of the directors, representing the "public," were to be appointed by the Federal Reserve Board; the remaining six were to be elected by the member banks of the district. [Only] three of the six locally elected directors could be bankers. . . . The Federal Reserve Act made membership in the system compulsory for national banks; state banks, upon compliance with federal requirements, might also become members. To join the system, a commercial bank had to purchase shares of the capital stock of the district Federal Reserve Bank. . . . A member bank also had to deposit with the district Federal Reserve Bank a large part of the cash it had previously held as reserves [and] after 1917, all the legal reserves of member banks were to be in the form of deposits with the Federal Reserve Bank. (Walton and Rockoff, *History of the American Economy*, 425)

Federal Reserve notes, to be printed by the Treasury Department, would be furnished to the Federal Reserve Banks in exchange for securities. The early method was described by Thurman Van Metre in the early 1920s: "Should the regional bank desire currency it places some of its commercial paper in the hands of its Federal Reserve Agent [appointed by the

Federal Reserve Board] and sets aside a sum of gold equal to 40 per cent of the amount of Federal Reserve Notes requested. The Federal Reserve Agent then gives the notes to the bank and holds in trust for the Government the commercial paper against which the notes are issued" (Thurman W. Van Metre, *Economic History of the United States* [New York: Henry Holt, 1921], 586). Following passage of the Gold Reserve Act of 1934—requiring all Federal Reserve Banks to turn over their gold to the Treasury in exchange for Gold Certificates that did not circulate beyond the Federal Reserve system—the amount of currency that could be furnished by Federal Reserve Banks depended on their Gold Certificate holdings. For a number of years there was an angry dispute between the board and the reserve banks about the power to set interest rates (discount rates). Economic historian Allen H. Meltzer provides details:

> The Board . . . sought control. One of its earliest acts was to rule that the reserve banks could not announce or change discount rates until they had been approved by the Board. . . . Early in 1915 the Governors Conference [a meeting of the presidents or "Governors" of the reserve banks] approved a resolution giving the reserve banks sole power to initiate discount rate changes "without pressure from the Federal Reserve Board." . . . In 1919 the Board was able to get the acting attorney general to interpret its power to include changing discount rates even if a reserve bank opposed the change. (See Allan H. Meltzer, in *A History of the Federal Reserve, Volume I: 1913–1951* [Chicago: University of Chicago Press, 2004], 77–78, 740.)

Over time, the power struggle was resolved through consensus-building via the Federal Open Market Committee (FOMC), established in 1923 as a subdivision of the Federal Reserve to coordinate the buying and selling of bonds. William Greider has observed that since the FOMC was effectively controlled by the Federal Reserve Board while nonetheless including in its membership some presidents of the regional reserve banks—the board had seven votes while the regional presidents had five votes, rotated annually among the regional banks—the "hybrid committee" was ideally positioned to serve as a forum for deciding "core questions of regulating money supply" in a nonconfrontational setting. See William Greider, *Secrets of the Temple: How the Federal Reserve Runs the Country* (New York: Simon & Schuster, Touchstone edition, 1987), 50.

22. Walton and Rockoff, *A History of the American Economy*, 250.

23. Irving Fisher, *100% Money: Designed to Keep Checking Banks 100% Liquid; to Prevent Inflation and Deflation; Largely to Cure or Prevent Depressions; and to Wipe Out Much of the National Debt* (New York: Adelphi Publications, 1935), 7.

24. William J. Baumol and Alan S. Blinder, *Economics: Principles and Policy* (Fort Worth, Tex.: Dryden Press/Harcourt Brace & Company, 1979; sixth ed., 1994), 727–28. In attacking this system, Irving Fisher explained in the 1930s that there is a "confusion of ownership" about checking deposits. "When money is deposited in a checking account, the depositor still thinks of that money as his, though legally it is the bank's. The depositor owns no deposit; he is merely a creditor of a private corporation. Most of the 'mystery' of banking would disappear as soon as a bank was no longer allowed to lend out money deposited by its customers, while, at the same time, these depositors were using that money as *their* money by drawing checks against it." Fisher further explained that this "double use of checking deposits" was based upon the legal principle (or loophole) providing that "the bank lends not money but merely a promise to furnish money on demand." See Fisher, *100% Money*, 11, 81, 7.

25. John Milton Cooper Jr., *Pivotal Decades: The United States, 1900–1920* (New York: W. W. Norton, 1990), 291.

26. John Morton Blum, *Woodrow Wilson and the Politics of Morality* (Boston: Little, Brown, 1956), 136.

27. Blum, *Woodrow Wilson and the Politics of Morality*, 140.

28. Cooper, *Pivotal Decades*, 297.

29. Cooper, *Pivotal Decades*, 298.

30. Cooper, *Pivotal Decades*, 312–13.

31. Woodrow Wilson, address to the U.S. Senate, July 10, 1919, in *The Papers of Woodrow Wilson*, Arthur S. Link, ed. (Princeton, N.J.: Princeton University Press, 1990), LXI, 436. On Wilson and the League, see John Milton Cooper Jr., *Breaking the Heart of the World: Woodrow Wilson and the Fight for the League of Nations* (Cambridge: Cambridge University Press, 2001).

32. Woodrow Wilson, address in Pueblo, Colorado, September 25, 1919, in *The Papers of Woodrow Wilson*, LXIII, 512–13.

33. See John S. D. Eisenhower, *General Ike: A Personal Reminiscence* (New York: Free Press, 2003), 4–5.

34. Eisenhower, *General Ike*, 6–13.

35. For details about the Hoover Dam project, see Lois Craig et al., *The Federal Presence: Architecture, Politics, and Symbols in United States Government Buildings* (Cambridge, Mass.: MIT Press, 1978), 280; Joseph E. Stevens, *Hoover Dam: An American Adventure* (Norman: University of Oklahoma Press, 1988); Andrew J. Dunar and Dennis McBride, *Building Hoover Dam: An Oral History of the Great Depression* (New York: Twayne Publishers, 1993); and U.S. Department of the Interior, Water and Power Resources Service, *Project Data: Boulder Canyon Project, Hoover Dam* (Denver: U.S. Government Printing Office, 1981), 79–88. For a brief history of the agency in charge of constructing Hoover Dam, see William E. Warne, *The Bureau of Reclamation* (New York: Praeger, 1973).

36. David Burner, *Herbert Hoover: A Public Life* (New York: Alfred A. Knopf, 1979), 143, 229, 230.

37. For coverage of Hoover's role in the flood disaster of 1927, see John M. Barry, *Rising Tide: The Great Mississippi Flood of 1927 and How It Changed America* (New York: Simon & Schuster, 1997).

38. See Pete Davies, *American Road: The Story of an Epic Transcontinental Journey at the Dawn of the Motor Age* (New York: Henry Holt, 2002).

39. See Dwight D. Eisenhower, *At Ease: Stories I Tell To Friends* (Garden City, N.Y.: Doubleday, 1967), 155–68.

40. See Walton and Rockoff, *History of the American Economy*, 499.

41. William Trufant Foster and Waddill Catchings, *Business Without a Buyer* (Boston: Houghton Mifflin, 1927; second ed., 1928), 19.

42. See Roy Harrod, *Money* (London: St. Martin's Press, 1969), 41–42.

43. See Lester S. Levy and Roy J. Sampson, *American Economic Development: Growth of the U.S. in the Western World* (Boston: Allyn and Bacon, 1962), 573–74. Hobson's major books were *The Evolution of Modern Capitalism* (1894), *Work and Wealth* (1914), *The Economics of Unemployment* (1922), and *Confessions of an Economic Heretic* (1938).

44. See Schlesinger, *The Crisis of the Old Order*, 85–86.

45. Walton and Rockoff, *History of the American Economy*, 497–99.

46. Walton and Rockoff, *History of the American Economy*.

47. Hixson, *Triumph of the Bankers*, 1.

48. See Walton and Rockoff, *History of the American Economy*, 508–10.

49. Walton and Rockoff, *History of the American Economy*, 496–97. Economists have been arguing about the causality of the Great Depression for a long time. For representative scholarly opinions, see Christina Romer, "The Great Crash and the Onset of the Great Depression," *Quarterly Journal of Economics*, vol. CV (1990), 597–24; Peter Temin, *Did Monetary Forces Cause the Great Depression?* (New York: W. W. Norton, 1976); Benjamin Bernanke, "Nonmonetary Effects of the Financial Crisis in the Propagation of the Great Depression," *American Economic Review*, vol. 73 (1983), 257–76; and Michael D. Bordo, Ehsan Choudhri, and Anna J. Schwartz, "Could Stable Money Have Averted the Great Contraction?" *Economic Inquiry*, vol. 33 (1995), 484–505. One school of thought down the years has de-emphasized the 1929 crash. Historian Maury Klein writes that "scholars . . . have yet to come up with convincing answers to the crucial questions of what caused the crash and what role, if any, it played in bringing on the grinding depression that followed" (Maury Klein, *Rainbow's End: The Crash of 1929* [New York: Oxford University Press, 2001], xiii). Historian David M. Kennedy argues that "most responsible students of the events of 1929 have been unable to demonstrate an appreciable cause-and-effect linkage between the Great Crash and the Depression" (*Freedom From Fear: The American People in Depression and War, 1929–1945* [New York: Oxford University Press, 1999], 39). But the logic of John Kenneth Galbraith remains compelling: Galbraith argued that "the stock market crash was not a slight affair. The economy was vulnerable to its blow, and given that vulnerability, the blow was a most important thing." Galbraith emphasized the heavy extent to which money from banks and corporations was diverted into stock speculation: "Loans to brokers for carrying securities on margin, i.e., for speculation, went up hugely—from $810 million at the end of 1921 to $2.5 billion at the beginning of 1929, with as much more being contributed by corporations and other nonbank lenders. There was a further vast increase—in the summer months by around $400 million a month—in 1929." Consequently, when the stock prices broke, threats of devastating loss prompted lenders to begin a big contraction, which spread and got out of control (*Money: Whence It Came, Where It Went* [Boston: Houghton Mifflin, 1975], 184–85, 177). In *The Great Crash, 1929*, Galbraith included more detail about the manner in which corporations were involved in the disaster: "During 1929, Standard Oil of New Jersey contributed a daily average of $69 million to the call market. A few corporations—Cities Service was one—even sold securities and loaned the proceeds to the stock market. By early 1929, loans from these non-banking sources were approximately equal to those from the banks." It seems probable that many corporations were hurt if the speculative investors to whom they lent the money defaulted due to stock market losses. See John Kenneth Galbraith, *The Great Crash, 1929* (Boston: Houghton Mifflin, 1954; Sentry edition, 1961), 36, 2, 94.

50. William E. Leuchtenburg, *Franklin D. Roosevelt and the New Deal* (New York: Harper & Row, 1963), Harper Torchbooks edition, 3.

51. Schlesinger, *The Crisis of the Old Order*, 250–51.

52. Leuchtenburg, *Franklin D. Roosevelt and the New Deal*, 22–23.

53. Levy and Sampson, *American Economic Development*, 489–90.

54. Leuchtenburg, *Franklin D. Roosevelt and the New Deal*, 24–25, 29.

55. John Maynard Keynes, "The World's Economic Outlook," *Atlantic Monthly* (May 1932), 525.

56. Frederick Lewis Allen, *Only Yesterday: An Informal History of the 1920s* (New York: Harper & Brothers, 1931; Perennial Library edition, 1964), 288.

57. Walter Lippmann to Newton Baker, July 29, 1932, Baker MSS, Box 149, cited in Leuchtenburg, *Franklin D. Roosevelt and the New Deal*, 10.

58. Charles Willis Thompson, "Wanted: Political Courage," *Harper's Magazine*, vol. CLXV (1932), 726–27, quoted in Leuchtenburg, *Franklin D. Roosevelt and the New Deal*, 10.

59. Henry C. Simons, *Economic Policy for a Free Society* (Chicago: University of Chicago Press, 1948), 54–55.

60. Leuchtenburg, *Franklin D. Roosevelt and the New Deal*, 50.

61. John R. Commons, *Institutional Economics: Its Place in Political Economy* (New York: Macmillan, 1934), 589–90.

62. Irving Fisher, "100% Money and the Public Debt," *Economic Forum* (Spring 1936), 406–20.

63. Fisher, *100% Money*, 18.

64. Fisher, *100% Money*, 8–10.

65. Fisher, *100% Money*, 81. Economist Lauchlin Currie, who served on the staffs of both the Treasury Department and the Federal Reserve Board, tried to get a "100% reserve" provision along the lines of Fisher's system inserted in the Banking Act of 1935. The Federal Reserve Board would have been renamed the Federal Monetary Authority in this proposal. See Meltzer, *A History of the Federal Reserve*, 474.

66. Some of the people who were calling for "dictatorship" were probably thinking of "the classics." College students were still taking Latin in the early decades of the twentieth century and people read Livy (Titus Livius), who told of the ancient Roman tradition when, in times of great danger to the state, the elected consuls and senators selected a Roman universally renowned for his courage, wisdom, and honesty, and vested him with sovereign power. Such was the dictator-hero Cincinnatus. See Livy, *The Early History of Rome*, books I–V of *The History of Rome from Its Foundation*, Aubrey De Sélincourt, trans. (London: Penguin Books, 1971), 16, 213, 285.

67. Alfred M. Landon, quoted in Schlesinger, *The Age of Roosevelt: The Coming of the New Deal* (Boston: Houghton Mifflin, 1958), 3.

68. Leuchtenburg, *Franklin D. Roosevelt and the New Deal*, 30.

69. Franklin Delano Roosevelt, first inaugural address, *Public Papers and Addresses*, II, 11–15.

70. Hamilton Fish Jr. to Franklin Delano Roosevelt, February 24, 1933, cited in Schlesinger, *Crisis of the Old Order*, 5.

71. Representative Robert Luce, *Congressional Record*, 73rd Congress, 1st Session, 70, 79.

72. Leuchtenburg, *Franklin D. Roosevelt and the New Deal*, 43–44.

73. Bronson Cutting, "Is Private Banking Doomed?" *Liberty* (March 31, 1934), 10.

74. For an assessment of the New Deal's conservative aspects presented with the disapproving slant of a New Left perspective, see Barton J. Bernstein, "The New Deal: The Conservative Achievements of Liberal Reform," in *Towards a New Past: Dissenting Essays in American History*, Barton J. Bernstein, ed. (New York: Pantheon Books, 1968), 263–88.

75. George W. Perkins, quoted in Schlesinger, *The Crisis of the Old Order*, 21–22.

76. This activity became the basis for the long-term federal school lunch program.

77. Leuchtenburg, *Franklin D. Roosevelt and the New Deal*, 70.

78. Leuchtenburg, *Franklin D. Roosevelt and the New Deal*, 122.

79. Franklin Delano Roosevelt, quoted in Leuchtenburg, *Franklin D. Roosevelt and the New Deal*, 122.

80. Lewis Douglas to Franklin Delano Roosevelt, November 28, 1934, quoted in Leuchtenburg, *Franklin D. Roosevelt and the New Deal*, 91.

81. Keynes, "The World's Economic Outlook," 525–26.

82. James MacGregor Burns, *Roosevelt: The Lion and the Fox* (New York: Harcourt, Brace & World, 1956), 330–35. Keynesian-tending measures in the early New Deal—job-creation projects such as the PWA, TVA, and CCC—were limited in their impact due to limited funding. In some ways FDR gave greater attention to monetary and economic experiments designed to create inflation. In addition to ventures in price maintenance via the NRA and AAA, FDR tried to reduce the buying power of the dollar by manipulating the precious metal basis of the money supply. At first to protect the nation's banks by stopping the withdrawal of gold deposits, FDR partially demonetized gold by forbidding its private possession, with a few exceptions. This policy, formalized by the Gold Reserve Act of 1934, required all citizens and banks to turn over their gold to the Treasury, with currency issued in return. With most gold in federal hands, FDR decided to alter the value of the dollar by purchasing additional gold above the world price. By thus devaluing the dollar (relative to gold), he hoped to weaken its buying power and thus prop up American prices. The resultant "high price of gold" in American dollars—along with the impulse in Europe to send away gold for safekeeping in America as war clouds gathered—prompted huge inflows of gold from abroad; this gold found its way through the banking system to the Treasury, which then monetized the gold by issuing additional Gold Certificates to the Federal Reserve in exchange for it. The great inflow of Gold Certificates helped build up the "excess reserves" within the system, thus expanding its potential to increase the money supply. FDR's authority came in part from an amendment to the AAA bill that gave the president discretionary power to create inflation through silver purchases, the issuance of Greenbacks, or alterations in the gold value of the dollar. Though FDR rejected Greenbacks, he approved of inflationary action via silver purchases, following the nineteenth-century precedents set by the 1878 Bland-Allison Act and the 1890 Sherman Silver Purchase Act. FDR was seeking not only to prop up prices but also to counteract the contraction of the money supply that resulted from the massive destruction of fractional-reserve checking deposits from 1929 through 1933. In purchasing silver the Treasury issued Silver Certificates in payment, which continued to circulate as cash. This off-budget "federal spending" (in actuality a pretext for generating currency by stretching the principle of mint-based coinage to encompass a nominal *purchase* of metal by the Treasury) constituted a direct expansion of the money supply through direct creation of money. For extended coverage of these issues, see Leuchtenburg, *Franklin D. Roosevelt and the New Deal*, 37–38, 42–44, 50–51, 78–84; and Broadus Mitchell and Louise Pearson Mitchell, *American Economic History* (Boston: Houghton Mifflin, 1947), 817–32.

83. Before the FHA, mortgages had tended to be short-term affairs with a high down payment and the principal due at the end of an extremely brief term. The FHA, through its loan guarantees, helped to usher in the modern fifteen- or thirty-year fixed-rate, self-amortizing mortgage that we all take for granted. Later in the 1930s, the new Federal National Mortgage Association ("Fannie Mae") was created to buy and sell mortgages, thus rolling more funds into the mortgage pool. The Federal Home Loan Bank Act of 1932 had created a system of regional home loan banks supervised by a Federal Home Loan Bank Board that was roughly analogous to the Federal Reserve system. The New Deal added to this institutional structure through the Home Owners Loan Corporation (HOLC), created in 1933 to refinance defaulted mortgages. It bears noting that the 1934 Housing Act created the FSLIC (Federal Savings and Loan Insurance Corporation) as the S&L counterpart of FDIC.

84. See "Realtors Applaud New National Housing Act," *National Real Estate Journal*, vol. 35 (July 1934), 20–22. See also Gail Radford, *Modern Housing for America: Policy Struggles in the*

New Deal Era (Chicago: University of Chicago Press, 1996), and *The FHA Story in Summary* (Washington, D.C.: Federal Housing Administration, 1959).

85. The best treatment of Long remains the excellent biography by T. Harry Williams. See T. Harry Williams, *Huey Long* (New York: Alfred A. Knopf, 1969).

86. Williams, *Huey Long*, 844.

87. See Marquis Childs, "They Hate Roosevelt," *Harper's Magazine* (May 1936), 634–42; and George Wolfskill, *The Revolt of the Conservatives: A History of the American Liberty League, 1934–1940* (Boston: Houghton Mifflin, 1962). No doubt the upper-class hatred of Roosevelt was preliminarily triggered by actions that appeared to be attacks upon the autonomous power of America's wealthy elite: the confiscation of gold, the regulation of Wall Street, and the high-level prosecutions of various magnates (including former treasury secretary Andrew Mellon) for tax evasion.

88. Federal bank examination authority was shared between the FDIC, the Federal Reserve, and the comptroller of the currency. The comptroller's office, established in 1863 pursuant to the creation of the national banks, continued to supervise these federally chartered banks even after they were absorbed into the Federal Reserve system. The Federal Reserve supervised state-chartered commercial banks that were members of the system, usually in partnership with state agencies. The FDIC examined insured banks that were not subject to supervision by the other federal agencies.

89. Wolfskill, *The Revolt of the Conservatives*, 107–8.

90. E. Digby Baltzell, *The Protestant Establishment: Aristocracy and Caste in America* (New York: Random House, 1964).

91. Franklin Delano Roosevelt, address in Chicago, October 14, 1936, *Public Papers and Addresses*, V, 487.

92. Franklin Delano Roosevelt, quoted in *William Randolph Hearst: A Portrait in His Own Words*, Edmond D. Coblentz, ed. (New York: Simon & Schuster, 1952), 178.

93. Carl Degler, *Out of Our Past* (New York: Harper & Row, 1959), 1984 edition, 445.

94. Burns, *Roosevelt: The Lion and the Fox*, 235, 238.

95. Burns, *Roosevelt: The Lion and the Fox*, 235, 237, 238.

96. Burns, *Roosevelt: The Lion and the Fox*, 237.

97. Leuchtenburg, *Franklin D. Roosevelt and the New Deal*, 345.

98. Alfred Smith, January 25, 1936, quoted in Wolfskill, *The Revolt of the Conservatives*, 152.

99. Lincoln Steffens to Sam Darcy, April 28, 1934, in *The Letters of Lincoln Steffens*, Ella Winter and Granville Hicks, eds. (New York: Harcourt, Brace & World, 1938), II, 983.

100. Franklin Delano Roosevelt, address delivered at the Democratic State Convention, Syracuse, New York, September 29, 1936, in *Public Papers and Addresses,* V, 384.

101. Harold L. Ickes, "Academic Freedom," *School and Society*, June 8, 1935, cited in Arthur Schlesinger Jr., *The Age of Roosevelt: The Politics of Upheaval* (Boston: Houghton Mifflin, 1960), 195.

102. Franklin Delano Roosevelt, address in Syracuse, New York, September 29, 1936, in *Public Papers and Addresses*, V, 389–90.

103. Franklin Delano Roosevelt, address in Philadelphia, June 27, 1936, in *Public Papers and Addresses*, V, 232–33.

104. Franklin Delano Roosevelt, address at Madison Square Garden, New York City, October 31, 1936, cited in Burns, *Roosevelt: The Lion and the Fox*, 283.

105. Williams, *Huey Long*, 761.

106. The Air Commerce Act of 1926 had given the Commerce Department responsibility for regulating civil aviation. The department's new Aeronautics Branch (renamed the Bureau of Air Commerce in 1934) oversaw air traffic rules, pilot licensing, certification of aircraft safety, and air navigation development projects such as lighted runways. In 1936 the bureau took over air traffic control. After the CAA was established in 1938, it was split into two separate entities, the Civil Aeronautics Administration (CAA) and Civil Aeronautics Board (CAB), in 1940. The CAA handled safety enforcement and air traffic control while the CAB promulgated rules and regulated fares and routes.

107. See Stephen K. Shaw, William D. Pederson, and Frank J. Williams, eds., *Franklin D. Roosevelt and the Transformation of the Supreme Court* (Armonk, N.Y.: M. E. Sharpe, 2003).

108. Leuchtenburg, *Franklin D. Roosevelt and the New Deal*, 249.

109. Harry Hopkins, "The Future of Relief," *New Republic* (1937), quoted in Leuchtenburg, *Franklin D. Roosevelt and the New Deal*, 263.

110. Hopkins, "The Future of Relief."

111. See Amity Shlaes, *The Forgotten Man: A New History of the Great Depression* (New York: HarperCollins, 2007). It has long been the mode among American conservatives to blame the New Deal for prolonging the Depression and preventing recovery. There are two things wrong with this claim: (1) it ignores the systemic breakdown of free-market forces (especially in banking) that prompted many businessmen to *call* for intervention by government early in 1933; (2) it understates the presence in the business community of *pessimistic sales expectations* that arose in reaction to reduced consumer buying power. Dim sales expectations put a damper on investment and hiring. It is smug to suggest that in a massive economic contraction such as this one the business community had all the right answers while the government was always in the wrong. Some New Deal measures were failures; others were resounding successes. Above all, without the New Deal—or something like it—the contingencies confronting the American people in the 1930s were frightening indeed.

112. Thurman Arnold, *Fair Fights and Foul: A Dissenting Lawyer's Life* (New York: Harcourt, Brace & World, 1951), 1965 edition, 143.

113. Merrill D. Peterson, *Lincoln in American Memory* (New York: Oxford University Press, 1994), 321–22. See also William D. Pederson and Frank J. Williams, eds., *Franklin D. Roosevelt and Abraham Lincoln* (Armonk, N.Y.: M. E. Sharpe, 2002).

114. See Burns, *Roosevelt: The Lion and the Fox*, 420.

115. Winston Churchill, radio address, June 18, 1940, quoted in William Manchester, *The Last Lion: Winston Spencer Churchill; Alone, 1932–1940* (Boston: Little, Brown, 1988), 686.

116. Franklin Delano Roosevelt, "Message to Congress Asking for Additional Appropriations for National Defense," May 16, 1940, in *Public Papers and Addresses*, IX, 199–200.

117. Even here, perhaps, he was copying Long, whose book *My First Days in the White House*, published posthumously in 1935, included the comic fantasy of Al Smith, Hoover, and FDR joining the Huey Long cabinet to help redistribute the wealth.

118. Robert James Maddox, *The United States and World War II* (Boulder, Colo.: Westview Press, 1992), 187.

119. Maddox, *The United States and World War II*, 188.

120. *St. Louis Post-Dispatch* editorial, quoted in Burns, *Roosevelt: The Lion and the Fox*, 441.

121. Franklin Delano Roosevelt, quoted in Burns, *Roosevelt: The Lion and the Fox*, 449.

122. Burton K. Wheeler and Franklin Delano Roosevelt, quoted in James MacGregor Burns, *Roosevelt: The Soldier of Freedom* (New York: Harcourt Brace Jovanovich, 1970), 44.

123. Franklin Delano Roosevelt, "Fireside Chat," May 27, 1941, in *FDR's Fireside Chats*, Russell D. Buhite and David W. Levy, eds. (Norman: University of Oklahoma Press, 1992; Penguin edition, 1993), 179.

124. Franklin D. Roosevelt, "Navy Day Address on World Affairs," October 27, 1941, in *Nothing To Fear: The Selected Addresses of Franklin Delano Roosevelt, 1932–1945*, B. D. Zevin, ed. (Boston: Houghton Mifflin, 1946), 297.

125. Peterson, *Lincoln in American Memory*, 321.

126. Franklin Delano Roosevelt, "Fireside Chat," May 27, 1941, in *FDR's Fireside Chats*, 186.

127. Burns, *Roosevelt: The Soldier of Freedom*, 190.

128. Maddox, *The United States and World War II*, 191.

129. *Historical Statistics of the United States, Colonial Times to 1957*, Bureau of the Census, U.S. Department of Commerce (Washington, D.C.: U.S. Government Printing Office, 1960), 1961 edition, 711.

130. Seymour E. Harris, "Fiscal Policy," in *American Economic History*, Seymour E. Harris, ed. (New York: McGraw-Hill, 1961), 151, 155.

131. Meltzer, *A History of the Federal Reserve*, 591.

132. Walton and Rockoff, *History of the American Economy*, 552.

133. Meltzer, *A History of the Federal Reserve*, 591.

134. Walton and Rockoff, *History of the American Economy*, 552.

135. Walton and Rockoff, *History of the American Economy*, 552.

136. Board of Governors of the Federal Reserve System, *The Federal Reserve System: Its Purposes and Functions* (Washington, D.C.: National Capital Press, 1939), 84–85.

137. Figures for the wartime spending have varied according to a number of variables, such as the issue of whether to include in the calculation the military spending of 1946, which included the costs of postwar occupation in Germany and Japan.

138. Meltzer, *A History of the Federal Reserve*, 588.

139. *Historical Statistics of the United States, Colonial Times to 1957*, 714.

140. *Economic Report of the President, Transmitted to the Congress, February 1988, Together with the Annual Report of the Council of Economic Advisors* (Washington, D.C.: U.S. Government Printing Office, 1988), 248.

141. Alvin H. Hansen, *The American Economy* (New York: McGraw-Hill, 1957), 26. For an unconvincing challenge to these views, see Robert Higgs, *Crisis and Leviathan: Critical Issues in the Emergence of the Mixed Economy* (New York: Oxford University Press, 1986) and *Depression, War, and Cold War: Studies in Political Economy* (New York: Oxford University Press, 2006). Higgs argues that "the war had taught the American people many lessons, some true, some false. Of the latter sort, a leading example was the Keynesian illusion" (*Crisis and Leviathan*, 226). He continues: "The notion that wartime 'full employment' had resulted from the huge federal deficits was false. Quite simply, unemployment fell mainly because of the buildup of the armed forces. . . . Any government that can conscript prime workers by the millions can eliminate unemployment." This is logic-chopping, for unless the soldiers were to serve without pay, a basic *finance method* was necessary. And since the method selected was taxes plus deficit spending via war bonds (as opposed, for example, to the issuance of Greenbacks, Civil War style), it follows that the deficit spending helped facilitate the full employment, not least of all because the deficit spending helped expand the money supply

through the Federal Reserve. (The very same method could have ended the depression via deficit-financed public works.) To this day, Higgs's work continues to be touted for exposing the so-called myth that the Depression was ended by the war.

142. Franklin Delano Roosevelt, radio address, June 6, 1944, in *Public Papers and Addresses*, XIII, 152–53.

143. Abraham Lincoln, "Response to a Serenade," November 10, 1864, in *Collected Works of Abraham Lincoln*, Roy P. Basler, ed. (New Brunswick: Rutgers University Press, 1953), VIII, 100–101.

144. Robert Fitzgerald, "Postscript," in Virgil, *The Aeneid*, Robert Fitzgerald, trans. (New York: Random House, 1980), 414.

145. Fitzgerald, "Postscript."

CHAPTER 5: THE LEGACY AS GREAT POWER STATECRAFT: FROM TRUMAN TO NIXON

1. Clarence Weinstock, "We Did Not Pant for War," in *World War II: Readings on Critical Issues*, Theodore A. Wilson, ed. (New York: Charles Scribner's Sons, 1972), 1974 edition, 23.

2. *So Proudly We Hail*, Paramount Pictures, 1943, Mark Sandrich, producer and director, screenplay by Allan Scott.

3. *This Is the Army*, Warner Brothers Pictures, 1943, Michael Curtiz, director, music by Irving Berlin.

4. Wendell L. Willkie, *One World* (New York: Simon & Schuster, 1943), 53–54.

5. Arthur Schlesinger Jr., *The Vital Center: Our Purposes and Perils on the Tightrope of American Liberalism* (Boston: Houghton Mifflin, 1949), Sentry edition, 1962, 165.

6. Reinhold Niebuhr, *The Irony of American History* (New York: Charles Scribner's Sons, 1952), 145.

7. Ludwig von Mises, *Bureaucracy* (New Haven, Conn.: Yale University Press, 1944; New Rochelle, N.Y.: Arlington House, 1969), 10.

8. Robert A. Taft, "Liberalism—Real or New Deal," *Young Republican* (May 1936), 6–7, *New York Times* (July 5, 1936), 12, cited in James T. Patterson, *Mr. Republican* (Boston: Houghton Mifflin, 1972), 156.

9. Robert A. Taft to Sumner Keller, February 18, 1941, Keller Papers, Yale University, cited in Patterson, *Mr. Republican*, 243.

10. Robert A. Taft to Herbert Hoover, June 26, 1941, Hoover Papers, cited in Patterson, *Mr. Republican*, 246.

11. Whittaker Chambers, *Witness* (New York: Random House, 1952), 471, 472.

12. Peter Viereck, *Conservatism Revisited* (New York: Collier Books, 1949), 1962 edition, Book II, *The New Conservatism: What Went Wrong?*, 17, 131.

13. James MacGregor Burns, *Roosevelt: The Soldier of Freedom* (New York: Harcourt Brace Jovanovich, 1970), 511.

14. Alonzo Hamby, *Liberalism and Its Challengers* (New York: Oxford University Press, 1985), 1992 edition, 71.

15. Harry Truman, quoted in David E. Lilienthal, *The Journals of David E. Lilienthal, vol. 2, The Atomic Energy Years, 1945–1950* (New York: Harper & Row, 1964), 434.

16. Harry Truman, quoted in Robert J. Donovan, *Conflict and Crisis: The Presidency of Harry Truman, 1945–1948* (New York: W. W. Norton, 1977), 62.

17. Harry Truman, quoted in Margaret Truman, *Harry S. Truman* (New York: William Morrow and Co., 1973), 349.

18. Donovan, *Conflict and Crisis*, 26–27.

19. For the links between the New Deal and the Fair Deal, see Mary H. Blewett, "Roosevelt, Truman, and the Attempt to Revive the New Deal," in *Harry S. Truman and the Fair Deal*, Alonzo Hamby, ed. (Lexington, Mass.: D.C. Heath and Company, 1974), 78–92.

20. For accounts of the GI Bill, see Michael J. Bennett, *When Dreams Came True: The GI Bill and the Making of Modern America* (New York: Brassey's, Inc., 1996), and Suzanne Mettler, *Soldiers to Citizens: The GI Bill and the Making of the Greatest Generation* (New York: Oxford University Press, 2005).

21. Alvin H. Hansen, *The American Economy* (New York: McGraw-Hill, 1957), 44–45.

22. John M. Vorys, cited in Donovan, *Conflict and Crisis*, 231.

23. For analysis of Truman's civil rights record, see Michael R. Gardner, *Harry Truman and Civil Rights: Moral Courage and Political Risks* (Carbondale: Southern Illinois University Press, 2002).

24. Winston Churchill, *The Second World War: Triumph and Tragedy* (Boston: Houghton Mifflin, 1953), 226–28.

25. For a latter-day version of the "Yalta sell-out" canard, see Robert D. Novak, "Betrayal at Yalta," *Washington Post* (August 18, 1997), A19.

26. John E. Rankin, *Congressional Record* (September 14, 1945), 8607.

27. George F. Kennan, *Memoirs, 1925–1950* (Boston: Little, Brown and Company, 1967), Bantam edition, annex C, excerpts from telegraphic message from Moscow of February 22, 1946, 594–95.

28. State-War-Navy Coordinating Committee, Subcommittee on Information Paper, "Information Program on United States Aid to Greece," March 4, 1947, quoted in John Lewis Gaddis, *The United States and the Origins of the Cold War, 1941–1947* (New York: Columbia University Press, 1972), 350.

29. Gaddis, *The United States and the Origins of the Cold War*, 353.

30. Gaddis, *The United States and the Origins of the Cold War*, 349.

31. Dean Acheson, *Present at the Creation: My Years in the State Department* (New York: W. W. Norton, 1969), 1987 edition, 219.

32. Cabell Phillips, *The Truman Presidency: The History of a Triumphant Succession* (New York: Macmillan, 1966).

33. National Security Council, "NSC 68: United States Objectives and Programs for National Security, A Report Pursuant to the President's Directive of January 31, 1950," April 14, 1950, reproduced in Ernest R. May, ed., *American Cold War Strategy: Interpreting NSC 68* (Boston: Bedford Books of St. Martin's Press, 1993), 24.

34. Ernest R. May, "Preface," in *American Cold War Strategy*, vii.

35. Ernest R. May, "Introduction: NSC 68: The Theory and Politics of Strategy," in *American Cold War Strategy*, 15.

36. Richard Rovere, "Communists and Intellectuals," in Richard Rovere, *The American Establishment and Other Reports, Opinions, and Speculations* (New York: Harcourt, Brace & World, 1962), 292–93.

37. Joseph McCarthy, quoted in Richard Rovere, *Senator Joe McCarthy* (Cleveland: World Publishing Company, Meridian Books, 1960), 11.

38. William E. Jenner, *Congressional Record*, 81st Congress, 2nd Session, 14914–17, cited in Acheson, *Present at the Creation*, 365. The life of General Marshall, an extraordinary patriot and public servant, is covered very well in the definitive biography, Forrest C. Pogue's multivolume *George C. Marshall* (New York: Viking Press, 1963–1989).

39. Robert A. Taft, quoted in Acheson, *Present at the Creation*, 364.

40. Richard Rovere, *Senator Joe McCarthy*, 41.

41. Rovere, *Senator Joe McCarthy*, 43.

42. Douglas MacArthur, Senate Committees on Armed Services and Foreign Relations, 82nd Congress, 1st session, *Hearings to Conduct an Inquiry into the Military Situation in the Far East and the Facts Surrounding the Relief of General of the Army Douglas MacArthur from His Assignments in that Area*, 3544, cited in Acheson, *Present at the Creation*, 520.

43. Hamby, *Liberalism and Its Challengers*, 86.

44. Hamby, *Liberalism and Its Challengers*, 82.

45. Joseph W. Stilwell, quoted in Burns, *Roosevelt: The Soldier of Freedom*, 375, passim.

46. Robert A. Taft, quoted in Hamby, *Liberalism and Its Challengers*, 106.

47. Hamby, *Liberalism and Its Challengers*, 109–10.

48. Hamby, *Liberalism and Its Challengers*, 110. See also Norman A. Graebner, *The New Isolationism: A Study in Politics and Foreign Policy Since 1950* (New York: Ronald Press Co., 1956).

49. Dwight D. Eisenhower, Philippine diary, September 23, 1939, in *Eisenhower: The Prewar Diaries and Selected Papers, 1905–1941*, Daniel D. Holt, ed. (Baltimore: Johns Hopkins University Press, 1998), 446.

50. Dwight D. Eisenhower, inaugural address, Columbia University, New York City, October 12, 1948, cited in Travis Beal Jacobs, *Eisenhower at Columbia* (New Brunswick: Transaction Publishers, 2001), 120.

51. Dwight D. Eisenhower to Edgar Newton Eisenhower, November 8, 1954, in *The Papers of Dwight David Eisenhower: The Presidency: The Middle Way*, Louis Galambos, ed. (Baltimore: Johns Hopkins University Press, 1996), XV, 1386.

52. Dwight D. Eisenhower, quoted in the *New York Times* (October 11, 1952), 8.

53. Steven Wagner, *Eisenhower Republicanism: Pursuing the Middle Way* (DeKalb: Northern Illinois University Press, 2006), 5.

54. Dwight D. Eisenhower, speech in Wheeling, West Virginia, September 24, 1952, quoted in Wagner, *Eisenhower Republicanism*, 5.

55. Fred I. Greenstein, *The Hidden-Hand Presidency: Eisenhower as Leader* (Baltimore: Johns Hopkins University Press, 1982, 1994), 247–48.

56. Stephen E. Ambrose, *Eisenhower: Volume One: Soldier, General of the Army, President-Elect, 1890–1952* (New York: Simon & Schuster, 1983), 521.

57. Ambrose, *Eisenhower: Volume One*, 536.

58. Stephen E. Ambrose, *Eisenhower: Volume Two: The President* (New York: Simon & Schuster, 1984), 95.

59. Robert R. Bowie, "Bowie's Commentary," in May, *American Cold War Strategy: Interpreting NSC 68*, 113.

60. Bowie, "Bowie's Commentary," 114.

61. Dennis E. Showalter, "Introduction," in *Forging the Shield: Eisenhower and National Security for the 21st Century*, Dennis E. Showalter, ed. (Chicago: Imprint Publications, 2005), 3.

62. R. Cargill Hall, "Clandestine Victory: Eisenhower and Overhead Reconnaissance in the Cold War," in Showalter, *Forging the Shield*, 119–20. See also Philip Taubman, *Secret*

Empire: Eisenhower, the CIA, and the Hidden Story of America's Space Espionage (New York: Simon & Schuster, 2003).

63. Ambrose, *Eisenhower: Volume Two: The President*, 174.

64. Dwight D. Eisenhower, quoted in Ambrose, *Eisenhower: Volume Two: The President*, 176.

65. In this connection it is useful to note Ike's early association with the Army Industrial College (later the Industrial College of the Armed Forces), created in 1924 to train army officers in procurement and mobilization of "industrial organization." Eisenhower attended the college, from which he graduated in 1933, and he taught there for several years thereafter.

66. Dennis E. Showalter, "Introduction," in Showalter, *Forging the Shield*, 4.

67. John Kenneth Galbraith, *Money: Whence It Came, Where It Went* (Boston: Houghton Mifflin, 1975), 262.

68. Hansen, *The American Economy*, 118.

69. Dwight D. Eisenhower, "Address at Eisenhower Day Dinner Given by the Citizens for Eisenhower Congressional Committee for the District of Columbia," October 28, 1954, in *Public Papers of the Presidents of the United States: Dwight D. Eisenhower, 1954* (Washington, D.C.: U.S. Government Printing Office, 1954), 983.

70. Robert J. Donovan, *Eisenhower: The Inside Story* (New York: Harper & Brothers, 1956), 213–14.

71. Ambrose, *Eisenhower: Volume Two: The President*, 301.

72. See Chester J. Pach Jr. and Elmo Richardson, *The Presidency of Dwight D. Eisenhower* (Lawrence: University Press of Kansas, 1991), 123–24.

73. Dwight D. Eisenhower, "Address at the Forrestal Memorial Award Dinner of the National Security Industrial Association," October 25, 1954, in *Public Papers of the Presidents of the United States: Dwight D. Eisenhower, 1954*, 953.

74. Galbraith, *Money*, 272.

75. Hamby, *Liberalism and Its Challengers*, 128.

76. Dwight D. Eisenhower, "Address at the Forrestal Memorial Award Dinner of the National Security Industrial Association," October 25, 1954, in *Public Papers, 1954*, 953.

77. Galbraith, *Money*, 241–42.

78. Many people who abhorred McCarthy wanted Ike to come out with guns blazing and attack the demagogue directly. The case can be made that the tremendous popularity of Ike would have made such a strategy effective. But that wasn't Ike's style; in some interviews with Walter Cronkite that were broadcast by CBS News in 1961, Ike made it clear that he deliberately refrained from ever mentioning McCarthy, in the hope that such behavior would make him more desperate and frantic, thus hastening his self-destruction.

79. Russell Kirk, *The Conservative Mind: From Burke to Santayana* (Chicago: Henry Regnery Company, 1953), 67, 75, 81.

80. William F. Buckley Jr., *Up from Liberalism* (New Rochelle, N.Y.: Arlington House, 1959), 1968 edition, 228–29.

81. Amid the vast and often sensationalistic literature on these subjects, an interesting study is William W. Keller, *The Liberals and J. Edgar Hoover: The Rise and Fall of a Domestic Intelligence State* (Princeton, N.J.: Princeton University Press, 1989). Especially abhorrent was Hoover's misuse of the counterintelligence "dirty tricks" program COINTELPRO against civil rights leaders such as Martin Luther King Jr. See Taylor Branch, *Parting the Waters: America in the King Years, 1954–1963* (New York: Simon & Schuster, 1988). COINTELPRO was initiated in 1956. Also abhorrent was the MK-ULTRA project in mind control that was

instituted by CIA director Allen Dulles in 1953. Among other misdeeds, the CIA administered mind-altering drugs to unwitting subjects. See Jonathan D. Moreno, *Undue Risk: Secret State Experiments on Humans* (New York: W. H. Freeman, 1999). On aboveground nuclear testing and its terrible human cost, see Carole Gallagher, *American Ground Zero: The Secret Nuclear War* (Cumberland, R.I.: MIT Press, 1993). Eisenhower was ambivalent on nuclear testing, but AEC Chairman Lewis Strauss and nuclear scientists like Edward Teller kept the pressure on. See Benjamin P. Greene, *Eisenhower, Science Advice, and the Nuclear Test-Ban Debate* (Stanford, Calif.: Stanford University Press, 2007).

82. See Ambrose, *Eisenhower: Volume Two: The President*, 252, 459–60.

83. Wagner, *Eisenhower Republicanism*, 104, 52–53.

84. Wagner, *Eisenhower Republicanism*, 54–57.

85. Arthur Larsen, *A Republican Looks At His Party* (New York: Harper & Row, 1955).

86. David A. Nichols, *A Matter of Justice: Eisenhower and the Beginning of the Civil Rights Revolution* (New York: Simon & Schuster, 2007), 43.

87. Nichols, *A Matter of Justice*, 56.

88. Nichols, *A Matter of Justice*, 78.

89. Nichols, *A Matter of Justice*, 83–88.

90. Barry Goldwater, *Congressional Record* (April 8, 1957), 5258–65.

91. Robert H. Ferrell, ed., *The Eisenhower Diaries* (New York: W. W. Norton, 1981), 288–89.

92. Robert H. Ferrell, ed., *The Diary of James C. Hagerty: Eisenhower in Mid-Course, 1954–1955* (Bloomington: Indiana University Press, 1983), 129.

93. Wagner, *Eisenhower Republicanism*, 115.

94. Greenstein, *The Hidden-Hand Presidency*, 3–4.

95. For the anti-heroic treatment of World War II after *Catch-22*, see Paul Fussell, *Wartime: Understanding and Behavior in the Second World War* (New York: Oxford University Press, 1989), and Edward W. Wood Jr., *Worshipping the Myths of World War II: Reflections on America's Dedication to War* (Dulles, Va.: Potomac Books, 2007). It should go without saying, though it needs to be said, that such writers understate (or fail to acknowledge) the implications of a global Axis victory. How they do it must remain their secret. It also bears noting that a pacifist anti-war literature accompanied the Second World War. Robert Lowell's poem "The Dead in Europe," which appeared in *Lord Weary's Castle* (1947), is a representative example.

96. See Irving Bernstein, *Promises Kept: John F. Kennedy's New Frontier* (New York: Oxford University Press, 1991), 128–29.

97. Robert Dallek, *An Unfinished Life: John F. Kennedy, 1917–1963* (New York: Little, Brown, 2003), 347.

98. U.S. Department of State, *Foreign Relations of the United States: Cuba, 1961–1962*, 177.

99. U.S. Department of State, *Foreign Relations of the United States: Cuba*, 178–81.

100. Kenneth P. O'Donnell and David F. Powers, *Johnny, We Hardly Knew Ye* (Boston: Little, Brown, 1970), 274.

101. Benjamin Bradlee, *Conversations with Kennedy* (New York: W. W. Norton, 1975), 122.

102. Hamby, *Liberalism and Its Challengers*, 213.

103. Dallek, *An Unfinished Life*, 418.

104. Dallek, *An Unfinished Life*, 420.

105. Dallek, *An Unfinished Life*, 422.

106. John F. Kennedy, "Radio and Television Report to the American People on the Berlin Crisis," July 25, 1961, in *Public Papers of the Presidents of the United States: John F. Kennedy, 1961*, 533–40.

107. Hamby, *Liberalism and Its Challengers*, 219.

108. O'Donnell and Powers, *Johnny, We Hardly Knew Ye*, 318.

109. Seymour E. Harris, ed., *The New Economics: Keynes' Influence on Theory and Public Policy* (New York: Alfred A. Knopf, 1947).

110. Galbraith, *Money*, 325–26.

111. Edwin L. Dale Jr., "When Will It Be Safe to Balance the Budget?," *New York Times Magazine* (January 24, 1965), 14.

112. Dallek, *An Unfinished Life*, 395.

113. Lyndon B. Johnson, quoted in Robert Dallek, "Johnson, Project Apollo, and the Politics of Space Program Planning," in *Space Flight and the Myth of Presidential Leadership*, Roger D. Launius and Howard E. McCurdy, eds. (Urbana: University of Illinois Press, 1997), 70–72.

114. Bernstein, *Promises Kept*, 172–75. According to Bernstein, the ARA created over thirty thousand jobs in community infrastructure such as "sewage and water systems . . . port facilities, natural gas, railroad spurs, airports, hospitals, industrial parks, and courthouses" and almost forty thousand jobs through commercial and industrial loans.

115. Carl M. Brauer, *John F. Kennedy and the Second Reconstruction* (New York: Columbia University Press, 1977), 240.

116. Arthur M. Schlesinger Jr., *A Thousand Days* (Boston: Houghton Mifflin, 1965), 966.

117. John F. Kennedy, "Radio and Television Report to the American People on Civil Rights," June 11, 1963, in *Public Papers of the Presidents of the United States: John F. Kennedy, 1963*, 468–71.

118. Kennedy, "Radio and Television Report to the American People on Civil Rights."

119. Isaiah Berlin to Arthur Schlesinger Jr., November 28, 1963, cited in Dallek, *An Unfinished Life*, 695.

120. Bernstein, *Promises Kept*, 298.

121. Dallek, *An Unfinished Life*, 708.

122. Arthur M. Schlesinger Jr., *The Cycles of American History* (Boston: Houghton Mifflin, 1986), 414.

123. Dallek, *An Unfinished Life*, 710.

124. Arthur M. Schlesinger Jr., *Journals, 1952–2000*, Andrew Schlesinger and Stephen Schlesinger, eds. (New York: Penguin Books, 2007), 291–92.

125. Jacob K. Javits, *Order of Battle: A Republican's Call to Reason* (New York: Atheneum Publishers, 1964), 304.

126. Milton Friedman, *Capitalism and Freedom* (Chicago: University of Chicago Press, 1962), 31.

127. Charles Mallar, Stuart Kerachsky, Craig Thornton, and David Long, *Evaluation of the Economic Impact of the Job Corps Program, Third Follow-Up Report*, prepared for the Office of Research and Evaluation, Employment and Training Administration, U.S. Department of Labor (Princeton, N.J.: Mathematica Policy Research, Inc., 1982), vi, 259, and Paul Taylor, "Job Corps Still Working," *Washington Post* (September 2, 1991), A1, A6, A7.

128. See, for example, Edward C. Banfield, *The Unheavenly City* (Boston: Little, Brown, 1970).

129. Lewis Sorley, *A Better War: The Unexamined Victories and Final Tragedy of America's Last Years in Vietnam* (San Diego: Harcourt, 2000).

130. Townsend Hoopes, *The Limits of Intervention: An Inside Account of How the Johnson Policy of Escalation in Vietnam was Reversed* (New York: David McKay Co., 1969), 53.

131. David Halberstam, *The Best and the Brightest* (New York: Random House, 1972).

132. An account of this process was provided thereafter by Townsend Hoopes, former undersecretary of the Air Force, in his book *The Limits of Intervention*, cited above.

133. Hamby, *Liberalism and Its Challengers*, 266.

134. Robert Dallek, *Lyndon B. Johnson: Portrait of a President* (New York: Oxford University Press, 2004), 376.

135. Hamby, *Liberalism and Its Challengers*, 263.

136. Galbraith, *Money*, 333.

137. Gabriel Kolko, *The Roots of American Foreign Policy* (Boston: Beacon Press, 1969), 29.

138. For a critical contemporaneous account of these developments, see Steven Kelman, *Push Comes to Shove: The Escalation of Student Protest* (Boston: Houghton Mifflin, 1970).

139. Richard Nixon, annual message to Congress on the State of the Union, January 22, 1970, in *Public Papers of the Presidents of the United States: Richard Nixon, 1970*, 13. See Russell E. Train, "The Environmental Record of the Nixon Administration," *Presidential Studies Quarterly*, vol. XXVI, no. 1 (Winter 1996), 185–96.

140. Richard Nixon, annual message to Congress on the State of the Union, January 22, 1971, in *Public Papers of the Presidents of the United States: Richard Nixon, 1971*, 53.

141. An early satirical account of the process was provided by Tom Wolfe in his book *Radical Chic and Mau-Mauing the Flak Catchers* (New York: Farrar, Straus & Giroux, 1970).

142. See William A. Donohue, *Twilight of Liberty: The Legacy of the ACLU* (Edison, N.J.: Transaction Publishers, 1994); Edward Leddy, *Magnum Force Lobby: The National Rifle Association Fights Gun Control* (Lanham, Md.: University Press of America, 1987); and Peter Harry Brown and Daniel G. Abel, *Outgunned: Up against the NRA* (New York: Simon & Schuster, 2003). The deinstitutionalization of the mentally ill was abetted on the legal front in the 1960s by a renegade psychiatrist, Thomas Szasz, who alleged that definitive proof of mental illness was impossible to furnish.

143. The provenance of the Cato Institute's name is worthy of comment. The institute claims no connection with the ancient Roman senators who bore the "Cato" cognomen: the elder and younger Marcus Porcius Cato. The institute's literature states that the organization "is named for *Cato's Letters*, pamphlets that were widely read in the American colonies in the early eighteenth century." But the pamphlets, written by the Radical Whigs John Trenchard and Thomas Gordon from 1720 to 1723, make it clear that the authors were inspired by the life of Cato the Younger (95 B.C.–46 B.C.), the Roman leader who committed suicide at Utica after Julius Caesar's victory over Pompey the Great. Trenchard and Gordon revered Cato as a champion of liberty; in *Cato's Letter* #23 (April 1, 1721), they attributed the following declamation to Cato: "No, says Cato, I scorn to be beholden to tyranny. I am as free as Caesar; and shall I owe my Life to him, who has no Right even to my Submission [?]" But if the founders of the Cato Institute consulted Roman sources instead of English eighteenth-century pamphlets, they would have discovered that their indirect namesake was regarded even by his friends as a rigid dogmatist. Marcus Tullius Cicero, for instance, who

eulogized Cato after his death, could not resist poking fun at his stubborn orthodoxies; see Cicero's speech *Pro Murena* (62 B.C.) in *Cicero: On Government*, Michael Grant, trans. (New York: Penguin Classics, 1993), 143, 145.

144. William Greider, *Secrets of the Temple: How the Federal Reserve Runs the Country* (New York: Simon & Schuster, Touchstone edition, 1987), 90.

CHAPTER 6: THE LEGACY IN RUINS: FROM CARTER TO GEORGE W. BUSH

1. William Butler Yeats, "The Second Coming" (1920), in *Selected Poems and Two Plays of William Butler Yeats*, M. L. Rosenthal, ed. (New York: Macmillan, 1962), 91.

2. Jimmy Carter, inaugural address, January 20, 1977, in *Public Papers of the Presidents of the United States: Jimmy Carter, 1977* (Washington, D.C.: U.S. Government Printing Office, 1977), I, 2.

3. Reinhold Niebuhr, *The Irony of American History* (New York: Charles Scribner's Sons, 1952), viii.

4. Jimmy Carter, State of the Union Address, January 19, 1978, in *Public Papers of the Presidents of the United States: Jimmy Carter, 1978*, I, 91.

5. William E. Leuchtenburg, *In the Shadow of FDR: From Harry Truman to Bill Clinton* (Ithaca, N.Y.: Cornell University Press, 1983, 1993), 190.

6. Leuchtenburg, *In the Shadow of FDR*, 194.

7. Interview of Jimmy Carter by David Brinkley, ABC News (December 18, 1981), cited in Leuchtenburg, *In the Shadow of FDR*, 194.

8. Arthur M. Schlesinger Jr., *The Cycles of American History* (Boston: Houghton Mifflin, 1986), 33. Sean Wilentz explores some of the same issues in *The Age of Reagan: A History, 1974–2008* (New York: HarperCollins, 2008).

9. Gary M. Walton, and Hugh Rockoff, *History of the American Economy* (Stamford, Conn.: South-Western/Thomson Learning, 2002), 606.

10. See Stephen Paul Dempsey and Andrew R. Goetz, *Airline Deregulation and Laissez-Faire Mythology* (Westport, Conn.: Quorum Books, 1992).

11. Japan in particular thrived on the teachings of W. Edwards Deming, a management consultant who preached the gospel of quality control and labor-management teamwork. The success of these methods for the Japanese was transferred later on to America when Japanese car manufacturers such as Toyota set up plants in the United States and hired American workers to make the Japanese cars. The Deming techniques worked as well in the United States as they did in Japan, although American corporate culture was largely resistant to such innovations, at least at the time. At this writing, of course, Toyota's quality control is slipping badly.

12. See Milton Friedman, "The Role of Monetary Policy," *American Economic Review* (March 1968), 1–17; and Milton Friedman and Anna J. Schwartz, *A Monetary History of the United States, 1867–1960* (Princeton, N.J.: Princeton University Press, 1963).

13. Wanniski touted the argument of Laffer, which he summarized as the belief "that the supply of goods creates a demand for goods and . . . the supply of goods can be increased by removing government impediments to production and commerce." He contrasted this view with "the alternative idea that has dominated Western economic thought for forty years, the

notion that the demand for goods creates its own supply and that the demand for goods can be increased by increasing the purchasing power of individuals through deficit finance or money creation." The terms of this dichotomy are highly oversimplified, omitting a wide range of economic as well as cultural/historical variables. But the gist of the assertions is clear on the level of the ideological *instincts* that organize data. It bears noting that Wanniski rejected both the work of Milton Friedman and the legacy of John Maynard Keynes. See Jude Wanniski, *The Way the World Works* (New York: Simon & Schuster, 1978), x, 162–65.

14. William Greider, *Secrets of the Temple: How the Federal Reserve Runs the Country* (New York: Simon & Schuster, Touchstone edition, 1987), 16–17.

15. Greider, *Secrets of the Temple*, 15.

16. Jimmy Carter, "Energy and National Goals Address to the Nation," July 15, 1979, in *Public Papers of the Presidents of the United States: Jimmy Carter, 1979* (Washington, D.C.: U.S. Government Printing Office, 1979), 1235.

17. Walton and Rockoff, *History of the American Economy*, 632.

18. According to Greider, "in December 1982, 12 million people were out of work, only 4.4 million of them drawing unemployment compensation. Another 4 or 5 million unemployed were not counted in the official statistics because they were no longer actively seeking jobs at the local unemployment office" (Greider, *Secrets of the Temple*, 454).

19. Alonzo Hamby, *Liberalism and Its Challengers* (New York: Oxford University Press, 1985), 1992 edition, 347, 349.

20. Ronald Reagan, diary entry, January 28, 1982, in *The Reagan Diaries*, Douglas Brinkley, ed. (New York: HarperCollins, 2007), 65.

21. Ronald Reagan, quoted in Jules Witcover, *Marathon: The Pursuit of the Presidency, 1972–1976* (New York: Viking, 1977), 97.

22. Ronald Reagan, quoted in *Time* magazine (May 17, 1976), 19.

23. Ronald Reagan, quoted in interview with Ben Wattenberg, December 1981, "Ben Wattenberg at Large," no. 113, cited in Leuchtenburg, *In the Shadow of FDR*, 219.

24. Historian Jules Tygiel observes that "Reagan uttered more untruths and misstatements than most presidents," though "he always believed what he said"; indeed, his aide Lyn Nofziger once remarked that for Reagan "the truth is what he wants it to be." See Jules Tygiel, *Ronald Reagan and the Triumph of American Conservatism* (New York: Pearson Longman, 2006), 148, 120.

25. Ronald Reagan, diary entry, March 30, 1981, in *The Reagan Diaries*, 12.

26. Ronald Reagan, quoted in *Raleigh News and Observer* (March 24, 1982), cited in Leuchtenburg, *In the Shadow of FDR*, 230.

27. Hamby, *Liberalism and Its Challengers*, 386.

28. Michael Schaller, *Reckoning with Reagan: America and Its President in the 1980s* (New York: Oxford University Press, 1992), 53.

29. Haynes Johnson, *Sleepwalking Through History: America in the Reagan Years* (New York: W. W. Norton, 1991), 13.

30. Pat Choate and Susan Walter, *America in Ruins: The Decaying Infrastructure* (Durham, N.C.: Duke Press Paperbacks, 1983), 1.

31. Edward N. Luttwak, *The Endangered American Dream* (New York: Touchstone/Simon & Schuster, 1993), 261–62.

32. Friedman's version of free marketeering got its test in Great Britain under Thatcher; the results were sufficiently disappointing that no elected leader of consequence has tried to use Friedman-style "monetarism" again.

33. For memoirs of the "supply-side revolution," see Paul Craig Roberts, *The Supply Side Revolution: An Insider's Account of Policymaking in Washington* (Cambridge, Mass.: Harvard University Press, 1984), and David Stockman, *The Triumph of Politics: How the Reagan Revolution Failed* (New York: Harper & Row, 1986).

34. William Greider, *The Education of David Stockman and Other Americans* (New York: E. P. Dutton, 1982), ix–x, vii, 14–27, 33–41, 47–51. The Stockman interviews were first reported by Greider in "The Education of David Stockman," which appeared in *Atlantic* magazine in November 1981.

35. Charles Peters, "A Neo-Liberal's Manifesto," *Washington Post*, September 5, 1982, C–1. See also David Harvey, *A Brief History of Neoliberalism* (New York: Oxford University Press, 2005).

36. Schaller, *Reckoning with Reagan*, 78.

37. For commentary of the S&L scandal, see Lawrence J. White, *The S&L Debacle: Public Policy Lessons for Bank and Thrift Regulation* (New York: Oxford University Press, 1991), and James K. Glassman, "The Great Banks Robbery: Deconstructing the S&L Crisis," *New Republic* (October 8, 1990), 16–21. True to the spirit of the age, Glassman's recommendation for avoiding any future banking crisis was to scrap deposit insurance.

38. Walton and Rockoff, *History of the American Economy*, 632. It bears noting, however, that after the recession-breaking ease-up of interest rates in 1982, the Federal Reserve shoved interest rates back up again to preempt inflation.

39. Kevin Phillips, *The Politics of Rich and Poor: Wealth and the American Electorate in the Reagan Aftermath* (New York: Random House, 1990), 21.

40. Walton and Rockoff, *History of the American Economy*, 652.

41. Kevin Phillips, *Boiling Point: Republicans, Democrats, and the Decline of Middle-Class Prosperity* (New York: Random House, 1993), xxi–xxii. See also, Richard Morin, "America's Middle-Class Meltdown," *Washington Post* (December 1, 1991), C1, C2.

42. Isaac Shapiro and Robert Greenstein, *Selective Prosperity: Increasing Income Disparities since 1977* (Washington, D.C.: Center on Budget and Policy Priorities, 1991), vii, passim.

43. *1991 Green Book*, Committee on Ways and Means, U.S. House of Representatives, 102nd Congress, 1st Session, Background Material and Data on Programs within the Jurisdiction of the Committee on Ways and Means, 1341.

44. Tygiel, *Ronald Reagan and the Triumph of American Conservatism*, 217.

45. Tygiel, *Ronald Reagan and the Triumph of American Conservatism*, 218.

46. Ronald Reagan, "The President's News Conference," January 29, 1981, in *Public Papers of the Presidents of the United States: Ronald Reagan, 1981*, 57.

47. Tygiel, *Ronald Reagan and the Triumph of American Conservatism*, 163, 171.

48. Tygiel, *Ronald Reagan and the Triumph of American Conservatism*, 152.

49. For coverage of "Star Wars," see Frances Fitzgerald, *Way Out There in the Blue: Reagan, Star Wars, and the End of the Cold War* (New York: Simon & Schuster, 2000).

50. Ronald Reagan, diary entry, April 6, 1983, in *The Reagan Diaries*, 142.

51. John Patrick Diggins, *Ronald Reagan: Fate, Freedom, and the Making of History* (New York: W. W. Norton, 2007), 348–49.

52. Ronald Reagan, diary entry, October 10, 1983, in *The Reagan Diaries*, 186.

53. Ronald Reagan, "Address Before the Japanese Diet in Tokyo," November 11, 1983, in *Public Papers of the Presidents of the United States: Ronald Reagan, 1983*, II, 1575.

54. Ronald Reagan, diary entry, November 18, 1983, in *The Reagan Diaries*, 199.

55. Ronald Reagan, "Address to the Nation and Other Countries on United States–Soviet Relations," January 16, 1984, in *Public Papers of the Presidents of the United States: Ronald Reagan, 1984*, I, 41, 44.

56. For a full-length account by a Soviet specialist and former CIA analyst giving Gorbachev, rather than Reagan, primary credit for the peaceful termination of the Cold War, see Raymond L. Garthoff, *The Great Transition: American-Soviet Relations and the End of the Cold War* (Washington, D.C.: Brookings Institution Press, 1994). Ironically, conservative commentators at the time—William F. Buckley Jr., George F. Will, Charles Krauthammer—criticized Reagan for trusting Gorbachev as much as he did.

57. For laudatory versions of Reagan's achievement with the Soviets, see Peter Schweizer, *Victory: The Reagan Administration's Secret Strategy that Hastened the Collapse of the Soviet Union* (New York: Atlantic Monthly Press, 1994); Paul Kengor, *The Crusader: Ronald Reagan and the Fall of Communism* (New York: Harper Perennial, 2006); and John Patrick Diggins, *Ronald Reagan: Fate, Freedom, and the Making of History* (New York: W. W. Norton, 2007).

58. George F. Will, "In Defense of the Welfare State," *New Republic* (May 9, 1983), 21.

59. George F. Will, "Congealed in Traffic," *Washington Post* (March 11, 1990), B7.

60. See Jason DeParle, "Latest Plan to Cure Welfare Troubles Borrows W.P.A. Blueprints of 1930s," *New York Times* (March 13, 1992), A14.

61. Felix G. Rohatyn, "Self-Defeating Myths about America," *Washington Post* (July 6, 1992), A19. For more recent commentary by this author, see Felix Rohatyn, *Bold Endeavors: How Our Government Built America, and Why It Must Rebuild Now* (New York: Simon & Schuster, 2009).

62. James P. Pinkerton, *What Comes Next: The End of Big Government and the New Paradigm Ahead* (New York: Hyperion, 1995).

63. David Osborne, "A New Compact: Sorting Out Washington's Proper Role," in *Mandate for Change*, Will Marshall and Martin Shram, eds. (New York: Berkley Books/Progressive Policy Institute, 1993), 240–41.

64. David Osborne and Ted Gaebler, *Reinventing Government: How the Entrepreneurial Spirit Is Transforming the Public Sector* (Reading, Pa.: Addison-Wesley Publishing Co., 1992), 252–53, 277.

65. Stuart Auerbach, "Clark Urges Iran to Release Hostages," *Washington Post* (June 4, 1980), A1, A24; and Stuart Auerbach, "Iran's Anti-U.S. Conference Calls for Peaceful End to Crisis," *Washington Post* (June 6, 1980), A15.

66. George Orwell, "Charles Dickens" (1939), in *A Collection of Essays by George Orwell* (Garden City, N.Y.: Doubleday Anchor, 1954), 111.

67. E. J. Dionne Jr., *Why Americans Hate Politics* (New York: Simon & Schuster, 1991), 14–15.

68. John F. Kennedy, press conference, August 20, 1963, in *Public Papers of the Presidents of the United States: John F. Kennedy, 1963*, 633–34.

69. Marc Fisher, "The Color of Anger," *Washington Post* (October 29, 1996), E1, E2. See also C. Eric Lincoln, *Coming through the Fire: Surviving Race and Place in America* (Durham, N.C.: Duke University Press, 1996), and Arthur Schlesinger Jr., *The Disuniting of America* (New York: W. W. Norton, 1992).

70. See Wilber W. Caldwell, *Cynicism and the Evolution of the American Dream* (Dulles, Va.: Potomac Books, 2006).

71. Richard Morin and Dan Balz, "In America, Loss of Confidence Seeps into All Institutions," *Washington Post* (January 28, 1996), A1.

72. Martha Sherrill, "Learning to Love Vulgarity," *Washington Post* (January 1, 1995), G1, G4.

73. Bill Clinton, acceptance speech, Democratic National Convention, July 16, 1992, *Washington Post* (July 17, 1992), A26.

74. Clinton, acceptance speech.

75. Clinton, acceptance speech.

76. Statement of Charles A. Bowsher, comptroller-general of the United States, *Major Issues Facing a New Congress and a New Administration*, testimony before the Committee on Governmental Affairs, United States Senate, January 8, 1993, United States General Accounting Office (Washington, D.C.: U.S. Government Printing Office, 1993), 11.

77. *A Vision of Change for America*, February 17, 1993 (Washington, D.C.: U.S. Government Printing Office, 1993), 29–30.

78. George F. Will, "Get Ready for More Government," *Washington Post* (February 25, 1993), A23; "Stampede for Statism," *Washington Post* (February 19, 1993), A21; "It's the Infrastructure Myth that's Crumbling," *Washington Post* (January 10, 1993), C7; "Do Americans Want Big Government?" *Washington Post* (February 28, 1993), C7.

79. Lloyd Cutler, "The Way to Kill Senate Rule XXII," *Washington Post* (April 19, 1993), A23.

80. Cutler, "The Way to Kill Senate Rule XXII."

81. Jeff Faux, *The Global Class War: How America's Bipartisan Elite Lost Our Future—and What It Will Take to Win It Back* (New York: John Wiley & Sons, 2006), 202. See also William Greider, *One World, Ready or Not* (New York: Simon & Schuster, 1997).

82. John Ralston Saul, "The Collapse of Globalism, and the Rebirth of Nationalism," *Harper's* (March 2004), 34, 36.

83. Saul, "The Collapse of Globalism," 38.

84. Sidney Blumenthal, *The Clinton Wars* (New York: Farrar, Straus and Giroux, 2003), 121.

85. Howard Kurtz, "Company for 'Harry and Louise' in Debate on Health Care Reform," *Washington Post* (February 13, 1994), A3.

86. Blumenthal, *The Clinton Wars*, 121.

87. E. J. Dionne Jr., "Lost Threads of a Presidency," *Washington Post* (August 2, 1994), A15.

88. Ann Devroy, "GOP Taking Joy in Obstructionism: Clinton Agenda Dying on Hill," *Washington Post* (October 7, 1994), A1, A16.

89. Dick Armey, *The Freedom Revolution* (Washington, D.C.: Regnery Publishing, Inc., 1995), 316.

90. John Harris, "Clinton Assails GOP Plans for National Parks," *Washington Post* (August 26, 1995), A4.

91. Stephen Barr, "Economic Advisers Placed on Block," *Washington Post* (June 24, 1995), A6.

92. Paul Starr, "State of the Union? Someday, Paralyzed," *New York Times* (January 24, 1995), A19.

93. Richard Kogen, "High Cost of a Balanced Budget Amendment," *Washington Post* (February 27, 1995), A19.

94. Gary Lee, "'Contract' Leaves Bad Taste with Food Safety Advocates," *Washington Post* (March 9, 1995), A19.

95. Kathleen Day, "Budget Cuts Slow Agencies Fighting New Bacteria Strains," *Washington Post* (June 27, 1995), A1, A6.

96. "Gingrich's Plan Sounds Fishy to Business," *Fortune* (March 20, 1995), 24.

97. Paul Taylor and Thomas B. Edsall Jr., "Disoriented Democrats Search for Direction," *Washington Post* (June 25, 1995), A1, A4.

98. See David S. Broder, "The Power of Our Discontent," *Washington Post* (September 6, 1995), A21.

99. Rick Weiss, "NIH Cancer Chief Vents Frustration," *Washington Post* (December 24, 1994), A7.

100. Ronald C. Moe, "Let's Rediscover Government, Not Reinvent It," *Government Executive* (June 1993), 48.

101. Bill Clinton, State of the Union Address, January 23, 1996, *Washington Post* (January 24, 1996), A13.

102. "The Record Is Relevant,' excerpts from Washington Post Interview with President Clinton," *Washington Post* (August 25, 1996), A19.

103. "Campaign '96: Transcript of the First Presidential Debate," *Washington Post* (October 7, 1996), A8; and Edward Walsh, "Dole Casts Clinton as Liberal Masked by Rhetoric," *Washington Post* (September 23, 1996), A11.

104. E. J. Dionne Jr., "Three of a Kind," *Washington Post* (June 11, 1996), A17.

105. Rick Weiss, "President Orders Overhaul of Meat Safety Inspections," *Washington Post* (July 7, 1996), A1, A10; Peter Baker, "Clinton Announces Registry of Nation's Sex Offenders," *Washington Post* (August 25, 1996), A16; Helen Dewar and Judith Havemann, "Water, Wage Bills Pass as Congress Recesses," *Washington Post* (August 3, 1996), A1, A8; Helen Dewar and Eric Pianin, "Pragmatism Drives Legislative Frenzy," *Washington Post* (August 4, 1996), A1, A24.

106. Henry Aaron, "The Myths of the Social Security Crisis," *Washington Post* (July 21, 1996), C1, C2.

107. Edward D. Berkowitz, "The Insecurity of Privatization," *Washington Post* (December 8, 1996), C1, C4.

108. Simultaneously commentators on the left began to criticize neo-liberalism. Democratic House Minority Leader Richard A. Gephardt called for a "new progressivism" and lauded the legacy of Theodore Roosevelt. See John E. Yang, "Looking Back to Theodore Roosevelt, Gephardt Calls for 'New Progressivism,'" *Washington Post* (December 3, 1997), A16. See also Michael Lind, "A Forgotten Founder Could Save the Democrats," *Washington Post* (November 23, 1997), C3. Lind's piece was a call for a "neo-Hamiltonian" movement in the Democratic Party.

109. See Eric Pianin, "Rep. Kasich Decries Highway Bill as Pork," *Washington Post* (March 28, 1998), A4; Eric Pianin, "Clinton Says Highway Bill Threatens Budget Accord," *Washington Post* (March 29, 1998), A4. See also Bud Shuster, "Once, Conservatives Knew the Value of Transportation," *New York Times* (July 17, 1999), A25.

110. George F. Will, "Maybe the Moon," *Washington Post* (August 13, 1995), C7.

111. George F. Will, "Road Work Ahead," *Washington Post* (April 25, 1996), A31.

112. William Kristol and David Brooks, "What Ails Conservatism," *Wall Street Journal* (September 15, 1997), A22.

113. David Brooks, "A Return to National Greatness: A Manifesto for a Lost Creed," *Weekly Standard* (March 3, 1997), 17, 20. See also George F. Will, "Conservative Challenge," *Washington Post* (August 17, 1997), C7.

114. Blumenthal, *The Clinton Wars*, 789.

115. See Joel Kotkin and David Friedman, "As Wall Street Pats Itself on the Back, Trouble Lurks Behind the Boom," *Washington Post* (May 24, 1998), C1, C4.

116. See Lawrence Mishel, Jared Bernstein, and John Schmitt, *The State of Working America, 1996–1997* (Washington, D.C.: Economic Policy Institute, 1997), 243–44.

117. Mishel, Bernstein, and Schmitt, *The State of Working America*, 97.

118. Robert Kuttner, "No Market for Civility," *Washington Post* (January 9, 1996), A15. See also Robert Kuttner, *Everything for Sale* (New York: Alfred A. Knopf, 1997).

119. Nancy Gibbs, "25 People to Blame: The Good Intentions, Bad Managers, and Greed Behind the Meltdown," *Time* (February 3, 2009), 22–23.

120. Charles Krauthammer, "To War, Not to Court," *Washington Post* (September 12, 2001), A29.

121. Robert Kagan, "We Must Fight This War," *Washington Post* (September 11, 2001), A–27.

122. Charles E. Schumer, "Big Government Looks Better Now," *Washington Post* (December 11, 2001), A33.

123. Robin Toner, "Now, Government Is the Solution, Not the Problem," *New York Times* (September 30, 2001), D14.

124. For the latest in a long line of analyses regarding the tension in conservative thought between authoritarian and libertarian tendencies, see Godfrey Hodgson, *The World Turned Right Side Up: A History of the Conservative Ascendancy in America* (Boston: Houghton Mifflin, 1996).

125. See Ceci Connolly, "The States Step In as Medicare Falters: Seniors Being Turned Away, Overcharged Under New Prescription Drug Program," *Washington Post* (January 14, 2006), A1.

126. Charles Tiefer, *Veering Right: How the Bush Administration Subverts the Law for Conservative Causes* (Berkeley: University of California Press, 2004), 4.

127. See Stephen S. Cohen and John Zysman, *Manufacturing Matters: The Myth of the Post-Industrial Economy* (New York: Basic Books, 1987).

128. See Justin Fox, "Tax Cuts Don't Boost Revenues," *Time* (December 17, 2007), 62: "Virtually every economics Ph.D. who has worked in a prominent role in the Bush administration acknowledges that the tax cuts enacted during the past six years have not paid for themselves."

129. Paul Krugman, "Stating the Obvious," *New York Times* (May 27, 2003), A25.

130. See Paul Krugman, "Delusions of Power," *New York Times* (March 28, 2003), A17.

131. Gregory Palast, "Some Power Trip: Put the Deregulation Genie Back in the Bottle," *Washington Post* (January 28, 2001), B1.

132. For an account of the Enron debacle, see Beth MacLean and Peter Elkind, *The Smartest Guys in the Room: The Amazing Rise and Scandalous Fall of Enron* (New York: Portfolio/Penguin Group, 2004).

133. Bob Woodward, *State of Denial* (New York: Simon & Schuster, 2006), 490.

134. Sidney Blumenthal, *How Bush Rules: Chronicles of a Radical Regime* (Princeton, N.J.: Princeton University Press, 2006), 145.

135. See Dana Milbank, "Colonel Finally Saw Whites of Their Eyes," *Washington Post* (October 20, 2005), A4.

136. On the issues and allegations regarding Social Security in 2005, see Roger Lowenstein, "A Question of Numbers," *New York Times Magazine* (January 16, 2005).

137. William Finnegan, "Watching the Waterfront," *New Yorker* (June 19, 2006), 52.

138. Del Quention Wilber, "Airline Safety Alarms Unheeded," *Washington Post* (April 4, 2008), A1.

139. For representative coverage, see Charles Morris, *The Trillion Dollar Meltdown: Easy Money, High Rollers, and the Great Credit Crash* (New York: Public Affairs, 2008), and Allan Sloan, "An Unsavory Slice of Subprime," *Washington Post* (October 16, 2007). A convincing account of Greenspan's partial culpability for the crisis was presented by the economist Benjamin M. Friedman in a review of Greenspan's memoir. Friedman wrote:

> Regulation of financial markets in the United States is spotty and fragmented among numerous agencies. . . . Poorly disclosed compensation arrangements for brokers, which would be illegal in the securities markets, have persisted in the mortgage market and give mortgage brokers substantial incentives to steer customers into loans that are excessively expensive or risky or both. . . . As early as 2001 the Treasury Department tried to get subprime lenders to adopt a code of "best practices" and to submit to monitoring, but the large lenders objected and the Treasury did not press the matter. The Department of Housing and Urban Development likewise proposed a set of rules for real estate transactions but then failed to follow through. . . . And the Federal Reserve Board, which under the 1968 Truth in Lending Act and other legislation is also responsible for regulating interest rate disclosures (and especially high-cost mortgages), likewise failed to act. This neglect by the Federal Reserve was hardly the result of lack of awareness. Both at the staff level and higher, numerous eyes were squarely on the problem. Edward Gramlich, a member of the Board of Governors from 1997 to 2005, frequently testified before Congress on problems in home finance and called within the Federal Reserve for action to halt abuses. . . . But Greenspan was consistently unsympathetic. . . . Greenspan's opposition to such proposals was consistent with the admiration that he expresses for unfettered markets and the sanctity with which he regards property rights. (Benjamin M. Friedman, "Chairman Greenspan's Legacy," *New York Review of Books* [March 20, 2008].)

140. James Lieber, "What Cooked the World's Economy?" *Village Voice* (January 27, 2009).

141. Scott Shane and Ron Nixon, "In Washington, Contractors Take on Biggest Role Ever," *New York Times* (February 4, 2007), A1. See also Taegan D. Goddard and Christopher Riback, "A Contrary Idea: Don't Run Government Like a Business," *Washington Post* (January 31, 1999), B2.

142. *Statistical Abstract*, U.S. Census Bureau, 2007.

143. Fred Hiatt, "She Brakes for Ideology," *Washington Post* (January 21, 2008), A15. See also Bob Herbert, "Our Crumbling Foundation," *New York Times* (April 5, 2007), A19.

144. Rauch, "What Ike Can Teach Us," *National Journal* (April 14, 2007), 14–19.

145. Andy Serwer and Allan Sloan, "The Price of Greed," *Time* (September 29, 2008), 37.

146. Alan Greenspan, quoted in Neil Irwin and Amit R. Paley, "Greenspan Says He Was Wrong on Regulation," *Washington Post* (October 24, 2008), A1, A10.

147. Francis Fukuyama, "The Fall of America, Inc.," *Newsweek* (October 13, 2008), 30.

148. Henry Paulson Jr., quoted in Serwer and Sloan, "The Price of Greed."

CHAPTER 7: HORIZONS

1. Joan Didion, "Obama: In the Irony-Free Zone," *New York Review of Books* (December 18, 2008), 18.

2. George Packer, "Obamaism," *New Yorker* (April 13, 2009). Packer also observed that the conservative side of "Obamaism" has failed so far to register with the American right, whose anti-government animus has become "abstract, hard-edged, and indifferent to experience and existing conditions." Two years earlier, another *New Yorker* commentator observed that there are moments when Obama "sounds almost Burkean." See Larissa MacFarquhar, "The Conciliator," *New Yorker* (May 7, 2007), 52.

3. Paul Krugman, "Money for Nothing," *New York Times* (April 27, 2009). See also Jo Becker and Getchen Morgenson, "Geithner, as Member and Overseer, Forged Ties to Finance Club," *New York Times* (April 27, 2009); Frank Rich, "Awake and Sing," *New York Times* (April 11, 2009); Philippe Boulet-Gercourt, "American Bankers Have Learned Nothing: Obama Versus Wall Street," *Le Nouvel Observateur* (May 7, 2009); William Greider, "Obama's False Financial Reform," *Nation* (July 19, 2009).

4. Michael A. Fletcher, "Recovery's Missing Ingredient: New Jobs," *Washington Post* (June 22, 2009), A1, A5; Michael Scherer, "What Happened to the Stimulus," *Time* (July 13, 2009), 38–41. On Lawrence Summers, see Ryan Lizza, "Inside the Crisis: Larry Summers and the White House Economic Team," *New Yorker* (October 12, 2009), 80–95.

5. Kevin Baker, "Barack Hoover Obama: The Best and the Brightest Blow It Again," *Harper's* (July 2009), 37.

6. See Alexi Mostrous, "President Says His Critics Lack Health Care Answer," *Washington Post* (September 8, 2009), A1, A7; Ceci Connolly and Michael D. Shear, "Obama Implores Congress to Act," *Washington Post* (September 10, 2009), A1, A8, A9; Ann Gerhart, "The Congressman Who Cried 'Lie,'" *Washington Post* (September 10, 2009), A9.

7. Donald Kagan, *Pericles of Athens and the Birth of Democracy* (New York: Touchstone/ Simon & Schuster, 1991), 2. Kagan's statement must be qualified by the fact that America's Founding Fathers in general believed they were founding a *republic*, not a pure democracy, and most of them followed the formulation of Polybius, who argued that the perfect polity embodied elements of rule by one person (monarchy), rule by a few people (aristocracy), and rule by many people (democracy). British eighteenth-century triumphalists believed that Britain's balanced constitution, embodying the mixture of king, lords, and commons, came closer than any other form of government to this ideal. The one-few-many formula found its way into our federal constitution via the pattern of president, Senate, and House of Representatives, the latter constituting the "democratic" element of government. Classical theorists from ancient Greece onward believed that any one of these elemental forms of power could become corrupt: monarchy could degenerate into despotism, aristocracy into oligarchy, and democracy into mob rule, for which reason a soundly engineered republic would always strive to balance these different forms of power *against* one another. Arguably, American political culture evolved into an openly *democratic* ethos by the age of Andrew Jackson and the rise of the Democratic Party, prompting de Tocqueville to write his classic study *Democracy in America*. For the one-few-many classification, see Aristotle's *Politics*, book III, chapter 8: "The civic body in every polis is the sovereign; and the sovereign must necessarily be either One, or Few, or Many" (*The Politics of Aristotle*, Ernest Barker, ed. [New York: Oxford University Press, 1962], 114). For the balancing of one-few-many, see Polybius, book VI: "Most of those writers who have attempted to give an authoritative description of political constitu-

tions have distinguished three kinds, which they call kingship, aristocracy, and democracy. . . . It is clear that we should regard as the best constitution one which includes elements of all three species" (Polybius, *The Rise of the Roman Empire*, Ian Scott-Kilvert, trans. [New York: Penguin Books, 1979], 303).

8. Kagan, *Pericles of Athens*, 3.

9. Kagan, *Pericles of Athens*.

10. Kagan, *Pericles of Athens*, 154.

11. Plutarch, "Life of Pericles," in *The Rise and Fall of Athens: Nine Greek Lives by Plutarch*, Ian Scott-Kilvert, trans. (New York: Penguin Classics, 1960), 178–79.

12. Kagan, *Pericles of Athens*, 154–55.

13. Even Washington National Airport, a modernist structure, was given a subliminally classical touch at FDR's insistence: a colonnade that was deliberately contrived to suggest and salute the columned porch of nearby Mount Vernon. The airport, built with New Deal funding via the PWA, was renamed later on for Ronald Reagan, a ridiculous and ignorant gesture equivalent to renaming Hoover Dam to honor someone like Calvin Coolidge. See James M. Goode, "Flying High: The Origin and Design of National Airport," *Washington History*, vol. 1, no. 2 (Fall 1989), 4–25. For FDR's intercession on behalf of classicism on the Mall, see Richard Guy Wilson, "High Noon on the Mall: Modernism versus Traditionalism, 1910–1970," in *The Mall in Washington, 1791–1991*, Richard Longstreth, ed. (Hanover: University Press of New England, 1991), 143–67. For commentary on the McMillan plan, see Thomas S. Hines, "The Imperial Mall: The City Beautiful Movement and the Washington Plan of 1901–1902," in *The Mall in Washington*, 79–100; and Jon A. Peterson, "The Mall, the McMillan Plan, and the Origins of American City Planning," in *The Mall in Washington*, 101–16.

14. Lois Craig and the staff of the Federal Architecture Project, *The Federal Presence: Architecture, Politics, and Symbols in United States Government Buildings* (Cambridge, Mass.: MIT Press, 1977), 401.

15. Edwin Rosskam, *Washington: Nerve Center* (New York: Alliance Book Corporation and Longmans, Green and Company, 1939), 141.

16. Mary E. Van Cleave, "We Pioneers," *Greenbelt Cooperator*, vol. 1, no. 1 (November 24, 1937), 4.

17. In a commencement address at Yale on June 11, 1962, JFK attempted to refute certain economic "myths." In the course of his address, he contended that budgeting parameters were artificial: "This budget, in relation to the great problems of Federal fiscal policy which are basic to our economy in 1962, is not simply irrelevant; it can be actively misleading." He also made the point that debts, whether public or private, "are neither good nor bad, in and of themselves." See Irving Bernstein, *Promises Kept: John F. Kennedy's New Frontier* (New York: Oxford University Press, 1991), 146–48.

18. For coverage of these controversies, see Robert Kuttner, "Cutting the Deficit Won't Cure the Economy," *Washington Post* (July 31, 1992), A23, and Hobart Rowen, "Growth and the Myth of the Deficit," *Washington Post* (October 8, 1992), A21.

19. Robert Eisner, "These Figures Spell Good Times, Not Bad," *New York Times* (December 24, 1995), 12. See also Max B. Sawicky, *Up from Deficit Reduction* (Washington, D.C.: Economic Policy Institute, 1994).

20. John M. Berry, "Economists Urge Investing Stimulus," *Washington Post* (March 31, 1992), C1, C4; Hobart Rowen, "What We Need Is More Debt," *Washington Post* (March 26, 1992), A21; Robert Kuttner, "More Important than the Deficit," *Washington Post* (April 7, 1992), A25.

21. David Alan Aschauer, *Public Investment and Private Growth: The Economic Benefits of Reducing America's "Third Deficit"* (Washington, D.C.: Economic Policy Institute, 1990). See also Fred R. Bleakley, "Infrastructure Dollars Pay Big Dividends," *Wall Street Journal* (August 12, 1997), 2.

22. Gary M. Walton and Hugh Rockoff, *History of the American Economy* (Stamford, Conn.: South-Western/Thomson Learning, 2002), 551.

23. Lee Iacocca, quoted in William Greider, *Secrets of the Temple: How the Federal Reserve Runs the Country* (New York: Simon & Schuster, 1987), 601. Iacocca continued as follows: "It was the middle class that made this country great in the first place. . . . If we don't watch out, I'm afraid we're going to find ourselves armed to the teeth—and with nothing left to defend but drive-in banks, video arcades, and McDonald's hamburger stands."

24. William F. Hixson, *A Matter of Interest: Reexamining Money, Debt, and Real Economic Growth* (New York: Praeger, 1991), 138.

25. James M. McPherson, *Battle Cry of Freedom: The Civil War Era* (New York: Oxford University Press, 1988), 447.

26. Irving Fisher, *100% Money: Designed to Keep Checking Banks 100% Liquid; to Prevent Inflation and Deflation; Largely to Cure or Prevent Depressions; and to Wipe Out Much of the National Debt* (New York: Adelphi Publications, 1935), 188–89.

27. Fisher, *100% Money*, 190, n3.

28. Fisher, *100% Money*, 191–92, 195.

29. John R. Commons, *Institutional Economics: Its Place in Political Economy* (New York: Macmillan, 1934), 589–90.

30. According to historian Franklin Folsom, Coxey was both an "earnest reformer" and a man of means, whose wealth was estimated at $200,000 in 1893 dollars:

> At the time Coxey heard [Populist Party organizer Carl Browne] propose a march to petition Congress for public works, he had already launched a program designed to help both farmers and the unemployed. He had drafted a Good Roads Bill and arranged to have it introduced in Congress. The bill called for hiring all unemployed men who applied for work at the then fairly decent wage of $1.50 for an eight-hour day. . . . The estimated $500 million needed to repair existing roads and build new ones would be obtained by simply printing paper (fiat) money, thus increasing the money supply, which Coxey thought desirable anyway. (See Franklin Folsom, *Impatient Armies of the Poor: The Story of Collective Action of the Unemployed, 1808–1942* [Niwot: University Press of Colorado, 1991], 181.)

31. William E. Leuchtenburg, *Franklin D. Roosevelt and the New Deal* (New York: Harper & Row, 1963), Harper Torchbooks edition, 50.

32. Hixson, *A Matter of Interest*, 121.

33. I first proposed this idea in December 2008. See Richard Striner, "How Lincoln Might Fix Our Economic Mess," History News Network (HNN) (December 1, 2008) (online publication). Accessible via http://hnn.us/articles/57568.html.

34. It bears noting, however, that Eccles was indignant at the profits accruing to the bond-holding banks during World War II, and he regarded the Treasury's war-funding policies as morally wrong. As William Greider observed,

> to ensure a successful bond sale and stable interest rates, the Fed expanded bank reserves by buying up outstanding government securities. The commercial banks lent the expanded money supply to private customers who would in turn lend it to the government by buying the new Treasury

issues. The customers then sold their new government securities to the commercial banks—and they eventually sold them back to the Fed when the central bank was again required to expand the money supply. In a roundabout way, the government was borrowing its own money—and paying a fixed fee to middlemen for the privilege. . . . Eccles wanted to prevent the "free riding" by limiting bank participation in the market chain of government securities and by issuing government bonds that could not be resold. He was never able to prevail. (Greider, *Secrets of the Temple*, 323)

INDEX

abortion controversy, 209
Acheson, Dean, 78, 139, 161, 164
Adams, John Quincy, 28, 29, 31,
  32–33, 36, 94
affirmative action controversy, 209–10
Afghanistan, 224, 233
Agnew, Spiro T., 176, 207
Agricultural Adjustment Administration
  (AAA), 104, 108
Agriculture, U.S. Department of, 38, 64
Air Commerce Act of 1926, 185
Airline Deregulation Act of 1978,
  185–86
Alien and Sedition Acts of 1798, 13
Al Qaeda, 223–24, 227
Ambrose, Stephen, 147, 150
American Civil Liberties Union
  (ACLU), 89, 180–81
American Liberty League, 107, 109,
  111–12
American Revolution, 24, 250n16
Americans for Democratic Action
  (ADA), 131
Amtrak, 177
Armey, Dick, 217
Arnold, Matthew, 3–4, 49
Arnold, Thurman, 117
Articles of Confederation, 24, 236
Aschauer, David Alan, 241

Bailyn, Bernard, 24
balanced budget principle, 103, 105–6,
  217–18, 240, 287n17
Bank of the United States: First, 11,
  18; Second, 27, 29, 30–31
Banking Act of 1935, 107, 244, 246
banks. *See* economics
Bellamy, Edward, 62–63
Bernanke, Benjamin, 231, 247
Bill of Rights, 25
Bismarck, Otto von, 9, 59
Blum, John Morton, 88
Blumenthal, Sidney, 216, 221–22,
  228
Brandeis, Louis D., 84, 86
Brooks, David, 221
Brownell, Herbert, 147, 156
Bryan, William Jennings, 67, 86
Buckley, William F., Jr., 153
Bureau of Public Roads, 93, 151
Burns, James MacGregor, 47–48, 81,
  82–83, 105–6, 110, 111, 133–34
Bush, George H. W., 199, 202, 205,
  206–7, 211, 212–13
Bush, George W., 223–32

Calhoun, John C., 27, 32, 34
Carlyle, Thomas, 8, 59, 75
Carnegie, Andrew, 60, 61

Carter, Jimmy, 5, 179, 182, 183–87, 188, 190–92
Catchings, Waddill, 94
Cato Institute, 181, 217, 277n143
Cato's Letters, 24
Central Intelligence Agency, 140, 153, 161–62, 274n81
centrism, 1–4, 7, 13–14, 41–43, 48–49, 76–77, 111, 113, 115, 134, 146, 171, 233
Chambers, Whittaker, 112, 133
Cheney, Dick, 223
China, 140, 143–44, 178, 205, 228
Churchill, Winston, 63, 118, 120, 138
Civil Aeronautics Act of 1938, 116, 186
Civil Aeronautics Board (CAB), 186
Civilian Conservation Corps, 103, 111
civil liberties, 13, 89, 153, 180–81, 225
civil rights movement, 51–54, 55, 133–34, 155–57, 158, 167–68, 178–79
Civil Service Commission, U.S., 57, 69, 70
Civil War, 36, 37–41, 42–43, 49
Clark, Ramsey, 208
Clay, Henry, 27–28, 29, 30, 36, 94
Clayton Anti-Trust Act, 84
Clinton, Bill, 5, 207, 211–22
Cold War, 130–33, 137–41, 160–64, 197, 202–4
Commerce, U.S. Department of, 71, 92, 116, 150
Commodity Credit Corporation, 104, 136
Commons, John R., 61, 100, 241, 245
Communism, 112, 113, 130, 138
Confederate States of America, 36, 38
Conkling, Roscoe, 57
Conner, Fox, 92
conservation movement, 64, 73, 76, 88
conservatism, evolution of, 8–9, 10–14, 57–63, 74–75, 113–15,

132–33, 152–53, 177–79, 196–97, 207–8, 221, 225, 250n9
Constitution, U.S., 25, 34–35, 49–53, 64, 75, 116, 236; amendments of, 25, 33, 51–53; broad construction of, 12, 28, 116; compromises in, 251n16; interpretations of by Supreme Court, 28, 34, 53, 64, 75, 116; Lincoln's view of, 49–51; strict construction of, 53, 64, 75, 108–9
Coolidge, Calvin, 91, 93, 94
Cooper, John Milton, Jr., 6, 73, 89
Corps of Engineers, U.S. Army, 28
Coxey, Jacob, 67, 95, 288n30
credit default swaps, 229
Crédit Mobilier, 55–56, 91
Croly, Herbert, 13–14, 48, 76
Currie, Lauchlin, 241, 244
Curry, Leonard P., 36, 38
Cutler, Lloyd, 214

Dallek, Robert, 162, 163, 169, 170, 174
Defense, U.S. Department of, 140, 161, 202, 227
deficit spending. *See* economics
Degler, Carl, 110
democracy, evolution of, 236, 286n7
Democratic Party, 29–30, 32, 84, 133–34, 155, 167, 176, 179
depressions. *See* economics
deregulation, 185–87, 191–92, 199–201, 206–7, 212, 222, 226
Dionne, E. J., Jr., 209, 216
Disraeli, Benjamin, 9, 58, 61, 75
Dole, Bob, 213–14, 219, 230
downsizing, organizational, 200, 201, 219, 229–30
Dulles, Allen, 153, 161, 162
Dulles, John Foster, 147, 154
Dunn, Susan, 47–48, 81, 82–83

Eccles, Marriner, 105, 107, 247,
  288n34
economics: and banking, 15–20,
  30–31, 84–87, 100–101, 102,
  107–8, 192, 199–201, 206, 222,
  229, 231–32, 246–47; cyclical
  nature of, 30–31, 94–95, 98; and
  deficit spending, 17–20, 39, 40,
  88, 98, 105–6, 124, 165, 198,
  217, 240–41; and depressions,
  30–31, 65, 67, 94–98, 124; and
  employment, 31, 94, 95–98, 124,
  150, 164–66, 191, 234–35; and
  financial panics, 30, 65, 67, 75,
  85–86, 95, 231–32, 265n49; and
  fiscal policy, 31, 94–95, 98, 105–6,
  116–17, 119, 122, 165–66, 234,
  241; and fractional reserve banking,
  16–18, 30–31, 85–87, 100–101,
  122–24, 245–46, 252n40, 263n24;
  and inflation, 135–36, 152, 164–65,
  187–91, 242–43, 246–47, 267n82;
  Keynesian, 105, 124, 127, 149–50,
  164–65, 241; and monetary policy,
  20–21, 38, 84–87, 95, 97, 122–24,
  246–47, 267n82; and money
  creation, 15–21, 30, 38, 66, 67,
  84–87, 96, 100–101, 122–24, 201,
  241–47, 252n40; supply-side,
  188–89, 198–99, 200, 225; and
  taxation, 68, 124, 198, 225, 226,
  240. *See also* free market ideology
education, federal support for, 26–27,
  38, 154, 225
Education, U.S. Department of, 225
Eisenhower, Dwight D., 92, 93, 230;
  bipartisanship of, 155; centrism
  of, 146, 155; character of, 145,
  146, 157; civil rights policies of,
  155–57; Cold War policies of,
  147–49; defense policies of, 147–
  49; economic policies of, 149–52;
  and "hidden hand presidency,"
  146, 153, 157; interstate highway
  program of, 150–51; Joseph
  McCarthy and, 153, 274n78; and
  nuclear deterrence, 148; and peace,
  147–48, 149; political instincts of,
  146, 153, 157; political philosophy
  of, 146, 157; Republican leadership
  of, 147, 157; Soviet Union and,
  147–48; and uses of government,
  145–46, and Vietnam, 149
Eisner, Robert, 240
Ely, Richard T., 61
Employment Act of 1946, 127, 150
Energy, U.S. Department of, 188
Environmental Protection Agency,
  U.S. (EPA), 177, 199

Fair Labor Standards Act, 115
farm loans, 66, 68, 88, 93
farm program, federal, 68, 88, 93–94,
  104, 115–16, 136, 154, 184, 220
Fascism, 112, 113
Federal Aviation Administration, 151,
  229
Federal Bureau of Investigation, 110,
  153, 274n81
Federal Communications Commission,
  106, 199
Federal Deposit Insurance Corporation
  (FDIC), 102, 107–8, 206, 218
Federal Energy Regulatory
  Commission, 206–7
Federal Housing Administration, 106,
  267n83
Federalist Party, 10–13, 27
Federal Power Commission, 108, 206
Federal Reserve System, 84–87, 89,
  95, 96, 97, 122–24, 229, 262n21
Federal Trade Commission, 84
Fifteenth Amendment, 52, 53, 55
financial crisis of 2007–2008, 229,
  231–32, 285n139
financial panics. *See* economics

fiscal policy. *See* economics
Fisher, Irving, 87, 100–101, 241, 243–44
Foner, Eric, 54
Food and Drug Administration, U.S. (FDA), 74
Ford, Gerald, 183
Forest Service, U.S., 73
Foster, William Trufant, 94
Fourteenth Amendment, 51–52, 53, 258n20
fractional reserve banking. *See* economics
Franklin, Benjamin, 20, 24
Freedmen's Bureau, 2, 41, 54
free market ideology, 3, 10, 11, 29, 145–46, 153, 171, 181–82, 184–87, 188–89, 192, 199–201, 206–7, 215, 217–20, 222, 269n111. *See also* libertarianism
French Revolution, 12
Friedman, Milton, 171, 181, 188, 201

Gaddis, John Lewis, 139
Galbraith, John Kenneth, 21, 131, 149, 152, 164–65, 175, 188, 252n40
Gallatin, Albert, 26
Gallatin Report, 26
Garn–St. Germain Act of 1982, 199–200
Geithner, Timothy, 234
GI Bill, 19, 124, 135
Gingrich, Newt, 217, 221
Glass-Steagall Act of 1933, 102, 222
globalization, 201, 215
global warming, 226, 239
Goldwater, Barry, 153, 157, 169, 171, 194
Goodman, Paul, 153, 159
Goodwyn, Lawrence, 65–66
Gorbachev, Mikhail, 193, 202, 204, 281n56
Gore, Al, 212, 216, 223

Grant, Ulysses S., 54–55, 56
Greenbacks. *See* economics, money creation
greenbelt towns, 108, 111; Greenbelt, Maryland, 238–39
Greenspan, Alan, 199, 229, 231, 285n139
Greenstein, Fred I., 146, 157–58
Greider, William, 181, 189, 198
gun control controversy, 181

Hamby, Alonzo, 134, 144, 152, 162, 163–64, 174, 175, 193, 195
Hamilton, Alexander, 10–14, 15, 18, 24, 26, 61
Hanna, Marcus Alonzo, 68, 71
Hansen, Alvin, 124, 135, 149, 150
Harding, Warren, 91
Harris, Seymour, 122, 160, 164
Hay, John, 47, 73
Hayek, Friedrich von, 132
Health, Education, and Welfare, U.S. Department of, 151
health care, federal involvement in, 136–37, 166, 177, 215–16, 220, 225, 234–35
Heller, Walter, 164
Higgs, Robert, 270n141
Hixson, William F., 85, 242, 245, 252n40
Hofstadter, Richard, 60, 76–77
Homeland Security, U.S. Department of, 225, 228
Homestead Act, 36, 38
Hoopes, Townsend, 173
Hoover, Herbert, 92–93, 95, 97–98, 99
Hoover, J. Edgar, 110, 153, 178
Hoover Dam, 92
Hopkins, Harry, 99, 103, 105, 108, 117
Housing and Urban Development, U.S. Department of, 172, 202

Humphrey, Hubert, 131, 176
Hurricane Katrina, 6, 228

Ickes, Harold, 7, 78, 103, 104–5, 234
income tax, federal, 39, 68, 198, 225
Indian Removal Act of 1830, 32
infrastructure, federal support for, 11,
    26–28, 31, 36–37, 38, 71, 92, 93,
    103, 104–5, 108, 150–51, 197,
    205–6, 213, 221, 230, 237–39
Interior, U.S. Department of, 31, 199,
    226
Interstate Commerce Commission,
    U.S. (ICC), 64, 73
Interstate Highway System, 19, 150–
    51, 197, 206, 230
Iran, 191, 205
Iran hostage crisis, 191
Iraq war, 227, 233
isolationism, 92, 117–21, 129, 144–45

Jackson, Andrew, 29–32
Javits, Jacob, 171
Jefferson, Thomas, 10–14, 25–27, 29,
    110
John Birch Society, 153
Johnson, Andrew, 54
Johnson, Lyndon B., 155, 157, 165,
    171, 172, 173–75
Justice, U.S. Department of, 64, 157

Kemp-Roth tax cut of 1981, 198
Kennan, George F., 138
Kennedy, John F.: centrism of, 160;
    character of, 159; civil rights
    policies of, 158, 167–68; Cold War
    policies of, 160–64, 170; Cuba
    and, 161–62, 163–64; defense
    policies of, 160–64; Democratic
    Party, leadership of, 167; economic
    policies of, 164–65; and FDR, 160;
    influence of Dwight D. Eisenhower
    on, 160–61; and Lincoln, 158;

political instincts of, 159–64, 170;
    space program of, 165; and TR,
    158–59; and Vietnam, 170
Kennedy, Robert F., 173, 174, 175
Kerry, John, 227
Keynes, John Maynard, 98, 105, 142.
    See also economics, Keynesian
Kirk, Russell, 153
Kissinger, Henry, 177
Kolko, Gabriel, 176
Korean War, 140, 143, 147
Krauthammer, Charles, 224
Kristol, Irving, 177
Kristol, William, 221
Krugman, Paul, 225–26, 234, 235

Labor, U.S. Department of, 71, 166
labor unions, 65, 67, 71, 200, 215
Laffer, Arthur, 188–89, 225, 278n13
laissez-faire. *See* free market ideology
Landon, Alfred, 78, 101, 111, 119
Larsen, Arthur, 155
Lend-Lease, 120–21
Lester, Richard A., 20–21, 241
Leuchtenburg, William, 96, 97, 98,
    104–5, 111, 185
liberalism, evolution of, 8, 10–14, 63,
    84, 110, 131–32, 154, 155, 179–80,
    207–8, 250n14
libertarianism, 23–25, 29, 153, 179–82,
    210, 235–36. *See also* free market
    ideology
Limbaugh, Rush, 207
Lincoln, Abraham: anti-slavery
    program of, 34–35, 39–43,
    49–50, 51; character of, 39–43,
    49–51; and conservative-liberal
    convergence, 1–3, 41–43, 256n56;
    constitutionalism of, 49–51;
    and deficit finance, 37–40; and
    Greenbacks, 38; Hamiltonian
    influence on, 40; and human
    nature, 2–3, 42–43; influence of,

1–3, 14, 35–45, 47–51, 73, 76, 118, 127; influence on Theodore Roosevelt, 2, 6, 14, 43, 45, 47–49, 73, 76; and infrastructure, 2, 31, 36–37, 94; Jeffersonian influence on, 40–41, 43, 50; philosophy of, 2–3, 31, 39–43, 49–51; political instincts of, 39–43, 49–51, 158; statecraft of, 41–43, 49–51; and use of government, 1–3, 31, 36, 38, 40, 43, 49–51
Lincoln Highway, 93
Link, Arthur S., 84
Long, Huey P., 106–7, 109, 113–14, 115, 269n117
Lucie, Patricia, 53, 258n20

MacArthur, Douglas, 98, 143
Macaulay, Thomas Babington, 7, 18–19
Madison, James, 12, 24–25, 26–27
Manhattan Project, 122
Marshall, George C., 120, 138–39, 142, 143–44
Marshall, John, 28
Marshall Plan, 19, 139
McCain, John, 232
McCarthy, Joseph, and McCarthyism, 112, 141–43, 153, 274n78
McGovern, George, 179–80, 184
McKinley, William, 68, 70
McMillan Commission of 1901–1902, 73, 237
McNamara, Robert S., 161, 173, 174
McPherson, James M., 36, 51, 243
Medicare, 166
Middle Way, Eisenhower's. *See* Eisenhower, Dwight D.
Miller, Perry, 8
Mises, Ludwig von, 132
Mitchell, William ("Billy"), 92
Mondale, Walter, 196
money. *See* economics

Morrill Act, 38
Moynihan, Daniel Patrick, 177

NAFTA. *See* North American Free Trade Agreement
National Aeronautics and Space Administration (NASA), 151
national bank system, 38
National Farmers Alliance, 66
National Institute of Health (NIH), 136
National Park Service, 88
National Recovery Administration (NRA), 103–4, 108
National Rifle Association (NRA), 180–81, 277n142
"National Road," 26
NATO. *See* North Atlantic Treaty Organization
Nazi Germany, 117–18, 121–22, 145
neo-conservatism, 177
neo-liberalism, 199
New Deal. *See* Franklin Delano Roosevelt, New Deal programs of
Newlands Reclamation Act, 71, 111
New Left, 153, 176, 179–80, 208
Nichols, David, 155–57
Niebuhr, Reinhold, 131–32, 184
Nitze, Paul, 141, 197
Nixon, Richard M., 141, 147, 176–78, 180, 183, 187
North American Free Trade Agreement (NAFTA), 215
North Atlantic Treaty Organization (NATO), 140, 144, 146
NSC 68, 140–41
nuclear weapons/war, 122, 140, 141, 202–4

Obama, Barack, 5, 232, 233–36
Office of Price Administration (OPA), 122
Office of Scientific Research and Development (OSRD), 122

Office of War Mobilization (OWM), 122

OPEC. *See* Organization of the Petroleum Exporting Countries

Operation Desert Storm, 211

Organization of the Petroleum Exporting Countries (OPEC), 187, 189, 193

Orwell, George, 131, 209

Osborne, David, 207, 211–12

Panama Canal, 72

Paulson, Henry, 231, 247

Pericles, 236–37

Perkins, Frances, 83, 99, 103

Perkins, George W., 79, 103–4

Phillips, Kevin, 201–2

Pinchot, Gifford, 73, 83, 111, 133–34

Populist Party, 66–67, 68

Progressive movement, 71, 261n71

Progressive Party, 78–79

Prohibition, 91

Project Apollo, 165

public works. *See* infrastructure, federal support for

Public Works Administration (PWA), 103, 104–5, 234

radicalism: left-of-center, 112, 113, 153, 175–76; right-of-center, 112, 153, 218, 235–36

Radical Republicans, 51–55

Reagan, Ronald, 5, 180, 184, 192–205

Reconstruction, 49–57, 167

Reconstruction Finance Corporation, 97, 104, 185

regulation of business, 11, 64–68, 73–75, 106, 116, 206

republicanism, classical theory of, 286n7

Republican Party, 34, 36, 38, 51–55, 57, 70, 133–34, 141, 142, 144–45, 152–53, 155, 157, 177, 196–97, 216–20

Resettlement Administration, 108, 239

Roberts, Paul Craig, 188, 189, 198

Rohatyn, Felix, 206

Roosevelt, Eleanor, 61, 82, 131

Roosevelt, Franklin Delano: bipartisanship of, 111, 119–20, 133–34; "Brain Trust" of, 102–3; character of, 81–83, 114, 115; conservation achievements of, 103, 111; conservatism of, 102, 109–11, 133; and conservative-liberal convergence, 2, 7, 111, 113; and Democratic Party, 83, 110, 115, 133–34; economic policies of, 99, 105–6, 116–17, 124, 127; family background of, 81–83, 114; farm program of, 104, 115–16; foreign policy of, 117–22; housing programs of, 106, 116; Huey Long and, 106–7, 109, 113–14, 115; influence of Lincoln on, 118, 121; influence of Theodore Roosevelt on, 2, 6–7, 81–83, 111, 113; influence on John F. Kennedy, 160; John Maynard Keynes and, 105–6; liberalism of, 110; New Deal programs of, 99, 101–9, 115–16, 269n111; political instincts of, 113–14, 115, 116–17; political philosophy of, 2, 7, 109–11; public works programs of, 103, 108; and regulation of business, 106, 116; rural electrification programs of, 103, 108; service as assistant secretary of the navy, 83, 88; service as governor of New York, 99; service in New York legislature, 83; Social Security and, 107; Supreme Court and, 108, 115, 116; Winston Churchill and, 118, 120; and World War II, 117–28

Roosevelt, Theodore: character of, 47–49, 68–79, 90, 159;

conservation achievements of, 73, 76; conservatism of, 61, 70, 75, 76, 90, 260n64; and conservative-liberal convergence, 2, 48–49, 76–77; family background of, 47–49, 69; food and drug regulation and, 73–74; foreign policy of, 69, 73, 90; and imperialism, 69, 90; influence of Lincoln on, 2, 6, 43, 45, 47–49, 73, 76; and infrastructure, 71–72; New Nationalism of, 77, 103; Panama Canal and, 72, 83; political ideology of, 5, 47–49, 69, 74–75, 90; and regulation of business, 69–71, 73–75, 77; and Republican Party, 48, 70, 76, 78; service as assistant secretary of the navy, 70; service as governor of New York, 70; service in New York legislature, 69–70; and Social Darwinism, 68–69, 75, 78; and Social Gospel, 68–69; social security and, 9, 77, 78; and uses of government, 48–49, 71–79; view of human nature, 74–75, 90; and World War I, 89

Rove, Karl, 223, 228
Rumsfeld, Donald, 224, 227
Rural Electrification Administration (REA), 108
Ruskin, John, 58–59
Russia. *See* Soviet Union

savings and loan (S&L) scandal, 192, 199–201, 206
Schlesinger, Arthur, Jr., 96, 131, 160, 161, 167, 170, 185
Securities and Exchange Commission, 106, 199
September 11, 2001, 223–25
Sherman, John, 38
Sherman Anti-Trust Act, 65, 71
Simons, Henry C., 100, 241

slavery in United States, 32, 33–36, 39–43, 51, 52
Smith, Al, 99, 112, 132
Smithsonian Institute, 33
Social Darwinism, 59–61, 69, 75, 109
Social Gospel, 61–63, 109, 111
socialism, 9, 57, 67
Social Security, 9, 59, 77, 78, 107, 136, 152, 189–90, 199, 220, 228
Soviet Union, 91, 112–13, 121, 130–31, 137–40, 162–64, 202–5
space-based surveillance, 148–49
Spencer, Herbert, 59–60
St. Lawrence Seaway, 92, 151
Stalin, Joseph, 113, 130, 138, 147
Stampp, Kenneth M., 54
"Star Wars" missile defense program, 203
states' rights, and slavery, 32, 34, 36
Steffens, Lincoln, 112–13
Stevens, Thaddeus, 53–54, 167
Stimson, Henry, 7, 73, 119, 231
Stockman, David, 198–99
Sullivan, Mark, 79
Summers, Lawrence, 222, 234, 235
Sumner, William Graham, 60
Supreme Court, U.S., 28, 34, 51, 53, 64, 75, 108–9, 115, 116, 155, 156; and *Brown v. Board of Education* (1954), 155, 156–57; and *Dred Scott v. Sandford* (1857), 34–35; and *Gitlow v. New York* (1925), 51; and *Lochner v. New York* (1905), 75; and *McCulloch v. Maryland* (1819), 28; and *Munn v. Illinois* (1877), 64; and *NLRB v. Jones* (1937), 116; and *Plessy v. Ferguson* (1896), 156, 157; and *United States v. Cruikshank* (1876), 53; and *United States v. Darby* (1941), 116; and *United States v. Reese* (1876), 53; and *Wabash v. Illinois* (1886), 64; and *Wickard v. Filburn* (1942), 116

Taft, Robert, 132–33, 134, 142, 144–45, 147, 152, 196

Taft, William Howard, 76, 78

taxation. *See* economics

Taylor, Maxwell, 162, 173

Teapot Dome scandal, 91

Tennessee Valley Authority (TVA), 103, 104

Thirteenth Amendment, 33, 40, 51

Tory reform, 9, 58–59, 61, 75, 110, 177, 205, 221

Train, Russell, 177

Transportation, U.S. Department of, 172

Troubled Asset Relief Program (TARP), 234

Truman, Harry S.: character of, 134, 140; centrism of, 134; civil rights policies of, 136; Cold War policies of, 138–41, 143–44; Democratic Party leadership of, 134, 140, 146, 147; Fair Deal program of, 136–37; farm policies of, 136; health care proposal of, 136–37; as heir to Franklin D. Roosevelt, 133, 135–37; and Korean War, 140, 143; and NSC 68, 140–41; political instincts of, 134; political philosophy of, 134; relations with Republicans, 137, 140, 142, 143, 144–45

Truman Doctrine, 139

Tugwell, Rexford Guy, 102, 108

unemployment compensation, 107, 191

Union Pacific Railroad, 38, 55–56

Viereck, Peter, 133

Vietnam War, 149, 170, 173–74, 176–77, 181

"Vital Center," 131, 134, 180

Volcker, Paul, 191, 193, 196, 242, 246

wage and price: controls, 124, 135, 174, 178, 187; guideposts, 164–65, 175, 187

Wagner Act, 108

Wallace, Henry, 102, 131

Wanniski, Jude, 181, 188–89, 278n13

War Manpower Commission (WMC), 122

War on Poverty, 166, 172–73

War Production Board (WPB), 122

Warren, Earl, 156

wartime agencies: World War I, 88; World War II, 122

Washington, D.C., planning of, 73, 237–38

Washington, George, 12, 24, 26, 235

Watergate scandal, 180

welfare state, 8–9, 57–59, 110, 205

Whiggism, 23–25

Whig Party, 30

Whiskey Rebellion, 12

Will, George F., 205, 213, 221

Willkie, Wendell, 118, 119, 120, 131, 133–34

Wilson, Woodrow, 78, 79, 83–91, 129, 174

Works Progress Administration (WPA), 108, 235

World War I, 88–91, 92

World War II, 19, 117–28, 129–30, 135, 138, 275n95

ABOUT THE AUTHOR

Richard Striner is professor of history at Washington College in Chestertown, Maryland, and senior writer for the Dwight D. Eisenhower Memorial Commission. He is the author of *Father Abraham: Lincoln's Relentless Struggle to End Slavery* and he has written for many publications, including the *Aspen Institute Quarterly, William & Mary Quarterly*, and the *Washington Post*. An interdisciplinary scholar, he works in the fields of political history, economics, architecture, historic preservation, English literature, and film.